NOTHING SO STRANGE

NOTHING
SO STRANGE

by
LORD FRANCIS-WILLIAMS

AMERICAN HERITAGE PRESS   NEW YORK
A Subsidiary of McGraw-Hill

First published in the U.S.A. 1970 by American Heritage Press

SBN: 8281-0044-6

Library of Congress Catalog Card Number: 77-95727

Printed in Great Britain

TO JESS
AS ALWAYS

There is nothing so strange as people

Contents

A Long Way to Oswestry

In those days it was a long way to Oswestry. We went there by pony and trap. Sometimes we went with my father but the journeys I most remember were with my grandmother. She had been a great rider to hounds when she was younger and although now in her seventies liked to go at a spanking pace and pass everything on the road. The other farmers would make a race of it and my sister and I would cling to our seats expecting her to lock wheels with the trap she was overtaking and spill us all out. But she never did. When we came home in the evening we would trot along more slowly and she would tell us stories of Shropshire eccentrics. Sometimes she would say they were relations of hers, sometimes not. But she did not really think of any of them as being eccentric, not even Squire Mytton who rode across country in his nightshirt.

There was one particularly lonely stretch of road where she would tell us how once when she was driving home alone two gipsies had jumped out of the hedge and caught her horse's head and tried to stop her. But she stood up in the trap and slashed them and the pony so hard with her whip that they screamed and let go as the pony reared. 'I suppose they thought I'd give them my purse,' she said. 'As if I'd be frightened of trash like that.'

And, indeed, it did seem silly to think she would be frightened of anyone when one saw her at the Griffin ordering her farm labourers about and keeping the big Irishmen who came over for the harvest up to scratch. If any of them had thought they would be able to take things easier after the Boss, her husband and my stepgrandfather, died they were soon brought to their senses.

She drove to Oswestry market with butter and eggs each week and sat beside her basket chit-chatting with everyone before she went to the Wynnstay Hotel for lunch and a hot toddy. She was often told that she ought not to be sitting in the market hall like this. But she would have none of it. She was proud of her butter and eggs and saw no reason for not making sure of the best price by selling them herself. Also she enjoyed the news she picked up about the goings-on of her friends. 'There's nothing so strange as people,' she said. It was on a market day that the First World War started in August 1914 and there were soldiers of the King's Shropshire Light Infantry with fixed bayonets on guard at the door of the market. I suppose they thought that if the Kaiser invaded Britain he would make for Oswestry first. So did my grandmother and I.

By the time the war came my father and mother and sister and I had left St Martins and gone to live in Lancashire in consequence of what my mother, who had a very conspiratorial view of life, was convinced was a plot to steal Rhos-y-llan, the farm where I was born, from my father. But we spent our holidays at the Griffin with my grandmother. Sometimes we also went for a few days to the Pentre to stay with our other grandparents. This was a rather dire experience. My grandmother at the Griffin liked everyone to have a good time and there was always a great stir and bustle going on, but at the Pentre it was very quiet and religious. Both my grandfather and grandmother Williams had been converted to Methodism and had abandoned frivolity and the Church of England. When we stayed there we were not allowed to look at anything but the Bible on Sundays.

My grandfather had become a noted lay-preacher and was very strong against wickedness, particularly if it had anything to do with the Church of England. He preached very long sermons and the yellow pine pews were very uncomfortable, but after the afternoon service was over we would go with him to high tea at the home of one of the leading members of the congregation and there would be enormous meals of cold ham, paste sandwiches, pickles, bread and butter and home-made jam, stewed fruit and jelly and blancmange and fruit cake. This was not in Shropshire though, but in Lancashire when he came to stay with us sometimes after Grandma died. When she was dying the doctor tried to give her brandy to revive her. But she clenched her teeth and died triumphantly with not a drop passing her lips.

Sometimes when we were at the Pentre we would go to see my father's aunt, our Great-Aunt Jane, who was very strange indeed. She had been in Paris when the Franco-Prussian war started and had lived through the siege of Paris. She had lived on rats, we were told, and we longed to ask what they tasted like but did not dare to. She was unmarried and lived alone in a cottage at the end of a long garden path and one of the effects of the siege of Paris on her was that she never bought any new clothes after it ended. She was always dressed in a long grey frock with mutton chop sleeves when we went to see her. She lived to be two days short of a hundred and never changed her fashion so that my own children and their cousins knew her and thought she was a witch. One of them who had been to see *Snow White and the Seven Dwarfs* went into hysterics when she offered him a large rosy apple from her orchard. Although she lived all alone and was reputed to keep her money in a big box with brass bands she was not nervous. She had a large black-thorn club and a pair of handcuffs beside her bed. The black-thorn club was to knock unconscious any burglar who might seek to molest her, the handcuffs were to fasten him to the bed-post with until she had time to go for the village policeman in the morning.

We liked staying at the Griffin best. It was almost self-contained. They baked their own bread, made their own butter and cheese and jams, killed and hung their own meat and ham, brewed their own beer and cider. There was really very little for which they depended on others. It was a world now entirely gone.

In the orchard there were apples and pears and plums and greengages and cherries. I once sat in one of the apple trees and ate thirty green apples straight off for a dare and afterwards was so ill that my mother, who waged a life-long war against germs and carried a bottle of disinfectant with her wherever she went, was convinced I had caught a germ. I was put to bed in a big four-poster with curtains round it and my sister smuggled a copy of *Dracula* by Bram Stoker to me. This I read by candle-light and the combined effect of the apples and the vampires was that I woke up hysterical in the middle of the night and one of the farmhands had to be roused from sleep and sent galloping on horseback to fetch the doctor.

This doctor owned the first motor-car I ever saw. When he gave my sister and me a ride in it we boasted to our friends for months. His senior partner, who must by then, I think, have retired, for he was a very old man, scorned such things and went his rounds on horseback. He was a distant relation of Admiral Lord Charles Beresford and a great hunting man and could be seen, I am told, taking the hedges in fine style as he made his way across country from farm to farm on his rounds.

When I was taking part in a television programme on Gordon of Khartoum many years later my father, who was then in his late seventies, told me that he remembered as a small boy being in a horse and trap with his father when they saw this Dr Beresford halloing and waving to them several fields away. When he came up to them he shouted to my grandfather, 'Those black devils have killed Gordon. Charlie and his gunboat couldn't get there in time.' And my grandfather, who was a strong Liberal as well as a nonconformist, replied, according to my father, 'Poor Mr Gladstone.' When my father told me this story I retold it to Mr Attlee and he nodded his head and said, 'Yes, they gave him a bad time in the House.' This made me see that politicians are a good deal alike.

I had a happy childhood and cannot remember hating either of my parents, both of whom were governed by one firm principle in their relations with children which was that they should be happy—all children, but their own especially. To make a child unhappy was in their eyes the unforgivable adult crime. This does not mean that they never lost their tempers with us. My mother, who had a strong dramatic talent, did so frequently. But she quarrelled with us on a basis of equality without any adult assumption of superiority and without any hard feelings when it was over. On such occasions she would frequently declaim with all the fervour of one of the melodramas she had known in her youth that something one of us had done had revealed to her that we were 'Rotten, rotten to the core.' The lovely cadences of her voice would invest this sentiment with all the world's burden of tragedy and betrayal and unfortunate acquaintances caught on the edges of the maelstrom would be convinced that family relationships were ended permanently, only to find us sitting down to supper a little later all happiness and gaiety, wounds given and received quite forgotten.

My father was more equable. His outbreaks of anger were so rare as to be legendary and followed, in our experience, an invariable course. When pressed beyond bearing he would become very still. Then he would walk quickly across the room, pick up the most valuable ornament his eye could light on, smash it to the floor and walk out, leaving us all, my mother included, much shaken, all the more so because what had happened was so contrary to his usual way, for he was kind and patient almost to a fault.

Like my mother, he never assumed, even in these rare outbursts, that to be angry was a prerogative of adulthood. He always treated us as his equals, acknowledging that we had as much right to criticize him if we thought he had fallen below the standards he set himself as he had to show his disapproval of us if we did. These standards were quite firm and were much concerned with honour and courage in an almost Conradian context. Conrad was, indeed, my father's favourite author and he introduced me to his books when I was very young, much as another man might have taught his small son to study the Bible. He particularly admired *Nostromo* and read it many times, the last time the week before he died.

My father thought that to go back on one's word, however onerous it might have proved to be, was the worst sin a man could commit—he was somewhat more tolerant, I think, of women in this respect. Close behind this came anything that seemed to him to be a failure in chivalry towards women. I remember my mother telling us, pausing dramatically at each stage in the story, of how, when they were just married, they went for a pleasure trip on a river boat and two very large 'toughs' (her word) frightened the ladies on board by rocking it and how my father who, although short in stature like many in the Welsh border counties, was immensely powerful, told them to stop three times. When they kept on, he stood up and without another word tossed each of them in turn into the river from which they had to be fished with landing-hooks.

He came of an old Shropshire farming family and was the only boy in a family of four. I think his own childhood must have been rather bleak after his parents took so strongly to religion and he himself would have nothing to do with religion when he grew up. Nor did he wish us bothered with it, regarding it, I think, as a pretext for making happy people unhappy and imposing upon them outside standards of conduct, whereas one should carve out one's own and abide faithfully by them. He was sent to school at Ellesmere College where he broke the bridge of his nose fielding near the boundary in a school cricket match. This gave him, as a man, a faintly piratical look which he encouraged by wearing hats punched into eccentric shapes. At Ellesmere College he learned mathematics and a little Latin —enough to make him decide to adopt 'Nil desperandum' as his motto for life—but not, I think, very much else, except, which was very important to him, a great taste for reading. When he finished school he was sent to a large farm the other side of Shrewsbury as a pupil before setting up on his own on a small farm in St Martins.

He was working in one of his fields beside the road when he heard a girl laughing and talking on the other side of the hedge as she went along the road. He was so enchanted by her voice— which, indeed, was very beautiful—that he said to himself, so he told us, 'That is the girl I shall marry', and throwing his fork on the ground raced to a gap in the hedge to see what she looked like. She was as beautiful as her voice. Not just pretty but of a really startling beauty. This beauty which was one of bone and structure she retained even in her middle and old age. In her youth she must have been quite breath-takingly lovely, light and delicate of bone with high cheekbones and a complexion like ivory with an inward glow to it, such as one sometimes finds in the Welsh border counties. He soon found out that she was a Miss Francis who had come to live at the Griffin with her mother and stepfather. Although very quiet he was a man of determination and it was not long before they were engaged—an event somewhat unpleasing to his parents who thought my mother's family ungodly and given to pleasure.

My mother—the girl on the other side of the hedge—was not a native of Shropshire but had been born in Montgomery, just

6

across the border into Wales, at a farm called Leighton—'a farm like a village' she used to say. The farmhouse itself was a black and white Tudor manor house. I saw it offered for sale in *Country Life* a year or two ago at a price which made me regret that I was not rich enough to buy it back into the family.

However, when my mother was quite young her father, who seems to have been a handsome, dashing, feckless, attractive fellow with a long list of local appointments of one sort or another as well as his farm but with a great passion for gambling, committed suicide in dramatic circumstances. He had been playing cards all night and drinking brandy too, no doubt, and lost heavily. In the early morning he got up from the card table, went into the harness room where there was a bottle of poison for killing rats, gulped it down and died almost immediately in great agony. The noise and commotion of the other card-players roused the household and my mother used to describe how she had run down the stairs in her nightdress and peeping around her mother's skirt had seen her father lying on the floor.

The sight naturally made a vivid impression on her, but not, curiously enough a very tragic one. At least it did not appear to have done so when she described it to us, as she often did, for she loved the drama of life and would always, I think, have preferred something terrible to happen rather than nothing at all. Perhaps her temperament was too volatile and her emotions too dramatic for deep tragedy. She did not harbour sorrow or indignation but released it in great torrents.

Her father's suicide meant the end of Leighton which had to be sold to meet his large debts. He left five young children—two boys and three girls—and Uncle John Francis, who was a Church of England clergyman, had to come to their rescue. Great-Uncle John was later to become much of a legend in the lives of my sister and myself. He was of striking appearance with a very large bushy black beard and when we occasionally stayed with him as children he always had for breakfast two large chops and a pint of old ale, a habit he had acquired when an undergraduate at St John's College, Cambridge. The silver tankard out of which he drank the ale had a glass bottom and we would look up from our breakfasts to see him peering at us through it. He was unmarried and was looked after by a niece whom my mother always referred to as 'the wicked Fanny

Kempster', being deeply convinced, although I am sure without any evidence, that she was plotting to get his money and leave nothing for his other nieces and nephews or their children.

It was not this, however, that made him so exciting to us but the fact that he was on the track of a vast fortune in America that would make us all rich. Although a clergyman he spent little of his time on the affairs of God. An earlier clergyman in the family, a great-great-uncle I think, is said, when accused of behaving in an unchristian way by a neighbour with whom he was involved in a deal over horses, to have retorted sharply: 'Sir, I will not be called a Christian. I am a member of the Church of England.' Great-Uncle John would no doubt have echoed his sentiments.

At any rate although a good Church of England man he wasted little time on spiritual matters and devoted most of his energies to directing from his study, with its first editions of Dickens and Thackeray, Tennyson and Wordsworth, the activities of lawyers whom he employed to hunt down what my mother would thrillingly describe as the missing documents. These if found would, we were told, establish that an earlier Francis ancestor, who had gone to America as a Colonist, had by some means or another got his hands on a large slice of the land on which down-town New York was later built, and although he had eventually sold it had done so on a ninety-nine-year lease and not in perpetuity so that it was by now due to return to the family.

My Grandfather Francis had dissipated his inheritance on cards and steeplechasers, Great-Uncle John spent most of what remained of the family fortune—except, that is, that part of it the wicked Fanny Kempster got hold of, according to my mother—in chasing the dream of owning Wall Street. No one in the family complained about this. As a family it was just naturally captivated by the idea of pots of gold at rainbow ends and got more satisfaction out of romantic visions of future wealth than out of money in the bank. It applauded Great-Uncle John's odyssey without reservation. When he let it be known that only one document—I never did learn which one it was—was still missing there was so much excitement and future planning that I think it would have been almost an anti-climax if it had actually been found.

8

My mother was convinced that sooner or later Great-Uncle John's quest would end triumphantly. Whenever she had to explain that we could not afford something on which we had set our hearts she would say, 'Never mind, we'll get it as soon as the American money comes.' Her whole attitude to life was that sooner or later something was bound to turn up, so that even when we were very poor, as we often were after leaving St Martins, she rarely let it depress her for long. This was partly because she refused to acknowledge unpleasant facts of the financial sort, assuming it to be a natural law, for example, that her children should have the best doctors and the most expensive dentists if they needed them and that these doctors and dentists would be honoured to wait for their money, but also because she had an indomitable faith in the existence of a treasure trove waiting to be found. The stone-flagged kitchens of the old farmhouses to which we moved from time to time provided her with many such hopes. Invariably she would find a stone flag that was loose, providing sure evidence that it had been lifted at some time or another for something to be buried under it. My father, who must have found her vagaries appealing and knew in any event that there would be no peace until he did what she wished, would thereupon abandon whatever he was doing to take this flagstone up and dig deep into the soil beneath to find what was never there. Nor did repeated failures cast her down for long. She went on believing that it would happen some day.

When her father committed suicide and my Great-Uncle John was compelled to come to the rescue he arranged for the two boys, John and Bert, to be sent to Christ's Hospital School —when we were children we greatly admired photographs of them in their long blue coats down to the ankle with leather girdles and shoes. The eldest daughter, Polly, and her youngest sister, Amy, were sent to a girls' boarding school at Ashford in Kent which allowed, I imagine, reduced fees for connections of the clergy. But, because she was her mother's favourite, my mother, Sally, was kept at home and never had any very formal education.

My grandmother had no taste for living on charity either as dispensed by her husband's brother or from the numerous members of her own family, the Edwards, who were for the most part practical-minded Shropshire farmers living in gloomy houses with a great deal of carved black oak in them; careful of their money and all having what my mother used to describe graphically as the Pentre David jib, a trick of sticking out their lower lips in a particularly stubborn way when asked to do anything they did not want to do. She, therefore, set out to earn her own living. This, somewhat surprisingly, she chose to do by means of a theatrical boarding-house in Leigh.

Here she was followed by a cousin, a formidable gentleman whose surname was Lawrence—I never knew his Christian name since by the time I knew him he was invariably called the Boss by everyone. The Boss had been in love with her long before she married the handsome, feckless Francis boy and he now renewed his suit with commanding vigour. He was at this time a salesman with the new American Singer sewing-machine company and had built up a substantial trade with farmers' wives all over Shropshire and the neighbouring counties, to whom the new sewing-machine came as a godsend. But he was not really interested in selling sewing-machines. He wanted to have a farm of his own and was simply selling sewing-machines to get the capital he needed. He soon broke down my grandmother's defences. They married and arranged to continue with the theatrical boarding-house where he joined her from his selling jaunts at the weekends so that they could jointly save more quickly for the farm.

My mother helped with the running of the boarding-house, working from morning to night as she would tell us dramatically 'like a child skivvy'. She did not like her new stepfather who was a domineering bullying sort of man who tyrannized so much over the two boys when they were at home for the holidays that both of them eventually ran away, one of them to join a circus and in good time marry a disappearing lady who was shot out of a cannon by a magician twice nightly, the other himself to disappear for several years until he turned up in Birmingham as a manager of one of the early cinemas.

My mother, who was a young girl of spirit and temperament, had no intention of letting him bully her and finally won his grudging respect by threatening to throw a pan of boiling fat over him when he shouted at her for not doing something or other quickly enough. She must have looked rather magnificent with the pan of bubbling fat poised in her hands, her eyes flashing. I daresay she would have thrown it if he had not retreated rapidly out of the kitchen. At any rate he thought so and thereafter treated her with considerable caution: she was, indeed, when I knew him, the only person to whom he ever showed any politeness. Because of this my sister and I were much better treated by him than were our cousins. He had a healthy fear, I suspect, of what she might do if he tried to bully us. His self-respect so far as I was concerned was assuaged when I accidentally shot an apple off a tree with my first air-gun. This allowed him to pretend that it was my prowess as a shot and not his fear of my mother that made him treat me so less roughly than he did others.

Despite her annoyance at being 'a child skivvy' my mother enjoyed the theatrical lodgers who made much of her and fed her natural liking for drama. My grandmother was persuaded to let her appear as a fairy in a Christmas pantomime and afterwards there were several suggestions by theatrical families among the regular visitors to the boarding-house that she should be allowed to go on the stage: they would, they promised, look after her just like one of their own children. I think a theatrical life might well have suited her, but my grandmother, who had no faith in theatrical morals, firmly resisted all such proposals. As a compensation she allowed my mother to have music lessons. In those days all young ladies were expected to take their music with them when they went visiting and new songs and piano pieces were as eagerly bought at the music shops as pop records are now. After her lessons my mother, who had a pretty, although not strong, singing voice, obtained a situation at a music shop playing the new piano pieces and singing the new ballads for customers who wanted to hear them before buying.

All the Francis girls were artistic. Polly painted and Amy played an instrument—the violin, I think—and in school holidays when Polly and Amy came home they would escape from the atmosphere of the theatrical boarding-house, which nevertheless had its compensations in free seats to the theatre, by playing their music together and dreaming of going to London where a second cousin, who was also known to be artistic, was making her way in the world in a very modern manner as a buyer at Liberty's and sometimes wrote to them about London's delights.

However, when the money for the farm was accumulated, Wigan and the theatrical boarding-house were put behind. Polly joined the staff of a private school and later started a finishing school of her own for young ladies, mainly Welsh farmers' daughters, in Lampeter. Amy went as a governess to a branch of the Cadbury family and became engaged to one of the sons. However, when he was sent to Africa to help manage one of the family's cocoa plantations she decided she did not love him enough to go so far and broke it off, dutifully returning her engagement ring which in due course his mother sent back to her with a sad letter telling of his death from yellow fever. She never did marry. But this was not so much, I think, because she could not forget her Cadbury as because she was temperamentally unsuited to matrimony.

As for my mother, she had to give up the music shop and go to St Martins where my father fell in love with her voice and persuaded her to marry him. They were married in the village church just opposite to Church Farm where they were to live. The church is still very much as it was then, with a square tower, a three-decker pulpit and tall box pews, one of them with a fireplace in it. My father's mother, to whom the Church of England was only a little less evil than the Church of Rome, took a deal of persuading to set foot in it for the ceremony.

By the time I was born in 1903 my mother and father had moved to a larger farm across the road, called Rhos-y-llan. They were at this stage rather prosperous, I think—a go-ahead young farmer and his beautiful young wife, very much a part of what would now be called the younger set; at any rate there were frequent whist evenings and parties at which, if we managed to stay awake, we would sometimes hear my mother singing at the piano. One of my own first recollections is of sitting on the lawn in front of the house and of my mother, looking very lovely in a long, high-waisted dress, dispensing tea to her friends in the mellow sunshine, and of finding a thrush's nest in the garden hedge and drawing her away to see it. I remember being taken to the village shop to buy pink sugar pigs—there were whole families of them—and long black sticks of licorice, and of watching the horses parade at St Martins' Show in the big field belonging to the Cross Keys public house, and of going with my father to call at the tents erected by Bibby's and other agricultural suppliers around the ground, and of being given drinks of fizzy lemonade while he took a tot of whisky and talked about cattle food and such like things.

There was a very tall elm tree at one side of the field, the tallest I ever saw, and I remember being told that my father had climbed to the very top of it when he was a boy and I wondered if I would ever have the courage to do the same. He was a famous tree-climber and taught not only Elsie and me but in due course our children. Even when he was in his seventies he would climb up and down a big walnut tree like a boy in his teens, picking walnuts for his grandchildren and showing them how best to manage the tricky bits as they followed him. 'I think he was the best tree-climbing Grand-dad in the world,' my son said when my father died.

I suppose if we had stayed in St Martins I might have become a farmer like my father and his father and his father's father before him, back through the generations and like my cousins and second cousins still scattered over Shropshire. But I doubt it, for I never had any inclination that way. As long as I can remember I wanted to be a writer of some sort. In any event our life at Rhos-y-llan came to an end when I was still very young.

I am not quite sure why, but it was something to do with my father and two farmer friends of his deciding that instead of sending their milk to a big milk firm they would buy a dairy business in Manchester and put a manager in charge of it, thus cutting out middlemen. I rather suspect that my father may have mortgaged Rhos-y-llan to raise the necessary capital for this venture. At any rate throughout our lives my mother would passionately warn us against mortgages, on which she had views very different from those held by Building Societies. They held place in her mind among the chief enemies of human happiness and the sanctity of the home, along with gambling and drink—a word that had connotations quite unrelated to the taking of a glass of whisky or wine or beer. This suspicion of mortgages may have been acquired from the melodramas at the Wigan Hippodrome in which wicked squires threatened to foreclose on mortgages unless they were allowed their will with innocent daughters. But I think it was more personal.

However this may be it eventually became clear to my father and his two partners that the manager they had appointed to handle their milk in Manchester was defrauding them in a large way and that if they were to save their money one of them must go and look after the Manchester business. I do not know why the choice should have fallen on my father. It may have been that he had involved himself more heavily than they had, or it may have been that the idea of moving to a city attracted my mother who was always restless and whose wishes were always very much my father's guide in life. Later, although she often hinted at dastardly work by people wanting to get their hands on Rhos-y-llan, she would also often say triumphantly, 'But if we hadn't moved what chances would there have been for you to get on a newspaper?' and later still, 'There you are, if we hadn't left Rhos-y-llan you would never have met Jess.' So I think she may have had a hand in what proved, so far as our standard of living was concerned, a somewhat disastrous decision.

Anyway to Manchester, near Victoria Park, we went and I never lived in Shropshire again. Yet it is St Martins and the Griffin that remain at the centre of my childhood memories—far more vividly so than any youthful recollections of Manchester.

The Griffin is much altered now. The walled garden at the front where grew greengages and apricots and delicious plums has gone and the front of the house which in those days was of a lovely mellow red brick has been covered with a sort of cement—to keep the damp out I was told. The huge open fireplace in the kitchen with the oven for making bread at one side and an oak settle at the other onto which the Boss would plump down when he came in from the fields and yell for a girl to take off his boots has been replaced by a modern tiled fireplace such as one may see in any suburban house. So have the fireplaces in the other rooms. Those who live in the country hanker after the facilities of the town. It is the town dwellers who go to live in the country who preserve and restore the old.

In my grandmother's day there was a huge table, scrubbed white, in the middle of the kitchen with hams clothed in muslin hanging from the beam above it and you went down a few steps to the back kitchen with its big stone sink with a pump beside it and a boiler for hot water in the corner. At the side a door went into the dairy, where the milk churns were, and there were great stone slabs with bowls of cream and butter on them and steps down into an arched cellar where there were barrels of home-brewed beer and cider and big stone jars of home-made ginger beer.

You turned right out of the small hall at the front door to go into the kitchen, although it was at the back door leading out of the back kitchen that the main traffic went on, left to go to the front parlour with its Victorian easy chairs with their anti-macassars and its oval mahogany table in the middle where we would play solitaire on rainy days on a beautiful board which I still have. Along a passage there was the back parlour which had a bookcase in it with a popular encyclopaedia and bound volumes of *Punch* and the *Illustrated London News* and the *Strand Magazine* and the *Wide World Magazine* to provide endless entertainment. The stairs, as I remember, went off the passage. Upstairs the bedrooms were low and sweet-smelling with huge four-poster beds in them such as the one in which I had a nightmare about vampires, and you could lean out of the windows and pick roses from the rambler growing up the wall. There were back stairs, too, which went up out of the kitchen to the poky little rooms where the servant girls slept: the un-married farm labourers had a dormitory reached by a ladder out of one of the farm buildings at the back.

Nearly everyone working on the farm lived in and ate at the big scrubbed table in the kitchen and there was always a great stir and bustle about the place. My sister, Elsie, and I were always packed off to the Griffin for a good part of the summer and sometimes, although not so often, I think, some of our cousins would be there too. I cannot remember us having much to do with any other children except when we were taken to visit my father's sister, Aunt Janie, who was married to a prosperous farmer at Gobowen and had four children, three boys and a daughter.

At harvest time we would take lunch to the field for the men; bread and cheese and onions and home-made pies and a stone jar of freshly drawn beer and another of ginger beer which we shared. We would sit beside the hedge while the long line of men with scythes moved across the field, one behind the other, sway-ing in a slow rhythm. Afterwards we would help to rake up the grass and play tag between the lines of haycocks. At the corn harvest there was the greater excitement of the hired self-binders each drawn by two horses following each other round and round the field in narrowing circles until only a tiny island was left to be scythed away in the centre, from which broke terrified rabbits and hares and perhaps a brace or so of partridge. I ought to have felt sorry for them as the ring of men, standing easily watchful with their shot guns resting on the crook of their arms, fired with a spatter of shots, but the pride of carrying back a big hare, its hindlegs linked together, put pity out of my head. When I laid it on the kitchen table the servant girls would exclaim admiringly almost as if I had shot it myself.

I do not ever remember being unhappy in those Shropshire days or ever being treated unkindly there or at home. I suppose I was sometimes scolded but the idea of physical punishment by an adult was totally outside my comprehension, although I knew that if I hurt myself, as I sometimes did climbing about in the big Dutch barn or in the lofts above the stables and cowsheds, it was unmanly to cry. Perhaps it was all very bad for my character, being surrounded by so much kindness, and being loved and appreciated by people who thought that children should be left alone and ordered about as little as possible, even when they were inclined, as I very often was, to dream the days away without any evidence of purposeful activity. There are those I know who regard so idyllic an existence as poor preparation for life in the adult world. I do not think I ever found it so.

CHAPTER 2

Pleasantly to School

When I was six years old I remember the newsboys racing along the streets shouting the death of Edward VII and my father going for a paper and telling us when he came back that when a king died you said, 'The King is dead. Long live the King', to show that the institution was greater than its holder and my mother talking about 'poor old Teddy' and saying that he was the peacemaker, and that when he married Queen Alexandra the papers called her 'the Snow Princess', but that it was Lily Langtry, the Jersey Lily, he was really fond of, and how sad it must be to be a king and not able to marry the one you really loved.

I have only to close my eyes for the sights and sounds of the Shropshire days to come back to me, but this is one of the very few things I remember from our life in Manchester. We lived in a terrace house. There was a sofa covered with horsehair, very shiny and prickly, in the front parlour. Horsehair is coming back into fashion again, I am told, although it seems to me to have no merit but durability and must be specially hard on those wearing mini-skirts. I can remember little else about this house except one winter afternoon when I sat in front of the fire in the parlour with my mother in the half light, eating buttered crumpets. It is a memory of absolute bliss and security. I vaguely remember, too, a shop at the corner of the road with a window packed with tier upon tier of glass jars of brightly coloured sweets and a big empty house in the overgrown garden of which we sometimes played, although I cannot remember any of the children I played with. And I can remember being taken for walks in the park and looking at big circular beds of red flowers and wanting to pick some and being told that you didn't pick flowers in towns, which seemed to me, as a country child, very strange indeed.

But that is all. Yet if I tried I suppose I could go on writing about my Shropshire childhood for many more thousands of words, which perhaps goes to show that children have a great capacity for remembering the pleasant and putting the dull or unpleasant out of mind.

My father hated living in a town. He hated not being able to feel soil under his feet and I find it hard to think how he survived without having cows and horses and pigs about the place. He had a great talent with animals. He could quieten the wildest or most frightened horse by talking to it in his soft, gentle voice until it would put its muzzle against his chest and he would softly stroke its neck as he told it there was nothing at all to be frightened about. When he had a farm all his cows had their own names which he chose to match their characters and they would come to him from the furthest corner of the field when he called to them. To him they all had their own individualities, as separate and unique as those of people. He respected their idiosyncrasies and was as tender to them as he was to those of children. I think he found it easier to commune with animals and children than with grown-up people. He understood them and they understood him.

Nor, I think, did my mother like Manchester as much as she had thought she would. She enjoyed the bustle of the streets and the shop windows, lit and glowing in the evenings, and occasional visits to the theatre—I vividly remember one evening at the Manchester Hippodrome when the whole of the orchestra pit and all the front rows of the stalls were flooded with water so that Mary could go call the cattle home in Charles Kingsley's pathetic poem, 'The Sands of Dee', which my mother recited to us with immense feeling on the tram going home. But she missed the sense of space and found it hard to confine her energies to a house which was tacked on to others and which it was impossible to believe contained any hidden mysteries. Nor could she get out of the habit of wanting to dash into the kitchen for half a dozen new laid eggs or a pound of newly made butter for visitors to take home with them. In a town house she was less than half a person.

Whatever may have been the ambitions that brought us to Manchester it was soon clear that it was an episode to be done with as soon as possible. Financially, I suppose, a little must have been retrieved from the wreck, although my father had small talent for business and my mother had no money sense whatever; to her money was simply something to be spent. However, within a year or two we were in a position to return to farming, although on a very reduced scale from that we had been used to at Rhos-y-llan. The new farm was on the Lancashire-Yorkshire moors between Bacup and Todmorden, one of the bleakest stretches of country you could come across. There were a few meadows on the lower slopes of the farm, but most of it was moorland with tufts of coarse grass suitable only for grazing sheep. There were no servant girls and farm labourers here as at Rhos-y-llan. My mother looked after the house on her own and my father did all the farm work except at harvest time when the Irish came.

The farmhouse was an ugly stone building on the hillside above the village of Britannia which was the site of the highest railway station in England. Yet I remember it as a place of great happiness. Although we were, I think, often in considerable financial difficulties I was too young to be much aware of them and they were disguised from me by my mother's skill in homemaking. She could invest the drabbest room with her personality and although when she was down, as she sometimes was, she would cry out in one of her favourite phrases that she had not the comfort of a workman's cottage, she made it, in fact, very warm and cosy. She also had a wonderful skill in turning odds and ends into tasty meals. I can remember a dish of shredded cabbage treated with butter and vinegar and spiced a little that was most wonderful and that made—as it often had to do—a splendid meal on its own. And she had a way of doing mushrooms fresh picked from the fields and slowly basted in the oven with a little gravy made of melted butter and water salted and peppered again and again as she went along that is unsurpassed in memory by any of the exotic meals I have since eaten in many parts of the world. The secret lay, I think, in the slowness with which the mushrooms were cooked and the constant attention she gave them while cooking. When the mushrooms were all gone one mopped up the lovely rich gravy with thin pieces of brown bread and butter. And she would make brawn from pigs' trotters, and many other things that I suppose were cheap but that under her touch became exquisite delicacies. She had a great sense of the ceremonial quality of a meal—particularly supper in the evening. If we had chicken, as we sometimes did, it had to be served with all its auxiliaries, including an exquisite parsley stuffing and crisp bacon and small home-made sausages and roast potatoes cut in halves.

My father's carving knife, worn to a thin sliver of steel by much sharpening, would flash in the light as it danced up and down, making music against the long steel in his left hand as he gave it its final exquisite edge. Carving was an art that he took seriously. He could scarcely endure to eat if he was forced to watch meat being hacked about by a clumsy carver when, as occasionally happened, we went visiting. He himself could carve a chicken so that it could be put together again when he had done it as though the knife had never touched it, and although I never reached his perfection I am deeply grateful for the pains he took over teaching me to carve well.

It is easier to be poor in the country than in a town—especially for children. And although we were often very short of money I never noticed it much. It hit my sister harder. She was a year or so older than I was and as a girl needed more things that it was not always easy to buy. However, she was a very pretty girl and could get along without much decoration. My mother, for her part, never allowed poverty to colour her outlook on life. She had a large family pride and always assumed that the world owed her deference. We were taught to think of the world as open before us. She had her snobberies but they were snobberies that assured her that anyone connected with herself—her children especially—had a naturally elevated place in the world with which money, which she treated with disdain, had nothing to do.

My father was more worried by unpaid bills than she was and was, I think, often hard put to make ends meet. But having adopted 'Nil desperandum' as his motto he stuck by it and felt it a matter of honour never to feel sorry for himself or allow himself to make comparisons with earlier easier times. He preferred to be poor and independent than be paid well for working for someone else. I remember going to him in great excitement one day and telling him that a boy I knew said his father earned a £1 a day for every single day there was. 'Even Saturdays and Sundays,' I said. It seemed to me an immense amount. 'Wouldn't you like that?' I asked him and he replied, 'Ah, but he works for someone else. I couldn't do that.'

Meanwhile, there was Great-Uncle John's American money to look forward to once that missing document was found and wicked Fanny Kempster to keep an eye on to make sure that she did not get it all for herself. While we waited for news of the finding of the missing document my mother did not waste her time. She cast a romantic eye over the floors and outbuildings of the farm for any hidden treasure that might be concealed within it. The farm was called Hogshead Farm and according to a local story, of which my mother soon learned, had once been a head-quarters for smugglers who brought brandy across the moors and stored it there until it could be disposed of in Manchester not many miles away. There was a vaulted cellar in the farm-house which gave some credence to this and since smugglers always have treasure to hide my mother felt sure that they must have left some bags of gold about the place somewhere. My father took up two stone flags in the kitchen which seemed to her to be loose and then conducted a major excavation in the vaulted cellar which my mother decided was part of a tunnel which had been walled off.

This proved to be the case, but when my father managed to break through the wall, it was not to disclose cases of gold coins or even hogsheads of brandy, but merely a rough tunnel used for digging coal out of the hillside. There were several such tunnels going into the moorside, some of them with rusted narrow-gauge railway tracks along which ponies had drawn coal tubs. Some of these tunnels went a long way under the moor and were ventilated by air shafts bored down from the moor surface. The low roofs of the tunnels were supported by pit props but with age and disuse many of these had rotted away and the tunnels were very dangerous. So were many of the air shafts which were of considerable size and were surrounded by inade-quate fences of stakes and wire to deter sheep from falling into them, which, however, they did with lamentable frequency.

These tunnels and air shafts fascinated my sister and me and one of them provided us with early and no doubt subsequently useful experience of how easy it is to invent evidence and carry it off with aplomb if only one has the right air of self-confidence. Although warned against the danger of these moorland shafts, we could not help envisaging the part they might play in one of those Sherlock Holmes mysteries we read with such avidity in the *Strand Magazine*. Our moor, although not as big as Dartmoor, was, we could not help but feel, quite equal to Dartmoor as a venue for mysterious happenings. Finally we wrote in ink in clumsy blotched letters on one of my sister's handkerchiefs the sad message, 'The horror is too much. I cannot face it longer. This is the only way.' This we put at the edge of the deepest and loneliest shaft with a stone to keep it from blowing away and left it hopefully for someone to find.

No one did and after a week during which the handkerchief was rained on a good deal, which made it look even more authentic, we discovered it ourselves and took it with much excitement to my mother. It provided a challenge she could not resist. Scarcely pausing to question us she caused an urgent message to be sent by the butcher, who was fortunately just delivering some meat at the house, requiring the policeman at Britannia to attend her immediately on a very serious matter. Within an hour or so the policeman was at the house panting more than a little after a long climb up hill, riding and pushing his bicycle. He was already in some awe of my mother whose looks, appearance and voice were so different from those usual to inhabitants of small Lancashire hill farms that he had formed the theory that we must belong to some eccentric but well-connected family experimenting in living the simple life. His natural shrewdness which would undoubtedly have guided him to the truth if he had been dealing with someone he understood better did not, however, entirely desert him. Did she not, he asked my mother, after painfully deciphering the message on the handkerchief, think it might be a joke. 'Perhaps,' he added nervously looking at us, 'by children.' At this my mother's eyes flashed and she drew herself up with all the formidable dignity of a Francis of Leighton. She was not used to being doubted by policemen and was not ready to let her children be impugned by anyone. 'Nonsense,' she said sharply. 'Of course it's genuine.

Just look at the handkerchief. How long,' she asked dramatic-ally when he still seemed undecided, 'How long are you going to leave that poor girl lying dead at the bottom without doing anything? You'd better be off to see your sergeant right away.' At this the policeman prepared to mount his bicycle, only to be called back for a glass of beer. 'I know we can rely on you,' said my mother, turning on him the full force of her charm as he drank it. 'If you have any trouble with your sergeant you send him to me.'

As the policeman rode away I looked across at my father who had been called in by my mother to lend unneeded support, but had not spoken. He gave me a swift secretive wink.

Next day to our excited amazement a police sergeant arrived with the local constable and two others. They had rope and winding-tackle fastened to their bicycles. My mother greeted them like a *grande dame* in a Victorian melodrama preparing to expose a dastardly drime and she and my father, with my sister and I beginning to feel that events were going further and faster than we had intended, walking nervously behind, set off across the moor to the shaft. There, to our horrified delight, a winch was set up over the top of the shaft and the youngest and most athletic policeman with his police torch secured to his chest and his whistle in his mouth was wound slowly down. He took a long time and many blasts on the whistle to reach the bottom, while my sister and I stood at a safe distance wondering what would happen when he reported there was nothing there.

However, when he was finally wound up again it was to report that the shaft led into a disused mine tunnel which was full of water. 'It's terrible black and deep,' he said, as much influenced by now by subjective judgement and my mother's conviction as the rest of us. 'The poor woman can't have had a chance. She must have floated right away.' Overcome by emotion and her own lively imagination my mother at this point dabbed her eyes and was patted on the shoulder in a fatherly fashion by the sergeant. 'There, there, madam,' he said, 'you mustn't take on. It's not your fault. The poor woman must have wanted to end it all very badly.'

By the time we got back home my mother was quite recovered and insisted on the police force having tea and home-made cake before leaving. As she presided over the table she concerned herself with how the poor girl's mother must be feeling not knowing what had happened to her daughter. 'You must find her,' she said. 'And you must cover up that horrible shaft so that no one can ever do it again. I shan't sleep a wink thinking of people throwing themselves down it.' As she talked we could all see a procession of deserted and betrayed young women making their way across the moor to end it all in our shaft. 'There, there, madam,' said the sergeant and added staunchly, 'Don't you worry, luv. We'll cover it up.'

And so, indeed, they did. Within a week a team of men arrived and built a brick roof to the shaft, afterwards surrounding it for additional safety with a strong fence. My sister and I could not help but feel that we had unwittingly accomplished some good in the world, although I sometimes wonder now that she is a magistrate whether my sister is ever troubled by the thought of committing a public mischief in this way.

My mother continued to enjoy the excitement and added the incident to her repertoire of stories, although she could not understand how it was that the police could never discover the girl's identity. Apart from the one swift wink, my father made no comment until many years later when he was in his eighties and my mother was dead. Then, one day sitting in his armchair by the fire, he chuckled and said, 'You and Elsie made it all up, didn't you?' 'Made up what?' 'That girl and that handkerchief. At Hogshead.' I admitted it and said, 'Did you know all the time?' 'Of course,' he said. 'But why didn't you say anything?' He looked at me with a bright beady eye and chuckled again. 'Sally enjoyed it,' he said. 'I didn't want to spoil it for her.'

When first we lived at Hogshead Farm we went to the village school at Britannia. Britannia was no more than two rows of stone houses opening direct on to a street of stone sets with their front-door steps holystoned to a shining whiteness and the Britannia Mill with its tall chimney at one end.

Those were the days of half-timers and in school the elder boys and girls who had started working half time at the mill when they were twelve would put their heads down on their desks in the afternoon and go fast asleep. They had to be at the mill at five o'clock each morning and were wakened just after four by a knocker-up who went round tapping bedroom windows with a long pole. They needed sleep more than lessons and the two teachers understood this and did not often disturb them or let us do so. Except for my sister and myself and a family called Watson who lived in a large decrepit house halfway along the road from Britannia to Hogshead Farm and whose mother was a Christian Scientist—later they emigrated to Boston and when I last met them there the eldest daughter, Phyllis, was working on the *Christian Science Monitor*, which seemed a very satisfactory ending to their emigration—all the children at the school wore clogs and most of the boys were clothed in rough suits of corduroy of a peculiarly evil-smelling kind. It was before science had discovered how to take the smell out. When the room became hot—there was only one schoolroom with two classes, one at each side of the room—the stench became almost unbearable, especially if it had been raining and the corduroy was damp. This had a good effect on my character. It made me careful to avoid getting into fights. I could not stomach rolling about the floor locked in combat with anyone who smelt like that.

The village depended entirely on the cotton mill and the men and women and children all worked in it. This did not affect their independence of character, no doubt because under the system then ruling in the cotton industry each family looked after a loom or set of looms and were paid on results. They were in a sense sub-contractors and, like my father, felt they were their own bosses. They conducted long, bawdy and derisory conversations across the floor of the weaving-shed by lip reading and called the manager and the overseers, who were among the chief butts for their wit, by their Christian names. The first week in August the mill closed for Wakes Week and practically everyone in Britannia except us went in a char-à-banc to Blackpool, taking their year's savings with them. All they left behind was a shilling or two in a tea caddy on the mantelpiece to tide over until pay day came round again after they got back. It was a point of honour to return with nothing in one's pockets.

Every now and then my mother would decide that Britannia school could scarcely provide an education suitable for her children and we would be packed off to Lampeter in Wales where my Aunt Polly had a school of her own. It was in a large old house in an untidy garden but was well thought of by the Welsh farmers' wives who sent their daughters there to be 'finished' by the fashionable Miss Francis, who was well known as a popular social figure at all the local balls. The school was an extremely inefficient establishment but had an untidy charm. Auntie Polly was what was known in those days as a flirt and had a constant retinue of suitors. She was out late at dances or concerts almost every evening and consequently found it difficult to get up in the morning so that she was often still in bed when school should have started. Sometimes she had a French mademoiselle to help her and we would all be given French lessons until my aunt came down. However, few of these French mistresses stayed long and when they left the farmers' daughters who boarded at the school were delighted to look after the younger children until my aunt felt in a fit state to face the world again. They did not seem to mind and, as she explained to them, it was all education.

My aunt was much admired for her paintings, which for the most part consisted of large canvasses of highland cattle or smaller ones of lovers saying farewell on rustic bridges spanning tumbling streams, and she was also well known for the dresses she designed for herself for fancy-dress balls. These were considered very dashing and added greatly to her artistic and social reputation. She had high cheekbones like my mother and dark black hair and although less delicately boned than my mother was equally temperamental and vivacious and a leader of Lampeter society, at least among the younger folk. Everyone, including my mother, expected her to make a brilliant marriage, which was the best thing a girl could do in those days, but she enjoyed flirtation too much and left it too late and eventually, to everyone's surprise, ran away with the manager of a confectionery business who was as big a flirt as she was and had nothing much to commend him except that he was a good dancer. They went to live in Barnstaple in Devon and spent their lives quarrelling furiously.

Like all her family Auntie Polly was devoted to children and would have liked some of her own. This proved impossible and she adopted a little girl who now lives in Chicago, where she is married to a very charming American man who is something rather abstruse in electronics. When my wife and I spent some months at Wisconsin University in Madison a year or two ago we saw a great deal of them and would scarcely have survived the rigours of life in a mid-Western winter but for their friendship and kindness. My debt to Auntie Polly, which was already considerable, was thus posthumously increased.

Although Lampeter had its excitements I soon grew tired of its predominantly feminine company and became homesick. At such times I would make paper darts in my bedroom and launch them through the window with messages appealing to passers-by to rescue me. These were brought back to my aunt by excitable and curious Welsh people and would often be followed by dramatic scenes in which they would join with her in bewailing the sorrows of the young and in trying to cheer me up with promises of future pleasures. However, if I remained inconsolable Auntie Polly would write to my mother and she would come by train to take me back. Sometimes my sister would come with us, sometimes she would stay on at Auntie Polly's school, which as a girl she found more fun than I did, although I do not imagine she got much formal education there, any more than I did. For the most part we both escaped being educated, so that our natural curiosity was not blunted. And as there were usually plenty of books about we picked up knowledge in our own way from these and from the conversation of our elders and did not much miss the formal teaching we never got.

At Britannia I could roam about the moors at will, walking and scrambling for miles until I was tired, when I would fling myself down on the short grass and give myself over to dreams as the peewits called in the sky above me. Usually I had an old collie dog as my companion and she would lie down close beside me and let me rest my head on her if I wanted to as though she were a pillow. Sometimes one or two boys from the village school would come with me and we would try to catch the horned sheep that roamed about the moor and see how long we could stay on their backs. If it was one of the big old rams we caught it would make straight for one of the high dry-stone walls and leap onto the top, leaving its rider sprawling among the stones.

On Saturday mornings we would sometimes walk across the moors to Bacup to a cinema hall known to everyone as the flea-pit, where we had the wonderful experience of seeing early Charlie Chaplin films, and Buster Keaton and the Keystone Cops and other such now legendary figures of the cinema's age of innocence. They came to us on a flickering screen with a piano strumming at the side without any preparatory warning, so that like Cortez on his peak in Darien we were struck silent with the wonder of it all, or would have been had we not been compelled to uncontrollable laughter. And there was one wonderful day when my father took us to see Buffalo Bill—the real genuine Colonel William Cody—and his circus in a field outside Bacup—that circus which as the posters weeks ahead had told us had been seen and admired by all the crowned heads of Europe, which did not surprise us, for what was a crowned head compared to Buffalo Bill and all the real cowboys and Red Indians he brought with him?

There was also a tremendous day when everyone lined the streets of Britannia to cheer the first tram from Rochdale to Bacup, decorated with flags and with the driver clanging his bell and the Mayors of Bacup and Rochdale riding on the platform wearing their chains. We felt as though now at last we were in the centre of things, linked to the world and all its wonders.

Such peaks as these were rare, of course. For the most part pleasures were more modest, like helping with the hay at harvest time. Two or three of my friends from Britannia school would come to help and at the end of the week, when my father paid the Irish labourers who came over in a team and who slept in one of the farm buildings, he would give each of us 3d for our week's wages. When we had it we would swagger down to Britannia and go to the fish-and-chip shop where we would each order a penny mixture—a bowl of peas with chips on the top—on which we would sprinkle salt and pepper and vinegar with a professional hand. We would buy a bottle of pop to drink—there was a glass marble in the neck which you had to press down before you could get the pop to come gurgling down your throat—and would sit on the bench at the side of the shop and eat our penny mixtures and drink our pop and listen to the grown-up conversation, and would not, as my grandmother used to say, have had the King for cousin.

In winter the moors were covered with snow and we would toboggan down the hill above the farm. When the milking was done and supper cooking in the oven my mother and father would join us and we would race each other down the long slope, my mother and I on one toboggan, my sister and my father on the other to make it fair, or so my mother would say, with a man to guide each one with heels ready to jam in the snow to swerve or stop. The moon would come up and all the world would be bright and glittering. Afterwards we would go in to supper and after supper my mother would cook chestnuts on the bars of the kitchen grate and we would read aloud to each other. We read most of Dickens on winter evenings round the fire and *Uncle Tom's Cabin* and a life of President Garfield called *From Log Cabin to White House*, of which my mother was very fond. She had a great taste for stories recounting the rise of famous men, particularly if they had difficulties to overcome along the way, and like many people was inclined to think rather disparagingly of fiction unless it had a polemical purpose. She also had a passion for disconnected facts. Like George Newnes, the Manchester fancy-goods salesman who made a fortune out of the magazine *Tit-Bits* when his wife bullied him into turning his hobby to practical use, she loved cutting things out of magazines and newspapers. But unlike him she did not paste them into a scrapbook, she stuffed them under the cushion of her chair so that as the years went by she sat higher and higher on a stratified mountain of clippings. She would never agree to destroy any of them, arguing that at any moment she might want to refer to one; when I announced fairly early on in my life that I wanted to be a journalist, she seized on this as another excuse for keeping them all. 'Think how useful they will be to Frank,' she would say.

Both she and my father hated going to bed. Life, they felt, was too short to waste in sleeping and although they knew in theory that children ought to go to bed early, they could never bring themselves to urge it on us in more than a half-hearted fashion—especially if it was a holiday and we did not have to get up early for school.

We had a pony called Nellie who had come from the Pentre. My father had taken me with him to fetch her and there had been a wonderful three days driving from Shropshire in an open pony trap and putting up at small inns where we saw that Nellie was comfortable and well fed in the stable before we took our own supper together in grown-up fashion. In winter the farm was often snow-bound and Nellie was shod in strong leather boots to pull the milk float, which was lifted off its wheels and put on home-made runners. To drive to the station by sledge in the cold first light of a winter day with the snow stretching for miles all around was like living in a Russian story in the library of international literature in twenty-four red half-leather volumes that my mother had bought.

We were still living in Britannia when the war came—although I was in Oswestry with my grandmother on the day it started. It did not affect us, or most of the people in Britannia very directly. My father was too old to join the Army and was told that it was his duty to stay and produce food. The Britannia mill was busy on contracts for army clothing, so that most people were better off than usual. Nor could even my mother persuade herself that there was much danger from German spies on the moors, although she kept a brisk look-out at night for mysterious lights flashing signals to Zeppelins. I was in the Scouts and on Scout nights we would be posted to guard a near-by reservoir—although against what was never quite clear. My mother longed to do something to help the soldiers and collected all that remained of her family treasures from Leighton, including several old and valuable candlesticks and early rush light-holders that ought to have gone to a museum and gave them all to jumble sales where they went for a few shillings to raise money for wool with which to knit Balaclava helmets for the men in the trenches. She was intensely patriotic and when she read atrocity stories, which she implicitly believed, about Germans cutting off the hands of children she burned with horror and indignation. But she thought it very wicked of people to hand young men white feathers and since she had no inhibitions about speaking her mind in public would round on anyone she saw doing so.

My sister and I were by now at a secondary school at Rawtenstall—a small textile town famous for its brass and silver bands which had won many contests in more peaceful days—and I can remember how we all gathered together in the main hall shortly after I went there to cheer the captain of the school and four other sixth formers who were leaving to go straight into the army. Within a few weeks three of them were dead, the first names on the school's roll of honour.

We did not, however, live out the war in Britannia, but moved soon after it began to Middleton, near Manchester, where my father had found a slightly larger and more cultivatable farm. I never went back to Britannia or Bacup after that, but I must still carry some evidence of life there in my accent. A year or so ago I was speaking at Guildford Cathedral where, although I am a Humanist—or perhaps because of it, for it is a very broad-minded and tolerant Cathedral Chapter—I had been invited by a very dear friend, Canon Chapman, to give the first of what are called the Guildford Lectures. These are an annual series of lectures on issues of social importance which attract audiences of getting on for two thousand and pack the Cathedral. At the end of my lecture I walked down the aisle with the Bishop so that we could stand by the door and say goodnight to members of the audience as they left. It was an audience of all denominations and of none and as I stood with Bishop Reindorp at the door, a nun came up to me. 'As I listened to you,' she said, 'I was trying to place where you spent your childhood. Was it Bolton? No, Bacup. That's it. You must have lived in Bacup.'

'For a few years when I was very young,' I said.

'I thought so,' said this Professor Higgins in a nun's habit and, with a small nod of satisfaction, hurried off after her friends into the night, leaving me with no explanation of how she had been able to pick out from my speech the cadences of this small town in the Lancashire hills which so far as I can remember has never, perhaps to my shame, been included in any of my references in *Who's Who* or elsewhere.

Middleton is now physically almost a part of Manchester and Batty Farm, where we lived, has become the site of a large Manchester Corporation housing estate. But in those days Middleton was still very much a place with its own character—indeed I dare say it still is for its sort of individuality is not easily eroded, however powerful the tides of development that engulf it. From our garden you could count more than a hundred mill chimneys sending out clouds of smoke all the way to Rochdale to the north and Oldham to the west, so that the whole landscape could only be seen through a grey haze. When the mills shut down in the depression that followed the war the sky suddenly became clean and clear and it was possible for the first time to see the true contours of hills and valleys. For the first time the grass in our fields was soft and green and if one touched it one's hand was no longer covered with grimy soot.

Although the mill chimneys and the tight-packed back-to-back houses spread across all the hills to the north and west with scarcely a break except for here and there a dirty recreation ground with football posts at each end, there were still a few green fields to the west where Batty Farm was and if one walked from behind the farm along the road to Birch it was almost possible to imagine oneself in the country.

Middleton is an old town with an ancient black and white inn in the High Street in the centre of the town and opposite it, in a park that climbed up to the church, there was a free public library. When my sister and I wanted tickets for this library my mother was horrified. In those days free public libraries were still considered to be institutions for those too poor to buy books for themselves. My mother felt it not only socially reprehensible for her children to borrow books from a free library, but also hygienically dangerous. She was convinced that any books obtained from such a source would be smothered in germs. When, therefore, we did manage to bring a book home from the library she would at once seize it from us and after sprinkling it with Jeyes Fluid, of which she always had a bottle handy, would put it in the oven beside the kitchen fire. She believed that if you cooked germs they died. However, she was easily diverted to other things and it would often happen that the book was forgotten until attention was drawn to it by clouds of smoke, whereupon flinging open the oven door she would seize the book in a pair of tongs and rush with it to the kitchen sink, where she would run cold water over it. After this procedure the brown charred, soggy mass was capable neither of being read nor returned to the library and the amount we had to pay in fines for 'lost' books astonished the librarian. When we argued with my mother about this method of dealing with books she would open her eyes wide with astonishment and say, 'But of course you must kill the germs.'

Many years later I told this story in a debate in the House of Lords on the Public Lending Right. I was arguing the case for library royalty payments to authors and pointing to the change in the public attitude to free libraries which have now become the main prop of middle-class reading. It was a long debate and a very interesting one. But, as I am sure she would have been delighted to discover, only my mother interested the *Daily Express*. It compressed the four-hour debate into one short paragraph: 'Peer's Mother Cooks the Books.'

Like most small Lancashire textile towns, Middleton was wonderfully free of class consciousness. It had the egalitarianist attitudes one finds in small American towns. This did not prevent there being great differences in wealth, but it checked the tendency among the rich to 'put on side'. Mill owners, managers and mill workers had usually gone to school together and still went to the same chapels and drank in the same pubs. This did not prevent them from hating each other's guts at times but it did prevent social life from being poisoned by the snobberies that afflict the south. Moreover, since most of the women as well as the men traditionally worked in the mills, there was considerable sex equality as well as social equality. It was a rough and materialist society but it was a free, open and jolly one with a healthy independence which, although it sometimes regarded rudeness as a positive virtue, was very encouraging to live in. I never cease to be grateful for having been brought up during my late childhood and adolescence in such a society.

It also offered me the immense advantage of education in a small co-educational comprehensive day school which had the good fortune to have a lazy headmaster at its head and a staff which, partly no doubt because it had been much attenuated by the war, did not worry itself about competing for academic honours but was content to take life easily.

Queen Elizabeth's Grammar School had been founded by Bishop Langley in the reign of Elizabeth I, had fallen into decay, been revived in the eighteenth century and eventually in the twentieth amalgamated with a girls' High School to become a co-educational Grammar School under the Local Authority. There were free places for scholarship children and an equal number for those—of whom I was one—whose parents paid a fee. The scholarship children tended to be more brainy than the others, or at any rate more serious in their addiction to study, the paying children more interested in social activities and in enjoying themselves. But all were mixed together in the same forms and joined in the same out-of-school activities. There was no attempt to create either an intellectual or social élite.

The Head was a local boy from Middleton Junction. He had

done well for himself by scholarships to school and university and having, in due course, achieved the peak of his ambition by becoming, no doubt with the help of a patriotic Education Committee, Headmaster of the Grammar School in his native town, saw no reason to struggle further. He believed in leaving staff and pupils alone as much as possible, although he would sometimes take classes in French, in which he had taken his university degree, and occasionally perambulate the school and pop into one class or another just to show he was keeping his eye on things. On such occasions he would bark a question or two before retiring again to his study. These attempts to strike awe into the school were never pressed far or with much vigour and when one small boy on whom he pounced replied, 'How should I know, sir, and why pick on me?' he let it pass without further to-do. His main efforts were directed to trying to cure as many of his pupils as he could of their Lancashire accents and as I already passed this test he troubled me rarely—especially after he had looked over my shoulder one day to see what I was reading and discovered that instead of it being, as he had suspected, a 'penny blood' it was *The Master of Ballantrae*—a taste that convinced him that I had better be left to myself.

The rest of the staff when I first went there in the middle of the war consisted only of a small group of women teachers—mostly Middleton born—who had long since let such fires of ambition as may once have consumed them die down into a kindly benevolence, and one elderly schoolmaster in a tattered gown, which caused him to be known as Shirt. Shirt had been in San Francisco during the great earthquake of 1906 when, so he assured us, his hair had turned white in a single night. He would sometimes organize out-of-school expeditions, instructing all who wished to take part in them to arrive at 9 a.m. with strong boots, a packet of sandwiches and an active mind. Although Shirt would occasionally remember former pedagogic aspirations and give lines for work undone there were few punishments. I can never remember the cane being used.

It never occurred to any of us that the fact that we were a mixed community of boys and girls might cause problems. I was later much astonished to find how terrified of co-education many English, although not, of course, American, educationists were and for what varied reasons—and how little many of them knew

34

of what had been common practice in a great many north-country grammar schools for a great many years. Their fears have always seemed to me to provide evidence of how remote from real life schoolmasters, particularly English schoolmasters, can become. In retrospect the relationships between boys and girls at Q.E.G.S. seem to me to have been friendly but also, or so I imagine it would seem to many now, remarkably innocent and sexless. Boys and girls went about a good deal together in small groups out of school but there were few complicated emotional tangles. We were neither bored by the other sex nor over-heated by its presence.

There were no dance halls in Middleton in those days nor much else in the way of entertainment except occasional school parties and tennis and cricket club dances and mostly we made our own pleasures. On Saturday evening we walked up and down the main street of Middleton, which was generally known as the Bunny Run, stopping and talking to other groups we met who were similarly occupied, or else talked and sang songs around the piano in each other's houses (not that I was very good at this: to my mother's great indignation the music master at Q.E.G.S. commented starkly in my school report, 'Singing: no idea'), or listened to Jack playing his ukelele.

Jack, who was my closest friend, and his sister, Jeannie, were figures of some glamour not only because of Jack's prowess as an athlete, which was considerable, but because every school holiday they departed for Canada with their mother travelling on a Canadian Pacific liner across the Atlantic and then by train across the continent to Vancouver where their father lived. This procedure was made necessary by their mother's Middleton distrust of tearing up her roots. When she and her husband were first married he was in a bank but he had an uncle who had emigrated to Canada and had been one of the first settlers in British Columbia, then for the most part farming land. He had settled on a farm in what was later to become the City of Vancouver and in process of time with the development of the city found himself rich; owner of, among other things, many building lots ripe for development, of a salmon cannery, an ice plant and the Vancouver race-track. He had no children and in due course summoned his only nephew to come and join him and help in the running of the business.

Mrs Wilkinson refused to have anything to do with this if it meant a break with Middleton. She would agree only if they kept their terrace house in Rhodes, which was a village joined on to Middleton famous for the largest mill chimney in the district, and if she could live there for at least half the year and send their two children to school in Middleton. So every school holiday Jack and Jeannie and their mother went to Vancouver to spend their holidays in some splendour in a large house in the best residential part of Vancouver and take part in a whirl of social events appropriate to their great-uncle's and later their father's position as men of prominence and wealth and at the end of each school holiday they returned happily to their small terrace house alongside Rhodes' mill chimney and to Queen Elizabeth's Grammar School. No one in Middleton thought this an odd thing to do. It seemed to them what any sensible Middleton woman would do in like circumstances.

Middleton had little to offer in the way of art or literary interest but Manchester was at the end of a short tram ride and Manchester was still benefiting from the great period of cultural awakening brought by the rich German merchants who had settled there before the war. The Hallé Orchestra was in full maturity at the Free Trade Hall and Miss Horniman was still at the Gaiety Theatre, although not for much longer. Scott was at the *Manchester Guardian* and C. E. Montague was writing leading articles for it of a wonderful penetration and grace. James Agate and Stanley Houghton and Harold Brighouse wrote on the theatre, Samuel Langford and later Neville Cardus on music, Eric Newton on art, Alan Monkhouse on books. James Bone was 'at the London end'. It was a university in itself for a boy enraptured by the diversity of life and determined to be a writer. In Manchester, also, there was the Literary and Philosophical Society to which 'Shirt' introduced me, and the Playgoers Club which read plays every Sunday evening. So I would take the tram to Manchester on a winter evening, swaying and swooping in the dark through that bizarre landscape of narrow streets and back-to-back houses, recreation grounds and corner shops, drab public houses and lighted chapels from which music came, that Lowry was to make famous, into a world of literature and art and liberal discussion that widened the horizons of my life in a way that nothing else could.

I wrote poems and had one accepted by *Country Life* and another by the *Weekly Westminster Gazette* and was much thought of for doing so by Queen Elizabeth's Grammar School, which was tolerant of achievement however eccentric or even useless it might seem. It was a school ideally suited to the following of one's own bent for it had no ambition to make its pupils alike or to compel them to follow a pre-ordained path of excellence, nor was it much concerned about examination results, which in any event did not loom so large in the lives of the young in those days as they do now. I suppose it followed many of the principles since popularized by progressive educationists. But it did so, I am sure, by accident and unselfconsciously.

Although I would never claim to be fully educated I learned many of the things I wanted to know at Queen Elizabeth's Grammar School and especially, which is one of the most valuable things one can learn, how to track down what I wanted. I look back on my schooldays as on the rest of my childhood with unfashionable pleasure and have often found myself commiserating with friends of mine who went to great and famous public schools. In so far as 'Pa B.' had a philosophy of education —and I may well be doing him an injustice in thinking that what he had was mainly a cover for natural laziness—it was that people learned what they wanted to learn and although they might go through school doing nothing very much in their early years would start working at a rapid pace once they found out what it was they wanted to do and saw some practical purpose in education.

Certainly his methods—if methods they were—suited me. And I imagine they must have suited others, too, for although it was a small school it produced a fairly rich crop of individualists, including a Suffragan Bishop, a ballet dancer, several quite good scientists, an All-England lacrosse player, one or two journalists, a county cricketer, a writer of stories for boys and several successful industrialists, as well as a considerable number of people adequately competent in their own line and very pleasant to know.

My mother, for whose children nothing but the best was good enough, was, it is true, sometimes concerned as to whether her son ought not to go to a larger and more famous school. She had her eyes on Manchester Grammar School which was then beginning under J. L. Paton to establish for itself its great reputation as a nurturer of talent and winner of open university scholarships. Finally she had her way to the extent that as my time at Q.E.G.S. drew to a close it was decided that I should try to gain an entry into Manchester Grammar School, which at that time took a certain number of late entrants from local grammar schools in its senior school. And so I took tram to Manchester for several days to sit an entrance examination. This, fortunately, I failed to pass.

I do not think I should have enjoyed Manchester Grammar School, although when I met Paton later at the Manchester Literary and Philosophical Society I got on with him very well and learned to like and admire him, and he was good enough to say he thought he would have enjoyed having me in his Sixth Form.

If I had gone to Manchester Grammar School there is, I suppose, a possibility that I would have passed from there to a university instead of getting a job on the staff of a weekly newspaper. This, perhaps mistakenly, I have never regretted. Moreover, not getting into Manchester Grammar School had one most fortunate consequence for me. Instead of making a new circle of friends I kept my links with Queen Elizabeth's Grammar School even after leaving it. And to Queen Elizabeth's Grammar School there came a young English mistress fresh from the university, about whom I first heard from Jack Wilkinson. She was, he said, very gay and special and young and full of fun and not 'like a teacher at all'. And so I met her and we talked for hours about books and went to the theatre in Manchester and Liverpool and on long cycle rides and wrote to each other about innumerable things and in due course fell in love and a very few years later married. And that was the best thing that ever happened to me.

CHAPTER 3

To Cover the Waterfront

So far as I know there had been no journalists in my family
until I decided to be one—nothing, in fact, but farmers and an
occasional country clergyman for, I suppose, some four hundred
years or so until I picked the idea of being a journalist out of
the air.

It was easier to say one wanted to be a journalist than to
become one. Manchester was an important newspaper town, but
although the people I managed to see at various newspaper
offices were kind and helpful they had no place for a schoolboy
without training. 'You must,' they said, 'get a start on a weekly
paper. Keep your eye on the advertisements in the *Daily
News*.'

So I did. It proved a disappointing procedure. However,
eventually a reply I sent to an advertisement for a junior
reporter on the *Bootle Times* brought a response. I was asked to
go and see them with a view to joining the staff at a salary of £2
a week.

My mother went with me. In retrospect this seems an
astonishing thing for her to do and one likely to inflict on me the
maximum of embarrassment. But I cannot remember that it
did or that I minded, any more than I did when as a small boy
lined up on Bacup Station to entrain for a Scout camp the curate
of the church to which the Scout troop was attached had
informed me in a loud voice that he had received a letter from
my mother instructing him not to let me sleep in damp sheets.
Instead of blushing, as I suppose the curate expected, I said

brightly: 'That's the sort of thing she would do, sir. Don't you bother your head about it.'

When she said she would come to Bootle I did not mind in the least. She might embarrass other people. She could not embarrass me. Also I knew that if she had made up her mind to come, there was no way of stopping her. She would listen in the most charming way to all your arguments, agree enthusiastically with what you said, and then do exactly what she wanted. So I said, 'Yes, do come' and we promised each other a pleasant outing in Liverpool after the meeting, which was with a Mr Smith, the Managing Director.

Mr Smith turned out to be a rat-like little man who also owned a slice of the local theatre, a situation inhibiting to sound dramatic criticism by reporters on the *Bootle Times*, as I subsequently discovered. However, he was extremely affable, especially to my mother. He jumped to the conclusion that she was a widow and fussed over her as if she were delicate porcelain to be protected from the harsh world. Whenever we met subsequently he would say to me, 'And how is your *dear* mother?' in tones that made it clear he thought me of too coarse a texture to appreciate her. He was a snobbish little man and much impressed when she observed that until I settled down I would stay with Cousin Sarah who lived, it turned out, in an expensive residential area of Bootle towards which Mr Smith himself had aspirations not yet fulfilled. I had never previously come across Cousin Sarah and wondered if my mother had invented her for the occasion. However, it turned out that she really did exist and was actually a second cousin related in some way to 'wicked Fanny Kempster' although innocent in my mother's eyes of that lady's crimes. She was large and gracious and, unlike my mother, genuinely a widow. Her husband had been a Liverpool merchant. We took tea with her in a drawing-room excessively full of china bric-à-brac and after much talk of distant Francis relations she said that she would be charmed if I would stay with her until I found respectable lodgings and that she always had tea at 4.30 and a light supper at seven o'clock and did hope that this would suit me and that I would not have to stay up very late at night. This made it clear to me that whatever the shock to Mr Smith I must find more plebeian lodgings as soon as I could.

In 1920 the offices of the *Bootle Times* were in a single storey
wooden building with a corrugated tin roof attached to Bootle
Station with a printing-shed behind in which there were two
linotype machines and an old-fashioned flat-bed press. The
paper has long since abandoned these decrepit premises and is
now installed in a slap-up modern building with the very latest
in web-offset production equipment: a year ago as a member of
the panel of judges for an annual newspaper design award I was
nostalgically pleased to vote it one of the two best-designed
weekly newspapers in the country. Such triumphs were not in
sight when I joined its editorial staff. This staff consisted of
Mr Light, the Editor, an amiable and witty man with a weak
chest and a liking for whisky who wrote a weekly column signed
Lux and had once been a sub-editor on the *Daily Sketch*, a girl
named Micky Kerrigan, who subsequently married an insurance
clerk in Liverpool called Cyril Morton who turned to journalism
and became News Editor of the *Daily Mirror* in its brashest,
yellow journalism days, and a young fellow serving indentures
called Bill Summers who after a period on the *People* and *John
Bull* came to the *Daily Herald* as its chief industrial sub-editor
when I was its Editor.

The editorial offices consisted of two rooms. There was an
inner room in which sat the Editor at a large desk with a box
at one side of it in which one had to put copy for him to attend
to. There were also two very small desks rather like school desks
by the window, the bottom half of the window being painted a
dark green to prevent people from looking in. At one of these
desks sat Miss Kerrigan. The other was given to me. This meant
one was under the Editor's eye except when he popped out
for a quick one at the Station Hotel. Fortunately he did this
frequently, preceding each departure with the remark, 'Got to
go and see a man about a dog.' Bill Summers sat in a small outer
room that also acted as a waiting-room for visitors. The walls of
both these rooms were hidden by ancient file copies of the paper
bound in black and if one tried to pull out one of these one was
likely to dislodge equally ancient beer and whisky bottles
stuffed down the back by long since departed members of the
staff. The corrugated tin roof had corroded in places above the
window and there was a row of jam jars on the window sill to
catch raindrops. As the junior resident of the Editor's room one

of my duties was to empty these jars before they overflowed. These decrepit conditions by no means disturbed me. On the contrary they added to the glamour of journalism. This, I thought proudly, was very different from a bank or other respectable agency of the hum-drum life.

The paper came out on Friday and on Thursday evening we brought sandwiches and flasks of coffee and stayed until about two in the morning reading galley proofs. At intervals the wail of a violin would come from the printing-shop. This belonged to the head printer, a small ancient man with a drooping white moustache much stained by the juice of chewing tobacco. Like many printers in those days he had at one time moved about the country earning his living as a journeyman. He had finally come to rest for no particular reason in Bootle. He was a single man and his violin was his chief companion in life. He brought it with him on Thursday nights to sustain him while he waited for the formes to be ready for clamping on the single flat-bed press. His favourite tune was the Barcarolle from *The Tales of Hoffman* and he played it with a mournful passion that seemed beautiful and haunting at one o'clock in the morning as we read the long galley proofs.

I was talking to Bill Summers in his little room on my first day when the porter came in from Bootle Station to tell us that a man had just hanged himself in the station w.c. The porter was an ex-seaman and a great friend of Bill's and he was writing a novel. His name was James Hanley and the novel was *The Furys*. It did not get itself published until more than ten years later, for novels of working-class life were not as much appreciated then as they later became, but it made a great impact when it did appear and was followed in due course by some thirty other books. However, when he dropped in to tell us about the suicide in the w.c., Hanley did not look like a distinguished novelist of the future. He looked like a small railway porter in a uniform too big for him. We walked over to the pub opposite and Bill stood him a beer for giving us the news and me one to welcome me to Bootle. Afterwards Bill and I went to the police station to check. The desk sergeant told us they had also just had a report that a man had been killed in a drunken fight outside a pub near the docks, so that I thought I was doing well, a murder and a suicide on my first day.

On this first day at the *Bootle Times* Bill Summers dropped a note on my desk as he went by to put some copy in the Editor's box. It read: 'How much are they paying you and are you a Socialist?' I dropped a note on his desk in reply when I went to the lavatory: '£2 a week. No. A Liberal.' Neither part of this answer pleased Bill. He was getting only 15s. a week as an indentured pupil and could not see why I, without any experience at all, should get nearly three times as much. Not that he bore me any malice; it was Smith, the exploiter, he was against. As for Liberals he regarded them with contempt. They were part of the wave of the past, only marginally better than Conservatives.

In fact, although Liberal was a label I had inherited from my father, I was remarkably unpolitical at this time. I wanted to be a writer and held that to be a good writer was much more worth while than being Prime Minister. I had not then met any Prime Ministers but subsequent acquaintanceship with several has not much altered my opinion.

All the same I cannot help but feel that my lack of interest in politics when I went to Bootle showed a certain insensitivity on my part considering what was happening around me. The truth is I had had a very sheltered life. Although we lived on the edge of an industrial area my father and mother were too preoccupied with their farm to have much part in it, except for occasional darts by my mother when her sympathies were roused by something. Bootle gave me my first experience of living and working in a world of ordinary people caught up in the general movement of events.

Bill Summers and Micky Kerrigan had been habitués of such a world from childhood. Both of them were the children of seamen and lived in streets where the loss of a ship could widow half the women in the street. They had known what it was to have fathers and elder brothers out of work for long periods. Bootle was a part of Merseyside. It lived very largely by and for ships. While the war was on there had at least been jobs for everyone. Now they became scarcer and scarcer. Among my first jobs on the *Bootle Times* was reporting the big open-air meetings of the unemployed in the docks, which hopelessly demanded Government aid while the police stood by on the outskirts waiting for violence to break out. Mr Light would knock out the adjectives when I brought back my copy. 'You're a reporter, not a crusader,' he would say. Sitting back in his chair and lighting a fresh cigarette from the stub of the old one he would give me a lecture on the need for the reporter to be detached, telling me for illustration, as I suppose thousands of junior reporters had been told in their day, of how General Booth of the Salvation Army, following his usual practice at the climax of a great revivalist meeting, had thundered, 'Are you saved?' and pointed a dramatic finger at a little man in a crumpled raincoat in the front row. Whereupon the little man had risen and replied with dignity, 'I'm the press.'

'You're not there to be saved or to save. You're there to report,' said Mr Light, drawing clouds of smoke into his tormented lungs and coughing ferociously. 'So cut out the adjectives. Reporters shouldn't be involved.'

I did not find this easy. Especially when I broke away from the crushing respectability of Cousin Sarah and sought less polite lodgings.

My landlady was a small quick woman with wispy hair who went out cleaning every morning. Her husband was an unemployed ship's engineer and they had one son, a thin young man with a cough who worked as a shop assistant in a chain shoe-store and was dying of tuberculosis, which at that time was usually called consumption. He had a white peaked face and his lips were blue and he longed to have a silk shirt with a pleated front but there was no money to buy one.

His father had been out of work for a year when I first went to stay there. In his youth he had been engineer on a pilot boat on the Ganges and had had a wonderful time. Afterwards he had served on ocean-going liners and had travelled the world. But when he got married he thought it was time to settle down and he got a job in a ship-building yard. He was a qualified man and at first he did well and during the war earned big money—or what seemed to him in those days big money. But he was fifty-four and was one of the first to be stood off when work fell away after the war. He had never forgotten his mother's teaching when he was a boy on Clydeside that if you were thrifty and put a bit by, God would see to it that you came to no harm so he had a bit saved when this happened and reckoned that they would be all right for a week or two until things looked up. By the time I went there all the savings had long since gone. But he still hoped. He could not believe that he was already on the scrapheap.

Every morning he got up at six o'clock and put on his dungarees and cut himself a piece of thick bread and margarine and went off to look for work. Sometimes before he went to bed he would say, 'I think I'll go and see McCulloch in the morning. Him and me used to be mates in the old days. He knows what I can do.' Or it would be someone else he used to know in the old days who knew that he was a skilled reliable man ready to do a good day's work. But they never did give him a job. There were no jobs to give. When he'd done the round of the docks he would go to the free library and queue up with the others to look at the jobs vacant columns in the papers—all the racing news was blacked out so that none of them should be tempted to throw their money away gambling. But there were rarely any jobs and when there were they had always been filled by the time he got there by someone who knew someone.

And so he would come home and sit on a chair in the kitchen with his hands on his knees staring at the fire, which was never lit until the evening. He would sit there for hours never saying a word.

Once a week his wife had friends in the front parlour. They sat around the table and had a spiritual séance and put their hands on the table and waited for the table to rap. They used to be visited by a Red Indian spirit and sometimes he would say that things would soon get better, although sometimes he wasn't sure. My landlady drew comfort from these visitations, and, I suppose, courage. She would try to persuade her husband to sit with them but he never would. He got so that he could not bear company of any kind. Sometimes in the evenings I would sit with him in the kitchen and try to get him to talk about the old days at sea or tell him about some meeting I'd been at in the docks. But as time passed it became harder and harder to get him to talk at all. You could see a man disintegrating before your eyes.

The *Bootle Times* was an Independent paper—which meant, of course, a Conservative one. Smith was against getting the paper 'involved in politics' and like many others he thought that to be Conservative was to be non-political. It was only Liberals and Socialists who wanted to drag politics into public affairs. Mr Light would have liked to give his 'young lions' a freer hand. But he did not dare get into trouble with Smith. He played safe and cut out our adjectives. We understood, and with the cruelty of youth, we loved him and despised him. We yearned, Miss Kerrigan, Bill Summers and I, to stir the public conscience and reshape the world.

Since the *Bootle Times* would not let us campaign we joined the Independent Labour Party and sang the Red Flag and the Internationale and dreamed of dying on the barricades. The meetings of the I.L.P. were held in a room above a fish and chip shop. 'Frying Tonight', it would say on the window and we would stop and buy threepennyworth of chips well sprinkled with salt and vinegar to take to the meeting with us. We would pass them round while we listened to the speaker and when the speech was over someone would pop downstairs for another threepennyworth so that the speaker could have some too. Although dedicated to solemn things like political justice and social equality and from each according to his means, to each according to his needs, these I.L.P. evenings were gay and jolly.

We were gay, I suppose, because it seemed so obvious that Utopia could not be long delayed. No one could want the world to stay as it was and everyone we admired was already on our side. Bernard Shaw and H. G. Wells, for instance, and G. K. Chesterton, although one could not always be sure of him, since he was apt to be carried away by his own paradoxes. And we were jolly because although there was so much misery and tragedy to be seen we were after all young and could not help enjoying ourselves. Even the middle-aged and elderly who came to the I.L.P. were young in heart. They had a quality of youthful innocence. They saw the world in blacks and whites, never in greys. Many had been members of Robert Blatchford's Clarion Cycling Clubs before Blatchford went jingoistic and they still carried little stickers in their pockets saying, 'God gave the land to the people' to paste on the flanks of the cows they met when they went cycling into the country. Although they sometimes talked about Marx they did not know much about him. They were followers of William Morris and Henry George.

We did not only talk about politics. We also talked about religion. Micky Kerrigan was a Catholic although sometimes, as she thought about the children crawling under their mothers' feet with never a break in the line in the poor Irish section of the dock area, a Catholic on the defensive. Bill Summers had been born a Catholic but had abandoned it and was now a Unitarian. He was very bitter about the priests who, he said, helped to keep the poor down by encouraging them to touch their hats to the bosses and do as they were told. I had been reading Shaw's *Back to Methuselah* and was a Creative Evolutionist—I even went to Bill's Unitarian Sunday School and gave a talk on it.

Not that our lives were entirely devoted to politics and religion and similar high matters. There were hot-pot suppers, and swimming galas, and bowling tournaments and amateur theatricals and weddings and police court cases and town council meetings and harvest festivals and practically anything else you can think of in the way of family entertainment to go to and report on. I suppose some of it seemed dull at the time, one sports day after all is very like another. But we were not often bored. We were tasting the pleasures of the journalist's life at their most innocent. For the most part there was nothing very exciting going on in Bootle, it is true, but we had front seats for everything there was. Moreover, a journalist's life has the immense advantage of taking one to things one would never dream of going to if left to oneself. It is odd to remember, looking back, how much pleasure there was to be got out of the click of the woods on a bowling green on a summer evening or even from the sound re-echoing against the walls as the swimmers dived into the green pungent water of the swimming bath. Even the town council meetings had a pompous gladiatorial quality that was great fun. They had to be reported at length and since I had found it impossible to acquire any real skill with shorthand this might have put me in a difficulty but for my good fortune in having the gift of almost total recall. By closing my eyes and concentrating I could see and hear the whole of a long debate. I have found this over the years a gift worth preserving and polishing in every way and have brought it to a pitch where I can recall speeches or conversations of a great many years ago. It seems so far as I am concerned a trick of visual memory. I see the person or situation quite clearly, as on a screen, and as I see them I also hear them.

Although Mr Light kept us away from politics as much as he could he encouraged us in other ways. He welcomed our descriptive efforts and encouraged me to write a weekly satirical poem on life in Bootle, it being understood that I must not satirize anything that really mattered. And all the time he drummed it into us that we must be interested in everything. He had no patience if you came back from an allotment show and said there was nothing in it but a list of the prize-winners. 'Then you haven't looked,' he would say.

Mr Light was a writing man and a reading man and a drinking man. As a writing man he hated sloppy sentences and mixed up paragraphs. 'Lucidity, lucidity, lucidity,' he would say, 'that's the thing. Don't try to be too fancy. Write like Daniel Defoe said,' and he would quote, letter perfect because he had repeated it so often, 'If any man was to ask what I would suppose to be a perfect style of language I would answer that in which a man speaking to five hundred people of all common and various capacities, idiots or lunatics excepted, should be understood by them all.' 'And if you can make it understood by idiots and lunatics as well,' Mr Light would add, 'that's a help these days.'

As a reading man he had a wide but rather nice taste. I soon found that if I wanted a weekend in Middleton the way to get it was to turn up on the Thursday with an armful of books for him to borrow. After looking them through and saying, 'That's very handsome of you, Squire, very handsome,' he would look at the diary and say, 'I don't see anything the home troops can't look after this weekend. You get off home.' But I had to be rather careful. When I lent him James Agate's *Responsibility*, which was making quite a stir at the time, and said my sister had lent it to me he was somewhat shocked. 'A bit hot for the distaff side surely,' he said when he handed it back.

He was neat and dandyish in his dress and very precise in his movements. He did not approve of us getting ourselves up in a bohemian fashion. 'When you go to see someone he should be able to see you're a gentleman,' he said. Even when he was the worse for drink he remained exquisitely polite, becoming, indeed, steadily more considerate as the evening passed. He drank, I suppose, half a bottle of whisky a day, perhaps more, sitting by himself for the most part on a stool in the saloon bar of the Station Hotel and keeping out of the drinking schools if

48

he could. But although a solitary drinker he was not a morose one. He had a word for anyone who came in and liked to get into uninvolved surface conversations without joining up with a group. He never invited Bill or me to have a drink with him. 'Keep away from it,' he would say. 'Do as I say not as I do. Whisky's ruined more good journalists than you can count.' We guessed he included himself among them. He had a nice but undemanding wife. It would, perhaps, have been better if she had wanted more of life.

He chain-smoked all through the day and he died when he was in his forties some years after I had left Merseyside for good. I was very sad when I heard the news. I had always thought I would make a trip to Bootle some time and drop in to see him unannounced on a Thursday evening when he was getting the paper out and perhaps give him a hand. I did so on my way to a Labour Party Conference at Southport just after I had become Editor of the *Daily Herald* and it was then that I learned that he had died a few years before. There was no one else I much wanted to see—Micky Kerrigan and Bill Summers had long since left—so I did not stay. I owed Mr Light a great deal both in knowledge and happiness and I would have liked to have been able to tell him so.

It was his training in always being on the look-out for stories that led to my leaving Bootle. I was chatting to a casualty porter at Bootle Hospital when he told me they had been having a bit of an argument in his local pub about a painting the publican had found stacked away in an attic and had hung in the saloon bar—a horse in a field it was, he said, very pretty. It was very old, he said, and on the dark side and someone had said it was perhaps worth a lot of money. So I went to the pub and persuaded the publican to let me take it to the Bootle Public Library to see if the Chief Librarian, who was a friend of mine and interested in pictures, could help to identify it. We went through a lot of art histories together and finally decided we had a Stubbs.

When I told Mr Light he said, 'Give it the full treatment, Squire, and then we'll try it on the nationals.' We had a photograph of the publican holding the picture and ran the story over two columns and Mr Light sent a paragraph to the Press Association. It made the *Daily Express*, the *Daily Mail* and the

Daily News under such headings as, 'Old Master In Pub Attic' and Mr Light and I shared the proceeds. I gave the porter at casualty five bob which made him happy. What was more important for me was that the *Daily Courier* in Liverpool sent a reporter to follow it up and a few days later the news editor asked me to call and see him and offered me a job on the *Courier* and its afternoon paper, the *Evening Express.*

I was sorry to leave Bill Summers and Micky Kerrigan, but although a bit envious they were very nice about it. Mr Light took me across to the Station Hotel for the very first time and gave me a farewell drink and Smith asked me to remember him to my dear mother and to tell her how pleased he was that I'd turned out so well.

The Beatles and the Liverpool sound were still far in the future but even at that time Liverpool was a rumbustious city bursting at the seams with energy: a wonderful city to be a newspaperman in. It was a nursery for Fleet Street. Apart from many reporters and sub-editors Fleet-Street bound there were a couple of future Editors, one of the *Sunday Express* and one of the *Weekly Dispatch* on the *Daily Courier* when I arrived and Arthur Christiansen, who was later to edit the *Daily Express* for close on a quarter of a century and completely reshape ideas about newspaper make-up in the course of giving it the largest popular circulation in the world, was soon to join us. At the moment he was a boy on the *Wallasey Chronicle* just across the river, dreaming of the day when he would have a paper of his own 'to sprinkle with star dust or whatever it is that women wear that catches the light at first nights', as he used to tell his staff on the *Daily Express.*

Politically the *Courier* was the mouthpiece of Liverpool Conservatism, a powerful force in those days under the formidable Alderman Sir Archibald Salvidge. Salvidge had begun his political life as a Conservative Working Man but was now a successful brewer and a close intimate of Lord Derby, the 'uncrowned King of Lancashire'. He had brought Lord Birkenhead into politics when he was a young advocate named F. E. Smith. One of the first political meetings I was ever sent to for the *Courier* was one at which Birkenhead revisited some of his old constituents in the Walton Division of Liverpool after being given a step-up in the peerage from Baron to Viscount. As often happened Birkenhead had dined well beforehand. When he rose to speak he swayed in an awe-inspiring way from side to side until he managed to get a firm grip of the table. But he was superbly at his ease and concluded his speech with a magnificent oratorical flourish. 'Gentlemen,' he said, with only a slight blurring of the consonants, 'you have known me as F. E. Smith, you have known me as Galloper Smith' (the name he earned for himself during the troubles in Ulster when he was an advocate of armed rebellion), 'you have known me as Sir F. E. Smith. Now I appear before you as Viscount Birkenhead. But, gentlemen, whatever vicissitudes of nomenclature I may suffer, I shall remain always your most humble, obedient servant.' I could not help admiring a man who could toss off a phrase like that.

Except for Schadhorst of Birmingham who built up Joseph Chamberlain's political machine in the 1870s, Salvidge was, I suppose, the only man in British municipal politics ever to rival the great City bosses of America. However, it is perhaps an encouraging indication of the independence of newspaper readers that despite his backing the *Courier* and *Evening Express* ran consistently second to the Liberal *Post* and *Evening Echo* in readership, so much so that by the time I arrived they had decided to play down politics and go after popularity. This made them easier to work for.

Colour stories were what the new *Courier* hankered after. They were not difficult to find. Pitt Street, which was where the Chinese lived, was always good for stories of opium smoking and orgies in low dives as well as producing even in the normal run of things more than its quota of brawls and knife attacks. In the Scotland Road area where the Irish lived there was a constant running battle between Catholics and Orangemen. On the anniversary of the Battle of the Boyne which, although it had taken place in 1690, meant as much to Scotland Road as if it had been reported in that morning's newspapers the Orange Lodges organized a vast picnic. As dawn broke a great procession with banners and bands would form up and march to the landing-stage where steamers already loaded with crates of beer and huge piles of sandwiches were waiting to carry the joyful crowd—with its attendant flying-squad of reporters—across the river to the Wirral Peninsula and a large open field. Here there were races for the children, brass bands and inflammatory speeches for the adults, and as much to drink as anyone could want. In the evening we would go back across the river singing all the way and at the landing-stage the procession would reform, but this time with the men in front, many of them carrying broken-off empty bottles as weapons, and the women and children in the rear.

Off we would march to Scotland Road, accompanied by a contingent of tough Liverpool police with batons drawn, ready to crack heads when the trouble started. There would be Orange songs and great roars of 'To Hell with the Pope and no surrender'. And shouts to the papists to come out and fight if they were men not rats. The Irish Catholics, big hefty dockers for the most part, with their heavy buckled belts in their hands for weapons, would come charging out while their women screamed from upstairs windows and emptied chamber-pots on the struggling mass beneath and the police went in with batons. It was a poor celebration when several hundreds were not knocked about.

On saints' days and on Catholic holidays or when the Cardinal was paying a visit, the women in the slum streets would be at work all night scrubbing and holystoning not only their frontdoor steps, which was usual enough, but the whole length and width of the roads so that the Catholic clergy should walk on uncontaminated ground. The men would mount guard to stop the Orangemen from throwing buckets of excrement over the stones and you could be pretty sure of a fight or two developing.

Apart from such manifestations of human prejudice the whole life of a great international seaport was there to explore and report. Liverpool had still not quite lost its ascendancy in the Atlantic trade to Southampton. The great Cunarders and White Star liners and the ships of the Canadian Pacific line still used it as well as the Booth line to South America and a host of smaller ships sailing to ports all across the world. I was given the job of covering the waterfront and a wonderful life it was for anyone with a romantic turn of mind. When a ship was coming in I would get a lift on a tug going out to meet her with a passenger list in my pocket to look for stories from the Captain and to get interviews from film stars, returning businessmen, lecturers and others of the famous and notorious before they landed.

I had helped to start a small literary group—the Pen and Ink

Club we called it. We met in the basement of a Kardomah restaurant where we read our own work and other people's plays and talked about life and art. Here I made friends with a small, wiry, pock-faced man with a raffish look who was called Crowther and had a slightly mysterious job which required him to visit ships—small ocean-going tramps for the most part—before they sailed. It was put about—by himself, I suspect—that he was a doctor who had been struck off. More probably he was a failed medical student. The job he had now, so far as I could make out, was as some sort of medical dispenser and part of what he had to do was to go round and check on the medical stores of ships that didn't carry a doctor and see that they had a proper supply of drugs for all emergencies. I took to going with him in the evenings.

This was a different world from that of the big liners I visited for the paper. We would go down to the docks at night and show our passes and then walk along the dockside taking care not to trip over a rope and take a header into the water until we found the ship we were looking for and hailed her and clambered aboard. Usually it was the second mate we had to see and we would climb down the steep stairs to his cabin and Crowther would hand over the medicines and then we would sprawl on the second mate's bunk and drink whisky with him and talk about where the ship was making for that trip: South America, or Malaga, or Java, or the Gold Coast, or Australia. It was like moving into a novel by Conrad or a poem by John Masefield, whom I had met in Manchester when he came to give a lecture.

Sometimes the ships we visited carried a passenger or two as well as crew and sometimes when it was getting late these passengers would come aboard and after stowing away their luggage would look into the second mate's cabin for a drink. There were repeated rumours in Liverpool at the time that some of the Sinn Fein leaders on the run had got to Liverpool and were waiting to be smuggled out of the country and by round-about ways to America to raise funds. I used to wonder some-times what I would do if one of these passengers who arrived late turned out to be a Sinn Feiner. Not that it ever occurred to me as a possibility that I should inform the police—my sympathies were all on the Sinn Fein side—but I could not help feeling an obligation to my paper and would try to devise ways by which I could give them a story without setting the police on the track. Fortunately the situation never arose, although some of these passengers were very rum characters whom one suspected of leaving the country for their own as well as their country's good. Some of them claimed to be traders and one or two said they were explorers. There was one, I remember, who said he was mounting an expedition to go up the Amazon to find Colonel Fawcett, but I never heard anything more of him. There was another who told us after a great deal of whisky that he hoped to get to Lake Titicaca in Bolivia, the land, he said solemnly, of the Incas and the Aymara Indians where the Incas had buried their gold when the Spaniards came. He said he knew where some of the gold was. But I never heard any more of him either.

When we had finished drinking the second mate's whisky we would sometimes walk along to the landing-stage opposite the Royal Liver building where the Mersey ferry boats came in and take a ride on a ferry boat to New Brighton and back just for the pleasure of being on the open river. There was no Mersey tunnel in those days and the ferry boats ran most of the night. They had great paddle wheels at each side and made a huge churning of the waters when they turned accompanied by much clanging of bells from the bridge to the engine-room. It was like being on a Mississippi river boat with Mark Twain. There was an all-night coffee stall on the landing-stage lit by an acetylene flare and when we got back from our trip we would drink coffee out of thick mugs and eat twopenny pork pies or a wedge of an extremely solid sort of mince pie. There was always a knot of people standing around the stall; seamen, perhaps, or printers coming off night shift, or drunks with nowhere to go and one or two tarts taking a rest away from their beats.

I remember a big Scandinavian seaman who said he was Jesus Christ and wanted to walk across the Mersey to Birkenhead. After we had quietened him down and sent him off in the general direction of the Seamen's Mission Crowther said, 'How do we know he isn't? What would we do if there was a Christ and he came back? Put him in a lunatic asylum, I suppose.' There was a little drunken Irishman standing next to Crowther eating a wedge and when he heard Crowther he put his plate carefully down on the ledge of the coffee stall. 'That's enough from you,

you blaspheming bastard,' he said, enunciating each word with the greatest of care, and threw a punch at him. But he missed and fell flat on his face and one of the tarts picked him up and dusted him down and then she, too, turned on Crowther. 'Why don't you pick on someone your own size, you great hulking coward,' she shouted and spat at Crowther, who may have been a couple of inches taller than the Irishman, but was certainly not more. At this the coffee stallkeeper banged on his counter with an O.K. sauce bottle and shouted, 'Now then, love, that's enough. Pack it up. You, too, mate. Ought to be bloody well ashamed of yourself coming here and kicking up a bloody fuss.' We walked off and Crowther, who seemed to me, the time of night being what it was, a deep thinker despised by the mob, put his hand on my shoulder and said, 'Do you believe in God?' And I said, 'No' and he shook his head and said, 'Neither do I.' And then he said, 'So do you know what it would have been if he had walked on the water?' And I said, 'No'. And he said, 'It would have been a mirage, that's what it would have been, a philosophic mirage. Like the chair.' 'What chair?' I said. But to this he made no answer.

Crowther lived in a decrepit Georgian house in a terrace not far from the docks. It was now a near slum but in the old days the houses had been lived in by Liverpool merchants and ship-owners and slave-traders, for Liverpool was a great centre of the slave trade and there was an old stone plaza down by the docks where you could still see great iron rings embedded in the walls where the slaves had been shackled when they were being offered for sale to American shippers. Crowther had only a couple of rooms furnished in this house of his; one on the ground floor and one upstairs, and not very well furnished at that. The other rooms usually had wooden packing-cases in them, containing, I assumed, medicines and drugs for the ships he serviced and when I stayed the night there, as I sometimes did, I would sleep on a mattress among the packing-cases.

Later Crowther got married to a rather pretty girl called Vera, with fair bobbed hair and a beautiful speaking voice, whom he met at our Pen and Ink Club. She was a telephone operator which no doubt accounted for her voice which was almost too perfect and bell-like for the normal transactions of life, and wrote rather sad little essays which seemed better than they were when she read them aloud. These essays were out of step with her real nature which was sunny and gay, although temperamental. I was the best man at their wedding, which was at a registry office, and when I called for Crowther he told me with considerable pride that she had thrown a vase at his head the previous evening. He took it as a guarantee that he would not have a dull married life.

After she and Crowther were married they went on living in Crowther's house but she cleaned it up a bit, although not too much, and instead of canned beans or bacon, which was all he had ever had to eat before, she would do Italian cooking which she had learned from a girl with an Italian mother at the telephone exchange. This was much less usual in English homes then than it is now and gave their hospitality a cachet all its own. If she did not feel like cooking one of her spaghetti meals she would send Crowther out to bring some Chinese food back from one of the restaurants in Pitt Street. He was always well served because he often gave medical attention on the side to the lascars who served in the ships he visited and many of whom had relatives living in Pitt Street where his reputation stood high in consequence. I sometimes suspected that he also, perhaps, handled a little opium for them from time to time. But I had no proof of this except for the impression created by the whispered conversations he would sometimes hold when I went to Pitt Street with him.

The Crowthers became my greatest friends in Liverpool and their house a regular calling-place. We would sit up until the early hours talking about artistic integrity and such like things and then I would go to bed among the packing-cases and think how very fortunate I was.

But, of course, there was much else in Liverpool besides the docks even although it was Liverpool the seaport that most engaged my romantic imagination. There was the Theatre Royal, all gilt and plush, then owned by a man called Kelly who smoked enormous cigars all day long and was an impresario of show business in the great tradition, so that when I met Lew Grade many years later I felt as though I had come across an old, much-valued friend. Kelly was married to a large Junoesque actress who had made a name for herself as Queen Josephine in a spectacular Napoleonic play. Kelly fell in love with her when this play came to the Theatre Royal and bought the rights in it when she accepted him, so that he could put it on at the Theatre Royal each year with her in the starring role. At the Theatre Royal, also, I saw Mrs Pat Campbell, old but still magnificent, although I cannot for the life of me remember what play it was she was in. I do not suppose it mattered much. It was she who mattered. I remember seeing *Outward Bound* there, too, and feeling more than a little superior because it did not impress me like it had some members of the Pen and Ink Club. And I remember being actively nauseated when I saw my first performance of *Peter Pan*, which seemed to me to be about a mawkish distaste for growing up. I was sorry about this because it was Barrie and his Arcadia Mixture that had first set me smoking a pipe and I much wanted to admire him. I thought better of *The Professor's Love Story* at the Liverpool Playhouse, which was then at the height of its repertory fame under William Armstrong's direction. This, however, was no doubt because Jess came from Manchester for the afternoon and we saw it together. We had coffee brought to our seats in the interval, which seemed rather dashing, and afterwards, still bathed in the sentimental glow of the professor's romance and the enchantment of the stage-set, with flowers ablaze through a french window and a bird singing in the garden, we had tea in the theatre café. It was a wonderful day.

Barrie was very much the rage in those days: I cannot count the number of times I had to report performances of *Quality Street* by amateur stage societies. We somewhat despised him at the Pen and Ink Club, except, perhaps, for the *Ten Pound Look*. We preferred Ibsen and Shaw and gave readings of *The Doctor's Dilemma* and *Candida*, in which I took the part of Marchbanks, borrowing Yeats's 'Tread softly because you tread on my dreams' for the poem at the beginning of Act III. For some reason play readings seemed to us much more advanced and sophisticated than amateur performances.

Except for the Playhouse, whose merits we acknowledged, especially when it put on something that lost money, we regarded ourselves as something of an oasis in a cultural desert. Indeed, although it made up for its lack of art by life itself, Liverpool had little of the cultural excitement of Manchester. If it had not been a great port it would have been in danger of being a dull bourgeois city. The teeming back-streets had not yet found a voice, or if they had, it was not one I had the luck to hear.

Away from the docks and the slum streets of Scotland Road Liverpool seemed characterless and conventional, too full of what in Manchester they called 'lace curtain stuff'. And whereas in Manchester and Middleton the Lancashire accent moved up the social ladder, in Liverpool the ugly, fascinating Liverpudlian twang was ironed out as one went up the income scale. The inhabitants of the rich suburbs were polite and kind and colourless—all, in fact, very much like 'wicked Fanny Kempster' when I met her at last.

I think she must have heard that I was in Liverpool from Cousin Sarah. At any rate, there was a letter from her at the *Courier* office one day. Since Great-Uncle John's death she had married—to someone who had been content to wait until she was free, the letter inferred—and she and her husband would be very pleased if I would care to take tea with them one Sunday afternoon. So off I set one Sunday to the rather grand suburb in which they resided in a mood of some anticipation. She turned out to be a gentle middle-aged lady with a profusion of beads and a fluttering manner acquired, no doubt, in entertaining Great-Uncle John's wealthier parishioners. Although she may have had a soul as dark as my mother suspected there was no external sign of it. Her husband was a solicitor of the precise not the thrusting kind and a keen photographer. They had recently been to Florence and Venice on holiday and we spent much of the time after tea looking at the photographs he had taken and discussing the art treasures they had seen. We had very thinly cut tomato and cucumber sandwiches for tea and small iced cakes and chocolate biscuits. It was served on a very delicate Wedgwood tea service with a pretty flower pattern ('That was my grandma's,' said my mother when I told her about my visit). They had a very nice Pembroke table ('That came from Leighton,' said my mother) and a Hepplewhite secretaire bookcase ('So did that,' said my mother triumphantly) and a good deal of other pleasant furniture. They were very agreeable and asked me if I enjoyed working on the *Courier* which they did not read but thought had changed for the worse. They read the *Liverpool Post*, themselves, feeling it to be more serious minded. When we had finished looking at the photographs and talking about art treasures we turned to current affairs. They thought it was a great waste of ratepayers' money to build Council house estates. 'They're all getting bathrooms, I'm told,' said Fanny Kempster's husband. 'There's a waste of money if you want one. What do they want with baths? They'll only keep coal in them.' He spoke as if 'they' were members of a different race. But then so did most other people of their kind at this time and I could no longer remember how often I'd heard about coal in the bath. I changed the subject to Great-Uncle John. 'Your Great-Uncle John,' he said, 'was a very strange man. He would never give up. I advised him to waste no more money on this matter but he would not be advised.' He dropped his voice. 'It was, I fear,' he said, 'the gambling instinct.' He shook his head and we said no more of Great-Uncle John.

However, although Great-Uncle John did not succeed in getting Wall Street for the Francis family, I had some reason to be grateful to him. I inherited £25 from him and with it I got to Fleet Street.

CHAPTER 4

London the Bloody World

Surveying his friends and the life of London from the marble and red plush of the old Café Royal, James Agate would sometimes recount the story of the cockney who was in Canada when the First World War started and who went to a recruiting office to enlist. 'Address?' asked the clerk after taking his name. 'London,' said the Cockney. 'London, England or London, Ontario?' asked the clerk. 'London the bloody world,' said the cockney.

Although Liverpool was fine and dandy in its way it was London the bloody world I wanted. But how to get there? I could not but admit to myself that it might be a long time before Fleet Street became sufficiently aware of my brilliance to send for me. Fortunately at this stage two events coincided. I got the money Great-Uncle John had left me in his will and about the same time a friend of mine on the *Liverpool Courier* called Austin, S. A. V. Austin, received notice from his girlfriend that she wished to have no more to do with him and was returning his ring. Austin, who was a few years older than me and had served briefly in the Royal Flying Corps towards the end of the war and then tried being a prep. school master before turning to journalism, was much cut up by this and told me about it over a beer at the press club. 'And what I shall do with the bloody ring now I don't know,' he concluded, producing it from his pocket. 'Sell it,' I said. 'I've got £25 coming to me and if we put the money together we could do something.'

This something we eventually decided on was a journey

through England with a horse and caravan. We thought we
would have no difficulty in getting a commission for articles and
that having established a reputation we would be sure of
rapturous welcome and many offers when we reached Fleet
Street. But Fleet Street remained unmoved until one wonderful
morning a letter came from the *Daily Herald*, then edited by
that veteran of all good radical causes, George Lansbury. Our
project must, I think, have awakened a nostalgic chord in his
sentimental heart, for although cockney bred he had been born
in a toll-house in Suffolk when his father was a time-keeper for a
firm of railway contractors and had spent his first years on the
road moving from place to place with the gangs of Irish 'navi-
gators' who were driving railroads through rural England. Or it
may have been Gerald Gould, the Associate Editor, whose fancy
was caught. Gould was a poet and a romantic whose most
quoted verses began:

Beyond the East the sunrise, beyond the West the sea,
And East and West the wander-thirst that will not let me be.

Whatever the reason the *Herald* offered to take two articles a
week. It could not afford to pay much, only two guineas an
article. But four guineas a week, we decided, would be more than
adequate for our needs, especially as we expected our horse to
live mainly off grass cropped by the roadside.

Austin would have preferred a paper more commonly seen in
prep. school staff rooms, but I could not have been better
pleased. To be travelling round England with a horse and
caravan writing articles for, of all papers, the *Daily Herald*
seemed to me to be the summit of human happiness. Indeed,
although by then it had passed its zenith, the *Herald* was a
newspaper to turn any romantic young man's head, particularly
of course, if he was a Socialist as I now was. It was—we had
Lord Northcliffe's word for it—'The Miracle of Fleet Street'.
And although it had no money not all the armies of unrighteous-
ness could silence it. It had become the focus of a generation's
passionate protest against war and social injustice. Osbert
Sitwell wrote leading articles for it—sometimes in verse,
Siegfried Sassoon provided its Literary Notes. E. M. Forster,
Havelock Ellis, Rebecca West, Rose Macaulay, H. M. Tomlin-
son, H. W. Nevinson, Ivor Brown, Aldous Huxley, Robert

Graves, W. J. Turner, Edward Garnett, W. H. Davies, Walter de la Mare all wrote for it. So for a time did Bernard Shaw. M. Phillips Price, famous as *Manchester Guardian* Correspondent in Russia during the revolution, was its Berlin Correspondent, Vernon Bartlett wrote its Paris Letter, the American, Frederick Kuh, sent news of revolution in Hungary and H. N. Brailsford as a travelling correspondent contributed dispatches on the state of Europe unmatched for brilliance. The Australian, Will Dyson, was its cartoonist, flaying the folly and evil of the world with a brush unequalled at that time anywhere else in the press. His cartoon on the signing of the Versailles Treaty was perhaps the most prophetic ever drawn. Clemenceau, Wilson and Lloyd George walk down the steps of the Hall of Mirrors in Versailles. 'Curious,' says Clemenceau, 'I seem to hear a child crying.' And in the far corner of the cartoon, half hidden by one of the pillars, there is a naked child with above its head a halo marked '1940 Class'.

So far as I was concerned, to have a chance to write for such a paper was like being invited to sport in Elysian fields.

With £25 from Great-Uncle John and a like amount from Austin's engagement ring I hurried to Middleton to seek my father's advice on the buying of a horse and van.

My mother was enraptured by the whole project. To her it represented one of those breaks with pedestrian reality for which she constantly longed. My father took a calmer view, but as always was ready to do whatever he could. We had hoped for a painted gipsy van but it soon became clear that anything of this sort was beyond our means, although how far beyond we did not fully realize until a month or two later in Tewkesbury when an ancient gipsy with whom we had made friends took us to see the new home waiting for him at the carriage builders and produced nearly £1,000 in gold, silver and notes secreted about his person to pay for a masterpiece of the craftsman's art, all gold and colour on the outside, with a coal fire and kitchen range, shiny black and steel polished like silver, in the living-room and a bed with brass knobs in the bedroom.

However, we were well content with a light four-wheeled flat-topped lorry such as greengrocers use, with three iron hoops over which was stretched a heavy canvas cover of green with flaps at the back and front. And with a Welsh cob to pull it and a lively roly-poly Old English Sheepdog puppy with a bob tail and an impressive sense of humour to trot alongside.

I have before me as I write clippings of the articles we wrote during our four months on the road. They are couched in a style which is in part an inferior copy of Borrow and in part an attempt to recapture the matey tone of Blatchford's *Clarion*. They have a good deal of the romance of the open road, the wickedness of civilization and the grasping nature of rural landlords in them, but tend to be short on facts.

But what comes back to me most from the musty smell of those clippings is the extent to which in those days Socialists— particularly in rural areas where they were few and scattered— felt themselves to be members of an idealist conspiracy, a guild, as it were, of the good, passionately anxious to meet and succour members of the same persuasion and share with them the delights of planning a new world which had very little to do with politics as they were fought in Westminster. When we were recognized by *Herald* readers they would find us a camping place and then take us home to supper.

After supper our hosts and the friends they had gathered to join them for this exciting occasion would tell us of their fights against rural injustices and ask us about Mr Lansbury and other beloved leaders whom we dare not confess we had not met, since they clearly regarded us as straight from the centre of things. Afterwards we would gather around a piano in the front room and sing 'England Arise' and 'Jerusalem' and the 'Red Flag'. Austin found these occasions hard going since he knew nothing about the Labour Party. But he enjoyed the ham and eggs or the hot meat pies thrust upon us with such generosity and I did my best to coach him in a few suitable sentiments. I was uplifted and warmed by such gatherings. I shared the enthusiasm and naïveties of those present and their fidelities seemed to me then—as they still do—wholly admirable. Although I sometimes felt like a pretender when I was assumed to have a knowledge of internal Labour politics I did not possess, I persuaded myself that this was forgivable since it so obviously made everyone happy to feel that they were moving a little on the inside of things. And I was sufficiently a journalist to make a little knowledge spread far.

We were sometimes able to offer the hospitality of an evening meal ourselves and with it a doss down by the fire for the night to ex-service men tramping from workhouse to workhouse, often with old newspapers stuffed in the holes of their shoes to keep out the wet. They were bitter about the treatment they got from workhouse masters.

The workhouse and its horrors had been a frequent theme in my mother's conversation when we were young, perhaps because the threat of it, like that of the calling-in of mortgages, had often come up in the melodramas she had been taken to by her mother's theatrical lodgers or perhaps because of the deep impression made on her by *David Copperfield* and other Dickens novels. 'We shall all end up in the workhouse,' she would cry when things were bad, or 'It's no better than living in the workhouse,' if the fire had been allowed to go out. But this was the first time I had met anyone who had actually been in a workhouse.

It is difficult, looking back from the comparative humanity of today's social services, to realize how substantial a part fear of the workhouse played in the anxieties of the poor even in the twenties and how harshly their regulations were interpreted in dealing with unemployed men searching for work. These unemployed were required to break an allotted number of stones used for road-making in return for a night's lodging. 'And it's no good showing your army discharge papers,' they complained. 'Spike-keepers don't give a sod about the war. They keep you breaking stones for your bowl of skilly until it's too late to have any chance of getting a job.'

Once or twice we joined a camp of gipsies. Not very pleasurably the first time, for half the night was spent in beating off attempts to persuade us to do a swap—of our van, of our horse, of the harness, of anything and everything we possessed, and at five o'clock we were wakened by dozens of small, dirty children stealing anything they could lay their hands on to a chorus of barking dogs roused by the growls of Bobs tied up under the van. Predictably when we described this in the *Herald* we asked, 'What would Petulengro have said?' Subsequent experiences with gipsies of purer blood were happier once their initial suspicions were broken down. I can still remember the flavour of a hedgehog baked in clay at a gipsy camp—it was rather like hare—and I think I could still tie the loop of a rabbit snare as demonstrated to me on the steps of a much-travelled caravan. But I could not hope to emulate the old gipsy who talked down a pheasant off the branch of a tree while I watched. His voice, cooing with curious sleepy sounds, seemed to hypnotize the pheasant until it fell like a dead thing off the tree into his cupped hands.

Many of the sights and sounds of those days still came back to me with a wonderful freshness: foxes barking in the night across a valley, the high-pitched snarling scream—it is the only time in my life that I have actually felt the hair bristle at the nape of my neck—of a wild cat heard in a wood in Herefordshire where a few of that now vanished breed were then still to be found, deer against the dawn skyline on Exmoor, an otter plunging into a river pool on the slopes of Dartmoor, fox cubs playing in a shaft of moonlight outside an earth in a Shropshire wood and, oddest of all, for why should this stay in my memory so long, the sound of an outboard motor starting up on a starless night across the waters of a lake and evoking for some reason a promise of excitement or adventure which remains as potent now as it was forty-five years ago, evidence, no doubt, of an incurably romantic nature.

We fell into a pattern of living which came in the end to have an almost hypnotic rhythm so that nothing seemed to matter but the business of moving on, as though the very act of walking along a country lane or a moorland track at our pony's head and pulling into the side for a meal or a sleep seemed all that mattered and life had no past or future beyond this simple act of travelling from one place to another. Towards the end I think we both began to feel that if we did not escape soon we would be caught for ever.

We ended our trip outside Salisbury, mainly because the pony needed shoeing and it suddenly seemed more sensible to put both pony and van up for sale than to go to that expense. We camped in a field until market day and I can still vividly remember lying in a sleeping-bag in the rain with a groundsheet over and under me on the last night, and feeling the sense of a whole way of life that I had come to love being lost for ever. We got, I think, £30 for the horse and van and divided it between us in the public bar of a pub near the market before going to Salisbury Station to catch a train to London with Bobs, who afterwards went back to my father, on the end of a piece of rope beside us.

The *Herald*, although welcoming when we called, turned out not to be in a position to offer either of us a job as we had hoped. George Lansbury's struggle to keep the paper afloat as an independent left-wing journal had finally failed and we arrived to find it in process of being handed over to the trade unions as an official organ. Lansbury had ceased to be Editor, although he stayed on for a time as General Manager, and Hamilton Fyfe, a distinguished war correspondent who had joined the Labour Party when he saw what the post-war world was offering to the men he had reported, had taken over in his place. He was pleasant but non-committal. 'Send in some articles from time to time,' he said. 'And if we should need any reporters we'll bear you in mind.' What is more, he actually meant it—although not, as it turned out, for some months.

By this time Austin had put on his old school tie and Harlequin scarf and retired to another prep. school. I heard no more of him for twenty years when I came across his name briefly in the Second World War in a report from our Ambassador in Iraq. He had helped to keep up the morale of the British community in Baghdad by organizing concert parties when they were all immured in the Embassy during a popular rising. When I was in Baghdad myself some years later I asked about him but by then everyone had forgotten him.

I found a back room above a public house in Pimlico with for furniture a bed, a wickerwork chair and a small square wickerwork table like those that aspidistras used to stand on. My room shared a gas meter with the one next door and long battles of will would develop over who put in a shilling when the gas went down.

My sister had got married and now lived at Acton where her husband was an accountant in the Treasurer's Department. They would frequently invite me to supper. On these occasions I would set out early from my room in Pimlico and walk to Acton. After supper I would leave as if to catch the last tube and walk back to Pimlico. I think I walked all over London in 1922, often patrolling the streets until two or three in the morning, absorbing the life of the place. It is surprising what you can find in the way of interest and amusement in London at night for little or no money if you put your mind to it: I agree with a man who said to me that London was the best city in the world to be poor in, although I am not entirely sure he was right when he added, 'And New York is the best to be rich in.'

When I had money I would finish my stroll at one of the all-night Corner Houses or one of the small Soho cafés with marble-topped tables and urns of tea and coffee at the end of a stained counter and have a cup of coffee and sit and speculate about the lives of the others who came in about two or three o'clock to rest their feet: waiters just off duty, prostitutes, petty thieves, street musicians, coppers' narks, provincials who'd missed their trains. These cafés were like clubs with their own regulars at almost every hour throughout the night. After a few visits one got accepted and became part of the freemasonry of the night, neither asking nor answering questions about one's reasons for being about, but sharing a certain sense of comradeship, cosy because of its deliberate withdrawal from judgement. The best place to eat, however, if one had a shilling or so was in none of these places, but in one of the printers' cafés off Fleet Street. Here one could get an enormous plate of sausage and mash or meat pie and chips, followed by a piece of Manchester tart, for a few coppers.

Afterwards I would walk home along the Embankment where in those days each bench would have its occupant wrapped in old newspapers against the cold. There would, perhaps, be a free soup kitchen on wheels standing there. I never came quite far enough down in the world to patronize that, although I was sometimes tempted. The all-night trams to Clapham and Battersea and places like that sailed magnificently by and on the river one might see a police launch nosing slowly along, on the lookout, perhaps, for suicides. I would walk past Scotland Yard and Big Ben to Birdcage Walk and finally to Victoria and my room in Pimlico where I would undress in the dark and fall asleep, tired out.

This was London the bloody world and I loved it, although I sometimes wondered whether I would be able to last out until Fleet Street was ready to open its doors to me. Hopefully but without success I made the round of all the newspaper offices and meanwhile survived by selling small paragraphs from time to time to the *Star* or the *Evening News*—you are very unlucky not to find a news paragraph or two if you spend your time walking all over London—and getting occasional articles in the *Herald*.

I could not yet claim to be a part of Fleet Street but at least I was on its fringe. Like the students at Berkeley, California, who, although they might never actually make contact with any of the dozen or so Nobel prize-winners on the Faculty, nevertheless, it used to be pointed out, had the privilege of sharing the same atmosphere, I breathed the same air as great men. G. K. Chesterton might still be seen scribbling his articles for the *Daily News* in the Cock Tavern. J. C. Squire, not yet ruined by too much whisky and cricket, edited the *London Mercury* just near by and was very kind to me when I tried to sell him some of my poems, although he did not buy them. One might see H. W. Nevinson, just back from the Gold Coast, striding down the street as though on safari and Hannen Swaffer, still, at that time, a drinking man, stopping to speak to a dozen or more people on his way to the Savoy Grill. He wore a black, stained Homburg hat and had the stub of a cigarette sticking to his upper lip.

I imagine if I had made an effort I could have got back on to the *Courier* in Liverpool. But I did not try. To have done so would have been to confess defeat.

However, in the end I did allow myself one small falter. My brother-in-law, Phillip, told me that the National Association of Local Government Officers, of which he was a prominent member, wanted a professional journalist to edit its monthly journal and offered to use his influence to get me considered for the job. I applied, he spoke for me and I got the job and most ungratefully hated it. It had nothing whatever to do with the sort of journalism I was interested in and I was also supposed to try to get advertisements which I thought a very lowering thing to do. But it made it possible for me to stay on in London when I had come very near to the end of things and in my sensible moments I was truly grateful to my brother-in-law. The salary was £350 a year, enough to enable me to go home for a weekend when I got my first salary cheque and, the weekend after, to travel to Otley in Yorkshire where Jess then was and to spend a wonderful two days with her and two friends of hers who became dear friends of mine, Madge and Bert Bland, with whom she shared a cottage in Wharfedale. We walked over the moors all day and ate enormous meals in the evening and talked half through the night about literature and life and politics and ourselves.

The offices of Nalgo were in Caxton Hall, which was the centre of a good deal of activity of one sort or another, including marriages between many famous or notorious characters in whom newspapers were interested, so that at least I had an opportunity now and then to stand on the edge of things and watch real journalists at work. And soon after I arrived Winston Churchill fought a by-election in the Abbey Division of Westminster as an Independent against the official Tory and I could nip out and watch how the battle went.

It was a ranting circus of a campaign with Churchill at his most mischievous and reactionary backed by Beaverbrook, Birkenhead and the *Daily Mail*, and uttering dreadful warnings of socialist horrors to come unless the defenders of 'the stately continuity of English life' were more vigorous. He desperately needed to win. He had lost his seat at Dundee following the breakdown of the Lloyd George Coalition and had been howled down by crowds whose 'passionate hatred' shook even him. He had tried to get back into Parliament as a Liberal in a by-election in West Leicester and had been badly beaten after a campaign in which he had frequently sunk to remarkable depths of ill-mannered vituperation against a much-respected and high-minded opponent, Pethick-Lawrence. Everything he touched seemed to be going wrong. He had no firm roots in any party and seemed to have lost even his own sense of direction. The legend of the Dardanelles followed him everywhere in his public appearances. There were many—including perhaps himself—who thought his political career in danger of coming to an ignominious end.

It was not a good occasion to see and hear him for the first time. Yet although I hated most of what he said and was constantly amazed that so great a man, as I felt him to be, could sink to such small-minded jibes, he made everyone else and particularly his official Tory opponent, a Captain Nicholson, look like mediocre sheep. All the fire and glamour were with him. I could not help but think how fortunate I was to have a chance of seeing him constantly at close quarters. Perhaps he

shone for me with an even brighter buccaneering glow against
the grey worthiness of the small bureaucrats with whom my life
was now cast.

On polling day most of us on the Nalgo staff were recruited to
help count the votes. It was a tense affair and Churchill made
little attempt to control himself as he prowled up and down with
his wife, pausing every now and then to glower belligerently at
Nicholson, who was doing his best to act like a gentleman. As
the count proceeded it seemed at first that Churchill was winning and he became wreathed in smiles and even cast a cherubic
glance in Nicholson's direction. But gradually Nicholson drew
ahead to win in the end by a narrow margin. As the final totals
were being checked I got up and moved across the room unable
to sit still any longer. I found myself standing beside Churchill.
The result was already clear and I saw that he was in tears. He
made no attempt to hide them. His face crumpled like a baby's
as his wife patted his arm. Absurdly I felt tears coming into my
own eyes in sympathy. He must have seen them and imagining,
no doubt, that I was one of the band of young men and women
who had been canvassing for him, he turned to me and said,
'Don't worry, young man, we will fight and win another day.'
'But,' I protested, determined not to be misunderstood, 'I'm
not really on your side. I'm not one of your supporters.' 'In that
event,' he said, 'your emotion does you all the more credit,' and
fully restored to good humour, took his wife's arm and prepared to follow Nicholson to meet the cheering, jeering crowd
outside.

Meanwhile I kept in touch with the *Herald* and in the end was
rewarded. Hamilton Fyfe kept his word and offered me a job
as a reporter. Although well meant it proved a brittle reward.
Not much more than six months later a new crisis hit the *Herald*
and the N.U.J. chapel was asked to advise on staff cuts. It
decided very properly that if the axe had to fall then it ought to
fall first on the unmarried. Lacking wives, I and two others
found ourselves out of a job.

I was back where I started. Or not quite. I had become in a
sense a Fleet Street man and Fleet Street, despite its reputation
for ruthlessness, does what it can to look after its own—or did
in those days. When I made my round of newspaper offices now
I was likely to be greeted with sympathy as a casualty of the

Herald's struggle to survive and given small reporting jobs on space to help tide me over.

There were a good many days when I went hungry—only very few when I could afford more than one meal. There were several occasions when I was so far behind with my rent that I dare not go back to my room for fear of meeting the landlord and slept the night in a station waiting-room. But I was almost unreservedly happy. I cannot believe that it matters much what happens to you when you are young so long as you are doing what you want to do and are sustained by the youthful belief that everything is bound to come right in time. Security is for the middle-aged. And always there was London.

One evening I was led—I cannot quite remember how, perhaps by an advertisement of a lecture—to Bermondsey, to the Bermondsey Bookshop. This had been started by a rich City man called Ginsburg, a commodity broker, I think, under the stimulus of his beautiful and artistically inclined wife who had decided, rather eccentrically, that what the East End needed was a good bookshop which should also be a centre for talk and music and poetry and discussion of the arts. They ran their bookshop without any show of patronage and it did, in fact, become for a time a bright light burning in the drab gloom of Bermondsey Street. Having found it I would walk there several evenings a week. Every Sunday the Ginsburgs inveigled an author to come and talk. I remember John Galsworthy, rather stiff and proper and almost excessively well intentioned, and R. H. Mottram, who had just written *The Spanish Farm* and was charmingly diffident, being convinced that no one could really have heard of him. Barrie was equally diffident, but not, one felt, quite so genuinely so. He was anxious to persuade us that he knew nothing about public affairs. 'I leave that sort of thing to Mr Wells and Mr Shaw,' he said. C. E. Montague, whom I worshipped for *A Hind Let Loose* and *Rough Justice*, came and H. M. Tomlinson, who knew the Thameside streets and the river better than any of us and whose bony face glowed with a gentle integrity.

The Ginsburgs reminded me a good deal of the rich, cultured, gentle Jewish families I had met in Manchester at play readings and other literary and musical occasions. They lived in White-hall Court and would usually entertain their visiting writers to dinner before taking them to the Bookshop. They got into the habit of often inviting me, too, so that, although young and poor, I soon knew a great many literary people of one sort and another, finding them, contrary to public report, for the most part friendly and kind.

Not content with the Bermondsey Bookshop the Ginsburgs published each month the *Bermondsey Book*, a literary journal of often remarkable excellence. It was edited by an assistant leader writer on the *Daily News*, of whom Mrs Ginsburg was very fond. He had lost an arm during the war and was a very dashing and romantic figure. His name was Heath, Captain Heath, but as this was also the brand name of a racing tipster on the paper and as racing tipsters are more important than assistant leader writers he had to fight a continuous and on the whole unsuccessful battle of identity. He was an attractive character. We became very friendly and he asked me to help him with producing the *Bermondsey Book*, which flattered me a good deal. He liked to have a few famous names as well as young and unknown ones and one weekend invited me to go with him to Dorset to see Thomas Hardy, who was by now well over eighty, and who he hoped could be persuaded to give us a poem for publication. He had already written and received in reply a stiff but courteous little note from Mrs Hardy, who had established herself as combined nurse and secretary to the great man she had married late in his life. The note said that Mr Hardy had heard with interest about the *Bermondsey Book* and would be pleased to receive Mr Heath (he had suppressed the Captain as inappropriate) if he would care to call at tea-time on Saturday. She added that her husband was now very old and frail and although interested in encouraging the young must not, as she was sure Mr Heath would understand, be made tired by too much talk. Mr Heath must leave as soon as she signalled to him that time was up.

When we got to the house I sat on the grass verge by the gate while Freddy Heath advanced up the drive to the front door with the promise that if it proved at all possible he would mention me and try to secure an invitation for me to come in. I had not been sitting on the grass more than a few minutes when I saw him beckoning to me.

'She's formidable,' he said, 'but he's sweet. I've told him

you're a young poet, worshipping at a distance. For God's sake don't let on that either of us are journalists.'

Hardy was sitting in a low chair by a brightly burning fire with a rug over his knees. There was a small round table beside him for his tea-cup and plate and on this there was the copy of the *Bermondsey Book* that Heath had sent with his letter and a small bundle of typescript. He looked small and shrunken and his hand when he gave it to me had scarcely more weight than a feather. His skin was ivory yellow, but of an ivory that had known a good deal of sun and rain. His eyes were clear and limpid and had a far-away country look. He did not speak much but when I was introduced he gave a quick bird-like nod in my direction and smiled as though he was glad to have company and when Heath was saying what a very great honour it would be for the *Bermondsey Book* to have one of his poems and what it would mean to the people of Bermondsey he winked at me. It was a quick, rather shy wink, immediately masked, as though he wanted me to know that at his age he was unlikely to be taken in by such talk, but would like this to be kept a secret between us. I was reminded of my father who would sometimes wink at me in much the same way when my mother was in the middle of one of her more extravagant fancies, disassociating himself from what was being said, yet affectionately so.

I was reminded of my father in other ways, but more particularly by the sense I had of a man who, although well aware of what was going on around him, had recesses of his own to retreat to which were intimately concerned with the country scene. My father, of course, was much younger at this time, but when he, too, reached his eighties he would sit very much as Hardy sat, courteous but abstracted and not hiding an occasional flicker of amusement—the ghost of a country joke—at the way some of his visitors conducted themselves.

When Heath stopped Hardy nodded, more to himself than to us, and then put his hand to the typescript on the table and picked out one sheet which he read through before passing it over. 'Will this do?' he said and when Heath burst into expressions of pleasure and gratitude he gave a rather depreciatory little smile.

He sipped his tea noisily with small sucking gulps and seemed to take a small boy's pleasure in the sandwiches that had been prepared for tea. There were also some small sweet cakes and he selected one of these in advance and rested it on the side of his plate, reserving it while he chewed a sandwich. His bird-like glance moved from Heath to me and back again and he seemed to enjoy our company but at the same time to be amused by the awe with which we regarded him. 'Have more tea,' he said, pointing a feather-weight hand in my direction and nodding encouragingly as though to show that he remembered from his own youth that the young had large appetites. But behind the silver teapot Mrs Hardy gave an authoritative shake of the head, indicating that the time had come to go.

After we had said goodbye we walked sedately down the drive to the gate. But once we had reached the road and the house was out of sight we broke into a little dance of triumph and afterwards walked over the hills to Cerne Abbas. We had supper in a pub in Cerne and drank a good deal of beer before striking into the hills again and walking back through the night in brilliant moonlight to Dorchester, where we rested in a station waiting-room before catching the first train back to London.

I had started to write a novel. As it happened it was a very bad one and no one would publish it when it was finished, for which I do not blame them. However, at the time I thought it a work of genius which would also sell in tens of thousands. My problem was how to live while I wrote it. I had established good relationships with a couple of pawnshops, one in the King's Road, Chelsea, the other in the Strand and they were very helpful.

Insufficient tribute has been paid to pawnshop managers. I found that once they got to know you and a relationship of mutual trust had grown up they would often go a good deal beyond the call of duty in helping one to grapple with one's immediate problems. In the little booths in which one conducted business with them there was no need for pretence. But I had not much to pawn and had already sold most of my books in Charing Cross Road. What I needed was some temporary capital and it occurred to me to try one of those affable gentlemen who offered to lend anything from £100 to £10,000 on note of hand alone. After writing to several I was offered an appointment at an office just off Bond Street. The lobby was panelled in confidence-producing mahogany, and I was taken to see a small, pneumatic man very smartly dressed in a decorous manner who looked as if he had just had a Turkish bath and then gone on to a manicurist. He had a rich over-stuffed office and when I was shown in to see him he grasped me warmly by the hand before putting me into a low chair beside his enormous desk.

On this desk there was my letter and a folder with a single sheet of paper in it—the start of my file, I supposed. He looked at it while I leaned back comfortably and crossed my legs in what I hoped was a nonchalant manner.

When he had finished reading, he embraced me with a benevolent smile and said, 'So you thought you'd like to borrow some money.'

'Yes.'

'I see you've written to several of my colleagues as well. No good, you know. We keep in touch with each other. We have a central register. No use trying to play off one against the other.' He brushed the fingers of his hand together. 'But that doesn't concern you,' he said magnanimously. 'This is the first time you've tried to borrow, isn't it? No question of any tricks. Now let us consider the circumstances.'

As we considered them he became not less benevolent but much less expansive. It seemed clear that I was unlikely to be much use to a money-lender who took his business conscientiously. 'Have you any expectations?' he asked and I could only say no, thinking regretfully of those unclaimable millions in New York. What clinched matters, however, was that I had no bank overdraft. 'Pity,' he said. 'There's nothing like a bank overdraft to give confidence. I'm always ready to lend money to someone who owes money to his bank. If they can trust you, so can I.'

I left with a warm invitation to return when I was better off. But it was not an entirely wasted morning. I wrote an article about it which I sold to the *Star*.

I began to think I would never persuade a newspaper to employ me and that perhaps the best thing to do while I finished my novel would be to try for some undemanding job which would pay me just enough to live on while I wrote. I thought that if I could get a job as a nightwatchman that would be fine.

I saw myself sitting in a little cubby-hole with a flask of coffee and a packet of sandwiches and nothing to interfere with my writing but an occasional walk round the premises.

However, just when I was wondering how to set about this a fellow I met in Fleet Street told me he had heard the *Sunday Express* was taking on a few part-time people.

'Tell the news editor you used to be on the *Herald* and got axed in an economy wave,' said my friend. 'He'll try to help.'

This turned out to be so. I was told I could come in on the Friday if I liked. There was not a great deal to do—a few telephone calls and the re-writing of bits of news sent in from lineage men—but I must have managed all right because at the end of the day I was told I could come along on the Saturday as well. In those days the *Sunday Express* paid you two guineas a day but Saturday was a double day. You started at ten o'clock in the morning and worked through until midnight or after and got four guineas. I was soon going in every Friday and Saturday and was then asked to look in on the Thursday as well to help with news features. This meant eight guineas a week and although it was a guinea below the minimum of nine guineas a week then ruling for a staff man I felt prosperous.

Also I was enjoying myself a great deal. The *Sunday Express* news room was full of curious characters whom it was a pleasure to know. There was a hard drinking ex-sailor who had written a couple of novels about the sea and was trying to keep himself in whisky while he wrote a third. They were rather good novels, as I remember, and should have done better than they did, but whisky killed him before he could find a real public. There was an ardent fisherman who told us proudly that although Lord Beaverbrook thought he had captured London society the Flyfishers' Club would blackball him if he put up for it. There was also a tall languid Etonian who was a cadet of a famous merchant-banking family and had been given a trial on the *Sunday Express* because he did not fit into merchant banking and his father knew Beaverbrook. We borrowed money from him when we were short, and he borrowed it from his father's butler. 'The thing about having a butler,' he said, 'is that you can always touch him for something.' Those were the days of the flappers and wild parties and he was often useful to the paper as a source of information about goings-on in Mayfair. In the end they finished him off. He was found dead at the side of a railway track after being swept off the roof of a train on which he was balancing to prove that he could. There was also an American girl from Topeka who was trying to work her way round Europe. And there was an Australian woman called Freda Sternberg who had a flat in Chancery Lane and a pleasant habit of inviting two or three of us home to share her cookery experiments from time to time.

Above all so far as I was concerned there was Tom Darlow, who became my closest friend until his death as a war correspondent nearly twenty years later.

In many ways Darlow was, I suppose, an amoral and even a reprehensible character. This was perhaps why I liked him. Later when I was Editor of the *Daily Herald* and Darlow was my Assistant Editor, he frequently caused me trouble by disappearing for days at a time with a young woman to whom he was attached and then ringing up from a rather grand hotel somewhere to announce that he could not pay the bill and as he was most anxious not to give the paper a bad name, would I have the money to meet it dispatched forthwith. But he was an excellent journalist and a staunch friend and I never knew him do anything to hurt anyone, which has always seemed to me a fairly good test of character in a thrusting world.

His father was a leading Congregational Minister, a great figure in the British and Foreign Bible Society and a close friend of Sir William Robertson Nicoll, Editor of the *British Weekly*. Darlow was a trial to his family and when he came down rather hurriedly from Oxford Robertson Nicoll suggested that the best place for a young man of his unconventional talents might be on the staff of a newspaper and had very kindly spoken to Lord Beaverbrook on his behalf.

Anyway, there he was on the *Sunday Express* enjoying it so much he said he would gladly work for nothing if he wasn't so much in debt. He was a large man, over 6 ft 3 ins in height and bulky in proportion like a small elephant, so that he was a very useful companion to have when he and I went, as we frequently did, in search of interest and excitement in the more dubious quarters of Soho and the dockland area of London. His appearance was off-putting to those who might have wished to cause trouble.

He had a great taste for the bizarre and was entranced when I told him that while pursuing a story about Aleister Crowley, notorious as a black magician and organizer of 'orgies', who was supposed to have returned to London from abroad—'The Devil is back in London' my story began, I remember—I had been introduced to a young woman who had been installed in a flat near Russell Square by a gentleman who was said to be the leading undertaker in London.

I introduced him and they got on admirably in a platonic sort of way. Closer friendship was prevented by the shadow of the undertaker. He was a jealous man and had installed a formidable companion to keep a watch on the lady's activities. We had afternoon tea with her very stylishly served on thin china. The whole thing could not have been more respectable and decorous. Among the other guests was an ex-army major and his mouse-like wife. He claimed to know Crowley and Darlow suspected him—rightly or wrongly I do not know— of being a go-between for gentlemen interested in flagellation. There was also an elderly lady of distinguished appearance who claimed to be a niece of Delane, editor of *The Times* in its mid-Victorian heyday. There seemed no reason to disbelieve her. It did not seem the sort of story anyone would invent, particularly in that company. As a child, she said, she had often heard how difficult he was and that he had been largely responsible for his wife's mental breakdown, which had set Queen Victoria against him.

We all left with many exchanges of mutual respect when the companion whispered in our hostess's ear that the undertaker had telephoned and would be coming in half an hour. Darlow wanted to hide on the other side of the street to see whether he wore his black top hat and morning coat for such occasions, but I thought this would be a breach of good manners towards our hostess and took him away.

Brooks, the news editor of the *Sunday Express*, came from Leeds where he owned a rather grand house in which his wife, who had impressive white hair and social ambitions, lived in considerable state. Brookie himself lived in one small derelict room in Clapham Junction during the week and ate at a Lyons or an A.B.C. Each Saturday evening he arrived at the office carrying a large linen bag full of washing. This he would take with him to Leeds on the midnight train, returning to London and work on the Tuesday morning. Later he got himself appointed Chief Northern Correspondent of the *News of the World*—a post which mainly involved combing through local newspapers for stories of rape, adultery and goings-on in public parks—and was able to take up residence in Leeds himself.

There was no Press Council in those days and not much concern about intrusion into private lives or bribing public officials to get stories, or other such matters. On the *Sunday Express* we took it for granted that the interests of the paper came before everything else. We had a great sense of élan and thought that nothing and no one had the right to stand in the way of our getting the story we wanted. Most ordinary people were in any event excited and flattered by a newspaper reporter's attentions—in the same way as they are now if a television camera turns in their direction.

Perhaps because I sometimes travelled up with him on the Leeds train when I was going to see Jess in Otley and had taken Jess to have a stately tea with his wife, Brookie treated me as a favourite son and gave me many of the best stories. As a result of this I found myself involved in a crime of some notoriety—a brutal murder by a young soldier following a theft committed while he was drunk. The crime itself was not uncommon. What gave it interest was that the young soldier's name was Lincoln and that he was the son of the notorious Trebitsch-Lincoln who had briefly been a Liberal M.P. and had left the country hurriedly when he was suspected of passing information to the Germans during the war.

Trebitsch-Lincoln was reported to have become a monk in Tibet and a story reached us from India that he was rushing back to England to intervene before his son was executed. According to this story he claimed to possess scandalous and sinister information about several Cabinet Ministers and would threaten publication unless they intervened with the Home Secretary for a repeal.

It was not a very likely story in all its details, although there was later confirmation that Trebitsch-Lincoln actually had started out, but it had enough drama and mystery to make it a natural for a paper like the *Sunday Express*. Brooks hurriedly dispatched me to Shepton Mallet in Somerset where the young

Lincoln was in the condemned cell at the local prison to report whether his father did turn up. Determined to get there before anyone else, I took the last train to Bristol and slept in a waiting-room on Bristol Station until I could get a local train to Shepton Mallet. I arrived there early on the Saturday morning, booked into a hotel and after a wash and a shave and breakfast went for a stroll. I walked round the prison which was in the centre of the town until I found a pub that it seemed likely might be used by prison staff. At opening time I was back. Inside there was an obvious prison officer having a drink. He was talking, as everyone in Shepton Mallet was, about the coming execution and when he saw me went into a violent tirade against the press and said that if any newspaperman approached him for information he would at once report him to the authorities. The violence of his language at once persuaded me that he suspected me of being a reporter and would be very willing to take a bribe.

I went outside and waited round the corner for him to come out. He was not long doing so nor did he take much persuasion to give me any information he had in return for £5, with another to come if he had anything else to offer later in the evening. I wanted to know whether Trebitsch-Lincoln had actually arrived and if so what passed between his son and him. If he should come and the warder passed out the news to me there would, I promised, be a lot more than £5 for him. Meanwhile I wanted any information I could get about the state of mind of the prisoner. It was an old prison, long due for demolition, and there was a window high up overlooking a lane running alongside it. The warder promised to be in the same pub at seven o'clock in the evening but if he could not get out or if anything happened after we had met, he would, he said, try to drop a note through this window into the lane below.

When we met at seven the warder had a graphic story to tell. He had been on duty in the condemned cell, he claimed, when Lincoln had been told his father was on his way and Lincoln had said to my warder, 'If you let him in here I'll kick his bloody face in. I'll top him. I may be a bloody murderer but I'm not a bloody traitor.'

I suspected this had been invented by the warder in the hope of a bigger hand-out, but in those days popular newspapers did not probe too deeply into their sources if a story sounded good. It was enough that it came from inside the prison and in high delight I went back to the hotel and phoned through a story of the murderer waiting to strike down his father as his last act on earth.

In the morning the story was splurged all over the front page under my by-line. No other paper had anything comparable.

My work was now done since there was no other issue of the *Sunday Express* before the execution, which was fixed for Monday morning. However, before I had finished breakfast the *Daily Express* was on the line asking me to hang on until their chief crime reporter, the legendary Stanley Bishop, arrived and to make myself available to him when he did. I had, it appeared, really set things going. By early afternoon Shepton Mallet was packed with newspapermen. The condemned man's brother and sister arrived and were followed everywhere by reporters and eager children.

Next day we all rose early and stood in a macabre group outside the prison waiting in the cold morning air for eight o'clock to strike. I found myself saying over and over in my head a verse from A. E. Housman with which the young soldier waiting to be hanged seemed to have a peculiar affinity:

> Strapped, noosed, nighing his hour,
> He stood and counted them and cursed his luck;
> And then the clock collected in the tower
> Its strength, and struck.

A few minutes before eight there was a stir in the crowd and an old country woman with a shawl over her head and a basket on her arm pushed her way through. She went up to the nail-studded door of the prison and knocked several times with the iron knocker. I looked at the man standing next to me, a reporter from the *Daily News*, and moved by a common impulse we walked over to the woman. 'You can't make a noise like that now,' I said. 'Somebody's going to be hanged.' She turned round, a pleasant, ruddy-faced body with a twinkle. 'Aye,' she said, 'and the hangman'll be needing his breakfast as soon as it's over. Proper hungry it makes him.' The door opened and she passed in.

We stepped back and as we did so saw a group of small

children racing round the corner of the prison. We followed them. They were in a lane with their heads against the rough stone of the prison wall. One of them looked up and said, 'Be quick, mister. If you listen close you can hear the drop.' He put his ear back to the wall as the prison clock began to strike.

More than forty years later I told this incident of the children listening for the drop in the House of Lords debate on the hanging bill to show the kind of climate that a hanging created. Several people, including the Earl of Longford, then Leader of the House, and Victor Gollancz, who was in the gallery, told me later that it made a great impression and affected, they thought, a number of votes. I hope it did, although the vote against hanging was sufficiently large not to need me to influence it.

For me the macabre affair of the Lincoln execution brought good fortune. Brooks invited me to come in on Wednesdays as well as Thursdays. This meant four days—ten guineas a week. On such an income Jess and I could get married.

We had got engaged a few months before, sitting under a tree in the rain on the banks of a stream running into the Wharfe near a village called West End which has since been flooded and now lies at the bottom of a reservoir. We were married on 19 April 1926 rather to the anxiety, I think, of Jess's father and mother, who had small experience of journalists, although later we became good friends, and to the delight of mine who loved Jess dearly. My mother, who had always been a great one for women's rights, was particularly entranced by the fact that Jess was a university young woman—university young women were rarer in those days than now—and told everyone how clever she was. 'But not a bit of a bluestocking,' she said. 'Not a bit of one.' We went to Exmoor for our honeymoon and cut our visit short by a day so that we could afford to buy a terrier puppy we called Chip after an old wooden doll Jess had had as a child. Two days after we got back the General Strike, which had been looming all through our honeymoon, started and I had to leave Jess alone with Chip in a furnished flat in Wimbledon.

CHAPTER 5

Lord Beaverbrook Proposes

Fleet Street that Monday morning of 3 May 1926 was full of people walking up and down trying to sell old bicycles at a profit in the belief, no doubt, that whatever happened reporters must be mobile. A few buses were still running and I had managed to get a train into Waterloo after a long wait. Everything seemed remarkably calm and it was plain that most people were enjoying the break with normal life. In the *Express* newsroom reporters were standing about waiting to know what was going to happen. In one corner the N.U.J. chapel was in continuous session waiting for advice from Union headquarters as to whether journalists were on strike or not. The N.U.J. was not affiliated to the T.U.C. and was not, therefore, directly involved. But the N.U.J. chapel in each newspaper office was a part of the Imperial Chapel representing all newspaper unions—and the printers had been called out. So what did we do? Finally a compromise was announced. It was, said the N.U.J. executive, proper for journalists to assist the maintenance of a flow of news by helping 'in the production of makeshift papers . . . so long as the people who produce them cannot permanently displace the mechanical workers who are on strike.'

Soon every newspaper was producing some sort of makeshift version of itself and the *Express* office—Lady Louis Mountbatten headed the switchboard squad, I remember—was crammed with society girls with high-pitched voices running the canteens and telephones. Their husbands and boyfriends roared through the night in sports cars distributing the papers that came limping off the presses and the business offices were turned into dormitories. Gaiety and excitement everywhere prevailed. Those who like myself felt that if there was going to be a revolution we would rather be on the other side comforted ourselves with the thought that we were getting out the news the people needed and could not get from the *British Gazette* which suppressed everything its Editor Winston Churchill did not like or the *British Worker* which was as dull as a trade-union branch report. In any event it was already clear there was not going to be a revolution.

In the middle of all this Darlow and I found ourselves cast for heroes' roles as a result of an eruption of my farming blood. This introduced me for the first time to Lord Beaverbrook and began an ambivalent relationship with him that lasted for nearly forty years.

Darlow and I were standing together in the newsroom looking out of the window when we heard loud shouting. A lorry loaded with rolls of newsprint and drawn by a pair of huge and handsome Clydesdales had become the centre of a noisy crowd as it tried to turn into the narrow lane leading to the *Express* loading-bay. As we watched the horses swung round and galloped off. Some of the people in the crowd threw stones after them.

'They can't treat horses like that,' I shouted, all the blood of my father aroused, and with Darlow at my heels raced down the stairs. We found the lorry halted some way down Shoe Lane. The horses were still panting. The driver had climbed down from his high seat much shaken and was looking indecisively about him.

'I'll take them,' I said. Brushing aside his protests I seized the reins from his hands and after talking to the two Clydesdales with the gentle cooing note my father used when any animals of his were frightened climbed up to the driver's seat as though to the manner born—as indeed in some measure I was. 'Come along then,' I said and turning them round proceeded steadily back to the *Express* with Darlow walking purposefully alongside.

The crowd was still there. But overawed either by my professional look on the driver's box or Darlow's size they let us through quietly and with a loud 'Whoa there' I brought the lorry to a halt with a stylish flourish to a rattle of cheers from the *Express* windows. I climbed down, gave the two Clydesdales a gentle rub on their soft velvety noses, told them what fine fellows they were, handed them over to their driver, who had followed inconspicuously on foot, and walked modestly into the *Express* building with Darlow beside me, both of us doing our best to convey that to us this was nothing—we were all-purpose reporters ready for anything.

No sooner were we in the newsroom than we were seized by the Assistant News Editor and rushed to the lift. 'The Beaver wants to see you,' he said and we shot up to the top floor. Lord Beaverbrook was sitting, one leg under the other, in a deep armchair, three telephones on a side table by his right hand, his hair tousled, his tie large and floppy, looking exactly like a younger version of the famous figure that was later to become a feature of Low cartoons. A couple of the society lovelies who had hurried to help the *Express* to keep revolution at bay were lounging on a couch near a table loaded with drinks. When we came in Beaverbrook leapt from his chair. 'Good-day to you,' he said, advancing on us with outstretched hands. He scarcely came up to Darlow's chin, but he seemed to loom over both of us. 'That was well done,' he said in his famous Canadian rasp. 'Have some champagne.' We each had a glass of champagne and when we had drunk it he turned to the Assistant News Editor, who seemed to have been left out when the champagne was being poured, and barked, 'Are these young men on your staff?' 'No, sir,' said the Assistant News Editor, regretfully I thought, 'they work for the Sunday.' 'Tell Innes he should be proud of them,' said Beaverbrook. 'Tell him to give them a rise.' He swung back to us. 'See you get it,' he said. 'Goodbye to you.'

When the strike ended Jess and I turned to finding a house in Wimbledon which in those days still had something of a small-town atmosphere. The railway station was a couple of wooden platforms presided over by a ticket collector with a pegleg. There were red squirrels in the trees that lined the side roads leading up to the Common, and a horse was still stationed at the bottom of Wimbledon Hill to give a helping pull to other horses making the slow haul with vans to the top. Many of the shops, particularly at the top of the town, had a village air and even the All England tennis courts—the old ones near the Southern railway line—seemed made more for patball and flirtation than world championships.

Although an undistinguished part of an undistinguished row the house we found was pleasant enough for a start with a small garden at the front and a french window leading out to a slightly larger lawn at the back. In this house our daughter Betty was born and the lawn became a place for her pram and in summer for a playpen with Chip sitting on guard beside it, with a great air of self-importance on his rugged face.

Betty had started earlier than expected and as Jess and I lay side by side, waiting for the doctor, I told Jess about the boll-weevil. Why I should have picked on the boll-weevil I cannot at this distance of time remember, but Jess asked me to tell her a story and I think I must have been collecting facts about the boll-weevil, which was at that time attacking cotton crops in America, and about its incredible capacity to survive and bring up its children. It made a long and, as it seemed to us both, a fascinating story as we waited in the night for our baby to be born. Even now if she cannot get to sleep Jess will sometimes say, 'Tell me about the boll-weevil.' But, alas, I am no longer the expert on its habits that once I was.

By this time Lord Beaverbrook had again intervened in our lives.

Jacob Epstein had just completed his statue Rima. With official approbation, but modified public rapture, it had been placed in a secluded setting in Hyde Park. There it was at once smeared with tar. I wrote a feature article for the *Sunday Express* attempting to persuade its readers that although possibly a controversial artist Epstein was a considerable one and that the London public ought to count itself extremely lucky to have such an example of his work to look at. What the general response to this article was, I do not know—if anything it increased, I think, the number of tar-throwers. But it had two appreciative readers: Epstein himself, who sent me a message to say he had never expected to read anything so sensible in the *Sunday Express*, and Beaverbrook.

When I arrived at the office after the appearance of the article I was summoned to take the lift journey to Beaverbrook's flat again. Beaverbrook was lying on a couch being attacked by a small man. This turned out to be his masseur. Dismissing him Beaverbrook sat up, rasped his customary greeting, 'Good-day to you,' and without further pause said, 'That was a fine piece you did on Epstein, I want you to go to the City and write about finance.' I did not hide my amazement.

'But I don't know anything about finance,' I said.

'That's fine,' said Beaverbrook. 'That's fine. I've got plenty of people who know all the X.Y.Z. of finance. I want someone who'll start with the A.B.C.'

When I protested again he took me by the arm and walked me over to the huge window at the end of the room. We stood silently side by side looking out.

'The two greatest powers in life,' he said after a long pause, 'are God,' and he pointed to the dome of St Paul's, 'and money,' and he pointed to the office towers of the City beyond.

'But . . .' I protested.

He swung round. 'Young man,' he said, 'our readers know about God. I want you to teach them about money.'

'But . . .' I said once more.

He took no notice, but seizing me again by the arm marched me to the door. 'I'll tell Cranfield Hicks you're coming,' he said. 'Report to him next Monday. Tell them I say you're to have £15 a week. Goodbye to you.'

This was still the City of narrow alleyways and of brokers drinking champagne and stout out of silver tankards before lunch. Although it involved me in what was in many ways a new and unexpected career I came in the end to enjoy it a good deal. Nor did Beaverbrook leave me to swim on my own. He insisted on giving me personal introductions to a number of bankers, including, I remember, Sir Reginald McKenna, a former Liberal Chancellor of the Exchequer who had become Chairman of the Midland Bank, F. C. Tiarks, the senior partner of J. Henry Schroder & Co., the merchant bankers, and Sir Edward Peacock, Managing Director of Barings and a Director of the Bank of England, who like Beaverbrook himself was the son of a Canadian manse. These introductions were of a character to suggest that so far from being merely a young reporter I had some special relationship with Beaverbrook, who was much concerned that I should learn about finance from the best tutors. His correspondents must, I think, have got the impression that I was the son of a relative or old friend who would ultimately have a great fortune in his control: at any rate they were very nice to me.

For a man interested in human nature it was a wonderful time to be mixed up in financial affairs—an age of great rogues and speculators—and I was very grateful to Lord Beaverbrook for giving me a ring-side seat to watch them from.

Some I felt sorry for. Like Harman, 'King of Lundy Island', whose Rock Investment Trust brought him to jail. He was a rugged, bull-headed man more suited to his island in the Bristol Channel than the City and when the accountants were drawing close with the police at their heels he argued passionately to me that men such as he were the front-line troops of finance, the poor bloody infantry.

'We hold the exposed positions,' he said, 'while your banker pals keep out of range. We get the casualties. They get the cash.' Just over a decade later his son was awarded a posthumous Victoria Cross in North Africa for behaving in war as his father had liked to convince himself he had conducted himself in peace.

I felt a little sorry, too, for Samuel Insull, the American electric power tycoon who had begun life as a London clerk determined to model his career on the best precepts of Samuel Smiles and ended up in the dock after an undignified chase round the world. He is buried in Putney cemetery, London. One can still find his grave with some difficulty, but no one ever visits it.

I was sorry also for that very different figure, the tall, aristocratic, much beribboned Lord Kylsant whom I used to call on regularly when he was Chairman of the Royal Mail Steam Packet and whom I watched, standing stiff as a ramrod to receive his sentence in the Old Bailey. When we talked in his panelled private suite in the Royal Mail offices he seemed a very Forsyte-like figure and perhaps it was in the Forsyte tradition that he should be brought down by his own brother, the first Viscount St Davids, whose sense of financial rectitude in the conduct of the investment trusts he controlled left nothing over for brotherly pity when he came across suspicious claims in the accounts.

I remember, with more pleasure, Captain Alfred Lowenstein of Melton Mowbray, Brussels and Biarritz—a gambler, perhaps, rather than a crook. Lowenstein was a flamboyant character who habitually travelled the world accompanied by an entourage of four secretaries, two valets, a private detective and a masseur. Even when he went bathing in the sea at Biarritz the secretaries, the valets and the masseur went in the water with him, although the detective stayed on the beach, no doubt to see that his clothes were not stolen. When I knew him he was trying to get control of British Celanese, one of the first of the big artificial silk manufacturers. But he had many other interests and I sometimes wondered why he devoted so much of his time trying to unseat the Dreyfus brothers, the Swiss chemists who had created the company.

'Because I hate them,' he said when I asked him. But he would not explain why. 'Besides,' he went on with a cynicism I enjoyed, 'consider the potential of the artificial silk market. Every man wants to buy silk stockings for his wife and silk underwear for his mistress and when he's bought this underwear for his mistress his conscience pricks him and he buys more stockings for his wife again. All wives should begin to worry when their husbands shower them with presents.'

Lowenstein had a private airplane and on the last occasion I saw him he tried to persuade me to fly to Brussels with him so that we could go on talking over dinner. 'Then the plane will fly you back,' he said. I told him I had a column to write and could not spare the time. 'Column,' he said. 'I will give you many columns.' But to my subsequent journalistic regret I still refused. When the plane was over the Channel Lowenstein opened the exit door in the side and went down into the sea. Whether he killed himself deliberately or, as his friends stoutly maintained, opened the door in a fit of absent-mindedness was never wholly decided, but I could not help wondering if he would have gone through that door if I had accepted his invitation and' if he had, whether he would have said anything to explain his discourtesy before leaving.

As a character Lowenstein was a good deal more attractive in his flamboyant rogue-elephant way than Clarence Hatry. However, it is possible to feel a little sorry for Hatry too. Although he went to prison for forging Municipal Bonds on a massive scale, his forgeries were inspired by an attempt to ride the storm during the world-wide collapse in stock-market prices in the autumn of 1929 and so remain in a position to complete what was in many ways a far-seeing attempt at steel rationalization through the medium of his company, Allied Ironfounders.

He was sartorially a dandy, excessively vain of his personal appearance. 'Why,' said one of his secretaries to me on one occasion, 'Mr Hatry even has the *soles* of his shoes polished.'

Hatry did the investing public out of about £20,000,000. His frauds looked small when Ivar Kreuger blew out his brains in his flat in the Avenue Victor Emmanuel III in Paris after defrauding Governments, banks and private investors of at least £67,000,000 and possibly, for it proved impossible ever wholly to disentangle his affairs, as much as £150,000,000,—this by reason of a series of transactions made possible only because of the confidence placed in him by the criminally innocent bankers of New York, London, Paris, Brussels, Rome, Amsterdam and his home country, Sweden. Interestingly enough only the Russians suspected him. They turned down his offer of a loan in return for a match monopoly. Their Marxist dialectic—or perhaps Stalin's peasant suspicion of smooth capitalist operators—stood them, on this occasion at least, in better stead than the economic subtleties of the West.

I used to see Kreuger flitting in and out of the Bank of England, where he was accepted at his own valuation until the very last, and was introduced to him by a mutual banking friend who took care not to mention that I was a journalist. He was a cold fish. Most of the rogues I have known have had a certain attractiveness, a piratical wildness, perhaps, or impish humour. Kreuger had none. He was as dry of human sap as President Coolidge.

The secrecy that surrounded him persisted after his death. His associates went to extraordinary lengths to expunge the record. His native country did its best to wipe him from memory. To uncover even the most innocent details became a matter of difficulty as I found some thirty years later when I was making a television documentary called 'The Face of Fraud'. I wanted film material on Hatry, Kylsant, Samuel Insull, the Frenchman Stavisky—and, of course, Kreuger. But I at once came across a very odd situation. It was easy to find all the material one needed on the others. But everything relating to Kreuger had disappeared. We searched the film libraries of London, New York and Paris for newsreel concerning him. It had all gone. Even still photographs were almost non-existent. For a man who had made so many headlines it was incredible.

He must, we conjectured, have systematically bought and destroyed all newsreels and photographs taken of him during his lifetime. But this was not all. The newsreels and photographs shot in the Avenue Victor Emmanuel III after his suicide had also gone. So had everything shot during the investigation that followed. All that the most careful search could produce were some still photographs of his State funeral in Stockholm before his crimes were known.

At this stage we put advertisements in the newspapers of several cities offering a good price for any material. We got nothing. And then weeks later when we had given up hope an advertisement in a Swedish newspaper brought a response. A letter came from a woman who said she had known Kreuger and might be able to help us. My producer, Michael Tuchner, flew to Stockholm to see her. She turned out to be a former mistress of Kreuger's who was now living in respectable poverty, She had some photographs and a ciné-film she had taken during a brief summer holiday with him on an island in the Baltic and these she was glad to sell us. They were surprisingly domestic pictures and the film might have been the holiday film of any middle-class couple, except that he seemed to avoid looking at the camera. She remembered him with affection. Perhaps because she was Scandinavian, one of his own, he seemed to have treated her much better than he had any of the other paid mistresses he kept in most of the world's capital cities.

'One couldn't help feeling sorry for him sometimes,' she told Mike Tuchner. 'He worked so hard. And he was so quiet.'

Yet even Kreuger was merely Saul to the City's David and where he killed his thousands, the respectable men of finance killed their tens of thousands in the disasters that followed the Wall Street crash of 1929. Beaverbrook had said he wanted someone to write about the A.B.C. of finance. I began to feel as if I had had the whole dictionary thrown at me.

And then I left Beaverbrook. I did so with regret. I had often disliked and distrusted him. But I found it hard not to love him at times. By my standards he was an evil and mischievous influence in public life—although not, as his enemies declared, without principle for, surely few men have retained such loyalty to principle as he did in his lonely advocacy of what he called Empire Free Trade.

In his personal relations he was like a tempestuous, fascinating and unscrupulous woman who enslaves while she appals. He had eaten many young men whole, flattering them with money, gossip and the prospect of power until they slipped down the gullet like a well-marinated steak. If Jess had not loomed so much larger in my life than he ever could I might have suffered the same fate. She helped to keep him in scale for me.

Beaverbrook's gods were exciting gods, but they were not mine. I liked his buccaneering way with finance better than the solemn orthodoxies of the City fathers with whom I spent my days—and on most of the big economic questions, he was incomparably more right than they were. I enjoyed his iconoclasm, his endless curiosity, his mordant summaries of the characters of the great. But when it came to most of the things I cared about we were on opposite sides of the barricades.

I owed him a great deal. In money, for he paid me handsomely, showering increases on me. In opportunity. In reputation. I was grateful. But I knew that if I wanted to make something real of my life by the standards that seemed to me important I must get away. It was thus an immense good fortune so far as I was concerned when the *Daily Herald*, which had been staggering along under trade-union control since Lansbury's departure, made a deal with Odhams Press by which the paper while remaining politically labour came under the financial and commercial control of Odhams, and was turned into a large circulation popular newspaper. I was invited to become its Financial Editor.

When I wrote and told Beaverbrook I had been offered the City Editorship of the *Daily Herald* and because my political sympathies lay in that direction was thinking of taking it, a short, sour note came back: 'You have taken a one-way street. Goodbye to you.'

However, when I made a name for myself on the *Herald* he changed his mind and a pressing invitation to have lunch with him at his country house, Cherkley, near Leatherhead, arrived. The house was full of guests. Viscount Castlerosse was there, of course, and a group of lesser Beaverbrook satellites and fashionable beauties. I had thought it would be pleasant to re-establish friendly relations, but as the lunchtime conversation proceeded

I began to wonder. This was not, I decided, a galley of which I wanted any part. A Reuter's message was brought in reporting an incident in the Saar in which a British official—an observer, I rather think for the plebiscite that was to take place on the issue of reunion with Germany—had been man-handled by a group of Nazis and then arrested. Beaverbrook read it out with obvious satisfaction and remarked gleefully, 'That'll be a lesson to Eden to keep his nose out.' Taking their cue from him the rest of the company went into a happy sycophantic babble in support of Germany's right to do what she wanted in her own area of Europe. I found it hard to sit through this and was glad when the luncheon party broke up and I was taken by Beaverbrook into his study.

He sat down on a couch and patted the seat beside him. 'Sit here,' he said. When I was seated he turned to me with a warm embracing smile. 'I want you to come back to me,' he said.

'I'm very happy on the *Herald*,' I told him. He gazed at me like a friendly tiger. 'You're wasting your time there,' he said. 'You ought to be up at the front of the paper not writing about the City at the back. Come to me and I'll make your name ring through the land. You can have a regular column.'

I looked dubious. 'We're old friends. We won't argue about money,' he said. 'Tell me what the *Herald* pays you and whatever it is I'll double it.'

At this moment we were interrupted. The door opened and, presumably by prior arrangement, a nurse brought in his small granddaughter. The little girl ran to him and climbed on his knee and he chortled to her and asked her what she had been doing. As they played together he became everybody's grandfather, the darling man all men could trust. She was a pretty little girl and he clearly adored her so that I was perhaps ungenerous in suspecting that this touching scene had been put on for my benefit. At last the little girl climbed down and after giving him a large kiss and me a small one was taken away by her Nanny.

'Well, you've had time to think it over,' said Beaverbrook as the door closed. 'I told your old friend Chris I was seeing you. He'll be delighted when I tell him you're going to join us. I'll ring him. He'll want to welcome you.'

'But I haven't said I will,' I replied. I went on to explain as firmly as I could that I saw no chance of the arrangement he suggested working because he and I disagreed on so many things and I did not fancy writing to order.

On my saying this he protested that I should write as I wished. 'You shall be as free as Low,' he said. This I took leave to doubt. I did not think I had anything like Low's value to him and I thought there were more opportunities of conflict over a column than a cartoon.

Finally, seeing that I could not be persuaded to say yes on the spot, he made me promise to think it over and write to him in a day or two.

Although unpersuaded I could not help feeling flattered as I drove home. After all, I said to myself, it is not every young man who gets the chance to turn down such an offer and I thought I would make sure that Elias, the Chairman of Odhams, heard about it. When I got home I told Jess about it with some pride. 'But what are you going to say?' she asked. 'No, of course,' I told her and she nodded and said, 'You wouldn't be able to call your soul your own.'

Greatly encouraged that Jess's instinct, on which I had come greatly to rely, confirmed my own, I wrote to Beaverbrook the next day refusing his offer. I was, I said, greatly honoured that he wanted me to join him and I should always be in his debt for many things, but I was too much of an egotist to accept. I wanted to be Francis Williams, not Lord Beaverbrook's man. For this he did not forgive me for nearly a quarter of a century.

In *The Baldwin Age*, which he edited, John Raymond described the late twenties and early thirties as 'the smiling age'. And so it was. As I look back on that time or refresh my memory with group photographs of the Cabinet tastefully disposed on the steps leading from the Cabinet Room to the garden of 10 Downing Street, or of Ministers and ex-Ministers getting on or off trains or even—the more daring of them—airplanes they all seem to be smiling. It was no doubt the new version of keeping a stiff upper lip. They smiled even in the City although not, as I remember, in the Welsh mining valleys and the north country shipbuilding yards like those of Jarrow. 'I would like to feel we'd made people happier,' said the General Manager of Barclays Bank to me one day when I asked him about the objectives of banking policy. It seemed a modest if unbankerlike ambition. But not, as things turned out, a very realizable one.

I gathered around me on the City staff of the *Daily Herald* a small team well versed in the normal run of City business including V. J. Burt who came with me from the *Evening Standard* and W. Oughton who came from the Exchange Telegraph, and a brilliant young chartered accountant, Gordon Cummings, whom I set to work to gut balance sheets and company prospectuses in a much more searching way than was usual at that time.

I was determined, however, not to have merely a traditional City page dealing with investments and kindred matters. I headed my own column—which usually, in fact, spread over two or three—Finance and Industry, and so far from confining myself to the City took the whole world for my province. I aimed, in fact, to link finance with economic and political policy in a way that although common now was little done on City pages then.

The surprising result was that I found myself much sought after by what Mr Lloyd George had once described as the penguins of the City and eventually by the chief penguin himself —Mr Montagu Norman, Governor of the Bank of England. I had for a time, indeed, the curious privilege of being almost the only City Editor Mr Norman could bring himself to see.

The first approach from the Bank came, as was Mr Norman's way, somewhat deviously. He had recently introduced into the Bank as American Adviser a former Professor of Banking at Harvard, Dr Sprague, later described by Bevin as the Yankee at the Court of King Norman. One day I had a mysterious telephone call. 'Is this Mr Williams?' asked a Bostonian voice at the other end of the line. I said it was. 'This is Sprague here,' continued the voice. 'I don't think we have met, but we have many mutual friends and I think we should. I should much enjoy it if you cared to look in some afternoon. I'm at the Bank.'

So I went to see Dr Sprague and found him an engaging conversationalist rather academic in style but much less inhibited in his views than most bank officials. He was much older than me, of course, and our conversation went rather like a seminar between a truculent student and a faculty member with a reputation for open-mindedness, but I think we both enjoyed it. At any rate after we had taken tea out of a silver teapot he said he hoped I would drop in again and suggested a day the following week.

Next week found us sitting talking again. This time, however, we had not gone very far when in answer to a question of mine Dr Sprague said musingly over fingertips pressed lightly together, 'You know that's something the Governor could answer better than me.' I was tempted to say, 'So what!' but instead I smiled politely and said, 'No doubt. But it's unlikely I'll have an opportunity to ask him, so won't you try?' 'No,' said Dr Sprague giving an excellent impression of a man coming to a decision, 'I think you should ask the Governor that. Would you like to meet him?' 'Of course,' I replied. 'I told him I was seeing you,' said Dr Sprague. 'I think he may be free. I'll just go along and have a word with him.'

A few minutes later I was being ushered into the Governor's presence. At that time Montagu Norman had been Governor of the Bank of England for some ten years, the first time in the Bank's history, except for an interlude of four years or so during the war, that any man had held this office for more than what had come to be regarded as the statutory two years. He was to remain for another fourteen years. He was already at the height of his authority, a virtual despot and a powerful, perhaps the most powerful, influence on national economic as well as financial policy.

Norman more than any other single man had been responsible for Britain's post-war return to the Gold Standard at a rate that enabled the pound to 'look the dollar in the face' and in doing so had almost ruined the coal and other export industries and made the General Strike practically inevitable. He had been also the prime influence in persuading Mr Stanley Baldwin to accept a settlement of the American war debt on terms that his Conservative colleagues, including even his Prime Minister, Bonar Law, regarded as intolerable. Yet this man of great brilliance and integrity who sometimes seemed able to exercise almost unlimited authority over the economic lives of his fellow countrymen was suffering, although only his intimates knew it, from the permanent effects of a nervous illness that had, in his own words, turned him into a prisoner in 'a prison constructed on the lines of hell'. This neurosis made it intolerable to him to

96

be required to argue with equals or accept any criticism of his decisions, as he had manifested very clearly during the sittings of the Macmillan Committee on Finance and Industry. Here he had shown a remarkable antagonism to both Keynes and Bevin and an even more remarkable incapacity to explain his policies under questioning. 'His negatives,' as Sir Roy Harrod has said, 'were cold, aloof and relentless.'

However, he was extremely gracious when Dr Sprague introduced us, displaying an old-fashioned courtesy rarely met with even in those days and now almost disappeared from the earth. It was the courtesy of a man much concerned not only with good manners but with the manner in which things were done, with all the formal and ceremonial procedures of human relationship. I was reminded of one of Conrad's sea captains, confident in the world of which he was master and determined that all should be most proper and correct within it. Indeed, there was something about him that reminded me of Conrad himself although I had only seen Conrad once at a distance on the platform at a public meeting and knew him mainly from photographs. It was not only the trim pointed beard, although no doubt this contributed to the impression, but a sense of something at once detached, romantic, and, to use one of Conrad's favourite words, elevated, about his personality. Yet there was also, I thought, something of Beaverbrook in him, much although both would have disliked the comparison—a suggestion of something capricious, mischievous and beyond control. This similarity, if there really was one, struck me even more when I saw Norman outside the Bank wearing his broad-brimmed black hat which he slung carelessly in the air to come to rest wherever it would on his head and which endowed him with an appearance of irresponsibility and even eccentricity, a sort of wild recklessness such as Beaverbrook's black hat worn in much the same manner brought out in him also, although with him these qualities were always nearer the surface.

Even without the hat Norman's appearance was impressive. He had much grace of bearing. His clothes, meticulously valeted, were sober and correct but this sobriety and correctness were given an unexpected, almost an antithetical, touch of splendour by a magnificent emerald ring through which his tie was threaded in the old-fashioned way instead of being knotted in the more usual fashion. The sculpted face, deep-set eyes and strong nose with a high bridge gave him something of a sephardic Jewish look. He seemed a glittering foreign bird to find in the sober parlour of the Bank of England.

As Dr Sprague introduced us Norman rose and gave a small courteous bow as though I were a person of great consequence to him. It was, no doubt, a regular part of the charm he wielded to such effect. He took great care over seeing that I was comfortably settled in my chair before he resumed his own. By this time Sprague having served his purpose as an intermediary had murmured an apology and gone.

Norman's desk was clear of paper. Unlike smaller men he did not use it to demonstrate his involvement in important matters but rather as an ancillary to his own good manners, courteously clear of anything that might suggest to the visitor that he was intruding on a busy man.

He put his fingers together on the desk in front of him—they were extraordinarily delicate and well shaped, I noticed—and leaning forward slightly said, 'I have read some of your writings and Dr Sprague has spoken to me about you. So, too, has Sir Edward Peacock. I thought it might be interesting for us to meet. As I understand it you do not altogether approve of what we do.' His voice was attractive and melodious but he had a curious trick of articulating some of his words with unusual deliberation.

Thus confronted I could but say that although I felt sure he was concerned only to act in the national interest, I thought that too little weight was given in the Bank's decisions to the ordinary workers in industry.

He interrupted to ask, 'And this is the general opinion of the Labour Party and the trade unions?'

I perceived that it was as a small, unofficial window into this alien and unsympathetic world that the Governor wished to use me, though whether because he really wished to know what went on there or because it had been suggested to him that he ought to know, I could not make out.

He leaned back as I talked, paying me the flattery of his complete attention, but not, I thought, with any warmth or sympathetic understanding of what was being said. He seemed to treat what I was saying as a verbal document from which it

98

might be possible to extract scraps of information not previously known.

Afterwards he talked at some length, but pithily, about the international responsibilities of the City of London. It was clear from his manner that he was not prepared for or interested in argument, nor despite the precision and clarity of his actual choice of words was the case itself intellectually argued. It was an expression of beliefs intuitively held.

When he had finished we both rose and again formally shook hands. 'You will not quote me of course,' he said and I said of course not. 'I hope we may meet again,' he said. 'Let Dr Sprague know when you feel it would be helpful. He will arrange something.'

After this I saw Norman fairly frequently, although oddly enough most of the suggestions for our meetings came from him through Dr Sprague, not from me. I think I must have felt rather diffident. Also I was making increasingly bitter attacks on the Bank's policy of what was called industrial rationalization which had its most dramatic expression in the virtual destruction of the shipbuilding town of Jarrow, whose citizens headed by their M.P., my friend Ellen Wilkinson, staged a famous protest march to London, and did not feel I could disguise my feelings.

When we met our conversation followed the same pattern as before. He would indicate that he had read my articles and wished to know why I should write in that strain and especially whether my views were representative of those in what he already thought of as the alien and inferior world of industry and the trade unions. Then he would speak of the Bank's international obligations, sometimes with a controlled vehemence revealed in the emphasis and intonation he gave to certain words. There was never any argument or even discussion between us and no attempt at any exchange of minds. 'The dogs bark but the caravan passes on' he was to say at a Lord Mayor's Banquet and I had a strong suspicion that so far as he was concerned I was merely a barking dog, although perhaps housetrained and therefore capable of being allowed in the house.

I continued to find the man fascinating although I was often terrified to think of the power he exercised. He was, I thought, temperamentally an artist, intuitive rather than logical, and

like some other artists I knew contemptuous of the ordinary
herd, the outsiders who did not comprehend the mysteries of his
art. Like Madame Pavlova who when asked her interpretation
of Giselle replied, 'Why would I dance it if I could put it into
words?' he was contemptuous of explanations and in a comparatively genial moment said to Bevin at the Macmillan inquiry,
'You may complain, Mr Bevin, of me or of other bankers you
have seen that their evidence comes through their nose . . . I
plead guilty to it myself to some extent and it is a curious thing
that so many of those who inhabit the City find difficulty in
stating the reasons for the faith that is in them.'

He remains for me one of the most tantalizing of figures.
Undoubtedly he was a great man although I think a blemished
one. Of the persistence of his legend I had strong proof when
passages concerning him in a book of mine, *A Pattern of Rulers*,
published in 1965, were serialized in the *Sunday Times* and
brought a glut of denunciations from bankers who still revered
his memory.

Despite my unexpected introduction to Norman I still
continued to see Dr Sprague. Sprague, I think, missed Harvard
and was pleased to explore ideas with a younger man. He had
the American belief that great issues are best brought out into
the open for public debate instead of being kept to a private
circle. His mind was trained to assess rather than dogmatize
and since he was also to some extent in the confidence of
Benjamin Strong, Governor of the Federal Reserve Bank of
New York, and, although to a somewhat lesser extent, Strong's
successor, George L. Harrison, he was particularly useful as a
source of information when it became necessary in 1931 to
secure international credits to support the pound—a situation
that had a topical ring thirty-eight years later—and the Labour
Government collapsed and was replaced by a 'National' one.

It was Sprague's habit and one which I well understood, to
avoid explicit answers to questions but to turn them into the
starting-point for a wide-ranging seminar during which we both
enjoyed considering what was and what was not likely to
happen in a particular set of circumstances. This discussion he
would illustrate by examples and on this occasion I came away
without any doubt in my mind that stiff terms had been put
forward by the Americans and approved by the Bank and that

these included considerable economies in Government spending and particularly in spending on Unemployment Assistance, for which most American bankers had no great sympathy.

I felt very indignant about this pressure—not so much that it was being made by the Americans who could perhaps be forgiven for thinking they had a right to demand satisfactory guarantees, but that the Bank of England should be going along with it and demanding what I regarded as fresh human sacrifices for gold. So far as I was concerned the Gold Standard was not worth saving and as for credits to support the pound, it was, I considered, the bankers themselves who chiefly benefited from propping up the pound at an exchange rate manifestly too high for our export industries and I saw no good reason why the unemployed should be required to make sacrifices on their behalf. 'It's nothing but a ramp,' I said to Tom Darlow who was by now Night Editor of the *Herald*, whereupon he put up 'Bankers' Ramp' as a headline on the story I had written and thus launched into circulation one of the most famous phrases in modern politics which was to be debated over many years.

The collapse of the Labour Government and MacDonald's decision to break with his party and head a National Government predominantly Conservative in composition came as a bitter blow to Jess and myself as to most other Socialists although I should not have been greatly surprised. Immersed in economics as I now was it had been driven home to me for some time that having preached the coming collapse of capitalism for years MacDonald and his colleagues had no idea what to do when it happened. They proved totally incapable of reacting to it with even a tiny part of the imagination and decision that was soon to be shown by Franklin Roosevelt across the Atlantic. Their performance was not of a kind to give anyone confidence and I found myself increasingly disillusioned by the level of their capacity.

Snowden had already intimated his disapproval of the expansionist anti-Gold Standard line I had been taking in the *Herald*. I stuck to Beaverbrook's advice to remember the A.B.C. of finance and not get lost in the higher reaches of the financial alphabet and had early reached the conclusion that the attempt to hold on to the Gold Standard could not help but bring industrial depression and exchange crisis. This view I

expressed daily and was encouraged to find that my original
mentor in such matters, Beaverbrook, maintained it just as
strongly as I did. He was far wiser than his conventional critics
at this time. As for Snowden, although he complained regularly
and bitterly that the *Herald* was 'unhelpful', he had nothing to
offer when I saw him but the most orthodox and deflationary
of remedies. He seemed to be hypnotized by Montagu Norman
and Gladstone, whose portrait glowered down at him from the
walls of his study at 11 Downing Street.

As for the rest of the Labour Ministers, Arthur Henderson
was almost wholly immersed in a noble but abortive dream of
international disarmament. Even when economic issues forced
their way into his consciousness he was incapable, it seemed, of
applying to them more than the strictly practical and rigidly
conditioned expertise of a trade-union negotiator of the middle
rank. His character was rock-like and admirable, his conception
of the brotherhood of man elevated and noble, his intellectual
understanding of economic principles negligible. Sidney Webb
might have been expected to move more easily among these
mysteries. But he was too much of a Fabian gradualist to recognize a world depression when he saw it. He had the mind of a
bureaucrat and was in any event fully involved in running his
own Department, the Colonial Office. Even here he was a poor
Minister too much in the hands of his officials and was without
authority in either the Cabinet or the House of Commons: an
admirable research worker lifted above his political station.

Some junior Ministers, notably Pethick-Lawrence and Hugh
Dalton, had, I thought, a clearer understanding of the situation
than the Cabinet but they were without authority. With the
exception of Ernest Bevin, who had opposed the return to the
Gold Standard when it was done and had since learned a great
deal from his membership of the Macmillan Committee on
Finance and Industry, the trade unions were as baffled as the
Cabinet, although more staunch in resisting attacks on the
unemployed and the lower-paid workers. Relations between the
Cabinet and the T.U.C., were, as was made clear to me in my
numerous perambulations, as bad as they could be. MacDonald
had never found himself at ease with the leaders of the trade
unions, and even Sidney Webb, who should have understood
the trade-union movement better than most, referred to the

members of the T.U.C. General Council as 'pigs'. One way and another socialist brotherhood was at a discount all round—and so was socialism.

Yet even so the news that MacDonald had defected and after persuading his Cabinet to resign had agreed to stay on as Head of a National Government came as a shattering blow. I felt as I had years before in Bootle when a Labour Alderman had changed sides and become a Tory Mayor and Bill Summers and I had marched the streets half through the night declaiming to each other, 'Just for a handful of silver he left us/Just for a riband to stick in his coat/Found the one gift of which fortune bereft us/Lost all the others she lets us devote.'

I had never, it is true, been enormously taken by MacDonald —especially as I came to know him better. He had considerable charm and a gracious way with those who were very much younger than himself. But just when you seemed to be getting somewhere he would disappear into the mist like one of his own Highland peaks and one would find oneself ankle deep in a bog. His snobbery although urbane was obtrusive. He liked to talk of his friends the Londonderrys. The Royal Family featured frequently in his conversation. At Chequers he liked to play the country squire, and at Upper Frognal Lodge, Hampstead, the amateur patron of art and letters: he had a fine library and one or two good modern paintings. A portrait of Keir Hardie, as Tom Jones, Deputy Secretary of the Cabinet maliciously noted, was kept hidden away behind a door. He was a good talker especially about books and travel, but not, I felt, possessed of any great critical judgement—although that may have been merely the reaction of a rather arrogant young man. He never, in my experience, displayed any great interest in economic matters or for that matter in political ideas, but this perhaps was natural in a Prime Minister off duty. He was very conscious of the burdens he had to bear and would comport himself like a weary Titan anxious for sympathy. He obviously liked the company of women more than of men and much enjoyed adulation.

Yet I remembered him also as a public speaker and what it had been like to hear that golden Scots voice across a great hall, all doubts and criticisms suspended with the opening invocation, 'My Friends', and the noble sweep of what seemed, when one was young, an authentic vision of a new world idealistic and humane. It seemed a sad sideways ending to greatness. I could not help an intense sense of disillusionment.

I have often wondered why not only he but the rest of the Labour Ministers in 1931 made such a shoddy mess of government. They had their successes, of course, MacDonald particularly so in Foreign Affairs where he was always most at home. But they were hopelessly ineffective in handling the major problems of the time. The melancholy fact is, I think, that Labour got office both in 1922 and 1929 long before it was ready for it, as a consequence not of its own merits but of the disintegration of the Liberal Party and the political accident of a vacuum into which the British liking for a two-party system pushed it before it had acquired the real experience and capacity to move to the centre of the political stage.

I am willing now—although I was not then—to believe that MacDonald was moved by a genuine sense of the public interest when he became the titular head—of a National Government. But if so it was a public interest with which his sense of his own indispensability had become inextricably woven. And, indeed, apart from a greater willingness to cut Unemployment Benefit and the incomes of teachers and public servants, including naval personnel who mutinied at Invergordon as a consequence, the National Government showed no more understanding of the crisis than the Labour Government had. Nor did its existence save the pound.

Along with other Financial Editors I was invited shortly after the National Government was formed to meet Sir Warren Fisher, Permanent Secretary of the Treasury and Head of the Civil Service, so that we could be told of the measures—mainly further economies—proposed to check the run. We all sat, I remember, around a large mahogany table and drank tea as is the habit of the British at times of stress. When Warren Fisher had finished we were asked if we had any questions. Was the Treasury satisfied, I asked, that we either could or should remain on the Gold Standard? Would it not be better to accept the fact that it had become unworkable and that any attempt to save it must involve almost intolerable sacrifices for the great mass of ordinary people? Cecil Sprigge, the City Editor of the *Manchester Guardian*, who was an old Etonian and a classical scholar with a very precise mode of speaking, followed. 'There can, I think,' he said, 'be no possible room for doubt that in this matter the City Editor of the *Daily Herald* is correct. I hope, Sir Warren, the Treasury has weighed the situation.' The rest remained silent.

Not so Sir Warren Fisher. He could scarcely contain himself. He rose to his feet, his eyes flashing, his face flushed with passion. He looked first at me and then, even more uncomprehendingly, at Sprigge. He was like a housemaster who has caught two of his boys, one of them actually a scholar, exchanging obscenities.

'Gentlemen,' he said, leaving his seat and marching magisterially across the room to take up a dignified stance in front of the great marble fireplace—'Gentlemen, I hope no one will repeat such sentiments outside this room. I am sure all those of you who know the British people will agree with me that to make any such suggestion is an affront to the national honour and would be felt as an attack on their personal honour by every man and woman in the country. It is quite unthinkable.' Sprigge and I could only put down our teacups and slink away.

Less than a week later on the evening of Sunday, 20 September we were both summoned along with other Financial Editors to another meeting, this time at Hoare's Bank in Fleet Street—chosen apparently because of its accessibility to our head offices since the City was in its Sabbath sleep. We were told by a solemn but basically cheerful group of bankers that later that evening an announcement would be made that the Gold Standard was to be suspended and that Banks and the Stock Exchange would be closed the following day. When we had been given time to absorb the news we were asked if we had any questions.

'What,' I asked, 'do you expect the result of this to be?'

'I am sure,' replied the bankers' spokesman, 'it will mean an immediate improvement in our affairs and I am confident the whole country will welcome it.'

'And you do not expect any suicides?' asked Sprigge. 'Not even at the Treasury?'

'No, of course not,' said the banker. 'Why ever should there be? This is excellent news.'

After this experience I have always found it difficult to take seriously the weightiest pronouncements of Treasuries—especially when given under emotional stress.

Having been formed to defend the Gold Standard and having been compelled to abandon it, the National Government shortly went to the country in the complete confidence that it would receive the full support of the people. This confidence was justified. In the General Election the Labour Party was decimated. It had gone into the election with 287 Members of Parliament. It came out of it with only 46. Every Cabinet Minister but George Lansbury lost his seat.

When the result was known Jess and I went to a rally of the losers at Seymour Hall in London. We did not feel cast down by defeat but rather uplifted by a sense of our common belonging. George Lansbury, who had been elected Leader, spoke. His speech was like a warm cloak of comradeship. We each felt emotionally strong, purged of past imperfections, a small romantic band of brothers again. Clement Attlee, who had been elected Deputy Leader and whom Jess and I then hardly knew although later he was to become one of our dearest friends, spoke shortly and crisply as was his wont. We were glad he did not seek to use rhetoric. We had had enough of rhetoric with MacDonald. Now we wanted quiet men whom we could trust.

When the speeches were over we stood in a ring. Jess was on one side of me, Ernest Bevin on the other, and we all clasped hands and sang 'England Arise'. Although in the posture for it we did not sing 'Auld Lang Syne'. We were not in the mood for that.

CHAPTER 6

Ammunition for Mr Churchill

Lacking prevision of what the future had to offer *The Times* thought that 1931 might come to be known as 'The black year in the history of the world'. By now, I suppose, it means neither more nor less than any other year to those who did not live through it and even for those who did it is mostly overshadowed by what followed. Yet for a time it seemed as though this was the year to mark on our tablets as the one in which the system of international exchange on which civilization depends finally broke down.

Men, women and children starved in their thousands while granaries bulged with grain that could not be sold and went without clothes while cotton was ploughed back into the land because no one could buy it. In Brazil—this for some reason caught the popular or at any rate the newspaper imagination more than most things—coffee was piled into bonfires at the docks and burnt because it was no longer worth while shipping it to the thirsty breakfast tables of Europe and America. According to the International Labour Office more than thirty million people were unemployed and from the windows of their soaring Wall Street office blocks bankers and stockbrokers jumped to destruction like demented rabbits. We seemed in the grip of a cosmic madness now almost impossible to comprehend as one looks back on it from the comparative economic sanity of the post-Keynsian world.

In London life continued, at least in the West End, with phrenetic, brittle gaiety. It was still easy to have a good time if you wanted it that way. But in the Lancashire mill towns of my youth and the mining valleys of South Wales, on Merseyside and in the villages of Durham, and the shipyards of Tyneside and Clydeside men squatted silently on their heels facing with hooded eyes a future black with utter despair. It was not to prove so, of course. In the end the human race pulled through, although more by the unpredictable processes of the instinct to survive and the remedial quality of time than by any combined exercise of intelligence.

Looking back I cannot help but salute democracy. I have no patience with those who proclaimed sententiously as fascism spread, 'It could happen here.' The amazing, the staggering fact is that it could not and did not. Every economic reason for a breakdown of democratic government existed in Britain and America in those baffling years. But it did not take place. Where democracy was well rooted it survived undamaged what might well have killed it. We pay ourselves altogether too poor a compliment when we give credence to the thesis that we only avoided fascism—or perhaps communism—by the skin of our teeth.

Yet one has to admit that the resistance to economic common sense which existed at the time seems hardly credible now. It is sometimes argued that those in charge are not to be blamed since the economic policies that kept breakdown and mass unemployment away after the Second World War had not been invented then. But this is not true. There were reasonable alternatives available. But no one wanted to listen to their authors. Of these the chief, of course, was Keynes, whose stature glows and grows with time and whose 'General Theory of Employment Interest and Money' gives him, as A. J. P. Taylor has said, some title to be regarded as 'the greatest benefactor of the human race'.

I read the General Theory avidly when it came out as I had read his earlier 'Treatise on Money', although I had to ask F. W. Pethick-Lawrence, who had been a mathematics Wrangler and a Fellow of Trinity College, Cambridge, to take me through the mathematics. I was wholly convinced by him and still find myself amazed that it should have taken so long for his conclusions to be accepted by practical men.

Keynes was, I suppose, the most intellectually brilliant man I ever met. He wrote with a grace, a brilliance, a lucidity and a wit unusual in economics—modern economics at any rate. But he had outbursts of intellectual savagery that although excusable in the face of fools did not help him as a persuader. He was a superb talker, extraordinarily compelling in argument although not always entirely scrupulous. His mind was so quick, so flexible and so powerful in rejoinder that to watch him in debate with anyone of a class at all comparable to his own was like watching a men's singles final at Wimbledon in a year of champions. The ball flew so fast the eye could scarcely follow it. No wonder Montagu Norman, who found it so hard to put his 'insights' into words, disliked him so.

Moreover, unlike some brilliant men he was as good at the mile as the hundred-yards dash. He had so extraordinary a power of closely argued yet intensely exciting exposition that time seemed to stand still as he talked. When he gave evidence before the Macmillan Commission, having stepped down from the judges' bench into the witness box, he spoke for five days and so enthralled the Commission by the brilliance of his argument that when he finished the Chairman commented, 'We hardly notice the lapse of time when you are speaking.' Yet for six years he tried to persuade governments and Central Banks to take account of his recommendations and failed completely. He was to go on failing until war, that great *régisseur*, compelled a change of mind.

This failure was mainly due to the congenital resistance to new ideas of bankers and politicians. But his own intellectual arrogance had some part in it. This arrogance matched his brilliance. His political judgement often fell behind both. He also had an unexpectedly strong sense of social as well as intellectual superiority which made him disinclined to believe in the possibility of unlettered working men having anything to contribute to a solution of the world's problems. Although he had acquired a certain amount of respect for Ernest Bevin's sagacity in their clashes with Montagu Norman during the Macmillan inquiry, his general attitude to the Labour and trade-union movement was that it ought to touch its intellectual forelock and say thank you kindly, sir, whenever he condescended to tell it what to do.

This was a pity. There was a chance at one time that the

Labour Party, badly winded by the results of the 1931 General Election and passionately anxious to find a respectable alternative both to the economics of scarcity practised by the National Government and the Marxist theories which were rattled at it without pause from the left, might have become Keynsian much earlier than it did, to its own and very possibly the nation's advantage. Keynes thought so himself and when he found the National Government and the cohorts of the Establishment so unyielding came to see me at the *Daily Herald* to enlist my support in persuading the Labour Party to adopt his policies. Since I regarded him as a genius with solutions that could save the world, I was both delighted and flattered by the invitation. But not to much avail. Whenever Keynes actually met Labour or trade-union leaders he managed to insult them.

Later, when the General Theory was published we tried again. By that time I had become Editor of the *Herald* and had appointed Douglas Jay City Editor. When Keynes proposed a meeting at my office I therefore invited Jay along. After all, I thought, Jay is an academic economist and a Fellow of All Souls with a more than adequate sense of intellectual superiority of his own—a younger horse from the same stable. If he would listen to anyone, Keynes, I thought, might listen to Jay on the tactics of persuading trade unionists. But I was wrong. At the end of a long and rather daunting hour in which we tried unavailingly to make Keynes understand some of the prejudices that would have to be overcome and the political allowances that would have to be made Keynes left with no great hope on either side that understanding would be possible.

'I never appreciated until today,' said Jay when he had left, 'how much Keynes thinks like a rich man.' I could not but agree—not, of course, as regards his economic thinking, although a little even there, but in his attitude to what he thought of as the uneducated working classes among whom he was prepared to go slumming if need be but to whom he found it virtually impossible to make any concession of understanding. He was more at ease with the *New Statesman* than the *Herald*. It breathed the same Bloomsbury air and although it was often very silly by his standards, it was the sort of silliness he had grown used to in University Common rooms. However, the *New Statesman* was of little use to him in converting the trade unions. They considered it flibberty-gibberty and lacking in loyalty.

In default of the pure Keynsian doctrine I did my best to preach expansionism and monetary reform to the Labour movement by becoming an avid pamphleteer. 'The World Muddle', 'Democracy and Finance', 'The Bank of England and the Nation' . . . these and others came rolling off my pen with unfaltering self-confidence. The financial criminals whose hunting had brought such zest and interest to my first few years in the City had now sunk beneath the waters, drowned by storms too great even for their ingenuity. But I could not complain of boredom. Indeed, I could not avoid feeling a little guilty when I thought of the excitement and prosperity crisis had brought to me compared with the bad fortune of the mass of the people. I found some solace in arranging what would now be described as confrontations between bankers and Labour intellectuals, both equally at a loss as to what it was best to do in so daunting a situation. On one such occasion I persuaded Charles Lidbury, the Chief General Manager of the Westminster Bank—and one of the most formidable defenders of traditional banking policy —to come with me to a Fabian weekend at Tunbridge Wells. Here, I told him—but he scarcely believed me—he would meet the men who would make financial policy in the future.

Hugh Dalton, affable and booming with an ineffable air of doing his best to be polite to a barbarian, took the Chair and Lidbury made an excellent speech for which he was attacked with great ferocity by a mild-mannered young lecturer in economics whom I had not met before but whom Dalton later introduced over Scotch and soda in the hotel lounge as Hugh Gaitskell. I thus kept my promise to Lidbury. He met two future Labour Chancellors at one go.

Gaitskell I soon came to know better. One afternoon shortly after our Tunbridge Wells confrontation a City gentleman in a top hat called on me. He presented himself as a member of the Union Discount Company named H. V. Berry. Berry, now Sir Vaughan Berry, had gone into the Intelligence Corps from Cambridge during the war and later been a member of the Interallied Rhineland Commission before coming to the City. He had, he said, been convinced by the events of 1931 that a more intelligent and more socialist approach to financial affairs was necessary but that the Labour Party was woefully short on expert knowledge of the City's financial institutions.

Out of this came the X Y Z Club, so called because we wanted something anonymous that would not be capable of proving politically embarrassing to members who worked in the City and who might well be in no position to disclose their political sympathies publicly, but also, in my case, because it pleased me to have a title that indicated that the time had come to take a closer look at the mysterious final letters of the financial alphabet instead of simply sticking to the opening A.B.C. as Beaverbrook had instructed.

We met above a pub in a City alley crowded and noisy during the day but silent and deserted at night, and Hugh Gaitskell, then an economics lecturer at University College, London, became our secretary. Other members besides Berry and myself included George Wansbrough, an old Etonian and Cambridge rowing blue who was at this time a director of Robert Benson & Co.; Nicholas Davenport, who combined being consultant to a leading Stock Exchange firm with writing about finance in the *New Statesman* and later the *Spectator*; F. W. Pethick-Lawrence who had been Financial Secretary to the Treasury in the second Labour Government; Hugh Quigley, the Chief Economist of the Central Electricity Authority; Douglas Jay; Evan Durbin, then of the London School of Economics whose death by drowning off the coast of Cornwall shortly after the war brought to a tragic close a most brilliant career; Cecil Sprigge, Financial Editor of the *Guardian*; and a number of City people mostly young but sometimes of surprising rank and seniority whom Berry brought along. The X Y Z Club still exists although it now usually meets in a room in the House of Commons. Later members have included Harold Wilson, Roy Jenkins and John Diamond, First Secretary to the Treasury.

Over the years the X Y Z Club drew up a blueprint for Labour financial policy much of which, including detailed proposals for the nationalization of the Bank of England, was adopted by the first post-war Labour Government. It has indeed, I think, some claim to have exercised in a quiet sort of way more influence on future government policy than any other group of the time and to have done so in the most private manner without attracting publicity to itself. It briefly became the subject of a 'sensational disclosure' in a popular Sunday paper in the late 1940s, but that was well after most of its major work was done. It stands, perhaps, as an example of a democratic Socialist 'cell' which far exceeded in its success anything that the numerous much-vaunted communist cells of the time managed to achieve.

Although I helped to start it—and the main credit for that belongs not to me but to Berry who later had a big hand in the first bout of steel nationalization as a member of the Iron and Steel Corporation of Great Britain—I can claim little part in its achievements. I dropped out after a year or two when I became Editor of the *Daily Herald* instead of its Financial Editor. I have often thought, however, that it deserves a footnote in the economic and political history of the inter-war years and might provide a fascinating subject for one of those Ph.D. theses which have become so essential to academic success. Delighted as I was with Berry's visit and much encouraged by the evidence that some at least of those who lived by finance were not wholly complacent about its showing in the thirties, I was by no means inclined to spend my life in this particular pool. There was too much to rouse concern elsewhere.

I had by now turned my column in the *Herald* into what was virtually a commentary on world affairs—although with an economic base. The *Herald* must often have seemed to its readers to be running two foreign policies, one in its leading articles and in the contributions of its eminent diplomatic correspondent W. N. Ewer, the other on its City pages. Nor did the two policies by any means always coincide. I was a good deal more publicly suspicious of National Socialism from its very beginning than was Ewer who, whatever his private doubts, could hardly avoid reflecting in his news contributions a certain amount of the professional optimism of the Foreign Office—although he abandoned it long before the Foreign Office itself did.

I found it impossible to share this official optimism. I had read *Mein Kampf* and was shocked to find how many of my friends dismissed it as a farrago of hysterical nonsense. To me it seemed a clear statement of intent by a man of unbridled ambition and remarkable political talent. Nor had I any doubt from the information that now flowed to me from many places—and an international money centre is one of the best diplomatic listening-posts in the world if you know how to find your way about it—that Germany was expanding her military power at an alarming rate. Similarly as I studied for my economic purposes the expansionist programmes of the great Mitsui and Mitsubishi banking and industrial interests in Japan and their close links with extreme nationalist, aristocratic groups in the army I could not feel much confidence in Japan's intentions. I was very far from being a Marxist, or even an economic materialist, but since being flung into the waters of finance by Beaverbrook I had become increasingly impressed by the inter-action of economics and politics and by the importance of economic factors in assessing national policies.

By 1935 I had become convinced that we would have to be farsighted and clear-headed indeed to avoid another world war within a very few years. I wrote a series of articles to this effect and then expanded them into a book—my first. This opened with what turned out to be the highly prescient sentence, 'Three nations threaten war today—Germany, Italy and Japan.' The book created a small stir and a certain amount of con-troversy but sold no more than a few hundred copies. However, some of those who read it seem to have remembered it. Quite recently the wife of an eminent London paediatrician came up to me at a party and said, 'Do you remember writing a book years ago saying there was going to be war with Germany, Italy and Japan? You spoilt my honeymoon.'

I found it fascinating to try to plot the course of Nazi policy by the analysis of innocent-seeming statistics and years later during the war when I had some contact with British Military Intelligence was assured that my efforts had been noted and developed. I was aided in my efforts by the unheralded arrival at my office of a German Jewish refugee. He had escaped from Berlin just before the Nazis caught up with him and was an expert on metal and commodity markets—he is now on the staff of *Neue Zürcher Zeitung*.

With his help I compiled a list of what I somewhat drama-tically called the silent masters of civilization: the raw materials without which no great industrial civilization can survive—or could not in those days before synthetics and electronics. There were twenty-five of them and although some have since been demoted in the march of progress I write them down with due reverence even now: aluminium, antimony, cadium, chrome, coal, cotton, copper, fluorspar, graphite, iron ore, lead ore, magnesite, manganese, mica, molybdenum, nickel, petroleum, platinum, quicksilver, rubber, sulphur, tin, tungsten, wool, zinc. From these we extracted a list of the metals essential to large-scale armaments manufacture which Germany did not herself possess and had to import.

We kept a graph of fluctuations in demand and through his metal-market contacts my German friend was able to check how much was on German account. The results, which I published, indicated that Germany was rearming at a rate far beyond that generally realized.

I suspect it was these disclosures that led to my name being put on the Nazi black list as one of those who were to be captured and shot immediately Britain was invaded. My inclusion gave me much pride when I was told of it by someone in M.I.5 during the war. However, this pride was somewhat deflated at the end of the war when the full list was published and I saw what a scratch lot we were.

Whether it was these particular activities which put me on the black list or not, they had a much more important and immediate result so far as I was concerned. They brought me into touch with Winston Churchill.

One night I was rung up by Hannen Swaffer who, like me, had left Beaverbrook for the *Daily Herald*. He had just come back from the South of France where he had been seeing Churchill, an old friend.

'Churchill wants to meet you,' he boomed—Swaffer was always a great boomer especially down the telephone. 'He rushed on to the beach just before I left waving an air-mail copy of the *Herald* in his hand and shouting, "This proves it, this proves it." He's going to quote that stuff of yours about the Germans and the metal markets in the House as soon as he gets back and he wants you to get in touch with him and keep him posted on anything more you find.'

So it came about that ten years after that first brief tearful exchange of which I was tempted to remind him but never did, I met Churchill again. He quoted me generously by name in a major debate on arms policy, declaring that whatever one might think of some of the Labour Party, he had complete confidence in me and that I had produced evidence that surely even the Government dare not ignore—a piece of unusual optimism on his part. Thereafter I fed him with everything we were able to quarry from commodity market dealings and statistical reports and from other information that came my way. I had now become fairly well known and frequently quoted abroad, and a good deal of confidential information reached me from one source or another.

In his Oxford *English History 1914–1945* A. J. P. Taylor claims that many of Churchill's estimates of German rearmament were exaggerated—and 'made him more unpopular than ever with the Labour Party'. If this is so I must, I suppose, claim a small share of the responsibility, although to be unpopular among some of those on the extreme left who reacted in this way was an honour. There were, however, plenty of other reasons why Churchill should be unpopular at this time—his reactionary attitude to India being high among them. In fact there was very little on which I myself agreed with him except Germany, although for me that was enough.

It was a difficult, miserable period for him. He felt himself on the outside of affairs and unable to influence the course of events. He was also frequently hard up and not too particular about how he got the money for his lavish scale of living, whether from loans and financial tips from Beaverbrook and Rothermere or pot-boilers written for the *News of the World* and other such papers. From this latter chore Beaverbrook eventually rescued him with a contract to write a weekly article for the *Evening Standard*. Having signed the contract Churchill quite properly refused to write what Beaverbrook wanted him to. Percy Cudlipp, who was then Editor of the *Standard* and a talented mimic, used to construct a whole after-dinner entertainment out of his telephone conversation with the two of them.

First Beaverbrook would telephone and ask what Mr Cudlipp's distinguished contributor, Mr Churchill, was writing on that week. Cudlipp would say he had not heard from him yet and Beaverbrook would rasp down the telephone, 'As his Editor you should instruct him to pay more attention to the domestic scene, Mr Cudlipp. Now, the situation in the north-east—that is a very suitable subject. Turn Mr Churchill's mind to that, Mr Cudlipp. Let him stop boring your readers with his gloomy thunderings on foreign affairs and turn his mind to the domestic scene. You are the Editor, Mr Cudlipp. Keep him in order. Good-day to you.'

Later Churchill would come on the telephone and Cudlipp would say, 'I was wondering, Mr Churchill, whether you would care to turn your attention to the situation in the north-east this week. My readers would like to know . . .' 'Admirable, Mr Cudlipp, admirable,' Churchill would interrupt. 'A most important subject, I am sure. But not, I think, this week, Mr Cudlipp. This week there are more pressing matters for us to consider. This week I propose to write on the failure of Mr Baldwin to appreciate the growing menace of Nazism. I have it in hand. Send your young man to collect it at the usual time and it shall be ready. See that it is well displayed, Mr Cudlipp, and thank you for your suggestions. I always enjoy our talks. They are most helpful. Good-day, Mr Cudlipp. Good-day.'

During a good deal of this period Churchill was drinking heavily. This did not affect either his eloquence or his judgement. He could have said then as he remarked many years later, that in the course of a long and arduous career he had done more damage to alcohol than alcohol had ever done to him. But it did sometimes affect his temper, never of the most even.

This most affected his friends, for like a child, and there was always a good deal of the child in the fascinating mixture that made up the Churchill temperament, he tended to take out his ill-humour on those of whose affection he was most sure. Recovering from one such attack Brendan Bracken, the most constant and loyal of all Churchill's allies and disciples, said to me in a burst of fury, 'He's utterly impossible. I don't know why any of us put up with him.' And then, more calmly, 'Being friendly with him is like being in love with a beautiful woman who drives you mad with her demands until you can bear it not a minute longer and fling out of the house swearing never to see her again. But next day she smiles at you and you know there's nothing you wouldn't do for her and she crooks her little finger and you come running.'

Churchill could be extraordinarily petty as well as magnanimous and he was often intolerably unfair to those he disliked or who had aroused his jealousy. He rarely bothered to control his emotions and although I was not close enough to him to suffer the brunt of his bad temper his moods, which could change in a flash from elation to the blackest despondency or from an iridescent charm to a growling rejection, were never hidden.

It is not true, of course, that he was alone in perceiving the threat of German rearmament or in fighting appeasement. Duff-Cooper, Macmillan, Boothby, Bracken among his own circle of Conservatives were all equally convinced of the danger. So on the Labour side were Hugh Dalton, Ernest Bevin and several of the trade-union leaders. But Churchill was the most single-minded. One felt the need for action burning inside him like a fire. It was this and the force of his will behind his conviction that made putting up with his moods a small thing.

It is even more untrue that the British people had become at this time, as Stanley Baldwin convinced himself, anxious for peace at any price. Baldwin claimed that a by-election at East Fulham fought in the autumn of 1937 at which a previously safe Tory seat was lost to Labour by seven thousand votes had been won and lost on 'no issue but the pacifist', and later used this election result as an ignominious excuse for not putting through rearmament.

But John Wilmot who won East Fulham was a friend of mine and I campaigned for him throughout the election, speaking at scores of meetings in schools and church halls. To this day I never drive along the Fulham Road out of London without remembering as I go past the school on the right a meeting packed to the doors at which I concluded with a vehement peroration on the need to defend international law by force if necessary. I was still young as a public speaker at the time and had never before been applauded in such measure.

What won Fulham for Wilmot was not international policy but local housing conditions, which were shocking. It was Baldwin who made it into an anti-war demonstration, not the electors. The fact is he could not bear the idea of war in any circumstances. He was an agreeable and civilized man and, although unsuited to be Prime Minister at this particular time in history, had many good qualities. But he had a nervous horror of violence and a great fear of emotion, perhaps because there was so much pent up inside him that he was afraid to let it out. And he had an extremely vivid visual imagination. When he talked, as he often did, of the country delights of his childhood that had long since passed, and some of which had never existed, one could not but be aware that what he described he saw clearly before his eyes in every single detail as he spoke. I suspect that he saw also with that so vivid inward eye the wrecked bodies of women and children bombed from the air and could not bring himself to contemplate the scene or do anything that might seem to take it for granted.

When one first met him he gave a great impression of benevolence, although sometimes of a benevolence with a sly quality about it and also a sort of rural passivity. But as one got to know him better one could not but become aware that a good deal of this was a mask and that beneath it there was an untidy bundle of fears and anxieties that showed in the nervous tics to which he was prey. His love of the English countryside, although he sometimes exploited it grossly, was genuine enough, as was also his simple faith in a God with whom he could conduct a conversation when he was in doubt as to what he should do. He was in some ways more an essayist than a public speaker. His best speeches were spoken essays often on country themes and of a self-consciously literary character. But he had no talent for martial speech or for martial thought and although he had considerable political cunning he liked life to move forward placidly if he could so manage it. He genuinely enjoyed best the company of simple people and slow talk with long pauses. Attlee, who had a considerable fondness for him, frequently told me that when he came into the smoking-room of the House of Commons he would deliberately seek out some of the older trade-union M.P.s and sit with them rather than members of his own party.

Unlike Chamberlain he seemed not merely unwilling to listen to talk about German ambitions but genuinely uninterested in them. But if he was uninterested I soon had evidence that Russia was not. It was not only Churchill who had noticed my investigation into German dealings on the metal markets. One day I had an invitation to lunch at the Soviet Embassy. I assumed that it was a diplomatic party of some kind and was astonished to find when I arrived that it was to be a *tête-à-tête* between Maisky, the Ambassador, and myself.

This was the first time I had met Maisky. He was small and

neat, with impeccable good manners and a precise academic way of thinking and speaking which it struck me must have been a little like Lenin, of whom, indeed, his stature reminded me. It was common gossip at the time that while Maisky himself, like his foreign ministry chief, Litvinov, was Western in his attitudes and rather pro-English, he was under careful surveillance by members of his staff who had been planted on him by the G.P.U. which was not. Whatever truth there may have been in the general story about G.P.U. men, none were present on this occasion. We were quite alone.

We talked a little about a new play and the theatre in general and the literature of our countries—and a very agreeable and civilized conversation it was. Naturally I could not help wondering during it what it was that the Ambassador really wanted to talk to me about. This became plainer when the meal, which was a pleasant, light affair, was over and the very English-seeming butler had withdrawn leaving us to coffee and brandy. There was, I thought, perhaps mistakenly for I may well have been too much on guard, a subtle change in the atmosphere as he began to tell me how much he enjoyed my City column and how interesting he had found many of my disclosures. Although at first we talked mainly about my German intelligence the conversation was soon broadened to cover City attitudes generally; which institutions could be trusted to be watchful of German moves and which, if any, I suspected of being pro-Nazi. Also which City groups did I think had most influence with the British Government. I began to feel a little uncomfortable under this interrogation, courteously and diplomatically done though it was, and to be rather cautious in my replies. It came to me that in the most delicate possible way the extent of my 'reliability' from the Russian point of view was being probed. Finally Maisky said, 'This has been most interesting and I am most grateful to you. I do hope we can lunch together again.' And then with only the slightest of pauses and with what seemed to me—I may well have been wrong—an almost excessive innocence he added, 'I suppose you would not contemplate sending me written reports from time to time on City institutions and affairs in the City? I would find it very interesting if you could. There must be much that you do not find it possible to print. It would be most valuable and we' (the 'we' was stressed ever so slightly) 'would be most grateful.'

It came to me with a slight shock of surprise that I was being propositioned and that M. Maisky was trying, in the nicest possible way, to recruit me. I may have been too suspicious. But there was the very faintest tension in the air that suggested otherwise. I replied politely that I had much enjoyed our meeting but was afraid I really could not undertake to write regular reports about the City. 'I would not be able to find the time,' I said, 'and in any case I put everything I know into my published columns.' 'In that event,' he said politely, 'I must certainly continue to read you. It was only an idea. Let us both forget it.'

We parted amicably and if he was disappointed he gave no further sign. We remained, indeed, on friendly terms all the time he was ambassador and Jess and I were often invited to his Embassy receptions. Each Christmas he sent us a jar of caviar and a bottle of vodka with his compliments. But there were no more *tête-à-têtes*.

Most of the doors I felt inclined to approach were now open to me and I found the City an agreeable enough place to work in. Not, however, one to induce any great confidence that the financial affairs of the country were being handled, or were likely to be handled, in a manner serving any but the most immediate and private interests. The City possessed a few people of great intelligence and ability and a small number of exceedingly stupid and unpleasant ones, but for the most part its higher echelons were composed, then as now, of amiable and socially pleasant people who were living rather lush, comfortable lives not because they were possessed of ability beyond the ordinary but because they came from the right sorts of backgrounds, had been to the right sorts of schools, had the right sorts of connections and had inherited money from their fathers. Although most of them had acquired technical ability over the years and were, of course, much buttressed in their doings by the accumulated tradition of the City itself they struck me as on the whole much inferior in energy and initiative to most of the American businessmen I met or, for that matter, to the northern industrialists I had come across in my youth. They were better-mannered and nicer to talk to over lunch but a good deal less forceful and open in mind.

Those most successful at making money were often the least

attractive. Moreover this ability frequently seemed quite unrelated to general intelligence. Considerable acquaintance-ship with rich men of one sort and another over subsequent years has confirmed this. There seems to be a special money sense, a talent as unrelated to others as a good eye at ball games or the ability of a memorist. Certainly there are some people to whom money seems to be attracted, they have the golden touch whatever they turn to. For the most part such men tend to be dull dogs, perhaps because in them so much mental energy is taken up by translating whatever happens to them or the world into terms of financial opportunity that none is left for much else. Nothing, indeed, so reconciles one to not being rich as the company of rich men.

With so many of the rich around me I was glad to escape to civilization when I could and meet people not trapped by money. I had read Leonard Woolf's *After the Deluge* when it first came out and thought, as I still do, that it contained one of the most perfect descriptions of the virtues of civilization I had ever read; the testimony of a man to whom the pursuit of reason was in itself a sufficient religion. It was, I thought, superior to Clive Bell's *Civilisation* because more deeply rooted in life. Leonard Woolf did not disappoint me when I met him. He seemed to me one of the wisest and gentlest of men and, of all those I knew, the least likely to be taken in by hypocrisy or the claims of the spurious.

He was at this time, among his innumerable other activities, secretary of a couple of committees which advised the Parliamentary Labour Party on various aspects of foreign and colonial affairs. These meetings, of which Roden Buxton was Chairman, I frequently attended and got to know Woolf fairly well. Jess was a great admirer of Virginia Woolf's novels and so to a slightly more modified degree was I, although I thought some of her criticism better. For me, therefore, Leonard Woolf had a double halo, his own and his wife's. To discuss the problems of the world with him was an immense refreshment of the spirit even although one had to remind oneself that in practice reason rarely prevailed. He was the other half of the Bloomsbury penny. He had Keynes's lucidity without his arrogance—although he was not altogether without Keynes's contempt for fools and sometimes showed it.

He did not, I thought, get along much better than Keynes with some of the Labour and trade-unionist leaders he was thrown into contact with by these committees. This was not because he despised them or sought to patronize them as Keynes did but because he was frequently genuinely affronted by their toughness of fibre and dislike for theory—qualities which I for my part often enjoyed. He found it hard either to like or understand Ernest Bevin whose manners he thought boorish and whose attitudes he considered crude and insensitive. He was constantly hurt by the failure of politicians to live up to his expectations of them. I was surprised by this in view of his successful record as an administrator in the Ceylon Civil Service until I realized that in Ceylon administration had been unimpeded by any of the fetters the democratic process puts about the ankles of the politician.

After the stimulating but at times almost too high-minded discussions of the committees on foreign and colonial affairs it was sometimes pleasant to slip along to the more conspiratorial gatherings of the Union of Democratic Control which met in a tiny attic office in Victoria Street, now gone. The secretary was Dorothy Woodman, surely one of the most remarkable women of the age when one considers the range and cutting force of her numerous left-wing activities. She was a ball of fire when it came to organizing anti-fascist campaigns or denouncing the private manufacture of arms or giving the support to anti-colonial movements that has since made her into a sort of beloved foster mother of many new Asian and African countries.

Fresh from teaching and the Women's International League and glowing with determination to make the tiny, nearly bankrupt twenty-year-old U.D.C. a force in the world, Dorothy Woodman had the energy of a prairie fire. Nothing was allowed to stand in her way. She bullied and cajoled all who might conceivably be of the slightest use in any one of her campaigns, drafted so many Parliamentary Questions that it sometimes seemed that no one else could be asking any, penetrated Mosley's British Union of Fascists disguised as a county young woman with a double-barrelled county name, and dashed constantly from place to place and person to person in search of reliable—it had to be reliable and was tossed ruthlessly aside if it was not—news of the latest wickedness of the British

Government. How she also found time to fall in love with Kingsley Martin and he with her none of us could understand. But manage it they did and set up house together, becoming a sort of joint conscience of the left which brooked no weakening of the liberal will but which was fortunately also, despite its prejudices, a great deal of fun to have around.

My first contact with her was when I had a telephone call demanding that I report for duty at once without pause or hindrance in the matter of Sir Basil Zaharoff, that incredible figure of the times who as an international arms salesman—or as we preferred to call it 'Pedlar of Death'—and envoy in chief of Vickers Ltd, was thought to exercise vast influence in all the more dubious corridors of power. He was reported, I believe correctly, to have begun his business life as a pimp in the Tatarla quarter of Constantinople, but by now was a millionaire several times over and a Knight Commander of the Order of the Bath, as well as holding some 298 decorations from thirty other nations—a man as secretive in his operations as Ivar Kreuger and possibly even more sinister in his ambitions.

I had devoted a good deal of time off and on to Zaharoff and was glad to make available to the persistent Miss Woodman all I had—which, owing to his skill in covering his tracks, was neither as much nor as fully documented as I would have liked. She was at that time engaged in compiling a U.D.I. pamphlet on the arms trade called 'The Secret International' which was later to be responsible for inspiring the United States Senate to set up an inquiry into the private manufacture of arms led by Senator Nye.

After this I joined the Committee of the Union of Democratic Control thus adding yet another to the activities that seemed in those years to spiral constantly from my base in the City.

However, late in 1935 I received a summons to lunch at the Savoy Grill with J. S. Elias, Chairman of Odhams Press and the *Daily Herald*, which changed the direction of my energies.

CHAPTER 7

Daily Newspaper Editor

Sitting at a carefully inconspicuous table in a corner of the Savoy Grill we ate, I remember, a clear soup followed by roast lamb but drank no wine. Elias had a glass of grapefruit juice and I, not being quite able to bring myself to that, had a modest lager. He was a very small man dressed reticently in unobtrusive grey and when he signed the bill at the end of lunch he left, I thought, a rather excessive tip, as though anxious to assure himself always of the very best service. In the forecourt of the Savoy we said goodbye and as he drove back to Long Acre I walked to a telephone booth outside the Law Courts and rang Jess to tell her I had been made Editor of the *Daily Herald* and was to be paid £5,000 a year. I was thirty-two.

As it turned out I was a disappointment to Elias and he was a disappointment to me. But on the day I rang Jess the world seemed wonderful. Here was I a young man in my early thirties given charge of a great newspaper with which I was confident I could help to influence the course of history. Life, in fact, had been going marvellously for us ever since we married—too marvellously, Jess sometimes suspected, for her Presbyterian upbringing had left her convinced that God did not approve of people being too happy. Although she no longer believed in Him, she could not help looking over her shoulder now and then to see if He was creeping up on her with a club. She envied me my pagan unconcern. However, even I, although not in fear of thunderbolts, could not help feeling sometimes that I was doing too well out of the world's distresses. It seemed wrong that I should get paid more and more for writing about situations that grew worse and worse. I did not brood on this over much however. I was too happy. We had two healthy and as it seemed to us highly intelligent and beautiful children, Betty and John. John had been born in 1931 on the day of the Hoover moratorium which, by suspending all interest payments to the United States on war and other debts, seemed momentarily to pave the way for world economic recovery. I tiptoed up the stairs when I heard the news from my office and told Jess that our new baby had been born under a fortunate star.

We lived then in Hillingdon near my sister and her husband and had a small house with a garden which Betty peopled with imaginary characters so that when Bill Summers visited us from Liverpool he had to stand still most of the time for fear of treading on someone if he stirred. Later we moved a short distance away to a house in the middle of an enormous Elizabethan garden which had once belonged to Hillingdon Hall.

We rented this house from a military man called Lt.-Col. Hutchison who had written a best-selling thriller called *The W Plan* and subsequently got involved in a libel action with the Prince of the Belgians. He did his best to persuade us to buy the house for which, as I remember, he wanted what then seemed the large sum of £3,000. However, we resisted him. If we had given way and bought The Old Garden—and even more improbably kept it—we should now be rich. It was bought by the local authority as a site for a new housing estate a few years ago for over £100,000.

But our minds were set on a more country life and by the time I became Editor of the *Herald* we had moved to Holmbury St Mary in Surrey where we built a house which we called Coneybarrow, because of the rabbits, on a hillside looking down the valley between Leith Hill and Holmbury Hill. This we bought from a man named Barnes-Brand whose wife was the daughter of the author of *Charley's Aunt,* a fact which pleased us very much and did so even more when John was a little older and Jess and he became connoisseurs of the play, attending each new presentation with an eager eye for the slightest break with tradition—Betty and I fell away after the third year. Amy Barnes-Brand was a tall handsome woman and used to play the real aunt in her father's play. She had wonderful stories of what it had been like as a little girl to have fortune suddenly fall upon the family in a golden shower.

Although within the stockbroker belt, I suppose, or possibly a little beyond it, for there was no stockbroker actually in reach of us as far as I knew, Holmbury St Mary and its neighbouring villages of Abinger Hammer and Abinger Common, where we now live, were then very largely untouched by town ways. For that matter they still are, being buttressed against urban invasion by the great stretch of common land known as Hurt-wood, by National Trust possessions and, since the war, by planning orders preventing property development. I would not pretend that this stretch of land had the uncomplicated rural simplicities of Shropshire or the fine sense of space and harmony of Jess's beloved Yorkshire moors. It was rather too comfortably off for that. But it had a genuine beauty and quietness which caught and still deeply holds our affections.

At that time a large part of the actual village of Holmbury St Mary was still owned by one old lady who made her round of visits in an open landau and expected the village children to curtsey as she went by, looking somewhat like a reincarnation of Queen Victoria. As owner of most of the cottages, few of which had electricity, running water or sanitation, she exercised great power and when a young man in the village wished to get married would refuse to let him have a cottage if she considered he should stay at home and look after his mother. She naturally regarded the influx of new inhabitants such as us with extreme dislike, correctly seeing in it the unpleasing shadow of social change. She was particularly upset when we built a cottage for a gardener we brought with us from Hillingdon and had it designed by the same architect who designed our own house with many amenities including a rather charming bathroom, and an all-electric kitchen with a floor of a rather nice material that had first been used for the liner *Queen Mary*.

We were, she complained, putting ideas into the heads of the working classes, not realizing, poor lady, that the *Herald* which I edited existed for exactly that purpose. Another old lady who lived in a pleasant Queen Anne farmhouse near by had made a vow after an unfortunate love affair when young never to let a man pass her door. She would nod and pass the time of day if she met one outside but that was as far as it went; when she was ill in her later years and needed a fire in her bedroom her maids, who were of an age when carrying coal upstairs was beyond their powers, were instructed to order the gardener to put a ladder against her bedroom window. Up this he carried a bucket of coal which he had to hand to one of the waiting maids through the window, carefully averting his eyes the while.

As our immediate neighbour we had the pianist William Murdoch. He had built a large modern house with a huge combined music and billiard room two storeys high in which he and Lionel Tertis and Albert Sammons would sometimes give concerts for his neighbours. His wife, Flossie, was a sister of Ernest Simon who was a friend of mine and later Chairman of the B.B.C. when I was one of the Governors. They had two children very close in age to Betty and John.

Another near neighbour was Frank Smythe, the Everest climber, and over the hill in Abinger my friend Cecil Sprigge of the *Manchester Guardian* and his wife, Sylvia, who was the daughter of a famous Berlin Correspondent of *The Times* and was herself a great authority on Italy, had a cottage. They entertained largely but in simple style—a huge rabbit casserole with a rough red wine was the most frequent dish at dinner—and had a large open fire which smoked shockingly so that one frequently had to fight one's way through billowing smoke clouds to meet the current house guest from Venice, Egypt, India or some other distant place, sitting with streaming eyes but cheerful heart—one could not but be cheerful with Sylvia around—in the inglenook. E. M. Forster lived with his sister at Abinger Hammer—so-called because in the days before blast furnaces its resources of peat from the wooded hills surrounding it had made it a centre of the iron industry—and wrote the text of our local pageant, which was produced in a natural amphitheatre in the hills and afterwards published in *Abinger Harvest*.

He was a very shy man and avoided the results of his fame as much as he could. During the war when Murdoch made open house for his concerts with Lionel Tertis and Albert Sammons so that people who could no longer easily get to London could still enjoy music, Forster knocked shyly at the door one day to ask if it would be all right for him to come. 'I'm afraid I live at Abinger Hammer, not Holmbury,' he explained. 'With my sister. The name is Forster.' He and I both belonged to the

Reform Club and one day I had a note from him. 'I awakened last night,' it said, 'and suddenly thought how odd it was that you and I and Sir Cyril Osborne should belong to the same club.' The extremely right-wing Sir Cyril had no doubt just been denouncing something.

One way and another there was thus a good deal of social and intellectual activity going on in Holmbury and Abinger and even the strong Conservatives who predominated among our neighbours did their best in a neighbourly way to forgive us our socialism—like our nearest neighbour Mrs Pool who had an acid tongue and an unsurpassed local intelligence service but who much against her political judgement took Jess and the children to her heart. 'I satisfy my conscience,' she told me, 'by pretending you are a Liberal—although even that, Heaven forgive me, is bad enough.'

In those days it was still the excellent fashion to call on new-comers and leave cards so that we soon knew a great many people. In the village itself we made and still have many friends whose families despite the pull of London have lived there for generations and who still follow the crafts of their fathers with a skill, integrity and friendliness not often found in these days. I think it was Compton Mackenzie who once said to me that as he grew older he found that one of the most enduring pleasures of life was talking to simple people. This has been my experience too.

When I became Editor of the *Daily Herald*, Holmbury was in many ways a silly place to live because of the distance from London. But we could not bear to leave it, especially as Betty and John were settled at a progressive co-educational school near by, Hurtwood School, which was one of the reasons we had come in the first place. So I drove up to London each day and often did not get back until early the next morning. Sometimes I would make a great effort to get home early, only to find the telephone ringing as I walked in, with Tom Darlow, the Deputy Editor, or Arthur Webb, the Night Editor, on the line with news of some new move by Hitler. However, I had a quick mind in those days and much practice in ordering my thoughts to meet emergencies and when necessary would dictate a new leading article to a copy typist over the telephone without delay.

Jess and I were sometimes worried because we had slipped into a way of living more lavish than we had intended. Though modest enough by the professional standards of those days it seems very extravagant now. We had two living-in maids and a girl recently out of school to help with Betty and John, daily cleaning help from the village and a full-time gardener. We had horses which we stabled in the village and, since we were some miles from a station, two cars. We could no doubt have lived a good deal more economically in a North London suburb but saw no reason to—it was not, we thought, as if we were grinding the faces of the poor or exploiting any labour but mine!

However, we could not avoid realizing that at Holmbury we were somewhat embedded in the English class system. But I don't think this affected our habits or personal relationships. Although it is always a dangerous boast for an Englishman to make, neither of us was much inclined to fall into the social snobbery that played so considerable a part in middle-class life in those days. You have only to read the detective stories that provided the favourite middle-class escape literature of the times and especially its great stars—Agatha Christie, Dorothy L. Sayers, Margery Allingham and Ngaio Marsh, all women, but then women are usually more open in their snobbery than men—to see just how class-orientated a society it was. We, however, had the advantage of having been brought up in the industrial North where snobbery is less prevalent and has a more transatlantic flavour, being based on money rather than class. There is, however, no use denying that in Holmbury St Mary we were a good deal cushioned against the world. 'You're living in a fool's paradise. Do you know that?' said a friend from Batley—as drear a place as one could find on a day's march—taking a drink on the terrace in the sunshine. And so I suppose we were.

This fool's paradise had no place in the *Daily Herald* office. There life was real and, in so far as my relations with Elias were concerned, increasingly unpleasant. J. S. Elias, later Lord Southwood, is not, I think, much remembered now—except perhaps in the hospitals and other charities he aided. Yet he is worth recalling for he was in some ways one of the strangest of that strange group of men who owned or controlled the British newspaper press during the thirties.

As a man he was kindly and benevolent, good to children and his employees and much dedicated to charitable enterprises for which he raised more than £20,000,000. I came to hate him more than any man I have ever known. He lived a private life of impeccable dullness with a wife of uncertain health and retiring disposition a good deal older than himself of whom he was deeply fond and who shared his tastes for cosy evenings by the fire. During them, if he was not working, she would often read to him from an American religious paper to which she subscribed, called the *Daily World*. They had no children. He went abroad only once in his life—and that merely on a day trip to Le Touquet as a young man—and apparently had no interest in anything outside England—and not much outside Long Acre. Each summer he took a summer holiday of four weeks at the Grand Hotel, Eastbourne, where he had a private suite overlooking the sea and a private telephone line to Odhams. Each evening he and his wife listened to the Palm Court Orchestra. Their favourite tune was the 'Blue Danube' Waltz.

He had no intellectual interests. He rarely if ever read a book, never went to the theatre or the opera, was rarely known to take any active part in general conversation, had no interest in food or wine. When he bought a house in the country to support his rising status in the world he bought it as it stood complete with furniture and, when the owner took some of the pictures with him, instructed the Editor of *Ideal Home* to find replacements to cover the bare spaces left on the walls. His only extravagance was in clothes. Every six months he ordered a dozen suits from a tailor in Savile Row recommended to him by H. V. Morton, whose clothes he much admired. They were always in the same discreet shades of brown, blue or grey.

He was a salesman of journalism, not a journalist, and although he had almost all the private virtues he precipitated one of the most disreputable episodes in the history of British journalism simply by being true to himself. His only test of success for the *Daily Herald* was that it should sell more copies than the *Daily Express*. Since he lacked Beaverbrook's flair and felt that except for 'big name writers' who could be advertised on hoardings, money spent on editorial services was a waste, the only way he could see of achieving this was to bribe people to buy the paper by free gifts. Under his single-minded enthusiasm journalism almost ceased to be a profession and became an adjunct to a bargain basement.

It was in the middle of all this that I became Editor of the *Herald*. I have often wondered why Elias wanted me. It cannot have been that he had read and liked my articles for he rarely read anything. It was partly, I think, that Beaverbrook had tried to persuade me to return to him. If Beaverbrook wanted me he wanted me even more. Also—such are the things that determine a career—he had been much affected by the fact that when a car I was driving went out of control (the front spring snapped), hit a tree and ended up in the middle of the road with its wheels in the air I emerged unscathed after first switching off the ignition. He referred to this several times during our lunch at the Savoy. 'Such presence of mind,' he said, sipping his grapefruit. What finally clinched things, however, I am sure, was the fact that, Arthur Christiansen, the very successful Editor of the *Daily Express*, and I had started together in journalism in Liverpool. He assumed that we were peas out of the same newspaper pod and that if he made me Editor circulation would inevitably rise.

And so, indeed, for a time it did, although how much was due to me and how much to the quality of the cut-price goods he was offering I would not like to say. We reached a circulation of two million copies a day—then the largest of any newspaper in the world—and did so ahead of the *Daily Express*. But we did not keep ahead. Christiansen, who was uninterested in policy, was a much better Editor of a popular newspaper than I was and Beaverbrook a far better publisher than Elias. Moreover, Elias found that even when the circulation reached two million the advertisements did not come rolling in as he had expected. Perhaps it was political prejudice, perhaps it was that *Herald* readers were not thought to have as much money as *Express* readers had, perhaps it was that advertisers were shrewder than Elias had suspected and were not taken in by readers acquired in exchange for kitchen kettles and fancy underclothes.

Elias, however, had a simpler explanation. He thought it was my fault. I produced, he complained, oh! how he complained, a gloomy paper instead of a nice optimistic one that would make readers want to go out and spend money. 'In the *Daily Express*,' Christiansen told his staff, 'every day is a sunny day.' 'In the *Herald*,' I told mine, 'the news must be given straight, the dangers into which appeasement is leading us made plain.'

I was young, impetuous, high-minded, and, having come up quickly, not a little conceited. To me journalism was something demanding all one's integrity and honesty. I was deeply affronted by Elias's attitude to it. It was not for this that I had rejected Beaverbrook's temptations. Elias's attitude to newspapers seemed to me a kind of blasphemy. I had no sympathy for his aspirations, too little, perhaps, for his problems.

These were real enough. The *Herald* was losing heavily. Even when its circulation went to over two millions a day it still lost £10,000 a week. And such being the nature of newspaper economics lacking adequate advertising the more it sold the more it lost. There were times when Elias began to fear that his whole publishing empire would be put in jeopardy. I could not sympathize with him. It seemed to me that his difficulties were the natural, indeed in many ways the appropriate, consequence of his attitude.

He began to demand editorial economies, snapped that there was no need to waste money on foreign correspondents when we could get all the news from Reuters. Dunbar, whom he used as his mouthpiece, would ring me up and say mournfully, 'The little man is very disappointed. Thought you'd get down to things, Francis.' Every week I would have lunch with Dunbar in a private room in the Howard Hotel, Norfolk Street. We would have a glass of a peculiarly horrid sweet sherry Dunbar always ordered in advance and then over a wholesome but uninteresting lunch, he would moan at me while he drank tonic water and I drank beer. He and Elias were both great moaners.

However, once back in the office with Darlow and Arthur Webb to beguile me I usually cheered up. Webb had been on the *Irish Times* during the troubles and had a fund of newspaper stories which, allied with his bubbling enthusiasm for experiments in make-up, could always charm depression away. Moreover, the great thing about a newspaper is that tomorrow is always a new day. Grappling with the flow of news and the need for instant decisions, peering over page proofs with the Chief Sub, Peter Hall, or snatching a few words with the *Herald* correspondents in Paris or Berlin or Rome when they telephoned in with their stories one could forget Elias and his troubles. There is no fun in the world like that of bringing out a daily newspaper, no camaraderie like that of newspapermen working together to meet a deadline. Being an Editor was not turning out as I had imagined it would when I first sat in the Editor's chair with my head full of Barnes and Delane. But I was usually happy enough.

There were plenty of other problems to take one's mind off Elias. Some of them were common to all newspapers and arose from the nature of the times, which were dark and bothersome enough. Some of them were peculiar to the *Herald* itself and arose from its special position as the official organ of a political party.

Almost all newspapers, of course, tend to reflect a particular political viewpoint and to be on the whole fairly faithful allies of one political party or another. But the *Herald*, theoretically at any rate, was in a much more circumscribed position. It was the official paper of the Labour Party.

In practice the official tie did not prove as restrictive as it might have done. This was perhaps because the Labour Party was out of office and much divided. When the Executive took a line with which I disagreed on a matter on which I felt strongly, as it did, for example, on the Defence Estimates, I said so in a leading article. This made some people angry. But it pleased others. On one particularly controversial occasion when the political directors were asked to call me to order the attempt came to nothing because Ernest Bevin refused to have anything to do with it. As Walter Citrine (now Lord Citrine) records in his diary, he retorted, 'Williams has a mind of his own. If you want to keep him as Editor you must put up with it.'

In all this I had the advantage of the perhaps inflated reputation I had made for myself as the *Herald*'s Financial Editor. I was accepted as a shaper of policy as well as an interpreter, an authentic voice in the great debate on the party's future after the defeat of 1931, and for this reason had, perhaps, a greater degree of independence than subsequent editors were allowed. I can in fact remember no occasion when pressure was brought to bear on me by the paper's political directors. I regarded it of course as part of my duty not only to keep in close touch with ordinary members of the Labour Party and the trade unions but to develop a friendly relationship with all the leaders of the party. This was not always easy: many of them were far from being friends with each other.

Like most people at this time, except the Cockney men and women in Limehouse of whom he was superficially the so unlikely representative, I underestimated Attlee. In this I was at one with Ernest Bevin. When he came to know him better he developed a deep-seated and unshakeable affection for him. But at this time he thought little of him, often saying to me angrily, 'The Party's got no leadership.'

Nor did Attlee himself do much to help. In stature slight and unimpressive, he carried with him little of the aura of vitality and drama that one is inclined to look for when one is young in those who occupy a central place on the political stage. He was not easy to talk to. He listened but he did not give much and seemed more often to reflect a middle view than have one of his own.

'Let the *Herald* act,' boomed Hugh Dalton as he and I walked along the front at Blackpool during a Labour Party Conference. 'Unless someone does something soon we shall have no choice but a nonentity or a drunk.'

The nonentity was Attlee; the drunk, Arthur Greenwood, the Parliamentary Party's Deputy Leader. It was a judgement far too harsh on that amiable and talented man whom devoted campaigning had left too often with nothing for comfort after a day of speech-making but a diet of whiskys and sodas in dreary provincial hotels.

But who else was there? Dalton himself was exuberant and able. He was one of the few leaders of the Parliamentary Party to understand early the threat of Hitler's policy and the need to meet force with force. But despite his energy, his generosity towards the young—he was one of the first to spot Gaitskell and promote his career—and his wide-ranging conviviality he seemed always a curiously hollow man, more so than perhaps he was. He was also so notorious an intriguer, although in the most open and cheerful way, that it was impossible to think of him ever commanding sufficient loyalty to lead the Party. If he had become its leader he would have started intriguing against himself out of sheer habit.

On that walk along the Golden Mile at Blackpool he was trying to persuade me to put the *Herald* behind Herbert Morrison. This I could scarcely have done without wrecking such position as it had managed to establish for itself as an impartial voice in the Party. Nor could I find within myself the enthusiasm for Morrison that Dalton had, despite his obviously great ability, especially as an administrator. I recognized that he was the greatest party manager of the age. But I suspected what seemed a basic slickness and opportunism in his character and thought him fundamentally a narrow man.

Cripps, for all his intellectual powers, had shown himself repeatedly at this time a political fool. He was naïve to the point of imbecility.

Aneurin Bevan was a youthful shooting star zooming above the horizon in a cascade of fireworks. But he neither possessed nor at this time deserved solid support in the Party and had a talent for invective that seemed designed to ensure he never would.

On the whole I preferred the trade-unionists to the Parliamentarians. They might be dull. But they were solid. Their feet were on the hard ground of working-class experience. My closest alliance was with them. And above all with Ernest Bevin—whom no one could call dull.

When Bevin joined the War Cabinet as Minister of Labour and National Service in the Churchill administration, George VI asked him how in so busy and difficult a life he had managed to acquire so wide a knowledge of affairs. 'Sir,' he replied, going back to his days as a farmer's boy, 'it was grubbed in the hedgerows of experience.' And so it was.

Virginia Woolf once described the process of authorship as the writer 'trudging around, seeing all he can, feeling all he can' followed by a period of slow gestation 'until the veil lifts and there is the thing—the thing he wants to write about—simplified, composed.' It often seemed to me that this was also the way Bevin's mind worked. He skipped formal logic and arrived at his conclusions after reason, emotion and experience had gestated in a way he neither fully understood himself nor could explain to others. But he had a remarkable capacity for being right.

He had been right about the effects of Britain's return to the Gold Standard when almost no one else but Keynes saw clearly what it would mean. He was right well ahead of most people when he urged its abandonment in 1931, which was when I first got to know him. He was equally right about Hitler and was entirely truthful when he told his union in one of his quarterly reports that 'From the day Hitler came to power I have felt that the democratic countries would have to face war.' Two years before Munich he was warning that 'Czechoslovakia, one of the most glorious little democratic countries, is in danger of being sacrificed.'

In all this he was as prophetic as Churchill—indeed on many occasions talking to one or other of them I could not help thinking how close they were on this issue and what a pity it was that old hostilities kept them apart. But he was at first equally unsuccessful with his own Party.

By 1936 he was so angry with the political Labour leaders—Attlee included—that he came near to regarding the gap between the trade unions and 'the politicians' as unbridgeable. He repeatedly told me that it was a mistake for the trade unions to have tied themselves so closely to the Labour Party. They would, he said, have been in a much better position to bring pressure on Chamberlain if they had not been so committed to Labour that Chamberlain knew he had nothing to gain by taking notice of them. I did not take this very seriously. But it was an indication of his mood.

At meetings of the National Council of Labour where leaders of the political party, the trade unions and the Co-operative movement met to agree policy he would mark his disapproval in an ostentatious and to me somewhat embarrassing manner. He would arrive late and instead of taking his seat at the Conference table with his fellow members would plomp himself down by me in a chair against the wall and carry on a running commentary in my ear. Although not a member of the Council I had been given, or perhaps appropriated to myself, the right to speak and had perfected a technique of bringing along with me potent extracts from cables on the situation in foreign capitals. Bevin would constantly urge me to intervene with these and ostentatiously applaud if by so doing I made the Council pause.

Although he was never a politician and not much of an orator by formal standards Bevin was responsible for the most devastating political attack I have ever heard.

Lansbury was then still the Leader of the Labour Party, the man to whom it had turned to save it after it had been torn to bits and decimated at the polls by Ramsay MacDonald's desertion. He appeared before the Party's Annual Conference to explain why, despite Mussolini's attack on Ethiopia, he found it impossible as a pacifist and a Christian to reconcile with his conscience the sanctions against Italy the National Executive wished to support.

He was given a quite staggering ovation as he rose to speak. With the sole exception of a small group around Bevin the whole Conference came to its feet and spontaneously sang 'For he's a jolly good fellow.' He was unable to speak for several minutes. The cheering went on and on. When he did speak it was with immense feeling. He was listened to in a silence charged with an emotion as great as his own as he told of how in earlier days he had pleaded with strikers near to starvation in the days before the dole or Poor Law Assistance and urged them not to turn to violence. 'I say to myself,' he said, 'I have no right to preach pacifism to starving people in this country and preach something else in relation to people elsewhere.'

Probably few in the audience shared his absolute pacifism but the only cries of dissent came when he said he would understand and accept if he was asked to step down from the leadership. When he finished the delegates again rose to their feet and applauded wildly. Many of the women delegates were in tears.

This was the moment Bevin chose to speak. Rising massively from his place among the union delegates in the body of the hall where he had sat unmoved throughout Lansbury's speech, he walked with the slow, rolling, entirely self-assured gait that always distinguished him up the aisle to the rostrum, looking neither to left nor right. I knew he would oppose Lansbury. But I had expected, as I think had most people, that while putting the case for sanctions he would acknowledge Lansbury's sincerity and pay a tribute to his services in the past. Instead, he turned on him with a contemptuous anger that at first brought incredulous protests but finally stunned the audience into silence. In a phrase that seemed deliberately designed to produce the maximum hurt for Lansbury and the maximum shock to his listeners, he accused him of 'trailing your conscience round from body to body asking to be told what to do with it' and charged him with betraying decisions he had had a part in making. The case he brought was long and formidable, although in many parts unfair, for Lansbury had on several occasions differentiated between his own personal views and those he had felt required to endorse so long as he remained leader.

By the time Bevin had finished those who a few minutes before had been applauding Lansbury so wildly had swung against him completely. When Lansbury tried to reply he was refused the right to do so and the microphone was switched off so that he could not be heard. He climbed down from the platform palpably a broken man.

It was not a pretty thing to see. And to many of us it seemed unnecessary, for it was plain that Lansbury had himself already decided that he could not stay as Leader. He could have been allowed to go on a wave of affection.

When the day was over I and some others who were close to Bevin turned on him. 'Why did you have to be so rough on the old man?' we asked. Bevin glowered at us. 'Lansbury's been dressed in saint's clothes for years waiting for martyrdom,' he said. 'All I did was set fire to the faggots.'

He was equally forthright in attacking Stafford Cripps and Aneurin Bevan, who had put down a resolution in that high-flown revolutionese popular among the left accusing the Government of using sanctions to protect imperialist interests and calling on the Labour Party to concentrate its energies on defeating capitalist imperialism. This infuriated Bevin. 'People have been on the platform this day,' he said contemptuously, 'talking about the destruction of capitalism. The middle classes are not doing too badly under capitalism or fascism. The thing that is being wiped out by fascism is the trade union movement. . . . It is we who are being wiped out and who will be wiped out if fascism comes here.'

I was glad Bevin's views prevailed. I thought he was right all along the line. But I could not pretend to myself as I came away from that particular Conference that the Party of which I was a member and whose newspaper I edited was a nest of singing birds.

CHAPTER 8

The Dreadful Years

These were the dreadful years. The only light relief was in the Abdication.

Although no American audience I have ever spoken to—and they still ask about it—has ever believed me, it is nevertheless the case that the silence of the British press until Bishop Blunt of Bradford remarked to a group of theological students that the King was in urgent need of God's grace was not due to any order from Buckingham Palace or Downing Street or any request, official or unofficial. Nor was the suppression of American and Continental reports in the news magazines like *Time*, and *Newsweek* by W. H. Smith and other distributors a result of official censorship.

There were two reasons. One was the fear of libel. In the early stages Mrs Simpson was still married to her second husband, a nice respectable businessman according to all accounts. Suggestions that she was involved in an affair with someone else, whether royal or not, could, newspaper lawyers advised, constitute a particularly gross libel under British law. The second reason was that the newspapers remembered Edward VII. We saw no reason to be more strait-laced than our grandfathers, and that monarch, one of the most popular in British royal history, had been widely known to break the tedium of sovereignty by a succession of lady friends. If the new King found solace in the companionship of one particular American lady known to be both witty and entertaining, then there seemed no good reason why the press should spoil the relationship. Nor, of course, could anyone be sure it would last. It might burn itself out. The situation seemed best dealt with by printing Mrs Simpson's name occasionally in the society columns as a member of the royal party and leaving it at that.

Bishop Blunt's utterance altered this because it brought into the public domain a matter that had previously been left private, and made a plea of good faith in a matter of public interest more likely to succeed if actions for libel should result.

I knew the King slightly. I had first met him on his trips to factories in the North when he was Prince of Wales and I was still a reporter. He had even passed on to me a piece of advice given to him by his father which was never to miss an opportunity to empty your bladder. He seemed a pleasant and unstuffy character and made a considerable effort to interest himself in uninteresting things. He had noticeable black bags under his eyes. One suspected long, late nights. I did not know Mrs Simpson but some of my friends did and they assured me that she had made him a good deal happier and more positive than before they met. This was not, they said, something that would pass. It was for keeps.

My first reactions, therefore, were to wish the King well in this matter, although I did not feel, as some did, that he was likely to play any very significant role as monarch, with or without Mrs Simpson. However, it soon became clear from the reports that came flooding in from the East End of London and from industrial areas in the Midlands and North and in South Wales that the general mass of middle- and working-class readers of the *Herald* were deeply upset by the suggestion that a woman who had been twice through the divorce courts might become Queen. I talked to Attlee and Bevin, both of whom took the same view. 'Our people won't 'ave it,' said Bevin. He had previously been accustomed to criticize the *Herald* for giving more space to royalty than he thought it worth. Now he became convinced that royalty was an important popular institution which ordinary people wanted preserved without a stain on its character. Attlee took a strictly constitutional view. A King's marriage, he held, was a public not a private matter and in all public matters the King must act on the advice of his Ministers. Although Beaverbrook and Rothermere did their best to persuade Elias that the *Herald* should line up with them on the

King's side, the *Herald* opposed the marriage, although not, I hope, too sanctimoniously.

On the actual evening of the Abdication broadcast I was dining in a restaurant with Hugh Dalton and Walter Nash, the socialist Finance Minister of New Zealand and later its Prime Minister, and his wife. To Dalton's amazement the Nashes insisted that come what may they must hear the King's farewell broadcast, about which he and I had been rather aloofly sophisticated. We went to Dalton's flat to hear it only to find that the Daltons' radio was out of order. The Nashes were so upset by this that I rang the *Herald* and told them to rush a radio round immediately. It arrived just as the broadcast was due to begin, by which time Mr and Mrs Nash were getting very worked up indeed. We listened to the broadcast in Dalton's sitting-room and found it dignified and moving. Even Dalton, I think, was glad he had been made to listen to it and I certainly was. At the end of it Mrs Nash was in tears and Nash himself was very near to them.

The Abdication and George VI's Coronation sent the sales of the *Herald* soaring, especially in the poorest parts of industrial Britain and the East End of London and made even Elias temporarily happy. Intellectuals of the left were very indignant when we published long descriptive stories of the Coronation and the street celebration by Hannen Swaffer and H. V. Morton, together with pages of pictures to satisfy a taste they refused to admit existed. Bonfires were lit on the hills to celebrate the Coronation and with A. E. Housman ringing romantically in my ears:

> From Clee to heaven the beacon burns,
> The shires have seen it plain,
> From north and south the sign returns
> And beacons burn again.

I chartered a plane and sent Ritchie Calder (now Lord Ritchie-Calder) up in it to fly over the countryside and bring back a descriptive story. He was to land at Croydon and telephone his report in good time for the first edition. But the time passed and no story came. Then we got a message that a small two-seater plane had been seen soaring and dipping above the fires on the Surrey hills, zooming down almost into the flames and then up again and away. It was hours later that Ritchie finally came on the phone, shaken but indomitable. He had had a terrifying experience. The pilot of our small chartered plane had become unbalanced and had shouted that he was going to dive into the flames. When he saw the first bonfire rushing at them from the ground Ritchie said he thought that all was over. He could see the crowd of people who had been dancing round the fire looking up at them, frozen into horrified stillness. But laughing with intense pleasure, the pilot had swung the plane up at the last moment and flown off to find another fire, there to repeat the manœuvre. Only by forcing himself to remain calm and continue talking to the pilot as coolly as he could had Calder eventually managed to persuade him to land as the fires began to die down. After landing he called an ambulance to take him to hospital where he was treated for a mental breakdown. As Calder recounted the story to us it seemed like a bizarre commentary on the way the world was going.

The Coronation, like the Abdication, provided relief from world affairs. But the continuing story remained one of darkness and frustration. Several members of my staff wanted to join the International Brigade to fight in the Spanish Civil War and some did. I tried to persuade them not to. Perhaps because I felt guilty about not going myself and did not want them to make me feel more ashamed. Some members of my staff became communists. I recognized the force of their feelings, but thought their logic wrong. They, for their part, considered me a right wing reactionary when I refused to accept the guilt of all those in Russia Stalin accused. Not only communists but many among my friends accused me of selling out to the right when I opposed the campaign for a United Front of Communists and Labour and later for a Popular Front with Conservatives and Liberals as well. I thought both ideas impractical, an escape from the real issues, and had in any event no taste for co-operating with that ridiculous and disreputable body, the British Communist Party.

It was a time in which many friendships were strained with no compensatory sense of achieving much oneself. I was frequently disenchanted with the Labour Party. But I comforted myself with the thought that at least we had not got a Chamberlain. I grew to dislike Chamberlain so much that I found it hard to maintain even the normal courtesies when I met him. Those who knew him well assured me that in his home circle he was kindly and devoted. I could only reply that in that case the sooner he returned to it the better. He was unfortunate in his appearance. Black-haired, heavily moustached and corvine in profile he looked like an unkempt crow. His face seemed to wear a perpetual sneer even when, as must have sometimes been the case, no sneer was intended. His manner was frigid and condescending.

One could recognize in Baldwin the qualities as well as the defects of a man of many parts. One might distrust him but one also warmed to him. Not so with Chamberlain. He was the most charmless of men. It was understandable that there should be no quick warmth between us when we met. I disliked his opinions. He despised mine. But there have been plenty of people with whom I have disagreed violently whom I have found no difficulty in liking. 'You soon find the other fellow isn't necessarily a dirty dog,' Attlee once said to me, talking about party politics. To Neville Chamberlain, however, anyone on the opposite side was exactly that. There was no give and take in his mind.

I was staggered when someone, it may have been Walter Elliot, told me—for I was so baffled, or rather, affronted, by Chamberlain that I constantly probed people about him in the hope of finding a key—that he was a great admirer of Conrad and read his books often. I could not understand how such a man could read Conrad's books and remain as he was. It seemed as though Conrad himself had somehow betrayed me. Later, however, thinking much about it, I could see that Chamberlain in fact resembled some of Conrad's characters in his self-sufficiency and loneliness, although without, it seemed to me, the nobility of the best of them. His early life on the island of Andros, where his father had sent him as a young man to restore the family fortunes by growing sisal and where all had collapsed into failure, had, when one thought about it, a distinctly Conradian flavour.

I saw that he was perhaps a more complex character than I had assumed. But not a more likeable one or any better fitted for office at that time. When Hore-Belisha was Secretary of State for War I asked him over lunch one day what it was like serving under Chamberlain in Cabinet. 'It's like being a Departmental Director in a private company in which the Chairman holds all the shares,' he said. 'You are expected to report intelligently on departmental matters but keep quiet on everything else. It's your job to do as the Chairman tells you and keep your nose out of general policy.' There was no nonsense about *primus inter pares* when Chamberlain was Prime Minister.

Like many on the left of politics I had in the beginning put much faith in Eden and was much excited when on an evening in February 1937 Ewer rang me and said 'Anthony's resigning. The fight's beginning.' It seemed wonderful news. Both Ewer and I felt sure Eden would stump the country rousing public opinion and—which was even more important—conservative opinion, against appeasement. We saw him as a powerful reinforcement to Churchill. But as it turned out he did nothing. He was too gentlemanly to rock the boat.

Perhaps one should not blame him too much. It is easy looking back to think oneself more resolute than one was. Few of us were so all the time. I wrote a lot of leaders in the *Herald* which I am glad to have written but there were some of which I am ashamed. One could not but recognize how deep were the conflicts between the will, the intellect and emotion and how hard it was to strike a balance between them.

One knew intellectually that trying to appease Hitler was not going to get us anywhere except into a worse mess. One could feel with one's will that even if to stop appeasing meant war this was preferable to constant retreat, one could accept the fact that because we had not acted earlier war might well now be not only the logical end of policy but the best. But at the same time emotion refused to accept this logic as final. It cried out that to think of war as an inevitable and possibly even desirable consequence of policy was to cease to be a civilized human being and demanded that one stop thinking of war in the abstract and thought of its effect on human beings, on one's own children and those of millions of others. To see Betty, lithe and sunburnt, doing handstands on the terrace, or John standing by his first bicycle and saying, 'To think that I, John Williams, can balance on two wheels', such things and a hundred others came between intellect and will and cried out that it was worth doing anything to avoid war.

The British are a humane and civilized people and such feelings, common to everyone, could not help but influence opinion. When Chamberlain spoke of 'a quarrel in a far away country between people of whom we know nothing,' I said bitterly to the members of my editorial staff listening to the broadcast with me: 'He's giving in. There won't be any war.' Yet even as I said this I could not conceal from myself that my moral revulsion was accompanied by a spurt of sheer physical happiness at the thought that we were going to stay at peace. When Chamberlain waved his bit of paper after Munich and prattled absurdly about 'Peace in our time' both intellect and will rejected it. Yet there is no use pretending that emotion did not long to believe and even raised a muffled guilty cheer.

It was not easy to avoid shame. I felt it unbearably at a little private dinner for Jan Masaryk, the Czech Ambassador, which Maisky gave after Munich. At the end of the dinner Masaryk broke into tears as he thanked us for standing by his country and himself and said he knew he could always depend on our friendship. As I looked at the three or four others there I wondered if they felt as unworthy as I did. Afterwards Maisky, as host, made a speech that time was to give particular irony.

'You know that you can rely always on Soviet friendship, Jan,' he said, 'we shall not fail you. You and I will yet welcome together the return of freedom to your land.' Many years later after the war when the news of Masaryk's suicide—or perhaps murder, who can be sure?—as the communists took over the Government of his country reached me, I remembered that moment. And again when the Soviet tanks rolled into Prague in 1968 and I thought of the Czech writers and artists and teachers whom Jess and I had been talking to in Prague only a few months before and what would now be their fate.

The confused emotions I was aware of within myself sometimes made me feel more charitable to Chamberlain than I otherwise would have done. They did not do so, however, on 9 March 1939 when Maurice Webb, my political correspondent and later a Minister in the Attlee Government, brought me some astounding news.

This was that the Prime Minister had summoned him and the political correspondents of all the other leading newspapers to a private conference at 10 Downing Street and there had told them that the international situation had taken so remarkable a turn for the better since Munich that he hoped to call a disarmament conference before the end of the year. He was satisfied, he said, that as a result of the new situation resulting from the Munich Agreement there was good hope of reaching political, economic and military agreements that would bring permanent peace to Europe.

This, it is necessary to recall, was exactly six days before Hitler tore up the Munich Agreement, marched into Prague, and annexed what remained of Czechoslovakia. Every responsible newspaper in London was receiving and, except for *The Times* under Geoffrey Dawson, publishing reports from their correspondents in Prague and Berlin that made it quite clear that an early German invasion of Czechoslovakia was probable. A. L. Easteman, the *Herald*'s Chief Foreign Correspondent, had just come back steeped in gloom from an Eastern European tour, taking in Rumania, Yugoslavia and Poland. Everywhere the sky was dark.

When Webb told his story it seemed to us that Chamberlain's self-deception had reached such a pitch that he had lost all contact with reality. Ewer rang the Foreign Office. So far from consulting them Chamberlain had not even told them he was holding a press conference. I rang several Ministers I knew. They could not understand it either. Nor could any of the Labour leaders. Or Churchill. Or Eden.

The time between Munich and the declaration of war was, I suppose, the worst ever lived through by those who had not been old enough to feel the full weight of the First World War. We now knew that war was certain. We felt we were ill-prepared for it and we expected it to be indescribable in its horror. By an unfortunate coincidence a film based on H. G. Wells's *War in the Air* had been showing at the cinemas at the time of Munich and had added a macabre horror to the sight of slit trenches being dug in the parks by the light of acetylene flares as darkness fell. Although the *Daily Express* went on telling its readers, 'There will be no war this year or next year either' and invented a humorous cartoon character called 'Major Crisis', even Elias —or as he now was, Lord Southwood—ceased for a time to urge optimism and a cheerful front page upon us.

I now usually got home still later than before and often had to turn and go back when I arrived or spend hours on the telephone remaking the front page and dictating a fresh leader to keep pace with the changing news.

However, Holmbury St Mary continued, to our minds, to justify the trouble of living there. We made new friends when the artist C. R. W. Nevinson—the son of an early hero of mine, H. W. Nevinson—and his wife came to stay at weekends in a caravan. We possess still a signed print of a picture of his that we found put through an open window one day in apology for failing to turn up to dinner the previous evening. It is inscribed, 'To the Williamses—really we did not mean to be so rude as we were. I have just had a smash.' The 'smash', I remember apprehensively, was a hostile review of his autobiography in the *Times Literary Supplement.*

My mother and father now had a farm in Flaunden in Hertfordshire, near enough for us to visit them frequently and for Betty and John to go and stay with them fairly often, sometimes with their cousins, Bobby and Roger, or with other children. My mother and father still believed one of the major purposes of existence to be making children happy. My mother treated our children exactly as she had treated her own, that is, as fellow adults. She never had any inhibitions about quarrelling dramatically with them if they did something of which she did not approve so that life was constantly exciting and unpredictable—except for the never-to-be-doubted prediction that she would never do anything to hurt them, and that my father would always be available to help them in everything they wanted to do.

Betty and John were also lucky in the possession of a maiden aunt. Modern children suffer much, I think, from the virtual disappearance of this most admirable species. Jess's sister Tina, whom they called Nina, was a remarkably sweet and endearing personality who loved and understood them and would keep them occupied for hours with the most intense enjoyment, unmarred by the slightest wish to sit in judgement upon them or make them what they were not. She had been a teacher—she must have been an adorable one—but had fallen ill with diabetes at a time when that disease was more crippling than it now is and had been forced to retire on a small pension and give up most of her activities. This might have embittered many people, but it seemed only to deepen the great sweetness of her character. I never met anyone more sympathetic towards others or more tolerant, she was as nearly a saint as anyone I have known. She never sat in moral judgement and had a natural gaiety and childlike delight in life that made her a marvellous companion for all young people. She was a leading member of her Presbyterian church, but without pomposity. When Betty wanted to be taken to church as a tiny child she took her, but when halfway through the sermon Betty announced in a high piping voice, 'This isn't very instreting to children or bunnies,' she remained perfectly equable and without even a polite shush took her happily by the hand and walked with her down the aisle in the middle of the service to the open air where children and bunnies could enjoy themselves more.

Now that Betty and John were older and at school most of the day Jess thought she must have something on which to exercise her mind. She decided to work for a degree in psychology under Professor Cyril Burt at University College, London. This gave us both a new interest in life and one that has continued. Jess's subsequent career as a Consultant Child Psychologist at a London teaching hospital and in research among deprived and handicapped children has greatly extended my own horizons as well as hers.

When it neared the time for the examination I undertook to help with the philosophy. Not that I knew much philosophy but I felt that attention to Hume and Kant and Leibniz, Descartes, Berkeley and Spinoza might make a pleasant break from Hitler and Chamberlain. We rented a tiny service flat in London and there each evening Jess would toil away in preparation for the next day's papers, while in between answering telephone calls from Tom Darlow or Arthur Webb or Bill Towler, the Foreign Editor of the *Herald*, I would make digests of the main philosophical systems—as I understood them—on sheets of quarto paper, one sheet per philosopher, so that Jess could refresh her memory before taking the philosophy papers. At midnight I made coffee and sandwiches and we picnicked while we worked. We had a wonderful time.

We both felt anxious as we drove from Holmbury to the Senate House one Saturday morning to look at the result sheets posted in the entrance hall. Jess sat outside in the car while I went to look and then I rushed back to tell her that she had passed and put my head through the open car window and kissed her. Afterwards I got into the car and we drove to a celebration lunch in Soho. Six weeks later war began. We could stand upright in the world again.

I had assumed that with the beginning of the war my troubles with Elias were over. Even he, I thought, could scarcely wish for a paper dedicated to brightness and better times for advertisers when war was actually being fought. But with the period of the phoney war all his determination to put unpleasant things out of sight came back. The phoney war restored his faith in the commercial ethos. If we did nothing to hurt Hitler, he thought, Hitler would do nothing to hurt us. Having made our ritual gesture we could get together and come to a business-like settlement.

I could not believe this. I thought the *Herald* had a duty to arouse people to the expectation of dark times ahead.

When I heard from Ewer that Sir Nevile Henderson, our Ambassador in Berlin, had been given permission by the Foreign Office to write his story I decided to try to buy it. He had been one of the worst of the appeasers but I thought the record of the disillusionment of even such a man might help to convince people that this war was serious.

We lunched together at his club which was the St James's. I already knew a certain amount about him. He was an Etonian and had begun diplomacy, when it was still glamorous, as a third secretary in St Petersburg in 1905. He had moved around a good deal; Tokyo, Rome, Paris, Constantinople, Cairo, Paris again, Belgrade as Minister and then Buenos Aires as Ambassador for a year before being sent to Berlin. He knew nothing of Britain. Indeed, he had never, he told me, spent as much as four months at a time in the country since 1905. Nor before being sent to Berlin did he know anything about Germany. It was hard to see why he had been appointed. He had a reputation as a shot and according to Vansittart, who was cynical about such things, it was because he had much impressed one dictator, Prince Paul of Yugoslavia, with his talents as a slaughterer of birds and animals that it was thought that he would be a good person to deal with another. Or if not with Hitler himself, for

Hitler was known to have conscientious scruples about taking animal although not human life, then Goering.

His ideas of diplomacy seemed to me scarcely to have altered since his youthful days in St Petersburg. I was once again amazed at how ignorant of the real world Ambassadors could be. Even by the standards of those days Nevile Henderson was appalling. He was a ridiculous person. I could not help getting more and more depressed as our lunch proceeded and as I thought that this was the man who had been sent to Germany to represent us. No wonder Hitler thought he could do as he liked.

However, he had now definitely come to the conclusion that Hitler was a cad, although he still had a soft spot for Goering who, he said, had many agreeable qualities and loved animals and children. He seemed pleased at the idea of his story appearing in the *Herald*. He was writing it, he told me, because of something the stationmaster at Grantham, a Mr Gardner, had said to him one cold morning while he was waiting for a connection to London. Mr Gardner had invited him to warm himself by his fire. They had chatted about the war and Mr Gardner had said to him that people like himself knew nothing of the real facts of the case. It was to let Mr Gardner of Grantham and all the other Mr Gardners know how hard he had struggled for peace that he was writing his book and he assumed that many of them read my paper. I assured him we had a high circulation among railwaymen.

He promised to tell his literary agent that he would like the *Herald* to have his book and came to the door to see me off. As we walked across the dining-room he nodded at his fellow club-men and said, 'You know it still amazes me that these chaps are now so much in favour of the war. They don't seem to realize it will probably mean the end of our lot.'

Elias was pleased with the purchase of the Henderson story. He thought it would sell papers. He was less pleased with a second venture. This was an attempt to plant in people's minds a conception of the revolutionary social possibilities of the war by publicizing a Declaration of Human Rights with which H. G. Wells was concerned. Wells, expansive and farseeing as ever, wanted people to think beyond the negative destruction of Nazism.

I was fond of Wells despite his cantankerousness. On the whole I quarrelled with him less than most people did, although I remember him ringing me from the South of France one day and blackguarding me in the most atrocious language for more than half an hour. Only towards the end of the tirade which opened menacingly, 'I hope you're satisfied with your filthy work' and continued explosively like a series of unexplained blows in the face did I find out what it was all about. Apparently that day's *Herald*, which had just arrived by air, contained an article about writers on the Riviera. It mentioned in a perfectly agreeable way that a well-known woman writer and Wells were close neighbours. This was, in fact, an understatement. Wells and the lady had been lovers for a considerable time. It so happened, however, that their relationship had just ended—and had ended violently. I was not aware of this for it was quite impossible to keep up with every new development in Wells's love life, but even if I had known it would have made little difference since the article was a quite innocuous piece, not much more than a superficial list of names. But Wells would have none of this. He insisted that it had been inspired by 'that bitch' for the sole purpose of holding him up to contempt and ridicule. Manifestly I was on her side, although in fact I had never met the woman. When I told him he was being silly his high-pitched voice, convoluted by rage, squeaked wildly down the telephone, 'How dare you deny it. Every word drips with malice. You can't get away with this.' He slammed down the receiver.

I had not known him for very long then and thought wretchedly that a friendship I valued had ended because of some ridiculous misunderstanding. However, I was dining a month or two later at the Acropolis restaurant when Wells came in with a friend and waved to me in a friendly manner. Later he came over to my table and talked as if nothing had happened, saying, indeed, 'Why haven't you been to see me?'

Our relationship had now been unbroken by storms—or only by minor ones—for some time and I eagerly embraced his idea of a new Declaration of Human Rights. He proposed that he should draft the statement but was afraid that if it went out under his name everyone would say, 'Oh, it's only Wells again.' He therefore proposed to assemble a group of what he called 'liberal-minded thinkers', of whom I would be one, under the Chairmanship of Lord Sankey, whose name as a great judge and former Lord Chancellor would carry weight. His 'young friend', Ritchie Calder, who was on my staff and who 'knew all about such things', would act as secretary and the statement would eventually go out as the Sankey Declaration of the Rights of Man. Would I publish it? I said I would be delighted to but that I should want Wells himself to write a series of articles explaining it and why he thought it so important. This he agreed to do.

We met at Wells's house in Hanover Terrace. I do not now remember all those who took part in addition to Sankey, although Julian Huxley and Lord Horder, who was Wells's doctor, were there, I think, and a good many others. Although Wells insisted that it was not his declaration but that of the 'Sankey Commission' he would fall into a furious rage if any of us tried to alter a word or even a comma of what he had written. However, Sankey, who was fond of him and very properly regarded him as a great man, could usually soothe him down. Even at lunch Wells would have a scribbling-pad beside him so that no idea should be lost. He had scribbling-pads all over the house, even in the lavatories. In fact my last memory of him, only a few days before he died, is of watching him as he sat, a shrunken figure in an armchair, with a scribbling-pad on his knee on which he was keeping a record of every turn of his illness—'So that I can prove that old fool Horder wrong.'

The Sankey Declaration did not make as much immediate impact as we had hoped. But it is reflected very closely in the preamble of the Charter of the United Nations which Smuts wrote. It may even have had some influence on the Atlantic Charter and its four freedoms for Wells sent a personal copy to President Roosevelt. Wells had always, of course, been a voluminous writer. Now he was writing at a tremendous rate—perhaps because he had a feeling he had not long to live and still had an immense amount to say. 'It's no use telling me I write too much,' he said. 'If you're a writer you write. If you were to fine a writer a hundred pounds for every book he wrote—no a thousand—he would still go on writing though he had to do it in a debtor's prison.'

All this time my relations with Southwood were steadily worsening. The original cause of our incompatibility had been removed with newsprint rationing which meant that advertisers no longer had to be wooed but that they lined up for what space they could get in small papers. What lay between us now was that he thought I was determined to stir up the war.

'Keep your eyes open,' Walter Citrine, General Secretary of the T.U.C., who was one of the policy directors, told me. 'They'll get you out if they can.' And indeed it was plain they would. Tom Darlow was no longer there to watch over things at night. He had persuaded me to send him to France as a war correspondent. There after a few brilliant dispatches he died, leaving behind for me a personal loss which I found it hard to bear. We had laughed together so often that Fleet Street seemed empty without him. Percy Cudlipp, a former Editor of the *Evening Standard* who had grown weary of Beaverbrook, joined the *Herald* as my chief assistant in his place. Soon it became plain that, with the Beaverbrook glow still on him, he was in Southwood's eyes not merely an assistant but a possible successor.

Yet I still find it hard to understand what made Southwood pick the pretext he did for bringing things to a head.

In addition to my general editorial activities I was at this time writing a weekly signed article on the leader page which had a considerable following. In one of them I took as my theme the need to think in terms of organizing pockets of resistance behind the enemy lines. I quoted the success of Lawrence of Arabia's guerrilla activities with the Arabs behind the Turkish lines in the First World War and argued that we ought to prepare ourselves for the possibility of similar operations on a far wider scale and even train men to organize underground forces in occupied countries if the need should arise. The present stalemate, I concluded, could not continue.

As things turned out it was a prescient piece of writing, the first time I think any newspaper had talked about organizing an underground resistance movement. After I had corrected the proofs I went home well content.

When I opened the paper next morning the article was not there. I rang Percy Cudlipp and was told that it had been taken out on Southwood's orders. I rang Southwood. He was 'not available'. So I rang Dunbar and told him I proposed to offer the Board my resignation unless my powers and responsibilities as Editor were clearly established.

When the Board met, the policy directors, who were ready to support me but who were without Bevin who was abroad, found themselves faced with a legal opinion that under the company's constitution the position of the Editor was a matter not for the policy directors but for the whole board. On this Odhams had a majority and despite strong support for me from Citrine and others my resignation was accepted.

Afterwards Southwood asked me to go and see him. I was reluctant but eventually agreed. He said he was sorry I was ceasing to be Editor but asked me if I would stay on as his Editorial Adviser at a higher salary. I looked at him in amazement and refused. He seemed surprised. He was, I suppose, anxious to avoid trouble with the Labour Party and thought he could pay me to be good.

Neither then nor later was I able to find out from him why he had objected to this particular article but I assume that he feared that if it were taken seriously it might stir the war into greater activity and this he did not want. Although brave and resolute when the war did become more active, at this time he still hugged the illusion that if only we all acted circumspectly everything might yet end peacefully without anger on either side.

In this he was not alone. As Harold Macmillan has remarked in his memoirs there was at this time 'a smell of peace in the air'. Bernard Shaw was advocating a compromise peace in the *New Statesman* and from Churt, Lloyd George, whom I could not bear to meet in his defeatist old age, was flooding America with defeatist syndicated articles. At Cliveden Nancy Astor and her circle were still busy advocating appeasement, and from the American Embassy the United States Ambassador, Joseph Kennedy, a tycoon who seemed to me when I met him to combine all the disagreeable traits of all the very rich men I had ever met with hardly any of their virtues, had set flowing a constant stream of denigration of Britain backed by the assertion that we would have no chance against the superior power and discipline of the Germans when it came to real war and had better come to terms while we could. With the exception of his son John, then still in his early twenties, all his personal circle seemed to take the same view. Since most of them were, like Kennedy himself, arrogant and gauche, to meet them at dinner parties and diplomatic receptions had become a painful matter. I remember one such occasion when one of his staff sneeringly remarked in a loud voice that Britain deserved the fate that was coming to her for being too cowardly to resist Hitler earlier and I rose at the table and said, 'While the brave, resolute Americans were resisting Nazism at every turn, I suppose', and walked out of the room my meal uneaten. I never again went to the American Embassy so long as Kennedy was there.

So smelling 'peace in the air' when Southwood repeated his invitation to me to remain as his 'Editorial Adviser' and said winningly, 'I feel sure we can come to understand each other, the Chairman of a great company like Odhams has obligations hardly less serious than those of a Prime Minister, you know, and we don't want to make the war any worse.' I rose abruptly and left the kindly little man in full flood.

At the *Herald* the news was already circulating among the staff on duty. Some of them wanted to stage a strike but I told them it would do no good and drove home. Just as the war was beginning to take a positive course and genuine resistance to Hitler was shortly to begin I was out of a job.

CHAPTER 9

Churchill Tries to Muzzle the Press

I had always thought of myself as an internationalist. I was not aware of any strong sense of patriotism. A man, I thought, should have loyalties wider and deeper than to the spot of earth where he happened to be born. Even my concern that Britain should stand up to Hitler had been due, or so I thought, more to a devotion to certain principles of humanity and civilization than to national feeling.

And then suddenly the war exploded and I found that what I most cared about was England. England in its most tangible form. The soil of England, the fields and hills and lanes of England, the English sky. My feeling for England was as strong a physical emotion as falling in love. But like real love it was more than physical. It commanded the whole commonwealth of my being: mind and spirit and heart as well as body. I was astonished at the strength of my feelings for they seemed to deny many of the things in which I had formerly thought I believed. But I neither could nor wished to gainsay them.

As Norway fell and then Holland and Belgium and France, and much that I had predicted came to pass, I found it almost intolerable to be removed from near the centre of affairs where, or so I had been able to persuade myself, I had had a part to play, however small. Yet at the same time I felt within myself a new sense of harmony as though my life had been stripped down to its essentials—the essentials of home and family and country. My love for Jess and Betty and John and my love for England converged to give me a new feeling of identity. I seemed to become wholly aware of myself for the first time.

The Local Defence Volunteers—the Home Guard—was formed. We used William Murdoch's music room for our company headquarters and Murdoch was company commander. I was adjutant. We trained by day and at night guarded the telephone exchange and sent patrols across the hills on the watch for parachutists. A retired lieutenant-colonel of cavalry lectured us on how to deal with German tanks. The best way, he said, was to creep up quietly behind them and ram potatoes in their exhaust pipes. I thought this advice special to us until I discovered from the television programme 'Dad's Army' that it was a part of the general store of Home Guard wisdom.

By early L.D.V. standards our company was well armed. Murdoch had a sporting rifle. Frank Smythe had an elephant gun brought back from India on one of the Everest expeditions. I had a fairly powerful air-gun for target shooting, Peter Dunsheath, who was a director and chief engineer of W. T. Henleys, the cable makers, and subsequently had a good deal to do with the development of Pluto (Pipe line under the ocean) for D Day, had a German revolver from the First World War. There were one or two schoolmasters who did not have much in the way of weapons but were knowledgeable about map-reading. And the real backbone of our company, which was made up of farmworkers, gardeners and local craftsmen of one sort and other, had shotguns for rabbiting. With our knowledge of the country we thought we would be able to make a pretty good stand and go down fighting. When the L.D.V. became the Home Guard we got American army rifles and when we were not on night duty we slept with them beside our beds.

By day I wrote a book which took up the theme of my banned article, now even more urgent and topical, I thought, than when Southwood had thrown it out of the *Herald*. I called it *War By Revolution* and it was published in New York as well as London. So also was my second, longer book, which I called—perhaps optimistically—*Democracy's Last Battle*, which T. S. Eliot accepted for Fabers.

Eliot had moved from London to Guildford when the bombing started and hated it. Particularly, he told me, he missed being able to stroll round in the evening to call on his friends. Without that life was dull indeed. We lunched at the Oxford and Cambridge Club to discuss the book and afterwards he asked me about Priestley, whose broadcast postscripts after the nine o'clock news, full of good Yorkshire pudding and the promise of a social revolution at the end of the war, had had an enormous public response and were said to have made Churchill jealous.

Was it true, Eliot asked, grimacing slightly as he mentioned them, that the Priestley broadcasts had been taken off because of pressure by the Conservative Central Office? I said I'd heard that there had been approaches. 'I should have thought the Tory Central Office would have tougher problems to worry about than that teddy bear,' he said. We moved to the smoking-room for coffee. The place was full of people in uniform pre-occupied with martial talk and for a long time we sat ignored in a corner. Eliot snapped his finger every now and then as a man does who does not really expect any response but it was a long time before a waitress came. When one did she apologized pleasantly. 'I'm afraid I didn't notice you,' she said.

'Do not blame yourself, my dear,' said Eliot. 'It is in my nature not to be noticed.'

I thought of this remark many years later at the University of Minnesota in Minneapolis when I was taken by an English Professor to see a huge sports arena holding many thousands of people. 'It was packed when Eliot came,' he said. 'Not to hear him, of course. Most of them couldn't understand what he was talking about. Just so's they could say they'd seen him.'

But although it was pleasant writing books and talking to Mr Eliot it was not enough in the middle of a war. Nor was the 1941 Committee, formed by Priestley, Sir Edward Hulton, owner of *Picture Post*, and Sir Richard Acland to mobilize the new political forces Priestley was supposed to have brought into being by his B.B.C. postscripts. Although Priestley was genuinely for social reform and a new world, he had little skill, I thought, as a political thinker and even less as a practical politician. In such matters he seemed to me, like C. P. Snow later, to be in danger of overdrawing his intellectual account. As for the others, Hulton was an intellectual manqué with a lot of money who was passionately keen on social revolution so long as it did not hit him, and Acland a sincere idealist who understood little about ordinary people.

We met once a week at Hulton's house, where we were provided with a magnificent cold buffet altogether out of keeping with a war situation, and talked as though the war was already won and all that needed to be done was to see that the results of victory were distributed fairly. I never got around to knowing everyone who came but Dick Crossman, Kingsley Martin, Michael Foot and Tom Wintringham, who had fought in Spain, were among them. The general feeling was that the poor old Labour Party with its bourgeois leadership and trade-union impediment would be quite incapable of producing anything in the way of social revolution after the war and that a new political force, of which the 1941 Committee would be the spearhead, was necessary.

I soon tired of these meetings. They seemed to me as much out of touch with ordinary men and women as did some of the gatherings to which I was invited at Cliveden. Both, in fact, were equally symptomatic of the attitudes of many intellectual middle-class and upper middle-class people. They did not want to think of the war as a fight for survival. To talk about the future was one way of avoiding thinking about the present.

I was invited to Cliveden mainly, I think, because Nancy Astor, who had enormous energy but not much sense, had decided that I must have resigned from the *Daily Herald* because I did not approve of Churchill and his policies. She was a warm-hearted, hoydenish hostess who loved noise and bustle around her. When she discovered her mistake about me, or had it discovered for her by her constant adviser and political intimate, Tom Jones, who permeated the Cliveden scene like a Welsh Minister taking tea at the house of a rich member of his congregation, she was in no way put out. She was quite prepared to welcome an entertaining addition to her entourage, irrespective of his views. Cliveden, as Bob Boothby remarked, was about as selective as Euston Station.

Dinner there represented the other side of the penny of which the 1941 Committee was one face. I felt more sympathetic to the Priestley group than I did to the Astors and their friends, but I came to the conclusion both were a great waste of time. I abandoned Hulton's buffet suppers and when Nancy Astor invited Jess and me to Cliveden for a weekend we refused—Jess having no more liking for the company than I had.

Meanwhile I was bombarding everyone I knew for something real to do in the Services or out of them. The only response I got was an invitation to serve on a morale committee of the Ministry of Information.

Once a week I went to the Senate House of the University of London which the Ministry had taken over, filled in a form at the gate, passed through the hall where I had read Jess's examination results and made my way to a small room on the first floor. Here I greeted Julian Huxley, Harold Nicolson, Kenneth Clark, Lord Horder, Edward Glover, the Freudian psycho-analyst, Professor Arnold Plant of the London School of Economics and one or two obviously distinguished but rather silent merchant bankers who did not much like the company they found themselves in. Tom Harrisson, one of the founders of Mass Observation who was studying the English until such time as he could get himself dropped among the head-hunters of Borneo by parachute, was usually in attendance, and so was Mary Adams, a delightful liberal-minded lady whose husband was a Tory M.P. and who had come over from the B.B.C., where I had known her well from my first days as a broadcaster when the readers of the nine o'clock news wore dinner jackets.

We studied reports from 'the field' which were supposed to tell us about the morale of the British people and what questions they were asking. The morale seemed fine, the questions to indicate a desire that whoever was in charge should stop wrapping things up. We then drew up a report which was rushed by motor dispatch-rider to Churchill who, as we learned later, tossed it unopened in his wastepaper basket. However, copies, we were assured, also went to all Government Departments and were awaited eagerly. After a time we grew tired of never seeing any result of our activities and asked to see the Director General. He was at that time Sir Frank Pick, late of the London Passenger Transport Board, where his choice of posters for publicizing the London Underground had won universal esteem. Pick's position at the Ministry was, however, precarious. He had made the mistake of lecturing Winston Churchill on truth in propaganda and Churchill had given instructions that he must never again be troubled by that 'impeccable busman'. Pick was a well-meaning but tactless man in a state of confusion

—'the bull *and* the china shop' as Churchill said of him on another occasion. It was clear when we met him that he had no more idea of the purpose of our activities than we had.

We had chosen Huxley as our spokesman and Pick listened to him with a puzzled frown until Huxley reached his peroration. 'Unless we can have some assurance that our time is not being wasted,' said Huxley, 'we see no point in continuing.'

'Ah,' said the Director General, seeing a great light at last. 'It's a strike, is it?' He seemed as though he expected Ernest Bevin to come through the door.

Soon after this the Committee was disbanded and I lost even this frail touch with the movement of events. The first of the heavy bombing raids had begun and at night from the terrace of Coneybarrow we could see London burning. Earlier we had had official evacuees but they had gone back during the phoney war and we now had Betty and John's cousins, Bobby and Roger, who lived in Uxbridge, and two small boys from Eltham who were the sons of an old university friend of Jess's, Marion New. In the daytime the Battle of Britain, a symphony of silver in a sky of azure blue, was fought above us, and as the Germans switched their bombing raids to the industrial Midlands we became an unloading area for the bombers that were driven back with their mission uncompleted and were frequently straddled by sticks of bombs.

'Let's go to sleep and then it won't hurt if we wake up dead,' said Roger, and in the morning the children would go searching on the common for bomb splinters. The Murdoch children and many others had been evacuated to Canada but we could not bring ourselves to do this. It seemed a sort of disloyalty, an act of privilege altogether alien to the nature of this war, and we thought our children would not forgive us even if we could forgive ourselves. On Home Guard duty at night one saw the flak over London, the flashes of the guns and the balls of fire rising lazily in the sky as the searchlights probed, and low down the bursting bombs and the glare of flames against the sky. It was like watching from a theatre circle a play in which one longed passionately for a more active part.

I was, therefore, immeasurably relieved when I received an invitation from Sir Walter Monckton, who had just become Director General of the Ministry of Information and who had, so he said, been told by Churchill to get in touch with me.

I had dinner with Monckton and Cyril Radcliffe, who was then Controller of News and Censorship, at Windham's Club. There was an air raid on at the time and we drank champagne because, as Monckton said, it was too terrible to think of being killed and leaving some behind us.

I had met Monckton in the days of the Abdication when, as Attorney-General to the Duchy of Cornwall, he was King Edward VIII's legal adviser as well as being one of his closest friends. He had more charm than any man I knew. One could feel it spraying over one like a warm shower. He was so anxious to see the points of view of all the strange people at the Ministry of Information that he was like the chameleon who was dumped on a patchwork quilt and broke its poor heart.

In those days the Ministry of Information still had an eccentric amateurism of an extreme but attractive kind. One never knew who or what one would find if one opened one of its many doors. Professors, writers, artists, journalists, retired Ambassadors, retired Consuls, retired Indian Civil Servants, retired generals, retired admirals, advertising agents, publishers, film producers, barristers, anthropologists, theologians, every conceivable kind of expert and non-expert milled around while a handful of Civil Servants, cracking under the strain, tried unsuccessfully to weld them into bureaucratic shape. There were committees meeting everywhere. Until long into the night the lights burned and ideas crackled. There was even one committee officially called The Dynamo. In every room there were camp-beds and as one hurried along the corridors the sign 'Meeting in Progress' met one's eye on almost every door. It was said that one man summoned from the north of England for some urgent task had arrived with his family and finding it impossible to find a flat had simply taken over a temporarily vacant committee room, hung up a 'Meeting in Progress' sign on the door and installed them there in privacy and comparative comfort for several weeks. There were camp-beds already in position for them to sleep on and at regular intervals the tea trolley arrived with food and drink.

There were constant changes at the top. Ministers arrived only to disappear and Directors General trod on each other's heels trying vainly to bring order out of the chaos caused by the meeting of so many brilliant and undisciplined minds under one roof.

However, when Monckton and Radcliffe asked me to join the Ministry that evening at Windham's the worst was said to be over. Churchill had appointed as Minister Duff-Cooper, the only man with the guts to resign from the Chamberlain Cabinet rather than endorse the dishonour of Munich. Harold Nicolson was to be his Parliamentary Under-Secretary.

On the face of it Duff-Cooper and Harold Nicolson seemed made for the Ministry of Information; an ideal political team. However, this turned out not to be the case. Both were belated Edwardians. They treated the Ministry of Information as if it were a branch of Belles-Lettres.

It was impossible not to feel affection for Nicolson. He was so amusing, so civilized, so urbane, he wrote so well, talked so engagingly and had so many charming anecdotes that you could not help but enjoy being with him. After a time, however, even the famous urbanity began to worry you. It seemed to have eaten so deep into his soul that there was nothing left. He came daily to the meetings of the Executive Board and enjoyed himself hugely, persuaded that he was near the centre of things. But he rarely contributed much beyond amusing conversation. He was a wonderful gossip but seemed to know hardly anyone outside Westminster, St James's and Bloomsbury. He was quite ignorant of the habits and attitudes even of the middle classes. As for the working classes he seemed to regard them as barbarians to be feared, admired and placated. Never was there a man who represented so completely in himself the distinction between Us and Them.

Duff-Cooper, Nicolson and Ronnie Tree, Duff-Cooper's Parliamentary Private Secretary, were all members of what Nicolson called in his Diary 'our group'. Their joint presence at the top of the Ministry suggested an attempt to turn it into an annexe of White's or the Beefsteak. Tree was, if possible, even more innocent of the rough world outside than Nicolson, although equally well meaning. He had a delightful country house at which Churchill liked to stay, a rich American wife who was the widow of one of the Chicago Fields and a great many friends in what were still thought of as influential circles. Although without political sense himself he had heard so much talk of politics among his guests at Ditchley Park that enough of it had rubbed off on to him to deceive you at first into thinking him knowledgeable.

Duff-Cooper, of course, was a more substantial figure than either Nicolson or Tree. He had been a good First Lord of the Admiralty until Munich and his own sense of honour compelled him to resign. But like Nicolson and Tree he was a curiously inbred political figure and had by now become also a rather idle one. He preferred talking over lunch to doing anything. Later he was to win praise for his energy as Minister of State in Singapore—not that it was of much avail. He was good in Algiers in the closing stages of the war and an excellent Ambassador in Paris after the liberation. But at the Ministry of Information he was almost wholly ineffectual, although he came there with great enthusiasm convinced, after a lecture tour in America, that British propaganda was being bungled and that he was the man to put it right. He had a rather Churchillian style of oratory, although without the master's rough vigour, and signalled his appointment as Minister of Information by a broadcast in which he recited Macaulay's poem on the Armada in the no doubt sincere conviction that this was what the masses needed to rouse them.

He asked me to introduce him to editors and columnists at a series of lunches. These lunches tended to go on a long time and to give everyone present the impression that he had not much to do. One of them had a somewhat eccentric result. A good deal of brandy and vodka had been taken—the vodka to toast the Russians who were now our allies—and William Connor, Cassandra of the *Daily Mirror,* began to complain rather truculently that much more attention was paid to American journalists by the Government than British. He cited Quentin Reynolds, whose gifts as a raconteur had much endeared him to the Prime Minister and who had been given time on the B.B.C. to deliver a riproaring attack on Hitler, whom he addressed by his original name of Schickelgruber. He himself, said Cassandra, could have given a much better broadcast if given the chance, but they daren't let him on the air for fear that he might attack some of their pets.

Duff-Cooper, who by now had consumed a good deal of brandy, denied having any pets and was thereupon attacked by

Cassandra for doing nothing about P. G. Wodehouse, who had fallen into German hands when France was invaded and had made a couple of silly broadcasts about life in captivity which indicated a juvenile remoteness from real life and from the current mood of the British people rather than anything more serious. The argument ended with Duff-Cooper inviting Cassandra to broadcast on Wodehouse or to Wodehouse if he preferred to do it that way, with the promise that he could say whatever he liked.

Later that afternoon the script was produced. The B.B.C. refused to put it on the air. They considered it vulgar, extravagant and probably libellous. Conscious of his lunchtime undertaking and of what Cassandra would say if he failed to live up to it Duff-Cooper insisted. Thereupon the B.B.C. demanded written orders under the wartime regulation which suspended the B.B.C.'s independent constitution and made it subject to the direction of the Minister of Information. They wanted evidence that they had acted under duress if a libel writ arrived after the war. The written order was sent, the only one issued, I think, throughout the war, and was locked up by the B.B.C. in its vaults for safe-keeping. Some years later Hugh Greene told me it was still there. Duff-Cooper regretted the broadcast as soon as it was made, and so, later, did Cassandra himself.

Although few of the lunches were as disastrous as this they did Duff-Cooper little good. He was suspected of wanting to replace voluntary press censorship by compulsory—quite wrongly as it turned out, although such a scheme had been under consideration when he became Minister and had included what must surely be one of the silliest proposals ever hatched by the bureaucratic mind. This was that all newspapers should be compelled to publish the same headlines, written for them by the Ministry of Information itself. He also found himself saddled with the activities of a Home Intelligence Department under Dr Stephen Taylor, now Lord Taylor and President and Vice-Chancellor of the Memorial University of Newfoundland, which was conducting surveys of public reaction to wartime regulations by sampling techniques now universally accepted. Unfortunately my successor as Editor of the *Daily Herald* discovered the existence of these surveys and in a brilliant flash of sad journalese christened the investigators 'Cooper's Snoopers'.

One way and another it soon became clear to everyone, including Duff-Cooper himself, that he was not a success. He was sent to Singapore as Minister of State. Monckton, who had grown tired of propping up incompetent Ministers, got himself dispatched on a propaganda mission to Moscow and then to Cairo where a great friend of his, Sir Oliver Lyttelton, was in charge and where his experience in drawing up instruments of abdication came in useful when it was felt necessary to put pressure on the young King Farouk. Harold Nicolson was shipped to the B.B.C. as a Governor, a post of even less importance in war than peace. The desks thus cleared, Brendan Bracken was appointed Minister in place of Duff-Cooper and a Labour M.P., Ernest Thurtle, Parliamentary Secretary in place of Nicolson. Radcliffe succeeded Monckton as Director General and I succeeded Radcliffe as Controller of Press and Censorship. For the remainder of the war in Europe there were no other major changes. The M. of I. had achieved stability. This brought me into close touch with a new and, to me, surprising side of Churchill's character: his phobia about press criticism. Few Prime Ministers—or Presidents for that matter—like what the newspapers have to say about them. But Churchill carried sensitivity to an extreme and sometimes dangerous degree. He would praise the press in public and when he invited Editors to meet him at 10 Downing Street would refer to them fulsomely as 'men of great fidelity to the state'. But he worried constantly about what they might be writing about him and read all the papers before going to bed. If he did not like what he read—and he very often did not—he would complain bitterly to Brendan Bracken, who was a fairly constant midnight companion. If Bracken were not of the party, he would ring the Ministry of Information. When he did so his opening words to me were almost invariably the same.

'I understand you are Controller of Censorship, Mr Williams,' he would say. When I had admitted the charge he would continue, 'Then can you explain to me, Mr Williams, why you are allowing the *Daily Mirror*'—it was usually the *Daily Mirror* but sometimes the *Daily Mail* or the *Daily Herald*—'to criticize the Government in unbridled terms tomorrow. Am I to assume that you agree with these grave charges?'

I would explain that censorship was confined to facts and

had no control over opinion, but this he would never believe. If I told him that under the powers of censorship bestowed by Parliament it was impossible to stop what he wanted stopping, he would say, 'Impossible. Impossible. I have no patience with the impossible. You talk like a bureaucrat, Mr Williams.' Or if he was in sunnier mood he would listen to my exposition of what I had and had not the power to do and then dismissing such considerations as of no importance, would say, 'Nonsense, Mr Williams. You are a man of influence. Pray use it.'

Whether he growled or cooed one thing was always abundantly clear, he had no patience with a press censorship that could not do whatever he wanted it to do. His sensitivity to press criticism became one of the M.O.I.'s most persistent headaches. The *Daily Mirror*, which had set itself up as the uninhibited voice of the men and women in the services and factories, was a particular object of his ire, perhaps because he had written regularly for it before the war and thought it owed him particular allegiance. Even its repetition of a joke then much in circulation that Churchill had said of a memorandum from Eden that it contained every cliché except 'God is Love' and 'Please adjust your dress before leaving', brought a stern rebuke and the accusation that in printing this story the paper was activated by 'the spirit of hatred and malice'.

The climax to all this came when he persuaded the Cabinet that the *Mirror* should formally be warned that unless it mended its ways it would be closed down under the Defence Regulations for publishing matter 'calculated to foment opposition to the successful prosecution of the war'. He had at first wanted to close down the paper without warning but this was too much for the rest of the Cabinet. The excuse was a cartoon that the Ministry of Information was actually considering at the time as a possible propaganda poster.

Zec, the *Mirror*'s cartoonist, had begun a series of cartoons attacking waste. The price of petrol had just gone up as a result of tanker sinkings by submarines and the third cartoon in the series was designed to make motorists think of the real cost in seamen's lives. It showed a seaman in the last stages of exhaustion sprawling across a tiny raft in a black empty sea. The original caption had been 'Petrol Is Dearer Now', but at the suggestion of Cassandra this was altered to 'The Price of Petrol Has Been Raised By a Penny—Official'.

The cartoon had a great impact. It was posted in stores and at petrol stations all over the country and the Division of the Ministry of Information concerned with posters was considering asking for the *Mirror's* permission to reproduce it when the astounding news reached us that Churchill had declared it a subversive attempt to undermine the morale of merchant seamen. Nor was this all. Churchill's phobia regarding the *Mirror* had now reached such a stage that he ordered a search of its share register to find out if any shares were held by enemy agents. None, of course, were. Nevertheless the official warning was issued and the *Mirror* told that if the Cabinet had reason to complain again it would be closed instantly—'and for a long time'. When I protested about this to Bracken he shrugged his shoulders helplessly, 'It's no good appealing to me,' he said. 'He won't listen.'

As the war proceeded Churchill became increasingly autocratic. Apart from Bevin, who would brook no interference in his own area of operations and whom Churchill prudently left alone, few Ministers cared to challenge or try to curb him. Although deferential to the constitutional proprieties and occasionally over-ruled by the War Cabinet when his strategical ideas were altogether too wild and too much at variance with the Chiefs of Staff he governed in most matters as a virtual dictator, arbitrarily intervening even in the most trivial matters when the mood took him.

Because of this he tended to regard any press criticism of the Government as personal and by no means confined his hatreds to the *Mirror*. Criticism in Parliament was bad enough. But there he had an answer. He could demand a vote of confidence and stamp his critics into the ground. Criticism by the press was less easy to beat down. He remained absurdly sensitive to it. In March 1942 he actually contemplated political censorship of newspapers on the grounds that criticism of the conduct of the war could undermine public morale. This proposal was bitterly fought by the Ministry of Information and in the end defeated, but only after Bracken got Beaverbrook to help him.

Churchill's habitual suspicion of the press had at this time been reinforced by hysterical messages from the High

Commissioner in Australia, Sir Ronald Cross, a merchant banker who had been one of Chamberlain's Ministers. Cross was much excited by the tone of some press messages from London and by the printing in Australian newspapers of extracts from British newspapers, suggesting a good deal of criticism of the Government. There were also complaints from the High Commissioner in South Africa about the effusions of an unimportant left-wing correspondent who acted as London representative of a number of small weeklies. These impressed Churchill out of all relation to their real importance and even when he was restrained from trying to gag the British press he insisted on trying to put a stop to the free thoughts of overseas correspondents and what he regarded as their malevolent habit of cabling home anything nasty a British newspaper said about him.

The Ministry of Information was able to show that the material complained of represented only an infinitesimal percentage of the eleven million words cabled by newsmen from London each week, but in spite of this Churchill persuaded the Cabinet to insist on radical change in censorship policy. Overseas press censorship was widened to include any word or passage by telegram or mail likely to 'create disharmony' among the Allies, even if the offending words consisted only of quotations from matter which had already appeared in the British press.

Anthony Eden was Churchill's chief ally in this. He and his officials at the Foreign Office were terrified of offending the State Department. They even argued that criticisms of American policy by American correspondents themselves should be prevented under the disharmony rule. If such criticisms were allowed by British censorship, then, they said, the State Department would take it as evidence that London agreed.

Matters came to a head with the Anglo-American landings in French North Africa and Eisenhower's decision to recognize the right wing, anti-British Admiral Darlan as the representative of French authority in North Africa instead of General Giraud who had escaped from a German prison in the spring of that year and had been generally assumed to be the man with whom the Allies would co-operate. No doubt to Eisenhower—never very good at politics—this seemed a simple military decision. His interest was to bring resistance to the Allied forces to an end as rapidly as possible and Darlan, he was told, was the most likely person to achieve it.

There was, however, much more behind it. The actual negotiations with Darlan had been conducted by Robert D. Murphy, former Counsellor at the U.S. Embassy in Paris and Chargé at the U.S. Embassy in Vichy, who had been appointed Eisenhower's Adviser on Civil Affairs. An able, ambitious man, contemptuous of what he regarded as sentimental left-wing attitudes, Murphy worked closely under the direction of Admiral Leahy, Roosevelt's Chief of Staff who had formerly been U.S. Ambassador to Vichy and had developed an acute dislike of de Gaulle. He was determined to prevent him from being invited to North Africa or allowed to send a representative there as the British wished. This 'so-called leader of the French people' and 'highly advertised hero in England' had, he sneered, no standing with the French—and no future. Opposition to dealing with Darlan was, he declared, 'instigated by Jews and Communists'.

Leahy's opinions came down to me through a joint American-British Committee on which I sat to consider public reaction to the North African landings and whose meetings revealed very plainly the American desire to keep de Gaulle out.

I had had a good deal to do with de Gaulle myself and understood the hackles he raised. His arrogance often seemed like the basest ingratitude and he never tried to disguise his contempt for most of the people he met. I found his physical ugliness daunting and I lacked sufficient facility in French to enjoy, as I might otherwise have done, the precision and lucidity of his way with words. He refused to consider wartime regulations, including censorship regulations, as applying to himself and treated reminders of their existence as lèse-majesté.

As a result of this his broadcasts to the French people were a continual trouble to us. On at least one occasion I had to order the switch to be thrown and a passage in one of his broadcasts blacked out. When he discovered what had happened his anger was intense. 'Would we,' the Aide he sent to protest asked with cold polite fury, 'have dared to do the same to Mr Churchill? Or was it only the French leader who was humiliated in this way?' In the circumstances there was something magnificent about the insistence on equality with Churchill.

I recalled this incident in a lecture I gave in Toronto just after de Gaulle's Canadian visit and his support for the Quebec separationists. The result was that everything else I said was ignored and I thought I should scarcely escape without being given the freedom of the City.

Despite my own troubles with de Gaulle I was amazed at the venom of those who took the Leahy line. One had at the very least, I thought, to accept the fact that here was a man with a magnificent readiness to gamble everything for the glory of France. He had hardly any cards in his hand but he played them with a verve designed to frighten away every challenger. He was his own best, indeed only, trump card and even when one was irritated almost beyond bearing it was impossible not to admire his intense conviction of destiny and his determination to fulfil it. A subordinate role had no part in his conception of himself. The person on my staff with whom he had the best relations was Brebner, the Director of the News Division, whose wife was French and who was himself a fluent French speaker. He would sometimes invite Brebner and his wife to his home for a modest meal with Madame de Gaulle. From such occasions Brebner would return palpably moved by an awe that was contagious. To seek to set aside de Gaulle for a man such as Darlan seemed to me incredible.

Not all the intrigues with Darlan were known immediately to American and British newspapermen. But they could not long be kept hidden. Even before their full extent was disclosed the mere fact that a deal could be contemplated with the arch-Vichyite Darlan enraged a large body of public opinion on both sides of the Atlantic. The Foreign Office, terrified of annoying the State Department, insisted that under the new disharmony rule not only should American correspondents not be allowed to report British disquiet but that they should not even be permitted to comment critically on the State Department's attitude themselves. And it claimed it was doing so in response to State Department pressure.

In these circumstances neither I nor my principal assistant, the Chief Press Censor, who was a retired admiral, Rear-Admiral Thomson, much loved by the press for his sweet character, saw any reason to disguise from the American correspondents the fact that the censorship of their views was contrary to our own judgement and had been imposed by the Foreign Office at, we were assured, the request of the State Department. Whether the State Department really was imposing such pressure we had, we said, no means of knowing for certain: possibly the American correspondents themselves might be in a better position to find out.

They took the hint. Ray Daniell of the *New York Times* and Geoffrey Parsons of the *Herald Tribune* organized a joint protest from American correspondents in London to their Editors asking that the matter should be taken up urgently with the State Department. This was done. Thereupon the State Department rushed, as I had thought it might, for cover, threw the Foreign Office to the wolves and issued a public denial that it wished to interfere with the free flow of opinion or had sent any request for the censoring of American correspondents' copy in London.

This broke the back of political censorship. It was never again seriously used.

Although Brendan Bracken proved unable to argue Churchill out of his worst obsessions about newspaper criticism, on most things he had his master's ear—or gave the impression that he had, which was almost as important in his standing with other Ministers. Bracken had attached himself to Churchill and Beaverbrook as a young man and he never strayed far from either of them. Such political power as he possessed derived from Churchill and from Churchill alone. He was unpopular with the Conservative Party whom he had baited and badgered relentlessly during their cold-shouldering of Churchill. To many he seemed no more than a privileged jester at Winston's court, and his position did rest a good deal on his never-failing ability to be entertaining. But he was a good deal more than this. He made an excellent Minister of Information because he did not believe in propaganda but did believe in newspapers and thought it was his job to get them maximum facilities.

He and Cyril Radcliffe, the Director General, now Viscount Radcliffe and Chairman of more Government commissions than one can easily remember, were opposites. Bracken had the dash and exuberance, Radcliffe the judgement and lucidity. Radcliffe's career had been one of ordered brilliance conducted in the bright light of academic and legal success: Fellow of All Souls at twenty-three, Eldon Law Scholar at twenty-four, a

K.C. when he was thirty-six, admired in his own profession as one of the best legal brains of the century. Some people thought him cold and reserved in his personal relations and taciturn in conversation but I never found him so.

Bracken's beginnings on the other hand were shrouded in mystery, a good deal of it self-created. He was the subject of constant speculation among political friends and enemies. So far as could be discovered he had been born in Kilmalock in Ireland, the son of a small speculative builder, and had a brother who was a policeman. But he had broken with his family and emigrated to Australia as a boy—to join an uncle, according to some stories. Whatever it was that took him to Australia his stay was short and profitable. He turned up in England when he was seventeen carrying, according to persistent legend, a Gladstone bag full of banknotes. With this he set about trying to buy himself a public school education. He tried Winchester first but proved too brash for its headmaster to swallow and wound up at Sedbergh where he got himself accepted for a year, paying the fees in advance out of his Gladstone bag, or so the story ran. The deal proved much to Sedbergh's advantage for he later showed his gratitude by a succession of handsome donations to the school.

Bracken, a bachelor with many women friends, was a sort of confidence trickster in reverse. A large unfinished man with thick lips, fuzzy red hair and a voice that constantly broke into a snort, his favourite adjective was tough and he conducted himself most of the time like a bad actor playing the part of a Tammany boss in an old-fashioned melodrama. He would tell what seemed the most outrageous lies only for you to discover later that most of them were true. This was hard on sceptical newspapermen who were often misled by his manner. Frederick Kuh, who travelled about London by bicycle extracting scoops for his paper, the *Chicago Sun-Times*, from unwary diplomats of every persuasion, once rounded on him on such an occasion, 'Everything about you is phoney, Brendan,' he roared, 'even your hair that looks like a wig isn't.'

Bracken was important to Churchill because he was so different from the devoted band of competent officials who served on the Prime Minister's personal staff and whom he called his Secret Circle: Norman Brook, John Martin, Leslie Rowan, John

Colville, Ian Jacob. These were mandarins of the highest order and Churchill could not have done without them or others like them. But his demon also required livelier fare. He needed wildness and argument and the presence of boon companions to refresh and invigorate his senses. Above all he was a political animal and needed other political animals around him. Bracken was such a one. He loved political gossip and collected it assiduously. He adored the sense of being on the inside of things, and was fascinated by Prime Ministerial patronage, particularly of the ecclesiastical sort. I would often hear him shouting down the telephone with elaborate schemes for moving church dignitaries around in a game of political and ecclesiastical chess. He was flamboyant, malicious and indiscreet—although perhaps less so than he sometimes seemed. He could make Churchill laugh out loud.

Also, of course, like Beaverbrook he was an outsider, and one of the keys to Churchill's character was that the companionship of such men was vital to him. Like his grandfather, Jerome, the Wall Street speculator, his batteries ran down if exposed too long to respectable company only.

CHAPTER 10

The Crash of War

The wooded hills that stretch from Holmbury St Mary to Leith Hill had been turned into a concealed ammunition dump and whether because of this or because it was a convenient place for German bomber planes to dump their loads on the way back from the Midlands, the number of bombs falling near Coneybarrow had become so considerable that neither Jess nor I could any longer avoid the decision that in fairness to Betty and John we ought to get them away.

In normal times we would not have thought of sending our children to a boarding school for we found the British middle- and upper-class habit of dispensing with one's children's company at the earliest possible age unattractive. But the war had introduced a new element that could not be ignored and regretfully we decided that much as they themselves enjoyed searching in the woods for pieces of exploded bombs we ought not to keep them unnecessarily in danger.

We made several educational forays about the country, eating an unconscionable number of horrible school dinners and listening to a great deal of nonsense from headmasters and headmistresses. After toying with Bedales and Dartington Hall we decided on St Christopher School, Letchworth—a progressive co-educational school whose headmaster, Lyn Harris, was a man of great nobility of character with an immense respect for children and whose staff combined, in what seemed to us a very pleasant balance, the academic and the eccentric.

Here they both happily acquired such education as they

needed before in due course passing on to Cambridge—where Betty found Girton somewhat confining after the freedom of her school life.

With the children away Jess decided to follow her degree in psychology with a clinical training under one of the pioneers in child guidance in Britain, Dr Lucy Fildes, at the Child Guidance Clinic, which had been moved out of London to Oxford at the beginning of the war. Dr Fildes, a magnificent and indomitable old lady with a human sympathy as big as her considerable intellect, encouraged her in every way, thus starting her on a career which after work as a psychologist in Surrey Child Guidance Clinics took her to the Children's Hospital, Great Ormond Street, to University College and finally to Guy's Hospital as Consultant Psychologist and later Research Psychologist at the Newcomen Centre for Handicapped Children. It has been a successful and a happy career. It has given her much satisfaction and me much pride and has brought us many stimulating and adorable friends all over the world. I know of no better recipe for a happy, entertaining married life than that both partners shall follow careers which provide sources of mutual interest.

Jess went to Oxford each week during her training and I stayed in London, sharing a flat in Cliffords Inn with Ritchie Calder. Cliffords Inn had the advantage of being a strong modern building providing a certain amount of protection from bombs and with a bar in the basement. But otherwise I found it a depressing place to live in as did Leonard Woolf who was one of our neighbours. Woolf found it hard to adjust himself to the boxed-in ugliness of life in such a place, but it was nice to have him there to talk to as the bombs fell. Simply by his presence he reminded one of more civilized days.

Later we sold Coneybarrow which was increasingly difficult to keep up on a wartime income not much more than a third of what we had had when I was Editor of the *Herald*. We both hated letting it go and Jess particularly so, for it was alive with recollections of Betty and John, and Jess had designed and planted most of the garden and each plant and tree carried its own particular memory. In its place we bought an Elizabethan cottage called Cammocks with thick oak beams and clay and wattle walls in Hinxworth, in Hertfordshire, within easy reach of St Christopher School, so that the children could cycle over with their friends for tea at the weekends and could be there with Jess in the holidays.

During the week we lived in London in a set of chambers at 3 Essex Court in the Middle Temple. It had a tiny cupboard of a kitchen, a small cramped bedroom and an old-fashioned ramshackle bathroom but a fine panelled sitting-room with Grinling Gibbons carvings over the fireplace. The rent with rates was only £94 a year. When bombs fell near the building it would shake and the dust and soot of ages would cover the carpet, but it had a graciousness denied to the antiseptic modernity of the Cliffords Inn and we were very happy there. Hinxworth was cold and unfriendly after Holmbury St Mary and populated for the most part by people who regarded strangers with distrust, but we were fortunate enough to find a woman who had moved there from another village, Mrs Morgan, who came in to help us with the housework and who was gay and warm-hearted and to whom we became deeply attached.

This was a working countryside and there were few footpaths through the great stretches of wheatland. But we would go on long cycle rides along the flat roads with their vast expanse of sky and although at first it seemed to us cold and bare after the friendly woods and meadows and deep lanes of our corner of Surrey, yet on winter mornings when the stubble of the cornfields and the black earth of the ploughed land was touched with white frost, or in the evenings when the mist rose in the fields, we came to see that it had its own beauty of sky and cloud and earth and distance. This bare windswept landscape, with its golden corn ricks standing in columns like the tents of an army and its farmsteads aloof and self-sufficient with russet tiles overgrown with a green moss so that they seemed to have become part of the eternal background of fields and sky, was in no way ostentatious. One had to live with it to know it: it made no concessions to the transient traveller.

During the children's holidays when Jess stayed there with them I would get to Cammocks each night when I could manage it. In the morning I had to leave early, often before daybreak, and would catch a slow stopping train with its windows still blacked out. It progressed slowly and would sometimes be halted for as much as an hour outside Kings Cross Station if there was an air raid alert. I did not mind this slow tedious journey because I spent the time writing. I was busy on a novel which Heinemanns later published and in some ways this crawling, blacked-out train provided me with perfect conditions. I often did not realize that the journey had ended until people pushing past me nearly knocked the pen out of my hand and I would make my way to the Ministry so much immersed in what I had written that it was only with difficulty that I brought myself back to the present when I took my chair for the first appointment of the day. This was to preside at what was called the Duty Room Conference, a gathering of the Services, Foreign Office, and other advisers to the Ministry and the chief officers of the Ministry itself to consider the news interpretations and other material to be sent to our Embassies, High Commissioners and Information Services abroad.

War, of course, is a dirty business but I have usually found those who practise it professionally honourable and kindly men and much preferable to my mind to most of those engaged in making money. The service officers I now came to know so well in our daily discussions had an openness of character that was very appealing. It came, I think, as it does with many clergy-men—for although not a Christian I have frequently found myself much at ease in the company of clerics—from the fact that they followed an unmercenary profession and were moved by standards of conduct and honour often unfashionable in the world of business.

As happened, I suppose, to many people I was living at this time on several different levels of reality. There was the reality of my life with Jess which took on a heightened intensity when, as so often, we were in London together during heavy night bombing and I held her hand as the planes came closer overhead and the gunfire mounted, or when we had arranged to meet somewhere during the day and there had been a daylight raid and for her to be even a few minutes late was an agony of apprehension. There was my imaginative life as a writer, and finally there was my life at the Ministry, so full of administration problems and the immediacy of practical decision.

Yet even some of my work at the Ministry had a quality so unrelated to anything I had ever imagined myself doing before the war that I asked myself if it could really be I who was involved in matters so strange which yet by force of habit soon became almost humdrum.

One of the strangest, even macabre, was the preparation of what I suppose I should describe as obituaries for German spies. In the early days of the war spy stories abounded. Much official propaganda seemed almost deliberately designed to make everyone suspect everyone else. Nor was this spy fever abated by the bare notification of the arrest, secret trial and execution of spies such as Waldberg and Meir in December 1940, which was all that the newspapers were at the time permitted to publish. However, both security services and judges were finally prevailed on to agree that it was desirable that more than such bare bones of information should be published where possible. Thereafter whenever a spy had been caught, tried and found guilty I met members of M.I.5 and the counter-espionage division of the Secret Intelligence Service (S.I.S.) before the execution date to go through the evidence and decide what should be given to the Press on the morning of the execution.

As we sat together considering the history of a man waiting to die I developed a good deal of perhaps unfashionable respect for M.I.5 and some, although slightly less, for S.I.S., whose Director of Security was at the time Lt.-Col. Valentine Vivian, known to his staff as Vee Vee. Vivian was an elegant ex-member of the Indian Police with a monocle and looked, possibly deliberately, as though he had just strolled in from the pages of a gentlemanly Secret Service thriller. He had a great but sometimes misplaced talent for recruiting Oxford and Cambridge dons and other intellectuals to the service and was responsible for selecting and pushing Kim Philby, later to become notorious as The Third Man. However, no one had any reason to question this appointment at that time, any more than I or anyone else had reason to suspect a loud and drunken member of the Foreign Office News Division at the M.O.I., Guy Burgess, of being anything but an occasional public nuisance.

Most of the cases we went through were drab and even pathetic, the stories of little men ill-equipped and badly trained and usually surprisingly ignorant of Britain and the British people. These were for the most part cat-and-mouse affairs with the end at the Old Bailey and the execution shed foretold from the start. I could not help but feel sorry for them. One wondered what it could have been that had moved them to embark on this service for which they were for the most part so ill-suited and what would sustain them at the last.

I can remember only one case that seemed to me to have a touch of strangeness about it. It was the case of a Dutchman who had gone over to the Nazis when Holland was invaded; most probably he was already in their service. Because he had spent some of his youth in England in the London office of a small Dutch shipping firm he was landed by submarine on the north-east coast one dark night. He was more intelligent than most of the spies that fell into our net and although his knowledge was rusty he knew England fairly well. He had all the right papers and might have been more difficult to catch than most but for a very curious episode.

He was at a railway station in a God-forsaken part of Lincolnshire. It was a small junction and he was waiting for a train. He was on his way, it was later suspected, to meet an important contact, but this he refused to admit. The train was very late as wartime trains often were. It was a bitter night and he and three or four other passengers sat for a long time with what patience they could in a waiting-room that was dirty and unswept and without any heat. There was no fire although there was one in the porters' room. When they had been waiting nearly an hour a porter popped his head in and told them there had been a signal. Their train was delayed and would be another two hours at least. The Dutchman had not spoken to anyone but was sitting in a corner with a newspaper in front of him trying to remain as inconspicuous as possible. He said nothing when the porter brought the news but one of the other passengers asked if there was any chance of a bit of fire. The porter snapped back, 'Don't you know there's a war on?' At this a man sitting next to the Dutchman jumped up and shouted that in that case why was there a fire in the porters' room and the porter replied truculently that that had nothing to do with it.

The Dutchman kept to himself throughout this scene, avoiding notice. And then something quite extraordinary happened. There was a rather pleasant middle-aged woman sitting on the bench opposite, a doctor's wife prominent in her local W.V.S.

(what they still call in country districts 'a lady'). She had one of those rather high-pitched flat voices you often find in women of this class and she suddenly intervened and said, as though keeping order at a W.I. meeting, 'Please do keep calm. It's no use making a fuss.' And at this the Dutchman, whom to her knowledge she had never set eyes on before, got up and slapped her face.

And that was the end of him. The porter and one of the other men grabbed him and although the woman herself was rather nice about it and said all their nerves were on edge and she did not wish to take it further, the porter called the local policeman who took the Dutchman to the station. The station sergeant was an intelligent man and after he had questioned the Dutchman for a while he began to think there was something fishy about the whole business and reported to higher authority. In due course an M.I.5 man arrived and that was the end for the Dutchman.

The M.I.5 officer who had interrogated the Dutchman was one of those with whom I went through the case but he could offer no explanation as to why a man who otherwise seemed remarkably intelligent and resolute should have drawn attention to himself in this incredible way.

In those days it was the practice for the officer who had interrogated a spy to see him on the night before his execution. In such interrogations a curious and sometimes oddly sympathetic relationship often developed between hunted and hunter; they came to know each other in a peculiarly intimate manner. It had often been found that if his interrogator called on him at the very last to say goodbye even the most hardened spy would sometimes begin to talk and having begun would find release in going on and on, almost as though talk could keep death away.

I learnt afterwards, however, that although the Dutchman did talk for several hours on his last night, on this one thing he remained silent. Nothing would persuade him to explain.

I have since thought that the explanation must have lain somewhere deep in the past, perhaps in some long-remembered insult in his youth delivered in just such a voice and perhaps in those identical words which could have been very chilling and dismissive to a young man, a stranger from another country in the full flood of anger or passion. It must have been something very personal. A general dislike of that sort of remark by that sort of person, although understandable, would scarcely have been sufficient to make a man lose all sense of mission and personal safety as this did.

War, of course, plays havoc with normal moral judgements, to do so is part of its trade. This always struck me in a particularly individual way during my visits to Mountbatten's Combined Operations Headquarters to take part in the highly secret planning of Commando raids on the European coasts. Although these raids were military operations they depended to a degree much greater than most warfare on the deliberate training of individuals in very individual and personal ways of murder, often to be carried out in secrecy and silence and in cold blood.

My presence in the planning-room of Combined Operations was due to the peculiar problems of news and political warfare involved.

I had originally been a little prejudiced against Mountbatten. Possibly I had been influenced without realizing it by Beaverbrook whose papers had long conducted a campaign against him, founded, I fancy, on some imagined social insult at his hands in Beaverbrook's early days when he was trying to break into London society as a brash young Canadian millionaire. I thought him a playboy. My first impressions of Combined Operations tended to confirm me in this view, for he had gathered around him in addition to professional soldiers and sailors of the first class a diverse group which included several well-known socialites whom I remembered from my newspaper days. The whole set-up reminded one of a chapter from an Evelyn Waugh novel.

This impression did not, however, long survive closer contact and I came to have an enormous admiration for Mountbatten as a true professional. He was the most meticulous of planners, every detail had to be carefully considered and thought through. But he had also, which not all meticulous planners have, a brilliant and unorthodox mind superbly impervious to the pressures of convention and the entanglements of red tape. He was open to consider anything. Some people complained that he was autocratic, overbearing, and altogether too cocksure. They thought that being born in the top drawer had given him a built-in assumption of superiority to the common run of mankind that could be both annoying and dangerous. I never found this to be so.

Of course his birth and social position were an advantage to him and I daresay he made use of them. But he underpinned them with an immense amount of hard work and an intense application to professional studies of the most abstruse and technical kind. He never struck me as a man of particularly wide culture or much interested in abstract things. But he had great intellectual power in dealing with practical affairs and a vast interest in people.

There were several friends or acquaintances of mine on his staff, among them Robert Henriques who was a friend of Evan Durbin and had written a very good novel of the military life called, *No Arms, No Armour*. Henriques took part in several raids and later wrote a rather fine poetic novel about one called *Captain Smith and Company*, of which Stephen Vincent Benét wrote, justly I think, that it was 'not primarily a report on a raid but on man's spirit'. Another acquaintance of mine at Combined Operations was David Astor, now Editor of the *Observer*, whom I regarded as the most intelligent of the Astors.

There was great public interest in these commando raids because although small they gave an encouraging impression of British initiative at a difficult time. They had a whiff of singeing the King of Spain's beard about them. But it was clear from the first that unless we were very careful the propaganda might backfire. The nature of the operations and the need to maintain radio silence until ships were back in home waters meant that the first news given to the world was likely to come from German sources, for we could not hope for full and reliable news of how a raid had gone until at least some hours after it was over and the attacking party had returned. During the whole of this time the propaganda air had to be left free to the Germans.

At our meetings in Richmond Terrace, Mountbatten, his staff and I would first consider what the raid was intended to achieve and then how soon Goebbels and his Ministry could be expected to receive news of the landing from the German forces on the spot. We then tried to estimate what line they were likely to take, how far we could hope to counter it in our own communiqué and how quickly. All this was complicated by the fact that although in the case of the bigger raids we naturally wanted to make as much splash on the front pages of the world's press as we could, in the case of smaller raids, of which there were a considerable number, it was often the purpose to land, blow up particular installations and withdraw without discovery, leaving the Germans to believe that the damage had been done by local saboteurs. In such cases we hoped to avoid saying anything about the raid unless the Germans themselves did. We were thus bound to trail behind the German version if there was one.

As the raids increased in success and size the problem of getting something out before the Germans took over headlines and radio space became more important. Finally we came to the conclusion that although radio silence was imperative going in and coming back there was a moment when the troops were re-embarking and the ships were still standing off shore when it might be possible to break it briefly since the ships' position at that moment would obviously be known to the enemy. Three signals, one intimating that the raid appeared to have been a complete success, one that it was a partial success only, and the third that it had been a failure were, therefore, arranged and I drafted short communiqués to cover each eventuality. At the same time I drafted fuller private and confidential guidance letters to cover each situation.

I had started these private and confidential guidance letters to Editors shortly after I became Controller of Censorship to meet situations where a D notice, a flat prohibition on security grounds, would have been wrong and inappropriate, since no question of censorship properly arose, but where it was plain that background information would be helpful to newspapers and would be welcomed by them, particularly as a help in deciding how to treat enemy communiqués.

They proved their value during the Combined Operations raids. Written to go out with the first communiqué they explained what the raid had attempted and what, according to the first signal, seemed to have been the result. They indicated what propaganda line we believed the enemy would follow and suggested how this might be handled in order to keep the public informed in a balanced way until the raiders, sometimes accompanied by one or two war correspondents whose stories were pooled, returned. As soon as Combined Operations received a signal during the radio break I was called on a scrambler telephone and issued the appropriate communiqué with a guidance letter. I then joined Mountbatten at Richmond Terrace to hear those men who came back and give out a fuller story.

As a result of all this we took the propaganda advantage away from the Germans again and again. We did so, for example, with the brilliant attack on St Nazaire in which destroyers and light coastal craft took an old American destroyer, *Campbeltown*, packed with high explosive five miles up the estuary of the Loire and blew it up shattering the lock gates and putting out of commission for the rest of the war one of the biggest docks in the world and the only one along the Atlantic seaboard capable of handling the *Tirpitz*.

The far bigger Dieppe raid has usually been accounted a failure and harshly criticized: 'improvised muddle again brought discreditable failure,' says A. J. P. Taylor in his *English History 1914-1945*. It was far from being either, although casualties, particularly among the five thousand Canadian troops whose first battle experience this was, were far heavier than had been foreseen and the damage to German port installations smaller.

The raid, bigger and of longer duration than any previously undertaken, was from the beginning planned as a reconnaissance in force, an essential preliminary, it was believed, to a full-scale invasion. It had to simulate to a large degree the conditions of actual invasion. Large land, sea and air forces had to be employed and heavy equipment landed and the assault had to be carried out during the hours of daylight. Heavy casualties were unavoidable. In the event they were far heavier than had been feared and on these grounds the operation is open to the criticism it has received. Of the five thousand Canadian troops employed in the attack, three thousand three hundred an fifty were killed or wounded. An incidental consequence of this was greatly to increase Beaverbrook's antagonism to Mountbatten. The defences of the port were found to be so formidable that it was impossible for tanks when landed to break through and capture the town. The number of sappers sent in to destroy the heavy concrete blocks guarding the end of the narrow

streets leading from the harbour to the town proved insufficient
to do the job and although Commandos sent to silence the
batteries on the flanks succeeded in completely destroying
those on one flank and putting those on the other out of action
for most of the time, the raid regarded as a raid was a failure.

But as a reconnaissance in force—its main purpose—it did
much of what had been intended. Much of the information
brought back was in one sense negative. But it was nevertheless
vital for the future. It caused the previous idea of seeking to
capture a great port and establish an invasion bridgehead by
these means to be abandoned. It was directly as a result of the
Dieppe experience that the Mulberry harbour off the open
beaches of Normandy was conceived. Tactically the raid was a
mine of experience in amphibious training, in battle tactics, and
in the nature of the equipment required. Without it, it is doubtful whether D Day would have been possible at the time it was.

I had, naturally, nothing to do with these military plans.
What I was involved in was the fascinating intellectual exercise
of trying to guess what the German propaganda response to the
raid would be and how we could best meet it. Combined
Operations had by now a substantial Information Division of its
own but Mountbatten had acquired a flattering faith in my
flair in such matters and a somewhat exaggerated confidence in
my influence with Editors. Whenever he was engaged in high-
level planning on the political warfare side of the raid he would,
therefore, ask me to join him and we would engage in a sort of
chess game to decide the German moves and our responses.
Sometimes after an afternoon so engaged I would realize that
under the intellectual stimulation of such an exercise I had
forgotten the human side of the raid altogether, the men who
would be killed or wounded or captured during it, and would
see how easy it might be for generals and staff officers to
become immersed in battles as professional exercises and forget
the torn flesh and shattered bone.

It was clear from the first that the nature of the Dieppe raid
was bound to present the Germans with many propaganda
opportunities. Whether themselves deceived or not they might
very well try to present it as the beginning of invasion, and the
sea, land and air forces to be employed were sufficiently large to
lend credence to this.

The otherwise extremely successful St Nazaire raid had brought many brave French men and women rushing out to take part when the fighting began in the belief that this was the beginning of an invasion. They had subsequently been massacred by the Germans. We did not want to risk that again. Moreover when the Germans recognized, as they were soon bound to do, that despite its size the Dieppe raid was simply a reconnaissance in force they might hope that to present it as an invasion which had been beaten off would bring substantial rewards in depressing British and American morale. And, what was even more important, it might shake Russian confidence in Anglo-American ability to open a second front in the West.

To prevent French resistance fighters from being deceived into showing themselves it was arranged that carefully devised instructions to the French underground should be broadcast by the B.B.C. immediately I passed to them a signal that the first troops had gone in. To deal with world reactions alternative communiqués were prepared in advance for issue as soon as the signal that the raid had started was received and we had the first flash as to how it was going, and I drafted a confidential letter to be sent out at the same time telling Editors and bureau heads of the purpose of the raid and asking them to use German reports with caution.

The raid began on the night of 18–19 August 1942 and as a result of these advance arrangements by midnight of the latter day we were able to issue a one-thousand-word communiqué giving an intelligible picture of what was happening and the losses incurred. This was in addition to a shorter first communiqué and a long guidance letter and was rapidly followed by the issue of pooled dispatches brought back by fast motor craft from a small group of war correspondents with the attacking forces. These included a man I had picked as a war correspondent when I was still Editor of the *Herald* and who was later killed during the fighting in Italy, A. B. Austin, who went in with the Commandos under Lord Lovat.

When the raid ended and the survivors returned I spent a day with Mountbatten listening to reports from all unit commanders, including the commander of a detachment of American rangers. I was the only civilian present. At the conclusion of this sombre yet by no means disheartening recital I drafted a further long communiqué and another guidance letter giving the un-varnished background as fully as possible.

In all this we were breaking new ground in war-reporting and learning a good deal about news coverage in battle which was to be very useful on D Day. We also managed to keep ahead of German propaganda which changed its story in mid-flight and at one time was running mutually contradictory versions.

With the lessons of Dieppe now to hand, Lt.-General Sir F. E. Morgan was appointed at the Casablanca Conference as Chief of Staff to the Supreme Allied Commander, not yet named, and instructed to draw up preliminary invasion plans. Morgan, an able and a witty soldier, turned the initials of his title into COSSAC, which seemed appropriate in the light of the con-stantly mounting Russian demands for a second front. It was under this code name that the plans he and his staff drew up went forward to the Quebec Conference.

He asked me to meet him and I was happy to find him well aware of the need to plan for massive news coverage of the invasion. Although the Cossac plan was subsequently revised and greatly enlarged as the magnitude of the task became clearer in the light of experience in the Mediterranean campaign, Morgan's intelligent understanding of the requirements of mass communication as a result of our Dieppe raid experiments and of the need to integrate news coverage into the overall plan at an early stage had an important part in making D Day when it came the most massively and successfully reported military enterprise in history.

As the invasion planning moved forward a large part of the Ministry of Information was cleared to house the Public Relations and Press Censorship Divisions of SHAEF under Brigadier-General T. J. Davies so that all operations could be co-ordinated. John S. Knight, publisher of the *Chicago Daily News* and the Knight newspaper chain, had previously come to London—somewhat upset when he arrived because it was designated a field of military operations by the Americans and he was not allowed to bring his wife—to act as contact between myself, Admiral Thomson and Byron Price, Director of the American Bureau of Censorship. Together we devised a pre-D-Day code of censorship acceptable to both American and British newspapers.

There were by now upwards of three hundred American newspaper correspondents in London. To service them the great hall of the Senate House was turned into a map room for military briefings. Those correspondents, both British and American, press and radio, accredited to the invasion forces were sent on special courses of instruction and warned to tell no one where they were going. David Sarnoff, head of the Radio Corporation of America, flew in with the rank of Colonel, later upgraded to General. He and I, with representatives of SHAEF, and the Chief of my News Division, Jack Brabner, who had formerly been Director of Information at the Post Office, planned how the news of the invasion could be sent out to the world at the fastest speed.

We reckoned we would have to handle more words in less time than ever before in the history of the world. It was impossible to hope for firm radio links, until permanent bases had been established, and until then we arranged that the SHAEF Communications Division would lay on a service of speedboats from the beaches across the Channel to be met by dispatch riders who would rush the bags of copy to the Ministry for censorship and distribution. To move copy out smoothly Brabner was to get half-hourly reports from all cable companies and switch copy from one to another as needed. We were prepared, we thought, for every emergency.

I had already met General Eisenhower and after initial disappointment that the man put in charge of so vast a military operation should appear so very ordinary—just a nice guy from Kansas with a sackful of goodwill but little panache—I learnt to respect his infinite capacity for reconciling potentially disruptive temperaments and convictions.

So far as the British were concerned he had begun with the enormous disadvantage that they felt he had been foisted on them over the heads of far better and more experienced British generals, simply because he was American. We would have accepted Marshall. He was already a great name. But who, until the North African landings and the Mediterranean campaign in which he had admittedly acquitted himself well, had ever heard of Eisenhower?

That these criticisms were gradually dispersed was not due to any display of military genius on Eisenhower's part. Even if he had any such genius, which in the strict sense is doubtful, he never had any opportunity to display it as a field commander. He had had no chance to show himself one of the great captains and it seems unlikely he would have proved so even if the opportunity had been his. But it soon became clear, even to those such as myself caught up only on the periphery of military affairs, that what he possessed was, in the job he had been called to do, more important than battle experience, of which there was plenty about anyway. What he had was an infinite capacity to be a good chairman. His performance as such was superb. If he had a fault it was, perhaps, that he was almost too ready to listen to his advisers—and had too many. But he had a remarkable capacity not only for growing in stature with responsibility, but for inducing an increase in stature in those around him.

Some years after the war Marshal of the R.A.F. Lord Tedder said to me when we were both Governors of the B.B.C. that Eisenhower made the people around him bigger, but Churchill made them smaller. Tedder had always found Churchill difficult and did not much like him, so that he may have been biased. But I have no doubt that he was right about Eisenhower. He remained friendly and unassuming in a situation which would have turned many men's heads. This might have been a liability if he had been a field commander. Field commanders need, like Montgomery or Bradley or Patton, to seem a little larger than life to their troops. Flamboyance does not come amiss. But as Supreme Commander, tied for a large part of his time to the conference table, committed to getting on with many divergent characters and to persuading rather than demanding, this lack of pretension was supremely important. It engendered loyalty, affection and respect on a remarkable scale. I certainly felt it myself and was much touched when at the end of the war I was awarded the American Medal of Freedom on Eisenhower's recommendation.

Eisenhower had an impressive solidity. He also had, what from my point of view was no less important, a genuine belief in the importance of getting news to the people. This was not in any way linked with a wish for personal publicity but came from a straightforward, one might almost say small-town, conviction that ordinary people ought to be told about things.

On 3 June I was warned to expect D Day the next morning,

but later that day was notified that there had been a post-
ponement for at least twenty-four hours, because of weather. I
saw Admiral Thomson and although we had both been sleeping
in our offices for some nights we agreed we would both go home
so as to reduce the expectations of the newspaper men waiting
around in the building. It seemed likely, we thought, to be a
peaceful night. We did not know that what was potentially the
most serious—although accidental—censorship crisis of the
whole war was about to break.

Shortly before midnight the Admiral rang me in great agita-
tion to inform me that he had just received from the Duty
Assistant Director of Censorship the astounding news that a
cable flash had gone out from the London Bureau of the
Associated Press of America announcing that allied troops had
landed in France. The message had been cancelled within
seconds, but many radio programmes in both the United
States and South America had carried it before the cancellation
and it seemed certain that German monitoring services must
have picked it up.

Next morning Robert Bunnelle, Chief of the A.P. London
Bureau, and his office manager met Admiral Thomson and
myself in my office. The news of what had happened had
already been communicated to 10 Downing Street and SHAEF
Headquarters. There were no recriminations from General
Eisenhower—only a message that SHAEF would like to know
the result of my inquiry but had confidence it was not our fault.
I was grateful for this but very much aware of the incalculable
damage that might have been done and conscious that in the
final resort it was my responsibility. How could it have happened, Thomson and I asked ourselves.

Bunnelle brought the answer with him. The explanation was
very human, although not one that any of us would have
conceived possible. It was due to the keenness of a girl operator
at the A.P. office. Although the wire services had no knowledge
of when D Day would actually be they were, of course, well
aware that invasion was imminent. Their correspondents with
the first wave of the invading forces had been alerted to stand
by and their Bureau heads had joined Sarnoff, Brabner and
myself in plans for moving copy rapidly after the invasion
forces landed.

To news agencies seconds are vital and all of them had instructed their keyboard operators to rehearse so that there should be no delay when the first news flash came. That afternoon during a news lull one of the keyboard operators at A.P., a young girl from Streatham, filled in time by practising the news flash she was hoping to be the first to send, and send, perhaps, if her fingers were nimble enough, a second or so before any other agency got the news out, thus giving the A.P. a world exclusive. 'Urgent Press Associated NYK. Flash,' she tapped. 'Eisenhower's Headquarters announce allied landing.' Her machine was, of course, disconnected from the transmitter but just as she finished her first practice message she was handed a Russian communiqué that had just arrived and told, 'This is important. Get it out quick.' In the excitement she fed the end of the tape into the transmitting machine without remembering to tear off her practice invasion message and as she connected it up and began to tap out the Russian communiqué the invasion flash went out with it. It was spotted at Western Union, the Cable Company over whose lines the message was being transmitted, when an operator saw that it did not carry the letters P.B.C. (Passed by censor) and was also incorrectly numbered. He at once tapped out a cancellation, 'Bust that flash . . . bust that flash . . . bust that flash.' A second or two later Associated Press itself discovered what had happened and sent out its own cancellation. 'Bust Eisenhower flash . . . bust Eisenhower flash.' But it was too late. The false news had already reached a number of radio stations who broke into programmes to broadcast it. We could scarcely believe that the Germans would not be alerted by it to the imminence of invasion.

But they were not. We found out later that when the monitored message was passed to German Intelligence they dismissed it as an over-subtle attempt at nerve warfare. Its true meaning, they decided, was that the invasion would not be for some time. Far from jeopardizing the landings which took place at dawn on 6 June, two days later, the little girl from Streatham, who had been taken home in a state of complete collapse when she realized what she had done, had helped to mislead the enemy.

CHAPTER II

San Francisco the Golden

I was in San Francisco when the European war ended. That city was curiously unmoved by the event, its eyes on the Pacific. We English celebrated quietly at the Top of the Mark and felt a long way from home.

In his autobiography Kingsley Martin remarked that he would always remember the San Francisco Conference as one of the most extraordinary events of his life. The adjective is the right one—especially perhaps for those who like Kingsley and I had flown straight from blacked-out, rationed London into a fantastic world of glitter and light and extravagant parties and food and drink and constantly spiralling talk. It is the only time in my life that I have seen—at a reception in the Palace Hotel—a living chain of waiters passing bottles of champagne from hand to hand for hour upon hour. I had just been introduced to Orson Welles, partly for the reason that we had both been told we looked like each other and wanted to compare faces. We stood talking by a fountain banked by a mass of vivid red flowers and every now and then as the chain of champagne bottles moved past us Welles would lean forward and pluck one from a waiter's hand and say, 'Ours, I think, George', and we would deposit our empty bottle in the fountain and fill our glasses to the brim from a new one. I drank with particular pleasure because not long before I had expected that at this time I would be in a cellar deep below London.

Some months earlier I had been summoned to a most secret meeting by Sir Findlater Stewart who had been seconded from the India Office, where he was permanent head, for highly confidential security duties. It was the first of several such meetings at which we examined intelligence reports from agents in Germany and occupied Europe, all of which pointed to the development of a new weapon of terrifying proportions. These first reports, later confirmed by aerial reconnaissance photographs indicating that experiments were being carried out at Peenemünde in the Baltic, suggested that what was being developed was a pilotless winged bomb with some form of jet propulsion. Later reports suggested that these flying bombs might carry an explosive charge of twelve tons and that an even more devastating rocket missile was also being developed. Looking back these reported missiles may seem relatively ineffective harbingers of what science can do for war. But when we first heard of them they seemed as though they would bring to our lives a new dimension of destruction greater than anything previously imagined. Our meetings were grim and sombre, for unless a bombing raid on the Peenemünde installations could delay completion of these new missiles until the European invasion had been mounted and there was a chance of over-running the sites there seemed a distinct possibility that London might be flattened to the ground.

One of the first acts of the Churchill administration had been to tear up plans for Government withdrawal from London but now the prospect had to be considered that if these new weapons proved as devastating as intelligence reports suggested, the War Cabinet and the chief Departments of State might be compelled to move from the capital in order to carry on the war efficiently. It was agreed that even if this should happen an attempt would have to be made to maintain London, with its great web of cable and wireless communications, as a news centre. I was nominated for the somewhat chilly honour of running it.

We chose a cellar far below the Senate House and began linking it with cable and radio outlets and reinforcing and equipping it to house Admiral Thomson and myself with a small staff and such British, American and overseas correspondents as wished to continue working from there while a deserted London crashed above us. Here, it was hoped, we would be able to remain, sending out news from London until such time as the Allied forces in Europe could fight their way to the missile bases and destroy them. It was, as I remarked, a claustrophobic prospect for those of us who had not had Admiral Thomson's advantage of having spent most of his early life in submarines. In the event our redoubt deep beneath London remained unoccupied. The flying bombs and rockets came but the speed of the Allied advance forced the Germans to use them before they had been brought to their full potential.

I was at Essex Court with Jess when the first batch of flying bombs came. They came mixed in with ordinary piloted bombers and the first to fall, with flames streaming out of its tail, looked like a bomber that had been shot down. I guessed otherwise but was not free to tell even Jess what I suspected.

It was a relief to find the next morning that none of these flying bombs had any extraordinary explosive power but carried charges estimated only at between one and two tons instead of the twelve originally feared. Moreover they were imprecise and vulnerable missiles. Although eight thousand were launched in eighty days of practically continuous bombardment of London, only two thousand three hundred got through. The rest were either shot down by our defences or went wildly off target. By the time the Allied forces in Normandy over-ran and destroyed the last of their firing-sites only about 9 per cent were getting to target.

The rockets began on 8 September just as the flying bombs ended. They came while it was still daylight out of a clear sky—one on Chiswick, one on Epping Forest. But they, too, proved far less dangerous than had been expected. Because of the rapidity of the Allied advance they were still only at the experimental stage when they were first tried and were at the very limit of their range, which was about 220 miles. Almost one thousand were fired in all but only about half of these reached London and, like the flying bombs, they were a good deal smaller than had been expected. They did serious damage in the East End but there was no panic and no need at any time to consider a mass exodus. As a result I had the pleasure of celebrating the defeat of Germany in a cocktail bar looking across San Francisco Bay instead of from a cellar in Bloomsbury.

It is pleasant to be praised for doing what comes naturally

but I still remain surprised at the eulogy the British information team received in San Francisco.

'This,' wrote Erwin D. Canham in the normally tight-lipped *Christian Science Monitor,* 'is an open and only slightly abashed tribute to the British Information Services and the other methods by which Britain's position is being made clear to the world press here . . . it is a beautiful job to watch.' He went on to describe at length what he called 'the effortless perfection of the Williams system'. At this distance of time I can even forgive the description of myself as 'a chunky youngish fellow who stuffs the pockets of his ill-pressed clothes with papers and documents, rumples his hair and looks somewhere between Winnie-the-Pooh and an American courthouse reporter.' Canham, after all, did go on: 'In action he's a darb.'

Part of the reason for this praise was the contrast with other wartime conferences. Over all previous gatherings a pall of secrecy had hung—some of it inevitable because of the exigencies of war, some of it merely official habit. At Teheran, Casablanca and Yalta no press were allowed. When Roosevelt and Churchill met at Quebec, Steve Early and Robin Cruickshank, who were looking after the press, were reduced to feeding the hundreds of assembled newspapermen with scraps about what Mrs Roosevelt and Mrs Churchill were wearing or what Churchill had had for breakfast. At Cairo reporters were driven to fury by press releases about people sitting under palm trees.

It was obvious that this pattern of secrecy could not be extended to the San Francisco Conference. If we were engaged, as we were supposed to be, in devising a better, more democratic framework for international society in the post-war world, then one of the things the statesmen at San Francisco must accept was the right of the press to be told about it. As at least fifteen hundred reporters from fifty nations were expected—actually over two thousand turned up—there would be a lot of people to tell.

With Sir Alexander Cadogan, Permanent Head of the Foreign Office, and a small group of Foreign Office and legal experts, I flew off in the middle of April to get ready for the conference. We crossed the Atlantic in a converted Liberator, lying on the floor at the take-off to spread the load. We flew first to the

Azores, where the coloured houses shimmered in the hot sun and then after a night's pause to Gander in Newfoundland, on the very edge of frozen desolation. Here we were icebound for the best part of a day before flying on to Washington. Somewhere across the Atlantic one of the escape-hatches at the side of the plane blew open, rocking the plane with a rush of cold wind. Those of us who were awake jumped to our feet to hold the hatch in place until the flight engineer mended it, remembering uneasily that there had recently been a rather excessive number of crashed Liberators on long flights. However, Sir Alexander Cadogan, who had been in dignified slumber, his rolled umbrella by his side, maintained, I was glad to see, a correct Foreign Office calm. He stirred slightly, summoned his secretary to his side, observed crisply, 'there seems to be a draught. Tell someone to see to it', and once more composed himself decorously for rest.

Later when we came in over Washington at three o'clock in the morning he unrolled his already tightly rolled umbrella, rolled it still more tightly, smoothed a crease with his fingers, snapped the elastic band into position and hung it carefully on his arm, ready to step on to American soil with the composure to be expected of a British diplomat, whatever dark hour of the morning the exigencies of weather and air travel should compel him to arrive in a foreign capital.

Cadogan seemed to me at that time the very picture of an official man, indeed almost a caricature of one: cautious, reserved, incomparably proper, invariably discreet. Several years later, however, he wrote to me regarding a book I had written about Chamberlain, Baldwin, Halifax and others called *A Pattern of Rulers* which he had enjoyed, and during our correspondence I suggested that he ought to publish his memoirs —he had after all been head of the Foreign Office at the time of Munich, had been at all the great wartime conferences and had been Britain's first permanent representative at the United Nations. He replied engagingly that although he had committed to paper a number of memories he feared the greater number of them were 'rather personal and even flippant' and that after 'a long service burrowing into official archives' he felt too lazy to undertake the task of research required for a serious record. Reading this I could not help but wonder what had lain behind that discreet official exterior all these years. One should never, I thought, judge a man by his professional uniform.

We stayed in Washington for three days. It was a city still in mourning, as London had been when we left, for President Roosevelt. Even now the shock of his death comes back with an impact almost as fresh as when the news was first flashed to us in London. It seemed then almost incomprehensible and insupportable, although incomprehensible it should not have been, for it had been plain for some time, and especially at Yalta, that he was very ill. Indeed, so distressing was his appearance at the Yalta Conference that Bracken, Radcliffe and I had deliberately suppressed several photographs, feeling that to issue them might cause too great public anxiety. Despite this the news when it came was utterly devastating. One of the twin pillars on which victory and perhaps the future civilization had seemed to depend was fallen.

In Washington, the death of the President had cast a deep gloom over the coming United Nations conference, deflating optimism. No one as yet had anything very revealing to say about Truman. He was, I was told, a little guy from Missouri, tough as old boots, who had stayed honest despite the Pendergast machine, which said a good deal for his character. But as a world statesman, why, who could tell?

I saw several old newspaper friends and took a peek at Truman from the back of a press conference. A fighting cock sparrow of a man, I thought at first sight, a more expansive Attlee. Afterwards I flew with Cadogan and the others to San Francisco. We came down to refuel at Denver, Colorado, and were entertained by the U.S. Air Force. The smiling black waitress who served us asked where we came from and I told her London, England. 'Ah,' she said, flashing teeth, 'we'se all neighbours now.' It seemed a good augury for the conference. What followed was perhaps a more correct one. After lunch and ceremonial speeches we trooped on board our plane to salutes and the music of a military band and then after a long wait clambered out again. A defect had developed in the port engine.

I have always thought it a great pity that San Francisco was not chosen as the permanent home of the United Nations. I know of no place in the world better suited to promote optimism.

Despite the famous fog, which is not of a kind to incommode a Londoner or even force itself on his notice, San Francisco has a climate in which one can work and enjoy oneself until two or three o'clock in the morning and arise fresh and blooming for another day at seven or eight. Its citizens are among the most charming and hospitable in the world, its restaurants and bars among the most varied and engaging, vistas of the bay break round every corner as one makes one's way up and down the steep streets of Telegraph Hill or Nob Hill or any other of the seven hills on which the city dwells.

All the apparatus of optimism surrounded us as we went to the first plenary session at the Opera House. The doomed Alger Hiss, but we knew nothing of his doom then, sat on the platform as Secretary-General of the Conference, so much the clean-limbed, clear-eyed, earnest young American that it was almost painful to look at him, his head, it seemed, full of the best American thoughts, his manners implacably Ivy League. We took our seats and the proud platitudes poured over our heads from all the statesmen who had come to build the world anew. It was all too good to be true.

And so, of course, it turned out to be. When he was Foreign Secretary Ernest Bevin once said to me that he found it possible to get along with Stalin, who indeed in his friendlier moments had some of Bevin's own rough geniality, but that he could not abide Molotov. 'There's nothing there to warm yourself with,' he said. 'He laughs with his lips, never his eyes,' Attlee said.

In the opening days of San Francisco Molotov gave every indication of amiability. In the lobby of the St Francis where the Russian delegation was housed crowds of young and middle-aged women waited all day long just to see him. He would come through the crowds, his guards making a flying wedge around him, and bow politely. Sometimes he would even lift his hand in salute. He learnt 'O.K.' from Senator Vandenberg and used it profusely. It seemed quite possible to believe that the Soviet might have decided that with German power broken more was to be gained from co-operation with America and Britain—particularly, of course, America—than conflict.

This confidence was shattered by the affair of the sixteen Poles. At Yalta Roosevelt and Churchill had agreed, reluctantly, but there was not much else they could do, that the Soviet-nominated Government in Poland should be accepted as the basis of a new provisional government. But it had also been agreed that pending an election this Government should be widened to include members of the Polish Underground and the free Poles in London, and that their representatives should be given safe passage to Moscow to open discussions to this end.

This was a matter on which both America and Britain placed great importance.

We had news that the members of the Polish delegation had set off and that General Okulicki, their leader, had had a preliminary meeting with a Soviet representative in the suburbs of Warsaw, after which the other leaders representing all the major Polish political groups had joined him for the journey to Moscow. After that silence fell. Day after day in San Francisco Stettinius, the U.S. Secretary of State, and Eden pressed Molotov for information. None came until the evening of 4 May.

On that evening the British delegation gave a cocktail party in the Mark Hopkins Hotel. It was, of course, crowded. It happened that I was talking to Eden and Stettinius when Molotov, glass in hand, his interpreter as always at his shoulder, bodyguards close behind, pushed his way towards us. He bowed to Eden and congratulated him on the excellence of his party. Then with, so far as I could judge, no change in tone he turned slightly to include Stettinius in his remarks and said, 'By the way, those Poles you are interested in. We have arrested them.' Without giving time for a reply he moved away. The first shot in the cold war had been fired.

At this stage comedy took over. Stettinius had fixed a dinner party for the leaders of the Chinese delegation which for reasons obscure to the rest of us was being much cosseted by the U.S. in his suite at the Fairmont Hotel after the British reception. But he and Eden both agreed that a formal talk with Molotov could not wait until the morning and their secretaries were sent off to try to arrange a meeting with him before dinner. Meanwhile, Eden, his eye on his watch and his charm at full force, carried on with his duties as host, giving an excellent performance, as Stettinius did also, of a diplomat without a care in the world. I moved away to find if any whisper of the fate of the Poles had reached the press.

Frederick Kuh who, in San Francisco as in London, was never off duty, had, I learned, been looking for me, which seemed suggestive. When we met he told me that he had heard the Russians might be making a statement the next day which would have something to do with the missing Poles. Would the British be saying anything? I went back to the Mark Hopkins to find Eden who was just on his way to the Fairmont to meet Stettinius and Molotov and told him what I had heard. He asked me to go with him and wait, so I cancelled a dinner date and went over.

In those days the Chinese were still noted for their courtesy; it was, indeed, their only weapon. They had arrived on time and were now sitting with exemplary patience outside the room where Molotov, Stettinius and Eden were locked in a battle that seemed even more prolonged than I had expected. Time dragged on. At 9.30 a platoon of waiters arrived, wheeling trolleys loaded with food. The Chinese rose politely. But at the door the waiters were ordered away and the trolleys wheeled back. The Chinese sat down again. At 10.15 the waiters and the trolleys arrived once more. Again the Chinese stood up politely. Again the food trolleys were waved away and again the Chinese sat down. At 11.10 the door opened and Molotov, his interpreter one step behind him, stalked out looking grim. The door closed behind him. Two square men rose and followed them. The door remained closed. The Chinese sat down again. At last it opened and as the Chinese rose once more out came Stettinius, both hands outstretched his smile wide to welcome his dinner guests. It was only three hours or so late and the Chinese in their polite oriental way seemed to express by their bows and smiles their belief that time had no meaning.

'I'm staying on to help Ed with his Chinese,' Eden said. 'Then we're going to draft something. Will you be back in an hour?' Pierson Dixon, Eden's Principal Private Secretary (later British Permanent Representative at the U.N. and subsequently Ambassador in Paris) and I went down to the coffee room to get something to eat: it seemed appropriate that the elevator girls should be Chinese, although dressed for some reason like members of a Persian harem.

We wound up about three-thirty in the morning in Stettinius's bedroom. He had a group of advisers with him including, as I remember, Archibald MacLeish, whom Roosevelt had made an Assistant Secretary of State, and Adlai Stevenson, who was some sort of Personal Assistant. It had become clear more than an hour earlier that Stettinius was in no mood to make up his mind. It may have been the time difference between San Francisco and Washington that was against him but he clearly did not wish to commit himself to anything, although so far from being conciliatory Molotov had bluntly repeated that the Poles were in prison and would there remain and that the case against them would be made known when—not if—they were found guilty.

I remembered an American newspaperman saying to me after Roosevelt died that Stettinius was now a yes man with no one to say yes to. Tonight he was saying neither yes nor no. Adlai Stevenson and I kept producing drafts but Stettinius would have none of them.

'Perhaps,' he said finally, 'we should just say that we are anxious.' 'Perhaps,' said Eden, losing his temper, 'we should just say we are bloody angry.'

Possibly it would have been better if we had. But, of course, we did not. Instead Stettinius took off his tie and lay on the bed and said, 'I'm going to sleep. If you want to issue something do it on your own.' Eden apologized for losing his temper: 'I don't know how our friends put up with us, do you, Francis?' he said, which did not seem to me to call for a reply, and we said goodnight and went down in the elevator with one of the Chinese girls from the Persian harem and walked across to the Mark Hopkins, where Dixon and I drafted a short British communiqué which Eden approved.

There were to be other shocks at San Francisco. But this first one was the most important because it was the first. That the Russians should want friendly governments on their borders was natural. Perhaps their suspicion of some of the Poles was natural too. But it was the manner of the break that was ominous. The deliberate affront. The calculated rudeness. From this the conference never quite recovered.

If San Francisco had been a less exhilarating city or there had not been more than two thousand press and radio men to interpret every raised eyebrow we would perhaps have shown our depression more. But we were all now a part of a gigantic spectacular to which San Francisco was the backdrop. By a trick of history, or perhaps just of climate, San Francisco seemed at this time a city bathed in light. If one climbed to the top of Telegraph Hill and looked over the roofs of the painted houses to Oakland and Berkeley six miles away across the water and then, farther to the right, to the delicate thread of the Golden Gate Bridge against the vastness of the Pacific, the whole scene seemed composed of light, a world made over by an enchanting luminosity. As evening fell and the riding lights of the ships at anchor along the wharves were reflected with unnatural brilliance in the dark water they seemed like footlights to a vast stage soon to be lit by other lights everywhere, the lights along the bridges and in the tall buildings, the flashing lights of the advertising signs spelling perpetual messages of hope and avarice, and always the lights of the automobiles flowing in perpetual rivers of radiance.

The life of the city never stopped. Police cars, sirens going, raced up and down the precipitous streets conducting the great and important about their own or the world's business. The cable cars clanged romantically up the hills, and street cars whose direction indicators beckoned one austerely to 'The Ocean' glided towards the Pacific. Everywhere the diplomats, the journalists, the radio men, the newsreel crews, the special writers, the officials, the experts, the cipher clerks, the pretty girl typists, moved phrenetically about the city. The tide of movement never stopped. At the Top of the Mark the hum of conversation was like the beating of the wind against a tall tower. In the Happy Valley Bar at the Palace Hotel it was like the surf breaking ceaselessly on the Pacific shore. In hotel bedrooms that had been turned into annexes of foreign ministries harassed young men drafted telegrams to Washington or London or Moscow, asking whether 'shall' in paragraph (3) Clause (E) second draft could be amended to 'will', with a possibility that it might be necessary to compromise on 'should' when the draft went to the full committee and telegraph instructions, please, by return. At the William Tell Hotel in Clay Street the musicians in their shirt sleeves tuned up as the sailors and their girls got ready to dance, and in the private booths of tea-shops in Chinatown starry-eyed lovers and sedate Chinese families drank out of painted cups. The restaurants were always crowded: Vanessi's, Amelio's, Solaris, Julius' Castle, the Omar Khayyam, the Blue Fox and a score or so more, and at Fisherman's Wharf men and women talked and laughed in every tongue as they ate cracked crab or abalone steak and looked at the boats bobbing up and down in the harbour.

And always there was news—news true, news rumoured, news to chase down or to release, news to interpret or explain. There seemed hardly an hour of the day or night when someone did not want to cable something.

Yet although the conference had its fantasies and its longueurs on the whole it can, I think, be said to have gone well enough. If it exposed more major problems than it solved, that was only to be expected. Despite the magnificence of the production those in the star roles were understudies, not principals, and since the principals in Washington, Moscow and London could not agree it was not to be expected that the understudies would be in a position to do more than put a gloss on disagreement. Molotov could decide on nothing without first clearing with Stalin. Stalin's replies took a long time and were usually negative when they did arrive so that one got used to the experience of seeming to make progress only to have it sharply reversed a meeting or two later. Stettinius spent much of his time looking over his shoulder, head cocked on one side listening for a master's voice.

Eden, although professionally adroit—every inch, indeed, a Foreign Office official—and determined to show himself a Prince Charming, suffered from Churchill's dislike for much that the United Nations was concerning itself with, and also, one suspected, from Churchill's inclination to remind him at suitable intervals that heirs apparent should not give themselves airs. There would be tempestuous scenes in the suite high up in the Mark Hopkins when peremptory cables arrived. Eden would stamp about the room proclaiming to Dixon and myself and whoever else happened to be there that he had had enough. This time the old man had gone too far. He would show him he could not be treated like a naughty schoolboy. He would send him a rocket. But in the end the rocket would always turn out to be a telegram beginning, 'You are, of course, quite right, Prime Minister.'

I developed an affection for Eden. Even his vanity, which was extreme, had a little-boy-lost quality about it that was touching. Perhaps because I was not a member of his personal staff, I was spared his worst outbursts of temperament. Indeed, for the most part he treated me with a courtesy all the more remarkable since we usually met before breakfast, again in the middle of the day and last thing at night. Crowds, like those who attended Molotov's path but younger in age, would gather to catch a glimpse of him wherever he went and comment favourably on his appearance. On one occasion when he gave an entirely incorrect interpretation of the troublesome Big Power veto at a press conference we were saved from the embarrassment of issuing a verbatim record because the young American stenographers who had been engaged to do the report became so lost in wide-eyed admiration of his manners and appearance that they forgot to take it down. This explanation brought derisive comments about slick British cover-ups from American newspapermen. But it was absolutely true.

Often at our midnight meetings Eden would wear the cloak of a weary Titan and would tell me how much he longed for a rest from foreign affairs—if only there were someone else capable of taking his place. 'But there isn't anyone,' he would say with a sigh and would try to probe me as to whom I thought would become Foreign Secretary in the dreadful event of Labour winning the next election.

'In some ways a period of Labour in office might not be a bad thing,' he would say handsomely. 'If only there were someone one could be happy about leaving all this to. But I don't see anyone. Do you?' When I would smile but not reply he would say, 'But then I mustn't ask you, must I? It isn't fair.' He made it plain in the nicest way that he could well understand such talk to be embarrassing to a Labour supporter like myself since he could not but feel that anyone who had had the good fortune to know him, as I had, must be as convinced as he was himself of his indispensability. He had, in fact, superb professional skill as a diplomat and a great talent for finding formulae to disguise disagreements. 'If only there were more strength behind the charm,' I wrote later in a book called *Press*,

Parliament and People, 'what a great Foreign Secretary he would be.' It is perhaps characteristic of him that when we met shortly after this book came out—we were in the wash-room at 10 Downing Street together, I remember—he thanked me for being so kind to him.

Looking back I cannot think we did too badly at San Francisco. The Charter of the United Nations, although scarcely a formula for a peaceful world—but then there is no such formula—has proved more durable than that of the League of Nations. The social, economic, health and educational instruments deriving from it have been of much practical value. The Big Power veto in the Security Council was much criticized at the time and has been since. But it was quite impractical to imagine that an instrument could be devised in which small powers would have equality with great or in which the realities of power would be transferred to a world government.

It is logically easy to make a case against the existence of sovereign states, as the advocates of Federal Union have done, and as a fortunate friend of mine, Emery Reves, did when he made a fortune out of a silly, sincere book—now almost totally forgotten—called *The Anatomy of Peace,* which swept the world just after the war with editions in seventeen countries. Such propositions satisfy a profound human longing for simple solutions but the most that seems to be within the grasp of practical politics for as long ahead as one can see is an international system with sufficient checks and balances and sufficient mechanisms of discussion and delay to make it less likely that national systems will come into violent collision with each other. This was what the Charter of the United Nations set out to do and on the whole it has not done it too badly so far.

By the time the Charter was signed I had left San Francisco. The Germans had surrendered on Luneberg Heath. The great wartime Coalition was over. An early election was ahead. In such circumstances I had no desire to stay on at San Francisco or the Ministry of Information, no wish to remain a Civil Servant in any capacity whatever.

I was tired of the official life. But neither did I wish to become a politician, although when I got home it was to find Jess snowed under with letters asking me to stand as a Labour candidate. I refused twenty-six in all—any one of which I would, to judge by the election results, have won. But although I had boastfully told a press conference in New York, where everyone assumed I was going back to fight, that I was confident I could beat any Conservative who stood against me, that was merely in the general interests of political morale. I had never any intention of trying to get into Parliament.

I had no ambition to be a politician. I did not want power. Although I respected many public men I knew, I had no wish to emulate them. I wanted to be a private person. Above all I wanted to write. Already I had spent too much of my life concerned with public matters. I had been too successful too soon. I had enjoyed being a financial editor, but had as a result of it been trapped too early into being an Editor. I had been lucky in war in finding a pleasant and useful outlet for my talents. But my life had for a long time now been running in channels very different from those I had planned for myself as a young man. What I wanted was time to think, to be no longer a person of action and decision but a contemplative man. It seemed to me that there could be no life happier than that of sitting in front of a piece of white paper and finding the right words to say what one wanted to say. Like my father I would be my own master even if I could not make money at it.

I had, of course, to earn a living. But neither Jess nor I had ever much bothered our heads about money—not perhaps as much as we should have done. We had a feeling that if you trusted fortune it would not fail you and that no fate was so bad as to allow oneself to be enslaved by money. My first novel, *No Man Is an Island*, had just been published and although it had not made as much money as we hoped, it had made some. It had had a number of favourable reviews—although Philip Toynbee in the *New Statesman* had delivered a formidable blast against it on the grounds that 'well-known journalists and publicists' had no right to write novels, which should be left to those dedicated to such things from youth.

I intended to write another all the same and meanwhile had agreed to write a book about the Ministry of Information and the relations between Governments and newspapers which I was to call *Press, Parliament and People*. I thought I was well enough known in Fleet Street to sell such articles as I felt like writing. To be free was the thing. That should be my course from now on. I did not foresee how strong would be the pull of old loyalties or how difficult it would be not to want to shout Ha! Ha! among the trumpets when the smell of battle and the thunder of the captains drew near.

CHAPTER 12

At 10 Downing Street

National leaders who have led their countries to victory can commonly expect public applause and gratitude. Churchill received both. But not enough to compensate for his leadership of the Conservative Party. Its pre-war record was an albatross too heavy for him.

Political leaders who have led their party to unexpected success can usually expect to be immune from attack. Not so Attlee. No sooner were the 1945 election results announced than he found himself confronted with an extraordinary demand that he should step down.

When Ernest Bevin heard of this he fell into a great rage. From being one of Attlee's most persistent critics he had become, as he got to know him better during the war, one of his warmest supporters—just as I had. Also he had taken to reading political biographies and had conceived a great respect for Campbell-Bannerman, who had led the Liberals to victory in 1906 and presided thereafter with great success over a Cabinet containing many men more popularly esteemed than himself. 'You mark my words, Francis,' he said to me, 'Clem'll do for us what Campbell-Bannerman did for the Liberals.'

Herbert Morrison took a different view. He had never reconciled himself to his defeat for the Party leadership by Attlee in 1935 and wanted a chance to reopen the contest. Cripps was with him. He thought both Attlee and Morrison his intellectual inferiors but he considered Morrison the better politician of the two and the more likely to generate popular enthusiasm. Therefore he backed Morrison. So did Aneurin Bevan. He did not like Morrison but thought the world of Cripps and went along with him. Ellen Wilkinson, the previous year's Chairman of the Labour Party, had been Morrison's Parliamentary Private Secretary at Home Security during the war and worshipped him. She took on the job of organizing an anti-Attlee vote in the Parliamentary Labour Party and was enthusiastically assisted in this by Maurice Webb. Webb, a former parliamentary correspondent of the *Daily Herald*— a job for which I had picked him—knew everyone and had only been narrowly defeated for the post of General Secretary of the Party the previous year when Morgan Phillips won in the third round after trailing behind Webb on the two previous votes.

The constitutional case for challenging Attlee was provided by Harold Laski, that year's Chairman of the Labour Party and Professor of Political Science at the London School of Economics. He argued that under the Party's constitution an election for Leader of the Parliamentary Party was required at the opening of each new Parliament and that it was Attlee's duty when summoned to the Palace to ask for a delay of forty-eight hours until the new Parliamentary Party, which numbered 392 compared with only 154 when Attlee had been elected Leader in 1935, had met and made its choice. Many of the new members were middle-class and professional people straight out of the Services. Laski believed they knew little of Attlee, who had consistently backed out of the limelight during the war, but knew Morrison and Cripps, who had not.

It was an odd combination. Cripps, Bevan, Laski and Ellen Wilkinson were on the left of the party and in the past the Left had looked on Morrison as a right-wing Tammany boss whereas Attlee had been thought of as slightly left of centre. However, Laski had been Attlee's personal assistant at the Cabinet offices for a couple of years during the war and as Attlee rarely took his advice had come to the conclusion that his intellectual capacity was small. He believed Morrison would be more amenable to his influence.

Laski was a curious character. He had long been regarded as one of the leading Socialist intellectuals in Britain, indeed for that matter in the world, and was well known in the United

States where his writings were highly thought of by liberals. He had lectured at Harvard, Yale and Amherst. In India and the embattled colonial territories he was venerated by many active political leaders who had been his students at L.S.E.

He was extremely small in stature, with a large head, and looked all his life like a precocious Jewish schoolboy, but he was a brilliant teacher of the young and a popular lecturer to working-class audiences, whose attention he held by the lucidity and comprehensiveness of his exposition without oratorical flourishes. He had, however, one found out when one got to know him better, one strange and unexpected quirk— he was an almost pathological liar. The lies he told were most often about his relationships with the great and were quite unnecessary for he had a genuinely vast acquaintanceship among the eminent. Despite this he constantly invented stories of his conversations with them, the inventions usually being much less interesting than the reality. Possibly he wanted to boast of his friends without breaking their confidences.

He had a passion for being at the centre of things and was now much excited at the idea of having a hand in the making of a Prime Minister. He had once described me in his own writings as the ordinary man writ large but when I told him that ordinary people in the country would be utterly baffled if he had his way and Attlee refused to form a Government when asked by the King to do so, he refused to listen.

His argument that a new Parliamentary Party must elect its own leader had a specious logic that might have had more success but for two things. One was a miscalculation of the time at the plotters' disposal. They had expected to have at least forty-eight hours to canvass support among new M.P.s after the result of the election was known. Instead Churchill decided to concede victory on the afternoon of 26 July and at once advised the King to send for Attlee. The other and more important factor in the plot's defeat was Attlee's own imperturbability. When Laski wrote to him that it was his duty to refuse the King's invitation until the Parliamentary Party met, he merely replied, 'Dear Laski, I thank you for your letter, contents of which have been noted.' And when Morrison informed him at an informal meeting at Transport House when the outcome of the election already seemed plain that he could not agree to serve under him because the Party might want him as Leader instead he merely nodded.

'If you're invited by the King to form a Government,' he said to me later, 'you don't say you can't give an answer for forty-eight hours. You accept the Commission and you either bring it off successfully or you don't, and if you don't you go back and say you can't and advise the King to send for someone else. It used to happen often in the nineteenth century. Queen Victoria couldn't stand Gladstone so she'd send for Granville or Hartington and they'd have to come back and tell her they couldn't manage it. People like Laski who knew all about the theory of politics and nothing about its practice just didn't understand that.'

In the event Attlee received a summons to the Palace as he was having a late tea with his family at the Great Western Hotel, Paddington, and accepted the invitation to form a Government without quibble. Next day he met the Parliamentary Party and when Bevin moved a vote of confidence in the new Prime Minister was given a tumultuous welcome. The plot against him was over.

He bore no ill will against those who had tried to depose him. 'I don't mind these things,' he said to me. It would, of course, have been impossible for him to pass over Morrison who hastily forgot his earlier unwillingness to serve under him and asked for the Foreign Office. This Attlee refused. Instead he invited him to become Lord President of the Council and virtually Deputy Prime Minister. All the other leading plotters were offered seats in the Cabinet, Cripps at the Board of Trade, Aneurin Bevan at the Ministry of Health. Even Ellen Wilkinson, much to her own surprise, was offered a seat in the Cabinet as Minister of Education.

Characteristically Laski expected to be rewarded for his part in the plot with the Ambassadorship in Washington. He wrote to Attlee expressing the hope that 'you will find a way of using me at the Embassy in Washington' and continued, 'I do know America with a quite special intimacy; I have a great many friends all over the country; and I think I could do, not least with ordinary people, the kind of job of interpreting Great Britain to the United States which Bryce did in his day. . . . I know I could do a good job in Washington; and I care for that more than anything else. But at least I want the Beaverbrooks and the Brackens to know that my own party does not regard me as a leper it would not touch. . . .'

As with Laski's earlier letter Attlee noted the contents of this one but took no action. This, however, was much more because of his distrust of Laski's common sense than out of any animosity because of his intrigues.

The attempt to depose Attlee was a factor in his decision to switch Bevin and Dalton and make Bevin Foreign Secretary instead of Chancellor of the Exchequer as he had originally thought. Over a solitary lunch he came to the conclusion that Bevin's suspicion and dislike of Morrison had reached such a pitch as a result of his part in the intrigue that to put them together on the home front with Bevin as Chancellor and Morrison as Lord President of the Council would mean certain trouble. It was this plus his experience at the Potsdam Conference, where he had become quite convinced that there was no chance of a post-war honeymoon with Russia, that decided him that it would be best to send Bevin to the Foreign Office instead of the Treasury. He needed a Foreign Secretary who was tough and who could rely on massive support as Bevin could from the trade unions.

In so far as I still felt myself involved in public affairs, and one does not easily abandon the interests of a lifetime, my own commitment was now, I thought, to journalism, not politics. I remembered a conversation I had had with Cyril Radcliffe when I got back from San Francisco. He had made such a success of being head of a great department and seemed to have enjoyed it so much that I asked him whether he had any thought of going into politics. He answered that his loyalty was to the law and that with the end of the war he felt that there would be more need than ever to restore and sustain the independent values of the law. It was to this that he intended to devote himself. I felt the same about journalism.

We had sold our house at Hinxworth and moved back into Surrey, where we had bought six and a half acres of woodland in Abinger, just across the stream from Holmbury. We intended to build on it as soon as building became possible and meanwhile had taken a small house on a pleasant small estate near the neighbouring village of Peaslake. Here we had friendly and unusual neighbours. On one side were the Greenwoods who were the best sort of 'old-fashioned' Socialists. They had two lively and beautiful daughters. Over the way lived the Wicksteads. Joe Wickstead, who had at one time been a master at Bedales, was a leading authority on the prophetic books and paintings of William Blake and was engaged at this time on a study of the poetic undertones of *The River of Life*. He would dash across to our house at all hours of the day to tell us with high enthusiasm of some new significance he had just discovered. Next door to him was a very pleasant retired police inspector and his wife. Betty and John were still at St Christopher and Jess more and more involved in her clinical work as a child psychologist. I had finished my book, *Press, Parliament and People*, and turned to a novel which had been pushing its way to the front of my mind for some time.

All my plans, however, were shattered by a telegram asking me to go and see Attlee at 10 Downing Street.

Attlee as always came to the point immediately.

'As you know, Francis,' he said, 'I am allergic to the press.' This I did, indeed, know. Unlike later Prime Ministers he took no interest in what they might have to say about him, and although courteous to those journalists he met had no desire to seek out their company and no wish to bribe them with confidences. He took the old-fashioned view that politicians and journalists were likely to do their best work if they were not in each other's pockets.

However, it had been borne upon him that there was bound to be great public interest not only in Britain itself but across the world in the first Socialist Government with power in Britain and that arrangements ought to be made for the press to get the information it needed, and also that the Government itself would need advice on probable public reactions to its policies and what needed to be done by way of public explanation.

'We've already got into a muddle,' he said, 'and we want you to come and get us out.'

I reminded him that I had turned down several invitations to stand for Parliament because I wanted to get on with writing and asked whether it would not be all right for me to recommend someone to him instead. He was always a master of evasive

tactics and ignored this. 'I know you'll arrange things so that
you can come, Francis,' he said, and took me upstairs to
have lunch with Violet Attlee. ('Don't need the lift,' said
Attlee. 'Good thing to have some exercise.') He nodded at each
of the portraits of past Prime Ministers that hung on the walls
as we walked up the stairs. 'He was rather a rum case,' he said
of one, 'Bit of a soundrel,' of another, 'Great man' of a third
and of a fourth, 'I've already lasted longer than him anyway.'

Violet Attlee had the great advantage for a politician's wife
of knowing little about politics and never trying to interfere in
them, although she always accompanied her husband to meetings and listened to his speeches in the House. She surrounded
him with affection and loyalty and was much more sensitive to
attacks on him than he was himself. She and I had always got
on well together.

'I do hope you're going to join Clem,' she said. 'It will be nice
for me having you here. You always make me laugh when I'm
worried.' 'Do you need someone to make you laugh?' I asked.
She made a little gesture. 'It gets on top of me sometimes.
Everyone's being so helpful but I really like doing things for
myself. I suppose I ought to be grateful.' And then she said
something I thought very revealing: 'You know, Francis, it's
the first time in my life with Clem I've ever known financial
security.' I thought this was probably true and an interesting
commentary on the life of the wife of a politician who all his
life had worked to help other people, spending even such small
private money as he inherited on social work in the East End.

For the next two years my life was centred almost enirely
on Downing Street. It was the first time such an appointment
had been made by any Prime Minister and neither Attlee nor I
could at first decide what to call me. We finally chose Adviser on
Public Relations to the Prime Minister, which was not very
good, but served. There were a number of questions in Parliament about the constitutional position which seem odd now that
such an appointment has become accepted procedure, but they
soon died away.

Jess and I tore ourselves from the country and took the top
half of a house in Gordon Square in Bloomsbury. This suited
Jess as well as me because she had accepted an appointment as
Senior Psychologist to Great Ormond Street Hospital for Sick

Children. Each morning I had a talk with Attlee in the Cabinet Room. I saw all Cabinet minutes and papers and all important Foreign Office telegrams and although I did not, of course, attend Cabinet meetings went to such Cabinet committees as I felt would be helpful. It would, I think, have been impossible to have a closer working relationship with anyone than I had with Attlee or to have been given more freedom to deal with things as I thought best.

Ellen Wilkinson would sometimes say at parties, 'You'd better get Francis on your side. He's our *éminence grise.*' But this was an entirely wrong conception of my relationship with the Prime Minister. I was very far from being, or wanting to be, a power behind the throne. Nor could anyone who really knew Attlee conceive of one existing. He was not a man readily subject to influence. He made up his own mind. What he did possess in high degree, however, was a readiness not to interfere with those to whom he had given his confidence. He trusted them to come to right decisions and to know when they ought to ask his advice. In those things in which he thought them more expert than himself he listened to their opinion and usually took it. He was neither a worrier nor an interferer and when he had agreed on something believed in leaving people alone. He would say, 'My father used to say "Only a fool buys a dog and barks himself." Very sensible advice.' He did not think a Prime Minister needed to have a finger in every pie. As the obverse of this if someone did not turn out as good as he hoped, he told them so briskly without subterfuge and dispensed with their services. When John Wilmot was dismissed as Minister of Supply Attlee thanked him for what he had done and said he wanted his resignation. 'I asked him if there was any particular reason,' Wilmot told me, 'thinking he might say something face-saving about Government reconstruction or the possibility of another job later. All he said was, "Don't think you measure up to the job." And that was that.'

I do not think I had a disagreeable word with him all the time I was there and when, as sometimes happened, other Ministers would object to something I had said or done, he would reject their criticism curtly. Even when Bevin, who was his closest intimate among Ministers, complained about some information I had given to lobby correspondents he sent back a crisp memo: 'If your office was doing its job properly Francis would not need to intervene.' We did not usually need to discuss things at length but I think he sometimes liked having someone around without political ambition to whom he could open his mind. He seemed to take it for granted that he and I thought the same way and left it to me to say what I thought necessary as the Government's chief spokesman to the world press.

It was, of course, a great advantage to me that most of the Cabinet were old friends of mine. I was already well aware of some of the strains and tensions that existed—as they exist in all Cabinets. The second day I was at 10 Downing Street Pierson Dixon, who had stayed on as Principal Private Secretary at the Foreign Office, rang me and said the Foreign Secretary very much wanted to see me.

Bevin, looking even more massive than formerly, waved me to an easy chair and sat down beside me in as near to a conspiratorial attitude as his robust approach to life would allow.

'I'm glad you're coming to look after Clem, Francis,' he said, rather as if I had signed on as a bodyguard. Leaning closer and dropping his voice to a penetrating whisper, he went on, 'You keep your eye on 'erbert when I'm not 'ere, Francis. Let me know if he gets up to any of his tricks. I wouldn't trust the little bugger further than I could throw him.'

It seemed an ominous beginning. The Bevin-Morrison feud, which was more of Bevin's making than Morrison's and went back to the days of the second Ramsay MacDonald Government when Morrison had been Transport Minister and had been suspected of being ready to stay on with MacDonald in the National Government if invited, rumbled on as long as Bevin lived. There were at various times a number of other inter-Cabinet hostilities to contend with.

On the whole Attlee's method of government prevented these tensions from erupting into an open clash during his first administration. It failed to do so in his second when, sadly weakened by Sir Stafford Cripps's departure through ill-health, followed by Ernest Bevin's death, he was faced with the resignation of Aneurin Bevan, Harold Wilson and John Freeman after a policy dispute with Hugh Gaitskell who—much to Bevan's chagrin—had been made Chancellor of the Exchequer instead of himself. Even this might not have reached so damaging a climax if Attlee had not been seriously ill in hospital at the time and forced to leave the job of mediation to Herbert Morrison. This, at any rate, was Attlee's own belief.

Attlee's strength as a Prime Minister came not only from an integrity of character which was acknowledged even by his opponents, but from his remarkable self-sufficiency. He had learnt the business of leadership in a hard school. First-elected leader of his Party when it was in almost complete disarray after the political massacre of 1931 and the internal wounds of the argument over sanctions against Italy, facing a Government so strongly entrenched that there was small chance of even the most minor parliamentary success, he saw as his first and major responsibility that of holding the Party together. With such a task in circumstances so daunting he could not afford the luxury of intimates, still less sycophants.

His own nature in any event inclined him to a solitary role. He depended less than most on the support of others, or on their assurance that he was right.

These qualities were very well suited to maintaining a balance in a Cabinet of such strong and often disparate personalities. Bevin, Morrison, Cripps, Dalton and Bevan each out-topped Attlee in some respect, all had a more powerful public persona, each in their various ways was a more forceful orator. But he understood exactly the balance of forces within his party and took careful account of them in the building of his administration. In Cabinet or Cabinet Committee he relied much more on the dexterous but unobtrusive guiding of opinion than on the attempt to dominate discussion, although his conclusions when they came were sharp and clear. Those who assumed that his lack of personal vanity and unconcern for the external trappings of political power were due to doubts about himself often had a rude awakening. He had in fact great self-confidence and a strong streak of ruthlessness, and although he was an administrator of ideas rather than a creative political thinker he knew exactly what he wanted to do.

I asked him once if he found being Prime Minister a hard life but he said No. 'Great advantage living on the job,' he said. 'Means you can see your family. And with luck you get a bit of time off at weekends. I'm finding time to read Gibbon all through again.'

When he had been younger he had been a great reader of poetry and had written a number of very passable translations of Italian poetry himself. But now he stuck mainly to political history and biography. I asked him if he read T. S. Eliot but he said he had tried but could not get on with him. 'I'm the wrong generation,' he said. 'I don't go further than Browning.'

He had an almost fanatical sense of duty, perhaps a very Victorian one, and assumed that those in whom he had put his trust shared it and if they had given a promise or undertaking would not allow themselves to be deflected from it. I had an interesting experience of this quite early in our association.

Trygve Lie, who had been elected the first Director General of the United Nations, was anxious that I should become Assistant Director General in charge of Public Information at one of those fabulous salaries in the neighbourhood of £15,000 a year free of tax which ruled in the early days of the organization. Rather surprisingly both the Americans and the Russians, who did not often agree, signified that they would be pleased by such an appointment and Lie arrived in London to ask Attlee's formal authority to approach me.

Attlee listened to him politely, working away throughout, as he often did on such occasions, at an elaborate doodle. His method in doodling was to establish first of all the scope of the doodle. With a quick precise movement of his pencil he would draw a diamond, a circle or a star in firm outline. He would then proceed to fill this framework, or frontier, with a carefully balanced design, gradually bringing in more and more detail until the whole area was minutely covered, every part balancing another part. He produced these doodles at considerable speed and with what appeared to be great concentration. This was somewhat off-putting until one discovered that his interest in the doodle did not in any way diminish the keenness of his attention to what one was saying.

Although they had met, Trygve Lie did not know Attlee well, and as work on the doodle proceeded he found his voice trailing away. This was not at all what he had expected. At last rather lamely he came to a halt. Attlee looked up. 'Francis wouldn't be interested,' he said. 'Gave his word he'd stay here for at least a year. Wouldn't break it.' And rising politely he shook Lie briskly by the hand and conducted him to the door of the Cabinet Room.

When I heard about this I was much touched, feeling honoured that Attlee had so firmly assumed I would behave as his own sense of duty would have made him. But I may have deceived myself. He may simply have been exercising that polite ruthlessness in getting what he wanted which often distinguished him in public matters.

To work in No. 10 was a pleasant affair—a post-graduate course in politics in delightful surroundings. The fact that the house is the Prime Minister's home as well as his office and is staffed only by a small personal staff, the charming walled garden and the view of the trees in St James's Park from the main windows, all these give the impression more of a small country house in which the master is going through the estate papers in the library than of a great department of state. Each afternoon when the pressure of newspaper and other inquiries permitted I would walk along the corridor past the hooded footman's chair in the entrance hall and the pictures of old Imperial Conferences on the walls, to the Secretaries' room next to the Cabinet Room. Here I would take afternoon tea with the rest of the private staff: Leslie Rowan (now Sir Leslie Rowan, Chairman of Vickers) who had been Churchill's Principal Private Secretary and was now Attlee's and who, when not involved in Cabinet secrets, was likely to be concerned with the equally secret business of picking the English hockey team of which he was captain; Laurence Helsby, now Lord Helsby, who after beginning as a lecturer in economics at Durham ended up as Head of the Civil Service; Anthony Bevir, now Sir Anthony, with a place in County Mayo, the Secretary for Appointments who advised the Prime Minister on the making of bishops and other high church dignitaries and had, so he claimed, more experience of rectory teas than any man in England; and the Parliamentary Private Secretary.

The first P.P.S. was Geoffrey de Freitas, who had been at Attlee's old school, Haileybury, and in moments of excitement would entertain us by tossing a lighted cigarette in the air and catching it in his mouth as it came down. He was succeeded by Arthur Moyle, now Lord Moyle, whom I suppose to have been one of the best Parliamentary Private Secretaries any Prime Minister has ever had. A man with a fund of Welsh stories and a vast range of friends among M.P.s of all parties, he served

Attlee with exemplary and devoted loyalty as long as Attlee lived, refusing all chances of promotion to stay with him. His trust and affection Attlee wholly returned. Moyle was truly a man for all seasons. His fidelity never faltered and his common sense and knowledge of every mood of the party was an immense advantage to the Prime Minister.

In the Cabinet Attlee and Bevin were always the closest. Superficially they seemed an unlikely pair: Attlee small, precise, very middle-class, conservative in many of his habits—he suffered acutely if the port was circulated the wrong way at his dinner table—controlled in emotion and logical in thought; Bevin tough, massive, pugnacious, defiantly working-class, enormously egotistical and easily suspicious, moving more readily among large conceptions than precise definitions.

Yet there was rarely any serious difference of opinion between them and towards Attlee, whom he called 'the little man', Bevin adopted a strongly protective attitude like an uncle with a clever but sensitive nephew. He seemed to think Attlee so innocent of the wickedness of the world that unless one of us was constantly on the watch someone would be sure to get him and was much happier when there was Arthur Moyle, a good trade unionist, to watch over him as well as me.

For his part Attlee's relationship with Bevin was the deepest in his political life and he spoke to him more openly than to any other man. He liked to discuss every major problem with him, however far it fell outside Bevin's particular territory as Foreign Secretary, and on foreign affairs themselves had an implicit faith in Bevin's broad judgement. He did not think it appropriate to try to run the Foreign Office as an annexe to 10 Downing Street, nor did he set much store by summit conferences which he thought usually suffered from too much publicity and too little preparation. For this reason, Bevin was perhaps the last of the independent Foreign Secretaries.

On the other hand Bevin did not like to move far without talking things over with Attlee. He would frequently pop over to No. 10 for a quiet talk and when he was abroad would write him long personal letters. Bevin took hard the persistent attacks from the left wing of his own Party. The *New Statesman* had (I suspect still has) a built-in Judas Iscariot complex which made it see betrayal where betrayal was not, and sometimes seem actually eager for it. It was constantly full of anguished fears and moans. So were some of the constituency Labour Parties.

Laski was naturally among those to annoy him. His temporary position as Chairman of the Labour Party gave him a platform much over-rated abroad, and his interventions annoyed Attlee, too. When Laski sent him a copy of a complimentary article he had written in *Reynolds*, he replied crisply, 'I thank you for your kindly reference in your *Reynolds* article. I am, however, bound to point out to you that the constant flow of speeches from and interviews with you are embarrassing . . . a period of silence on your part would be welcome.'

On the whole, however, Attlee was more tolerant of the left wing than Bevin, and understood it better. To him their criticisms were a natural part of the political life. To Bevin, the trade-unionist, they were the rankest disloyalty. He was always, as Attlee said to me once, 'a majorities man'.

It was fortunate that Attlee himself was not a prima donna for Bevin was far from being the only egotist in the Cabinet. Cripps ran him close, the difference being, as Attlee once remarked, that Bevin's was the egotism of the artist while Cripps's was that of the altruist.

'Gentlemen, there but for the grace of God goes God,' Churchill had remarked during the war after Cripps had excused himself from a dinner party in which he had eaten only a plain salad and drunk only orange juice while discoursing at length on the need to satisfy the spiritual longings of the nation. As I struggled with Cripps's views on what was likely to persuade the British people to work harder and export more I frequently felt that Churchill had had something there.

In one's arguments with Cripps one had to keep one's wits about one and never forget that he was a lawyer. He employed all his formidable forensic powers to put over his case. If one were not careful one would wake up to find that one was being driven into a corner from which it would be impossible to escape without giving him what he wanted.

Perhaps fortunately he came early to the conclusion that I was not for saving. In our prolonged meetings over the perennial problem of Britain's balance of trade he often showed an almost excessive regard for what he seemed to think of as my journalistic immunity from austerity.

I remember with affection an occasion when we had been meeting in his room at the Treasury without reaching a conclusion and had agreed to continue in his flat after dinner. Scarcely had I got back to my room at 10 Downing Street when my telephone rang. 'Stafford here,' he said, 'I forgot to mention we don't have anything to drink at the flat, Francis. Bring a bottle of beer with you.' 'That's all right,' I said. 'You may not think it, Stafford, but I can actually get through an evening without a drink.' 'No, no,' he said, 'do bring a bottle of beer for yourself.'

When I walked round to Whitehall Court about 9.30 the first thing he said when he opened the door was: 'But you haven't brought any beer.' I did my best to reassure him. But after we had been working for about half an hour he broke off to say to Lady Cripps, 'Do you remember that bottle of vodka the Russians gave us when we left Moscow, Isobel? Have you any idea what we did with it?' Isobel thought carefully. At last she said, 'I'm not sure but I think I last saw it on the floor of the wardrobe in the spare room.' 'I thought Francis might like some of it,' said Cripps. 'I'll go and look.' He came proudly back bearing a nearly full bottle of the best vodka. 'The only thing is,' he said, 'we don't have any wine glasses. Would you mind drinking it out of an egg cup?' 'An egg cup would be fine,' I said.

His and Isobel's austerity in eating and drinking had been due more in the first place to their adoption of a nature cure diet for health reasons than ethical principle, but their austere approach to life in general was very much a moral matter. Cripps was a man of immense integrity but it was an integrity of that dangerous sort that assumes that its possessor is the only man capable of giving the country the leadership it needs. In earlier times he might have been a Prince of the Church and sent his enemies to the stake in the sure conviction that he was doing God's will. His appearance, tall, emaciated and intense, fitted the part but the intense nervous strain he lived under was shown by the fact that he never stopped smoking, his only vice. He was a considerate host, immensely attentive to even the youngest or least important of his guests, whom he would draw out with great skill. But one had the feeling with him that one was no more than a document. When he was talking to you he extracted everything useful in the way of ideas or information, giving you during the process not half his mind as many people do in conversation but the whole of it. But when he had finished he put you away as he might have put papers into a dispatch box.

He was a great lawyer but he understood little about ordinary people and had small sympathy with the prosaic ambitions that moved them. Because of his reputation for ascetism he was sometimes compared to Gandhi. But they were not really similar and when they met in India Gandhi found him personally unsympathetic. 'In his heart,' he said to a friend of mine, 'there is not enough humility.' Cripps for his part thought Gandhi more politically slippery than suited a saint. He got on better with Nehru, who had some of his own intellectual coldness and aristocratic disdain for the ordinary and who frequently stayed with Cripps at his house in the country before the war: it was there I first met him.

There are occasional moments that throw a revealing light on personality, sometimes indeed on the personalities of several people. One such for me was the evening when Hugh Dalton had to resign from the Chancellorship of the Exchequer because of a ridiculous indiscretion as he walked into the Chamber to deliver his Budget speech. As he went in he met an old journalist friend of his—and mine—John Carvel, Lobby Correspondent of the *Star* and father of Robert Carvel, now the Political Editor of the *Evening Standard*. In reply to a joking question Dalton let slip some scrap of information which he assumed Carvel would regard as confidential and which in any event he thought too late for him to use. But on an impulse, which I hope he later regretted, Carvel went to a telephone and phoned his newspaper. He claimed to me later that he had only intended to give them background so that they could prepare their layout in advance. Be this as it may, the *Star* rushed the news into the stop-press of an edition which was on sale on the streets while Dalton was still talking.

The leak was a small one and came only a few minutes ahead of the parliamentary announcement. But by parliamentary tradition Dalton had no alternative but to offer his resignation. Attlee, a stickler for the proprieties, accepted it.

I knew nothing of all this until Leslie Rowan rang me at my Gordon Square flat just as I had finished dinner and told me the

Prime Minister wanted to see me urgently in his room at the House of Commons. When I arrived I was told what had happened by Rowan and went in to see Attlee.

'This is terrible about Hugh,' I said. 'Behaved like a fool,' said Attlee. 'Can't see why anyone should want to talk to the press.' When I had finished talking to Attlee I went into the ante-room. Herbert Morrison was there. 'This is a bad business, Francis,' he said. 'How do you think it'll affect the Gravesend result?'—a by-election in which Sir Richard Acland was standing as Labour candidate. I sat down to wait until Attlee showed he was ready for me to see the political correspondents and Ernest Bevin walked in and slumped down beside me. 'Poor old Hugh,' he said. 'It's easy done. Might just as well have been me. I'm always opening my bloody mouth too wide.' Then Cripps arrived. He beckoned me and when I joined him said, 'The P.M.'s asked me to take over the Treasury. I'd be glad if you could come over to see me in the morning. There are several things I'd like to discuss with you.' He made no reference at all to Dalton.

A few days later Jess and I travelled down to Chequers for the wedding of Janet Attlee. We shared a compartment with Arthur Moyle and Aneurin Bevan, Arthur and I in usual wedding clothes with morning coats and top hats, Nye in a blue suit and a black beret. Jess and Nye had a friendly argument about housing. Jess thought he was far too complacent in view of the plight of many of the families she saw at Great Ormond Street and to the delight of Arthur Moyle and myself gave him much better than she got. At this point Bevan changed the subject. He began to talk about Dalton and added his own comment to the store I had collected, when I remarked that I was astonished that so experienced a politician as Dalton should fall into such a trap. But Bevan would have none of it. 'Something like that was bound to happen to him,' he said. 'There's no immaculate conception of disaster.'

There was rarely an occasion when Bevan did not have a phrase for it. I suppose Lloyd George may have equalled him as a parliamentary debater although by the time I heard him he had passed his best so that I had no means of judging between them. Certainly no one else did, not even Churchill, although Churchill was better for the grand occasion. Sometimes Bevan's power over words was his undoing. One could see him pause to taste an insult that had leapt to his mind and knew that nothing would stop him from the pleasure of uttering it, however much damage it might do him in the long run. I have never known a man who enjoyed his own speeches so much.

Bevan was not one of the inner group on which Cabinet unity depended. This consisted of Attlee, Bevin, Cripps, and Morrison, and since both Cripps and Morrison would frequently have been delighted to see Attlee out Cabinet stability effectively rested on the relationship between Attlee and Bevin. However, there is little doubt that if Attlee had been challenged, as Cripps would have liked him to be in 1947, the majority of the Cabinet outside the inner group would have been firmly on his side—particularly such stalwarts as Chuter Ede, A. V. Alexander, Jim Griffiths, George Hall, George Isaacs, Tom Williams and George Tomlinson.

In such Cabinet intrigues as there were Herbert Morrison played a smaller part than Cripps, despite Bevin's constant suspicion of him. This may have been because he continued to regard himself as Attlee's natural successor and did not think Cripps's projects likely to advance his chances. But it was also, I think, because he was very busy and enjoyed what he was doing. He would have liked to be Prime Minister but he was too much of a politician to repine for what was not while what there was was so considerable.

More than any of the others Morrison was a politician of the absolute sort. With Attlee, Bevin, Cripps, Bevan, one was aware of inner mysteries, territories of the soul that had nothing to do with their public lives. But for Morrison politics was everything, the only reality. In political action he expressed every part of his being. He had also to an extreme degree that instinctive awareness of the political consequences of unpolitical events which marks the genuine man of politics, just as a similar awareness of the financial consequences of unfinancial events marks the true man of money.

He was touchy about precedence, watchful about proper respect to his position to an extent that the other four were not; Attlee because he did not care, Bevin, Cripps and Bevan because they took their own pre-eminence for granted. But short of greatness, he was a superb politician, shrewd, able, honest and energetic, as well as being the best party manager in the business until the Tories hit on his equal in Woolton. It was easy to admire him for he had courage and guts and tenacity as well as ability and I wished I could have liked him more. Perhaps I found it hard to do so because there seemed nothing else beneath the politician's skin. Despite the cockney swagger and the touchiness he was a machine man. There were no complexities to explore. Yet he quite lacked the simplicities that made such a man as George Tomlinson, who succeeded Ellen Wilkinson as Minister of Education when she died from an overdose of sleeping pills, so lovable—or gave the intellectually much more sophisticated Secretary of State for India, F. W. Pethick-Lawrence, former Captain of the Oppidans at Eton, Cambridge Wrangler, Fellow of Trinity, such a quantity of unpretentious goodness.

The Pethick-Lawrences were near neighbours of ours in Surrey, with a house in the next village of Peaslake. They had early come to an arrangement consonant with the principles of sex equality for which they had both gone to prison during the Suffragette struggle. Under this arrangement she managed their household affairs while they were in London, in Old Square, Lincoln's Inn, and he took over when they were in the country. When Jess and I had tea with them he would offer us the excellent scones and cakes he had baked and would show us his jam and bottled fruit. Sometimes I would take American visitors staying with us shopping and point out the Secretary of State for India standing in a queue outside the village fishmonger's at Shere with a roll of old newspapers under his arm to wrap his fish in.

On the whole I found most of the politicians I spent my time with during this period admirable people. Contrary to public legend, it is in fact my experience that politicians of all parties are as a class nicer, more public spirited and a good deal less watchful of their own interests than either businessmen or academicians. No doubt there is from time to time a certain amount of intrigue and close dagger work among them. But there is much less of it than in boardrooms or in the senior commonrooms of universities. This may be because the close communal life of Parliament itself readily reveals the spurious and unmasks the pretentious, but in so far as I could judge, the virtues of the political life were equally apparent in politicians of other nations. Certainly I would find it hard to nominate within my own experience more admirable repositories of the true American virtues than President Truman, or in a different way President Eisenhower, or than Marshall when Secretary of State, or Harry Hopkins, or Adlai Stevenson.

Of course politicians are often compelled to work within conditions not of their own making. This sometimes makes them seem to operate by double standards. Reading the preamble to the Constitution of the United Nations, for example, one could scarcely help but feel that Smuts, the political philosopher, who drafted it, was a very different person from Smuts, the Prime Minister of South Africa with its lack of enthusiasm for the human rights of black Africans. He was well aware of the dichotomy himself. I had got to know him well in San Francisco. The last time I saw him was at a Commonwealth Prime Ministers' reception at Lancaster House. He was tired and was resting a little apart from the general mêlée. I joined him and passed some rather empty compliments about a speech he had made at the Conference that day. He looked at me with the steady open-air stare which was one of his characteristics and said, 'I know what you young liberals think when you hear me talking like that. You say: Why doesn't he do better by the Africans in his own country instead of talking to us about human rights? Well, my friend, some day you'll appreciate what an avalanche I've been holding back.'

I felt a little impatient at these excuses which were to be so justified by events. I tried not to show it but perhaps he guessed because he stood up and said, 'Well, we shall see' and moved away, an old, great man, ramrod straight.

CHAPTER 13

Attlee and Truman

Attlee was extremely fortunate in having President Truman
at the White House while he was at No. 10. Their friendship had
not the fine romantic flavour of the Roosevelt–Churchill
alliance. But it was practical and stable, based on an appreciation of each other's qualities all the greater, perhaps, because
each had come to power in the shadow of a greater predecessor.
They were both small men who were a lot bigger than they
looked.

They had first met briefly in Washington when Attlee was on
his way to the San Francisco Conference. They met again at
Potsdam where Truman came to know Attlee well and appreciate what he described as his 'deep understanding of the
world's problems'. As for Attlee he came quickly to the conclusion that the new President was 'One of the best'. 'His instincts
were right,' he said, 'and he learnt fast. A very courageous
fellow and a good friend. You could always talk to him.'

He felt the need for such a talk a few months after becoming
Prime Minister. He was increasingly concerned about international control of the atom bomb, in the development of which
scientists of the United States, Britain and Canada had jointly
participated and a good deal of the original impetus for which
had come from Britain. As early as 1941 an expert committee
under Sir George Thomson had been set up to co-ordinate
research into the release of energy by atomic fission begun
before the war in Oxford, Cambridge, Imperial College, London,
Liverpool and Birmingham and had become convinced that

there was every possibility of producing an atom bomb in time to be of use in the war. At this stage American scientists doubted it. In view of the conflict of views the British Cabinet decided that, if need be, they would go ahead with an independent British project in Canada where the necessary sources of uranium were available and where the plant would not be vulnerable to air attack as it would be if built in Britain. However, at the Washington Conference of 1942 the evidence produced by the British–Canadian team convinced Roosevelt. He agreed that America should come in.

As Deputy Prime Minister Attlee had been privy to these arrangements. In the interests of security however he had refrained from seeking detailed information of progress and did not know of the successful culmination of the atomic project until Potsdam when President Truman told Churchill and him of the detonation of the first atomic bomb at Alamogordo, New Mexico. With Churchill he had acquiesced in the use of the bomb against the Japanese.

At this stage he thought the atom bomb comparable to conventional bombs already used by both sides in bombing raids, only bigger. Later, when I passed to him the *New Yorker* report on Hiroshima by John Hersey which had much horrified me he waved it aside with the remark that the damage was simply an extension of what had been done by high explosives in the German raids on Britain and the British and American raids on German cities. Subsequently he told me, not in defence but in support of a frequent argument of his that it was misleading to judge the past through the eyes of the present, that at the time of the Potsdam decision neither he, nor, as far as he knew, President Truman or Churchill, knew anything of the genetic effects of the atomic explosion or the long-term consequences of fall-out.

'Whether the scientists, British and American, directly concerned knew or guessed,' he added, 'I do not know. But if they did, then so far as I am aware, they said nothing to those who had to make the decision.'

The medical and scientific evidence on the effects of the bombs on Hiroshima and Nagasaki came to him, therefore, as a grave shock. They had a profound influence on his thinking. He expressed his anxieties in a long personal letter to Truman on

25 September 1945. The world, he said, was now facing entirely new conditions which had not, and could not, have been present in anyone's mind when international security had been discussed at the United Nations Conference in San Francisco or at Potsdam.

The destruction wrought by the Germans through their air fleet on Warsaw and Rotterdam [he wrote] was startling enough but subsequent attempts to do the same to London were defeated, though without much to spare. Our own attacks on Berlin and the Ruhr resulted in the virtual destruction of great centres of industry. In Europe the accumulated material wealth of decades has been dissipated in a year or two, but all this is not different in kind from what was done in previous wars in Europe during the Dark Ages and the Thirty Years War, in America by your own Civil War. Despite these losses civilization continued and the general framework of human society and of relations between peoples remained. But the emergence of this new weapon has meant, taking account of its potentialities, not a quantitative, but a qualitative change in the nature of warfare.

Following this letter a meeting was arranged between President Truman, Prime Minister Mackenzie King of Canada and Attlee for 9 November. After speaking at a luncheon at the Mansion House Attlee flew to Washington with a small party, of which I was one. As we got into the plane he beckoned me to sit beside him. We lit our pipes—one of the advantages of flying in a private party with the Prime Minister was that there was no one to say cigarettes only please—and talked about cricket: his choice not mine.

Early on in my association with Attlee I had learnt that one of the necessary chores of friendship was a close study of *Wisden*, 'Always good reading for settling the mind,' he said. What I acquired in the line of duty never, however, equalled what he absorbed out of love and after much speculation on who would have a place if one were picking the best English test side of all time, I managed to move him into what were for me more rewarding pastures by asking if any of the same principles applied in picking a Cabinet.

He said yes, he thought they did. You needed, he said, some good all-rounders ('Like Herbert. He's a good all-rounder, a professional. Stafford on the other hand has not got many strokes, but he can score a century on his day. So can Ernie. He hasn't much style, but he can lift them out of the ground when his blood's up. Dalton's a bit erratic but he's got great zest. Loves having a knock'). And you needed good fast bowlers ('Like Nye. There's no one to touch Nye when he's got his length. Doesn't always find it though'). But you also needed some good solid chaps not necessarily brilliant but reliable ('Like Chuter Ede. Very safe pair of hands, Chuter. And Addison. Wise old bird. Very steady').

'The thing you have to remember in picking a Cabinet,' he went on, dropping the cricket analogy, to my relief, 'is that although you want some brilliant people you also want some ordinary fellows who can tell you how other ordinary fellows are feeling. Nothing so dangerous as a Ministry of all the talents.'

Later, after dinner and a gossip about old friends, I asked him what as a First War soldier—we had been talking about the days in the Labour Party when he was always known as Major Attlee and in Limehouse simply as The Major—he thought of generals in the Second World War and how they compared with those in the first.

'Very much more intelligent,' he said. 'And they worked well as a team. Very unusual. No intrigues. In the first war the top lot intrigued all the time.'

'Who was our best?'

'Alanbrook. A very cool judgement and decision. He knew his own mind. A fine strategic brain. And Marshall among the Americans. I didn't know MacArthur, but those who did told me he was good. Alanbrook himself put Marshall as the biggest man on the Allied side. He had the appearance of a big man. His lines were sound and he had a good knowledge of strategy— although I thought Alanbrook matched him. It was hard luck on both of them that they didn't have top command in the field. It had to be an American, of course, which was hard on Alanbrook who'd done very well when he had a command in the field earlier. He would have been first class. But the Americans were providing the biggest number of troops so it was right the European command should go to them.

'We expected it to be Marshall and I think he would have been a brilliant success but Roosevelt felt he was too important at home. Eisenhower worked to Marshall, of course. He accepted him as his superior and took his advice. Ike did very well. He's a very good fellow, an extremely good diplomat, the man to get people working together. And plenty of courage. Took important decisions without hesitating. But not as good a soldier as Marshall. Not a major strategist as Marshall is. Hadn't a very good strategical conception, as a matter of fact. His idea was to have every available man fighting. He never thought much of strategy or coming up round the back. He was all for mass. But a great man for running a team.'

Of the others Attlee described Alexander as a man who 'didn't just look at the battle. He looked ahead at what was going to happen and had a broad strategy of the war. He was the man for a campaign, Montgomery for a battle.'

He would not listen to criticism, common among many generals and politicians at the time, of Montgomery's 'theatricality'.

'Nonsense,' he said. 'What they call theatricality was the realization that men wanted to know their generals. Quite different from the First World War. The Divisional Commander was as far as it went then. The Corps Commander was a name. You might possibly just see him, but I never remember seeing anyone higher up. Monty made himself as well known to his troops as Napoleon or Marlborough. Made them feel they were all in the show.'

Of the American generals he picked out particularly Bradley, 'a first-rate man,' and 'that startling fellow, Patton; too much of an individualist, always out for his own show, but a good fighting man.'

He surprised me by saying that although Roosevelt was not in anything like such continuous contact with his Chiefs of Staff as Churchill was, he had a penetrating strategical outlook. 'He knew the essentials of attack and assault, how to deploy your troops to advantage and punch where the enemy was weakest. And he had a long view. I remember talking to him in Washington in his yacht on the Potomac in October 1941, nearly two months before Pearl Harbor and the Americans coming in. We were discussing the probable course of the war and he pulled out a map and put his finger on Algiers and said, "That is where I should like to have American troops." A remarkable piece of prevision.'

We drank up our brandies. A bed had been made up for Attlee and there was another which Leslie Rowan, who had been working on dispatches while Attlee and I chatted, told me was intended for me. But I insisted that he should have it instead since I knew that when we arrived in Washington he would be kept much harder at it than I would and I was perfectly happy sitting back in my seat.

Attlee and I had talked about many things, but not about the purpose of the meeting with Truman.

'I shall be asked about the reason for your visit and what you're aiming to do as soon as we arrive,' I said as Attlee got up from his seat. 'What shall I say?' 'You've seen the letters and telegrams,' he said, 'I leave it to you. Don't say more than you have to.'

Attlee was staying at the White House and I went to see him that evening. He had been put in what had been Lincoln's bedroom and his sense of history was very much engaged as he showed me his rooms. He had already had a meeting with Truman and was just as impressed as before by his common sense and sincerity—qualities which always appealed particularly to Attlee.

I had had an off-the-record meeting with the Washington correspondents of the British newspapers in the afternoon. I had not told them much more about the purpose of the meeting and Attlee's hopes from it than Attlee had already told the House of Commons and had said at his Mansion House speech before leaving. However, as often happens, because what I said was 'off the record' it assumed in many newspapermen's minds much greater importance than when it had been said publicly. Presented by newspaper correspondents with all the necessary garnishing of 'informed circles say' and 'I am reliably informed that' and passed on by them to their American colleagues, it created something of a stir. It was hailed by several leader writers in London as heralding a new approach to world affairs, pregnant for good. By the weekend even the *New Statesman* had temporarily put aside its habitual suspicion of its friends and allowed itself a modest cheer. As for the

American newspapers, they gave banner headlines to the story and expressed their approval of what they called the Attlee approach. Since they had not themselves been present at my off-the-record talk and felt no obligation to honour any promise of confidence, they complained bitterly that the only news on the talks was coming from me. Drew Pearson referred to me as 'that well-known British leak' and an old friend of mine from San Francisco days, Bert Andrews of the *Herald Tribune*, wrote a piece headed, 'Williams Rides Again'.

All this made me unpopular with the British Embassy which governed its activities on the principle that nothing must ever be done to annoy the Americans and that an appearance of British initiative would. The White House and the State Department were, I was told, very upset. When I met the President he showed no signs of being so. He gave me a friendly grin and said, 'I've been hearing about you.' 'Good things, I hope, Mr President,' I ventured and he grinned and said, 'What do you think?'

I found him on this occasion as on others always easy to get along with. He had a basic dignity and sense of office that needed none of the solemn garnishings of lesser men to sustain them and although he recognized protocol he never let it clutter up his feet. He seemed to me to embody a great deal of what is best and most attractive in the American character and that urbanization is in some danger of destroying. He was a kind of grown-up Huckleberry Finn. On his desk in the White House he had a pile of bookmatches which had printed on their covers the message 'I snitched this from Harry Truman.' I never had the nerve to take one but later my son John did.

Attlee remained unperturbed by the Embassy's excitement and deflated my critics by rather ostentatiously coming across to me at an Embassy party and engaging me in friendly conversation in the middle of the room for nearly ten minutes. As for Mackenzie King, he was so impressed by the amount of favourable publicity Attlee was receiving that he decided he needed a similar 'adviser' and sought me out to ask for my ideas on the sort of person he should appoint if he got himself one, which he did immediately he returned to Canada.

The talks themselves were 'successful'—but in the end unproductive. Confident of their own good intentions Truman and

Attlee assumed too readily that Russia would be content to accept the high-minded assurances of her wartime allies and leave control of the atom bomb to them until such time as complete international control through the U.N. proved possible. This euphoric attitude was well illustrated in informal speeches at a State banquet at the White House. Truman, after a pleasant compliment to the ability of the British Empire always to construct a foreign policy that the British people would support whatever government was in power, expressed his hope that the United States could do likewise, and went on to envisage as a major part of this policy a programme for the use of atomic energy 'that would be world wide and continuous and that will include every nation in the world without exception'.

Attlee responding said that what was even more necessary than a foreign policy for Britain and a foreign policy for the United States was 'a universal foreign policy, a foreign policy that is directed not to any immediate aim of any particular country, but a foreign policy that is conceived in the interest of all the people of the world. That does not mean that we don't take into account our particular differences but it seems to me today that the over-riding interests of world civilization come first.' He concluded on what was for him rather an emotional note, urging that in all their counsels they should seek to bring about 'what I believe is the supreme need today—the lifting of the bonds of fear from the human spirit and the setting free of the human spirit so that science instead of a menace, as it is being looked on today, shall be looked on as something that is throwing open wide the gate to a fuller life for us all.' They must, he said, ever keep in mind that what they were trying to do was 'devise a world policy of the common man'.

It is perhaps difficult now not to record such sentiments in something of an ironic tone of voice, easy to feel that such Utopian dreams, and even the proposal for a United Nations Commission on Atomic Energy Truman and Attlee put forward at the end of their talks, had little relation to reality and were evidence either of hypocrisy or excessive innocence. But they were not hypocritical and the innocence was noble. I think it does neither of them any discredit to remember their words. They may be criticized for their euphoria now but it was for their refusal to go even further in euphoria that they were criticized then. Washington was a hopeful place in those days— and gay. Not quite so hopeful or so gay as San Francisco had been, for it had the weight of the atom bomb on its conscience. But nevertheless confident of its own good intentions and equally confident of its power to direct events to serve them.

On our last night some of the newspapermen and others who had been at San Francisco gave me a party. The host was Charles Campbell, head of what was known as the down-town office of the British Information Services, and surely one of the most extraordinary characters ever to grace the British foreign service, much as that service has always been given to cherishing a few eccentrics to break the monotony of its surface proprieties.

A small, florid, pop-eyed man with an inexhaustible capacity for taking in hard liquor, an equally inexhaustible supply of anecdotes, mostly of a scabrous and witty kind, and an apparently unfailing attraction for women, almost all of whom wanted either to love him or mother him, he was the intimate and cherished friend of the entire Washington press corps. This friendship they expressed on one occasion by a standing ovation to him at a National Press Club dinner to Winston Churchill. Later they christened him affectionately 'Her Majesty's Charlie'.

His father had been a ship's captain sailing out of Liverpool who finally settled in South Carolina. He instilled in his son a sturdy English patriotism which prevented him from adopting American nationality, although he lived all his life in the United States. Charlie liked to tell of his first day at school in South Carolina when he was found in tears. 'Why are you crying, Charlie?' his teacher asked him. 'Because the boy behind kicked me.' 'Why did you kick him?' asked the teacher. 'Because he wouldn't salute the flag,' said the boy behind. 'Why didn't you salute the flag, Charlie?' asked the teacher. 'Because I'm English,' said Charlie. 'Kick him again,' said the teacher. Despite this initiation Charlie continued all his life to love America only a hair's breadth behind England. He was news editor of a paper in South Carolina when Britain declared war on Nazi Germany and immediately threw up his job, kissed his wife and children goodbye, took train for Washington and there presented himself for duty at the British Embassy—any duty, anywhere. At Washington he remained, incredible, irreplaceable, a constant source of legend, and perhaps the most brilliant spokesman for Britain ever known anywhere.

The B.I.S. was at that time full of brilliant and dedicated people recruited during the war, Aubrey Morgan, Jack Winacour, René MacColl, and D'Arcy Edmondson among them. But the only figure to compare with Charlie in influence and élan was Bill Ormerod (now Sir Berkely Ormerod) at the New York end. He was of a very different personality but of a plumage no less extraordinary in the official life of the times.

Ormerod had been an officer in the regular army, a gunner major and a county cricketer. He was a member of Boodles, the M.C.C., the Royal and Ancient (St Andrews), Knickerbocker (New York) and the Travellers (Paris). After being badly wounded in the First World War he turned to stockbroking and wrote a learned treatise on *The Dow Theory Applied to the London Stock Exchange* before moving to Wall Street as an investment consultant. From this unlikely background he migrated to the British Information Services in New York when the Second World War started and abandoned finance to become the confidant, friend and trusted adviser of about every leading American newspaper columnist and radio commentator you could think of.

He lived in considerable splendour at the Pierre Hotel overlooking the park and I never knew a man with so many eminent friends, all of whom loved him even when they hated each other. A curious but admirable quality of goodness and simplicity, unusual in a man so versed in financial matters and so good at making money, shone from him so that even the most egocentric accepted his strictures—when he felt such to be necessary—without protest. You could give him your confidence without question. It was never betrayed.

He had a strongly hypnotic power. You found yourself hanging on to his conversation even when it was about something of which you knew more than he did, for he seemed able to transmute everything into gold of his own devising. I remember lunching with him and Walter Lippmann and hanging spellbound on his words as he explained some aspect of British policy. How fascinating, how revealing, I said to myself, wherever did he learn it, only suddenly to realize that it was all based on what I myself had told him that very morning.

He was at this time a bachelor and so we all expected him to remain. But in 1962 when he finally retired from the B.I.S. after presenting the case of both Labour and Conservative governments with equal sympathy—patriotism being his one test of virtue in such matters—he went to a party before setting off on a world tour during which he had been invited to stay with Nehru and several Heads of State who had become his close friends during his official activities. At the party, he—then being sixty-five and having never before shown any inclination to matrimony—met Beatrice Sigrist, the widow of the aviation pioneer, and fell immediately in love—so much so that although he started on his world tour he found himself unable to bear being separated from her and abandoned it to return to New York to ask her to marry him. This she did, much to the delight of his friends all over the world. They now live in the Bahamas.

For our farewell party in Washington Charlie Campbell stocked up with a roomful of liquor and called up not only most of the Washington Press Corps, who surged in and out throughout the night as their duties permitted, but a contingent from New York, including Sylvia Porter, America's best known woman financial writer, and Margaret Parton of the *New York Herald Tribune*, who had become a great figure in the San Francisco scene and a close friend of mine at the United Nations Conference. She had lived in San Francisco as a girl and had written a fine nostalgic book about it called *Laughter on the Hill*, publication of which was artfully timed by her publishers to coincide with the opening of the Conference: she later went to India and wrote a fine book about that too. And there were, of course, as fixed planets in the changing scene, my close friends Robert Waithman of the *News Chronicle*, Arthur Webb of the *Daily Herald* and Jack Winacour of the B.I.S., along with a young man from the State Department who had been invited because he had a fine voice for Negro spirituals which he sang whenever there was a pause in the conversation.

The party went on all through the night and about halfway through it, I remember, we went to the apartment next door and borrowed a piano from the girls who lived there and who got up to join the party, taking off the door of the apartment to get the piano out and in. We did not finish until nearly ten the next morning when it was time to go to a final press conference at the Embassy presided over by Lord Halifax. At this Charlie and I, finding a convenient wall at the back of the room to lean against, went fast asleep on our feet. Afterwards I caught the train for Ottawa with the rest of the Attlee party. We were piped out of the station at Ottawa by an M.P. in a kilt and were entertained by Malcolm MacDonald, the High Commissioner, who disappointed me by not walking on his hands and waving his feet in the air as I had been told he often did. Instead he tried to persuade me to go with him in a canoe at 4.30 the following morning to watch wildfowl, which I thought a poor substitute.

We had a rather grand dinner with Mackenzie King and his Ministers and Attlee spoke to both Canadian Houses of Parliament, including in his speech a few French sentences about peace which he had found in Rabelais. After this we flew home. England was shrouded in fog when we arrived and our plane had to fly from airport to airport looking for somewhere safe to land while the radio reported our erratic passage to the anxiety of our friends and relatives, including Jess.

Although Attlee and Truman cemented their personal friendship during the Washington talks, their relationship was not without strain. Scarcely was Attlee back in London before the danger of summit conferences, at which national leaders forgather with considerable publicity for a few days and produce rotund communiqués designed to indicate that all is harmony between them, became plain.

Both he and Mackenzie King—and, I think, Truman too—had ended the conference believing that although the wartime agreement on exchange of atomic information between the three countries was under considerable strain on the American side, these difficulties could be ironed out. All three wanted the first clause of the memorandum they signed to mean what it said: 'We desire that there should be full and effective co-operation in the field of atomic energy between the United States, the United Kingdom and Canada.' They soon found that although statesmen proposed it was Congress that disposed and Congress was by no means ready to allow information to be pooled. It regarded the 'know-how' on the atom bomb and on the development of atomic energy for peaceful purposes as the exclusive property of the United States and had no inclination to share with anyone—not even the wartime allies who had contributed so much in scientific knowledge to what had been achieved. There were a series of sharp telegrams between Attlee and Truman. But the MacMahon Bill prohibiting all disclosure of information was passed by the Senate and 'full and effective co-operation' came to a final end.

Attlee did not blame Truman. 'He was ready,' he said, 'but the Senate wanted everything for America.' It was in these circumstances that Attlee reached what seemed to many when it became known the somewhat extravagant decision that Britain must make an atom bomb of her own.

He always insisted that it was the right decision. 'It cost us a lot more than if we'd had the help and information due to us from America,' he said when we talked about it later, 'but we had to go ahead. I don't blame Truman, but there it was. We had to hold up our position *vis-à-vis* the Americans. We couldn't allow ourselves to be wholly in their hands. And we had to bear in mind at that time that they might withdraw and become isolationists again. This was before NATO, remember. I wanted international control of the bomb. I wanted it completely under the United Nations. But that was going to take a long time and meanwhile we had to face the world as it was. We had to look to our own defence. We couldn't just leave it to America.'

The need to keep close to America yet independent of her was a major purpose of foreign policy to both Attlee and Ernest Bevin. In steering a course between the two great powers, America and Russia, they considered it inevitable, for many good reasons of kinship and outlook, that this course should take Britain closer to America than Russia, but they were much concerned not to give the Soviet any reason for feeling isolated or to put any obstacle in the way of a response to a gesture of friendship from Stalin.

Bevin was more hopeful of such a gesture than Attlee. Typically Bevin had persuaded himself when he became Foreign Secretary that Stalin would remember the service he had done the infant revolution in 1920 when 'his dockers' had refused to load the *Jolly George* with munitions for Poland for use against the Bolshevists, and the Council of Action of which he was a leader had forced Lloyd George to abandon plans for military intervention against them. 'They've reason to know I'm a friend,' he said to me several times. 'L.G. and Winston would have downed them at the start but for me.'

It is now sometimes argued that Attlee and Bevin abandoned hopes of Russian friendship too early and concentrated too completely on an American alliance. I did not think this at the time and do not now. However, it is certainly the case that both of them became increasingly convinced by Soviet response to their approaches that one of the main objectives of Russian policy was to take advantage of Britain's post-war weakness and so cripple her role in Europe and the Middle East as to create a vacuum into which Russian power could move. They perhaps paid insufficient attention to the effect of Russia's immense war-time losses on her own international thinking or to the intensity of her continuing hatred and fear of Germany. They were constantly aware of the danger of two massive antagonistic blocs developing. Soviet coolness to the Four Power Treaty proposed by the United States dashed Bevin's hope that 'a bridge between East and West could really have been built and the antagonism which is growing so fast in the United States would have been checked'.

In a long personal letter to Attlee from the meeting of the Council of Foreign Ministers in Moscow, which Attlee later showed me, he wrote: 'It was very sickening and saddening to see such an opportunity thrown away. The best description I can give of Molotov's statement is that it was a product of an irascible mind and very, very much like the old discussions that used to go on in the old International pre-1914 where they argued for days about words and theories of the most impractical kind.' He concluded sadly, 'It looks to me as if we are getting perilously near a position in which a line-up is taking place. I had hoped when I came to Moscow it could all have been avoided and I think a little more salutary attitude on the part of the Russians and better methods of handling their problems would have succeeded. ... There is courtesy, there are no high words being used, no tempers, but all of it is cool and calculated and between the two big boys looks to me to be pretty determined.'

Neither Attlee nor Bevin thought the Soviet wanted war. But they began to fear that Stalin might find he had released forces that even he could not control. This opinion Bevin expressed in the plainest terms replying to a question from Field-Marshal Smuts at a Commonwealth Prime Ministers' Conference at Downing Street. 'We are,' he said, 'forced to recognize that the Soviet policy of expansion backed by her historic national ambitions and her Communist belief has engendered its own dynamite which may prove too strong for Stalin despite all his shrewdness and his power. I don't think he's planning for war. But he may be unable to control the forces he's started. We have always got to be prepared for that.'

This was the period when Admiral Leahy, whom Truman had for the time being inherited as his Chief of Staff, was advising that Britain was prostrate economically and relatively impotent militarily and that the only sensible thing was to accept the Soviet as 'the unquestioned all-powerful influence in Europe', and when Harry Hopkins was reporting back from his mission to Moscow that he saw no major conflict between Russian and American interests in any part of the world and thought it essential that the United States should not allow itself to be manœuvred into a position of lining up in a bloc with Britain against Russia to implement Britain's European policy.

Although Truman himself was less happy than some of his advisers about Soviet policy Attlee and Bevin had therefore to be very careful not to do anything that might suggest that Britain was trying to put the United States in the position of standing bond for her.

The Foreign Office was even more scared than they were. It was thrown into a great tizzy by Churchill's Fulton speech, on which neither Attlee nor Bevin nor our Embassy in Washington had, of course, been consulted. This consternation grew when the first telegrams from the British Embassy in Washington reported that the speech had been widely interpreted as expressing British official policy and had been seized on by a good deal of American opinion as the beginning of an attempt to manœuvre America into a dangerous new alliance.

Bevin came over to Attlee to discuss this. The two of them

were together when a telegram marked 'Personal from Churchill for the Prime Minister and Foreign Secretary' arrived. In it Churchill, well aware of the Foreign Office and Embassy reaction, reported that although he had not, of course, consulted any member of the American administration about the text of his speech he had shown the President a mimeographed copy in the train on the way to Fulton.

'He told me,' he cabled, 'that he thought it was admirable and would do nothing but good though it would make a stir.' Mr Byrnes, the Secretary of State, had been equally pleased 'both before and after'. What was even more significant, said Churchill, was that in conversation on the train the President had told him that he intended to take diplomatic advantage of the sudden death of the Turkish Ambassador in Washington by sending his body back to Turkey in the American battleship *Missouri*, the strongest battleship afloat, accompanied by a strong task force which would remain in the Sea of Marmora as an evidence of American interest in that part of the world. With its somewhat macabre use of a dead Ambassador as an instrument of diplomacy this news pleased Churchill greatly. It pleased Attlee and Bevin too.

Churchill went on to say that after nearly three days of intimate contact with President Truman and Mr Byrnes he was satisfied that they were no longer ready to put up with further treaty breaches by the Soviet in Persia or with the pressure for Russian expansion in the Mediterranean at the expense of Turkey and Greece, and had come round to the British view that some show of strength and resistance was necessary to secure a good relationship with Russia. He predicted that this would soon be the prevailing opinion in the United States.

This long, frank and friendly personal telegram was the first benevolent gesture to the new Government and its international efforts Churchill had made and pleased Attlee and Bevin greatly for that reason as well as for its contents. Churchill followed it up five days later with a speech at a National Press Club lunch in Washington strongly supporting the proposals for the American loan which were then before Congress and ridiculing the idea that it could in any way be regarded as a 'subsidy for socialism'. For Congress to turn the loan down, he said, would be a disaster—although even in those circumstances the

British would come through in the end, for they 'could never be beaten'. Churchill had emerged from the black mood which had followed his defeat at the General Election. He was now vigorously implementing his principle that one should always support one's country abroad even when relentlessly opposing its Government at home. Attlee sent him a personal telegram thanking him most warmly and suggesting a long talk on international policy when Churchill got back to England.

Truman's action in sending the *Missouri* to Turkey was a curtain-raiser to the Truman Doctrine of a year later which established security in the Eastern Mediterranean as an American interest and thus removed Attlee's and Bevin's worst fears of an American return to isolation.

Not all matters went so smoothly. Almost the first document put in front of Attlee when he became Prime Minister was a memorandum on Jewish immigration which the President had addressed to Churchill two days before the result of the British election was known. This asked for the lifting of the restrictions on Jewish immigration into Palestine, first imposed before the war in the British White Paper of May 1939. 'They contrive,' said Truman, 'to provoke passionate protests from Americans most interested in Palestine and in the Jewish problem.' At this point Attlee could only reply that he could not make any statement of policy until he had had time to consider the matter, but thereafter Palestine was continually to sour the relations between President and Prime Minister.

So far from the further consideration promised bringing Truman and Attlee closer, it moved them further apart—the more so because both Attlee and Bevin came to the conclusion that the real steam behind the President's request for the lifting of restrictions came from domestic pressure by American Jewish voters who had little interest in long-term attempts to secure peace between Jews and Arabs in the Middle East.

Rightly or wrongly this view was fed by the State Department. A bitter fight had developed inside the American Administration. While Roosevelt was alive the State Department had been sure of Presidential backing in its dealings with the Middle East. It had several times with his authority, as the Foreign Office knew, promised Arab leaders that no decision affecting the basic situation in Palestine would be taken without full consultation with both Arabs and Jews. A few months before his death Roosevelt had, himself, assured King Ibn Saud, who had taken care to let the British know, that he 'would make no move hostile to the Arab people and would not assist the Jews as against the Arabs'. Roosevelt's view, like the State Department's, was that the Zionist aim of a Jewish State in Palestine could be established and maintained only by military force.

Much of the bitterness that developed between Downing Street and the White House came from Attlee's and Bevin's suspicions, sometimes deliberately fostered by the State Department, that what had been accepted as settled American policy was now being thrown overboard without regard to the long-term future simply to satisfy the Democratic Party machine. This suspicion seemed confirmed when the State Department passed on the news that Robert E. Hannigan, the Postmaster General and chief fund-raiser for the Democratic Party machine, was urging the President to demand entry for a hundred and fifty thousand Jews into Palestine in order to assist him in raising funds for the Democratic National Committee.

Because of these suspicions both Attlee and Bevin underestimated, I think, the influence on the President of humanitarian sympathy for the sufferings of the Jewish people. Attlee and Bevin shared this sympathy. But it loomed smaller in their thinking than his because they had not a Jewish electoral machine to contend with. Also Britain's links with the Middle East compelled them to be concerned about the future of Arabs as well as Jews.

One of Bevin's first acts at the Foreign Office had been to circulate a document called 'Peasants Not Pashas' in which he directed that future British policy should concern itself much more with raising the standards of living of the poverty-stricken masses in the Middle East and much less with keeping often corrupt ruling groups in power. It was a somewhat starry-eyed document in that it assumed that Britain had much more political influence in the Middle East than was left and much more capacity for economic aid than was any longer the case. But it was very genuinely felt and it was in this context that Bevin reacted to the pressure for a Jewish State and the

President's demand for the immediate acceptance of a hundred thousand Jewish immigrants into Palestine.

When I talked to him I found him fired with the vision—I choose the word designedly for although so matter of fact in so many ways Bevin needed visions to sustain him—of a partnership between Jew and Arab that would invigorate and revitalize the whole of the Middle East. When he publicly pledged himself to achieve a settlement it was of this that he was thinking, and it was this he thought threatened by what seemed to him the President's precipitate demands for quick action to satisfy the Jewish Agency.

I well remember the shock caused by the letter from the President calling for the immediate entry of a hundred thousand Jews into Palestine and the comings and goings that followed when the Foreign Office reported—a shade self-righteously, I thought—that the President had proposed this against the strong advice not only of the Secretary of State, James Byrnes, who had plainly told the President that he could be associated neither with such a policy nor with the criticisms of Attlee and Bevin who, he thought, had been placed in a most difficult position, but also against that of James Forrestal, the Secretary of Defence, and John Snyder, the Secretary of the Treasury. There followed a somewhat tart message to the President from Attlee saying that such a decision at this stage seemed to repudiate the solemn undertakings of President Truman's predecessor and might set aflame the whole Middle East. 'I know you realize,' he added acidly, 'that as things are the responsibility for preserving order with all the consequences involved rests entirely on this country.' He ended by proposing an Anglo-American Commission of Inquiry.

This was the stage at which things were when we went to Washington. American Zionist leaders had urged the President to reject out of hand the proposal for an Anglo-American Commission and stick tight on the demand for a hundred thousand immigrants at once. However, although he was far less friendly in these discussions than in those concerned with atomic development, the President did finally agree on American participation in a Commission.

This pleased Attlee. He returned to London convinced he had made a significant advance. It did not work out that way. The

Commission's report simply widened the breach between the two of them. Truman refused to have anything to do with that part of it that 'expressly disproved' that Palestine had ever been granted to the Jews as their own State, recommended that the attempt to establish an independent state should be ruled out as impracticable and that the long-term objective should be neither a Jewish State nor an Arab State. Attlee and Bevin for their part refused to accept that part of the report which supported the issue of a hundred thousand immigration certificates, the one recommendation the President favoured. Despite Attlee's argument that the report must be considered as a whole a Presidential statement endorsing the hundred thousand was issued without Attlee being informed.

When the news of it reached us I was called into the Cabinet Room where Attlee sat glowering with Bevin glowering even harder beside him. They asked me to call the press together and tell them that the President had issued his statement without British knowledge or support. And for the first time in my experience Attlee asked me to make it plain that in telling the press this I was not speaking just for background guidance but as the Downing Street spokesman and could be quoted as such.

Matters were not improved when after much persuasion Truman agreed that a joint British-American expert committee representing the State Department, the Foreign Office, and the Treasuries and Defence Departments of both countries should examine the practical implementation of the Commission's report.

The experts met against a background of mounting terrorism in Palestine culminating in the blowing up of the King David Hotel in Jerusalem. Both the British and the American experts supported the British view that the admission of a hundred thousand Jewish immigrants could only be carried out with the agreement of the Arabs and ought to be conditional on this. They recommended a federal system for Palestine made up of an autonomous Jewish state and an autonomous Arab state with a central Government with powers over Jerusalem and the holy places. To both Attlee and Bevin this seemed a workable long-term solution—or at any rate the beginnings of one. Not so to Truman. He considered he had been let down by his own experts and angrily cabled Attlee that the report could not be issued as having joint authority.

I was with Attlee when he received the President's message. Even his habitual placidity was dented by it. As for Bevin, he was so enraged that he declared he would no longer keep an appointment to see the President when he was in the States for a meeting of the U.N. Security Council. 'I couldn't trust myself to speak to him,' he said. 'He's smashing everything I'm working for.'

I had already heard from Charles Campbell that the President was equally enraged by the British attitude, and indeed some of Bevin's public utterances on American policy had been far from diplomatic. They caused the President to describe Bevin to members of his Cabinet as 'uncouth and hostile'. The prospect of a public quarrel if Bevin started talking when he reached New York seemed considerable and I cabled Bill Ormerod, for whom Bevin had a great fondness, warning him of the danger and urging him to keep Bevin away from pressmen as much as he could. In the event, after much diplomatic coming and going, Bevin did go to the White House and the President and he got on well enough. But only by avoiding the subject of Palestine and talking about their youthful days down on the farm.

It is one of the tragedies of the age that Attlee, Bevin and Truman, each no doubt with the best intentions and highest humanitarian ambitions, never managed to get together on this issue. There was a breakdown of communication for which the price is still being paid. And I can't help feeling that the heaviest responsibility was Truman's.

The White House was more sympathetic towards Britain's problems in India, perhaps because it was not directly involved. However, sometimes two strands of opposing opinion would become clear in American comments: one that Britain was dragging its feet and was still the captive of its colonial past, the other that it was stripping itself of imperial power too wantonly.

Among the steady stream of overseas visitors to Downing Street at this time the only one to whom I took a strong dislike was Jinnah, the Moslem leader in the India talks. He seemed to me not only rigid in his ideas but the sort of man who would think nothing of having your throat cut and your body sewn into a sack and dropped into the river at night if you dared to cross him and he had the power. As he walked down the corridor to the Cabinet Room you had a sense of a cold implacability of a most unpleasant kind. I found that Attlee, who had to spend much more time in his company than I did and had known him since 1927, felt the same. 'A nasty fellow,' he said.

Attlee had been involved with India ever since he had been a member of the Simon Commission in 1927 and had no doubt about the difficulties ahead. He admired Gandhi but thought him a tricky combination of saint and politician. Gladstone, he remarked to me, must have been a bit like him to deal with. But whereas with Gladstone the politician was uppermost, with Gandhi it was the saint: 'Which doesn't,' he said, 'make it any easier. Saints don't fit into a democracy any better than criminals.'

He found Nehru easier, although difficult to pin down: 'He enjoyed splitting hairs for their own sake, like most Indians, and was at first inclined to put everything wrong in India down to the British and avoid responsibility himself. However, he was more ready to take responsibility than most and in the end he did. He was quite a great man.'

Attlee had hoped for a united India but all his attempts to move towards such a settlement splintered on Jinnah's opposition. It was this and his own experience of how timeless negotiations with Indian leaders could become that brought him to two decisions, both of which caused sharp controversy. One was to set a timetable and tell all the Indian parties that whatever happened British rule would end on that date and India would be handed over to them. The other was to sack Wavell as Viceroy.

For Wavell as a soldier Attlee had very great admiration. He put him in the same bracket as Montgomery but with some of Alexander's qualities, and thought him very unfortunate in the number of impossible tasks he had been given to do. But he considered him badly cast as Viceroy. 'He's a great soldier,' he said when we talked about him, 'but a singularly silent one, a curious, silent bird altogether. And the Indians are very loquacious. Silent people can't make much of a relationship with them, you know.'

Also he felt that Wavell had become completely defeatist about India. At one stage he had actually drawn up a plan for evacuation by stages which to Attlee read like a plan of retreat following military disaster. It shocked Attlee. He could well imagine Churchill denouncing it in the full flow of magnificent rage as 'an ignoble and sordid scuttle'—and being right.

But who to send in Wavell's place? The idea of Mountbatten came as an inspiration out of the air. Attlee was doodling one afternoon and thinking of how unsuited Wavell's great military qualities had turned out to be for this particular task when by association he thought of Mountbatten's success as Supreme Allied Commander in South-East Asia and how he had got on well with all sorts of people, including particularly the Burmese, whose military leader, General U Aung San, had been talking about him to Attlee in glowing terms during a visit to London only a little while before. 'I thought to myself,' he told me, 'that he was also blessed with a very unusual wife and that that would be a great help too. He was abroad on leave. But I asked for him to be recalled to come and see me.'

Mountbatten was by no means keen. His greatest ambition was to be First Sea Lord, the position from which his father had been forced at the beginning of the First World War because of his German blood. He did not want to jeopardize his chances of it by taking 'a shore job'. But Attlee promised to talk to their Lords of the Admiralty and rather reluctantly he agreed, stimulated perhaps, by Attlee's estimate that the odds were about six to four against success. Attlee then went to see King George VI. He had expected to find him doubtful about committing a member of the Royal Family to an enterprise in which there was such a strong chance of failure. But the King played a sympathetic role in the Indian negotiations right up to the end, when he willingly put aside the imperial crown and accepted the title of Head of the Commonwealth and he warmly approved the Mountbatten appointment.

A further complication now arose. Stafford Cripps, who had had a big part in the previous talks and knew all the Indian leaders, was enthusiastic for Mountbatten's appointment. Too enthusiastic, in fact. He expressed his willingness to go with him as an Adviser. Both Mountbatten and Attlee were appalled by this suggestion. Mountbatten feared that if Cripps went he himself would be regarded as no more than a royal figurehead with Cripps there to do the real work. And Attlee, who did not believe in running authority in tandem anyway, wanted Mountbatten to start with a clean sheet. But it needed careful diplomacy to turn down Cripps's genuinely magnanimous offer without deeply offending him.

Once these and other obstacles were out of the way, Mountbatten as always embarked on his plans with immense gusto. He picked a staff of able personal friends to help him, headed by General Lord Ismay, known to his friends as Pug, who had been one of Churchill's closest intimates during the war and a strong backer of Mountbatten's Commando operations, and Sir Eric Mieville, a former Assistant Private Secretary to the King, who also had had experience in India on a former Viceroy's staff. As always, in any Mountbatten operation, there was due regard to publicity. He appointed as his press officer a young man who had served on his staff in south-east India in the same capacity, Wing Commander Campbell-Johnson. 'We shall get nowhere,' he said when he told me about this appointment, 'unless we make the Indian people believe in us and if you want the people to believe in you, you have got to make the press trust you.'

Although neither the Mountbatten appointment nor Attlee's own efforts produced the United India both had wanted they were satisfied that the best that was possible had been achieved. A surprising degree of friendship for Britain remained in both India and Pakistan after the withdrawal. I remember Margaret Parton telling Jess and myself when she came to visit us in London of her baffled astonishment as the daughter of American liberals when she found the British so popular when she arrived there as chief correspondent for the *New York Herald Tribune*.

'They seem to like you and dislike us,' she said with the indignation of one who had spent her youth denouncing British imperialism in India.

The wave of inter-religious massacres that started in Bengal and then moved on to the United Province and from there to the Punjab appalled Attlee, as they did everyone else. But he insisted that the death-roll would have been far higher if we had tried to hold India. Between him and Mountbatten a remarkable confidence developed. Although so different, they had a surprising appreciation of each other's qualities.

Almost the last occasion I remember at 10 Downing Street before, after staying twice as long as I had originally intended, I persuaded Attlee to release me and went to America for the

Observer, was the celebration of another independence—that of Burma. I remember it particularly because it was such a jolly occasion. We gathered in the Cabinet Room for the signing of the Treaty of Independence and the Burmese delegation, small, dark and happy in the coloured dress of their country, put their palms together in salute and Thakin Nu, the Prime Minister, laughed, and we all shook hands and said, 'Congratulations. Congratulations and good wishes,' and the Burmese said, 'We thank you all very much.' And laughed again. A few days later most of them were dead, murdered by one of their number, U Saw—'a nasty smiling fellow' Attlee had called him when we had talked about the delegation earlier. U Saw sent hired assassins with sten guns to a meeting of the Executive Council and killed everyone present, although fortunately Thakin Nu had just gone out of the room when the gunmen arrived.

It was a startling demonstration of the difficulties and dangers that, along with so much that was good, the tide of independence, sweeping across the world, would bring.

CHAPTER 14

Washington Summer

Washington is not one of my favourite cities. I prefer New York. New York's violence may appal or even frighten one but at the centre of the New York storm there are oases of stillness always to be found: tucked-away houses, small squares, quiet bars in which intimacy grows all the more intensely because of the sense of the vast, compulsive frenzy outside.

Washington is beautiful, of course. There are few cities lovelier when the cherry trees are out. But its beauty has always seemed to me that of a public monument more than of a city with a deep and complex life of its own. The best cities, like the best people, are those that respond with new mysteries the more one gets to know them so that one feels oneself constantly on the edge of fresh intimacies. Washington is a city on the surface, so much conditioned to one function, government, that there are no depths to explore. One spends one's time moving from party to party, meeting the same people, circulating the same gossip. It is not really an American city but a vast international goldfish bowl in which politicians, diplomats and journalists swim round and round in search of each other.

That summer it was a goldfish bowl from which the steam rose, humid and enervating. Air conditioning was still comparatively rare then. One found it in restaurants and cinemas and the most advanced public building, but not much elsewhere. For our apartment Jess and I hired a large electric fan and at night lay with all our clothes off panting in the stale air it circulated. It was the humidity that made the heat so

difficult to bear. When we could pant no longer we would dress
in as few clothes as decency, less broadminded then than it is
now, permitted and go to an air-conditioned all-night cinema.
We went to more cinemas than in any other place or time in our
lives. In the morning the office girls going to work in the street
cars would carry a load of clean frocks on hangers—three or four
each—to change into during the day, and when one walked
out of an air-conditioned restaurant after lunch into the street
it was like opening an oven door. One could understand why
Congress, which was forced by the pressure of business to sit
late that summer, lost its temper so often. Eve Waithman
claimed that lying in a bath full of cold water trying to keep
cool she had actually seen an empty rubber hot-water bottle
hanging on a hook on the bathroom door melt before her eyes
and drip, drop by rubbery drop, on to the floor. But she did not
like America, which her husband loved with deep passion, and
may have been exaggerating. However, the summer months
had one advantage. There was live theatre in the parks. For the
rest of the year the Theatre Guild refused to allow its members
to play in Washington because at that time there was segregation in the theatres. But the park regulations did not allow
segregation in the parks and the summer companies came and
it was wonderful to sit in the still air and watch them.

It would be absurd to pretend that despite these tribulations
to the flesh and the spirit Washington was not an exciting place
to be in during the months after President Truman's inaugura-
tion or that there were not great events to write about. I
remember the signing of the North Atlantic Treaty—'This is
one of the greatest days in my life, Francis,' Bevin said when I
met him at the ceremony and he was visibly glowing with
pleasure as he walked to the platform with his usual rolling
step to a burst of applause greater than that given to any other
of the visiting Ministers. Jess and I flew to Boston for Churchill's
speech to M.I.T. Outside the hall there were small groups
parading up and down with banners that said, 'Send this
bundle back to Britain', and there were a few boos when he
arrived. But inside the hall the huge audience was ecstatic.
Churchill looked much older even than when I had last met
him: no doubt release from the daily pressures of office had
given age a chance to move in at a smarter pace. But as he

climbed the steps to the rostrum years seemed to drop away from him at every step. I had a copy of his speech. It was, as always, set out like blank verse. When he reached the rostrum the audience rose to him and he threw back his head in a characteristic gesture and seemed to sniff the air like an old lion daring the young contenders to get in his way. When he began to speak his voice rang out with all the old magic and with the same calculated hesitations and the same search for the word already there before him. It was a tremendous performance. At the end as he gave the V sign to a frantically applauding audience he looked young and vigorous again. But when he turned and went down the stairs age seemed to come up to meet him like water in a pool.

I remember, too, the death of James Forrestal, Truman's first Secretary of Defence, a man of probing intellect and a sensibility too extreme for politics. I had a letter of introduction to him from a very old friend of mine, A. V. Alexander, the British Defence Minister who had been First Lord of the Admiralty in succession to Churchill during the war. But Forrestal had been taken to Bethesda Naval Hospital and I never presented it. I looked forward to meeting him when he was well again. I was told this would be very soon. But one night when Jess and I were dining with the Waithmans at the National Press Club restaurant Bob Waithman arrived late. 'Forrestal's killed himself,' he said. 'The news has just been released. He went out of a sixteenth-floor window in Bethesda during the night.' Forrestal had been copying some verses from Sophocles' 'Chorus From Ajax' in Praed's version out of Mark Van Doren's *Anthology of World Poetry*. At three o'clock in the morning he put down the book and went to the small kitchen, where there was an unguarded window through which he climbed. It was a death containing within itself a significant statement on the pains and stresses that Washington imposed on the best of its servants.

Those pains and stresses were fortunately incapable of making any dent in the sturdy spirit of the President himself. Meeting him again and watching him at White House press conferences it seemed to me that my original assessment, although high, had been a long way below what was justified. Truman's stature grew with every test. I came to see him as one of the great Presidents. Although always conscious of the dignity of his office and careful that it should not be diminished this in no way affected the ease and naturalness of his own personality. He seemed to me less personally affected by the vestments of power than any man I had known—even less so, if that were possible, than Attlee.

I acquired, too, an even greater admiration for Marshall than Attlee and Bevin had already passed on to me. He seemed to me to possess the very best of the soldierly virtues and to combine with them a powerful and penetrating intellect. He was a man on whose fidelity one could depend to the farthest limit and whose integrity would never falter.

I had thought Eisenhower such a man also and I still like to think that in many ways he was. But I could never feel the same about him after he agreed during his Presidential campaign to delete from a major speech in Milwaukee a personal tribute to Marshall, the man to whom he owed more than any other man in the world, in order to get Senator Joseph McCarthy to sit on the platform with him. It had sometimes seemed to me when I knew Eisenhower during the war and worked a little with him that his desire to secure agreement among those with whom he worked occasionally bordered on the excessive. But this had then been one of his great assets and there had never been any indication that he would be ready to sacrifice principle to it. In Milwaukee it seemed to me he did so and in a manner peculiarly shocking. It was a flaw in the character of a great man that I found it hard to think of without shame.

In that summer in Washington, however, McCarthyism was still no more than a sluggish drain underground. The man himself was as yet without any sort of fame although Richard Rovere of the *New Yorker*, who was in Washington for the North Atlantic Treaty, went to see him about some gross allegations he had made about maltreatment by American soldiers of Nazi stormtroopers under sentence in Germany for a peculiarly horrifying massacre and had come away utterly baffled, confessing himself incapable of making any sense of what McCarthy produced as evidence.

But although there was no McCarthy there was the first of the Alger Hiss trials. Hiss at San Francisco had seemed to me well intentioned but dull, with that peculiarly opaque dullness that one sometimes finds in the high-minded. When I talked to him at San Francisco he sometimes seemed congenitally incapable of seeing any issue from any standpoint other than that of a believer in America's God-given right to lead other nations along the path of righteousness. One could not, however, help but like him: he was always so polite and helpful.

When I first heard of the charges thrown at him by Whittaker Chambers they seemed grotesque—as did Chambers himself. Later, thinking things over, I came to the conclusion that it might just be consistent with Hiss's character as I understood it for him to have handed over a few not very important confidential papers to a free-lance journalist for whom he had developed a regard, without too much concern for the strict security proprieties—after all, the giving of confidential information to favoured journalists is almost an industry in Washington. But when I said this to Bert Andrews, then Chief of the Herald Tribune Washington Bureau, who had spent many months on the case he dismissed it scornfully and said, 'He's as guilty as hell. He deserves what's coming to him. And by God I hope he gets it.'

The note of what seemed almost self-satisfied vindictiveness in this observation shocked me. And yet because I had a long-established respect for Andrews's perspicacity as a newspaper-man it shook my own confidence. The split jury in the first trial well reflected, I think, the feeling of many of us. After many hours of talk and thought I found myself unable to decide where I stood.

I still am. I find it infinitely harder to make up my mind about Hiss than any of the others I have known who have been involved in charges of treachery to their country. Some commentators—including Alastair Cooke—have argued that the confession of Klaus Fuchs, the naturalized young British physicist who passed atomic secrets to Russia, confirmed in a way the views of the jury who found Hiss guilty in the second trial, that after this it was impossible any longer to believe, as the defence in the Hiss case had tried to argue, that 'gentle, trusted types' like Hiss were not likely to be capable of disloyalty.

But there is really hardly any point of comparison between Hiss and Fuchs, between the young Ivy League American and the young German driven into the arms of communism as a boy by hatred of Nazism, escaping from it when he came to England, brought back to it when the country of which he then longed to be wholly a part seemed to reject him by interning him in Canada at the beginning of the war, and then later caught up by a misty idealism that convinced him that because of the delay in the second front he had a personal obligation to help Russia and was saving the world by passing on the knowledge that had come to him as an atomic physicist. Fuchs presents a study in abnormal psychology which can brook pity as well as anger, but it has no parallel in the case of Hiss.

Nor do I find much parallel in the cases of Burgess and Maclean, whom I also knew, Maclean only slightly but Burgess quite well during his time in the Foreign Office News Division at the Ministry of Information and later when he was personal assistant to my friend Hector McNeil, the Minister of State at the Foreign Office. Burgess and Maclean bore the marks of inner instability on their foreheads like the mark of Cain. As they moved from one drunken disaster and emotional crisis to another it was not possible to disguise from oneself their unreliability. One could only wonder how it was possible for even the loyalties of the Establishment and the old school tie to keep them where they were. Nor does there seem any parallel between Hiss and the much more formidable but no less neurotic character of Philby. I knew Philby slightly, his background better. His brilliant, mad father, the Arabist St John Philby, was for a time one of my correspondents in the Middle East when I edited the *Daily Herald*. What deceived one about these three was not that they were so steady and respectable but that they seemed more drunken and irresponsible than any spy could afford to be.

None of these were like Hiss, who, if indeed he was guilty as the second jury decided, carries his secrets within his own breast with an exemplary fortitude that none of the others have matched. I continue to find it impossible to make up my mind.

Many years after Fuchs's discovery and confession I talked to a woman who had been friendly and kind to him, Mrs Skinner, the wife of his immediate Chief, Professor Skinner. She was Viennese and in his days at Harwell she befriended him, nursed him when he was ill, went to concerts with him, tried to make him a more complete member of the enclosed Harwell community.

We talked in her apartment, eating sweet cakes from a little round table, and I asked her what it felt like to his friends when they learned the truth about him. Even after all these years she found it hardly possible to speak because of the strain of remembered emotion. 'It wasn't just that we were shattered,' she said. 'I mean we were . . . how can I put it . . . it made us question everything about ourselves because in the end the point was not so much what he had done but who were we? Did we see only what we wanted to see? Could we any longer trust ourselves when we had been so fantastically misled as to think that we knew him in the way we knew ourselves, or our children? Was anything real any more? What would ever be real again . . . ?'

I think many who knew Hiss must have probed themselves similarly. In such a case questions of one's own judgement, almost of one's own identity, of 'who were we that we saw only this and this?' inevitably arise. In Hiss's case these questions hang still in the air because there is as yet no final answer to the central question.

Even in more mundane matters certainty is hard to grasp in this half-world of treachery. On 2 June 1945 Fuchs passed over to his American contact, Gold, at the Castillo Bridge in Santa Fe what must, I suppose, have been the most important news transmitted by a traitor in the whole history of treachery—the news of the completion of the atomic bomb and all that it signified. Some six weeks later, on 16 July, again in Santa Fe near a church, Fuchs met Gold for the last time and told him that the bomb had been exploded in the Alamogordo Desert.

Yet the evidence suggests that Stalin knew nothing of this until he was told by President Truman at Potsdam some seven days later and even then had no understanding of the full potentialities of what had been done. Even when informed that an atomic bomb was to be dropped on Japan he showed so little understanding of what its effect would be that he continued to haggle about the date the Soviet would declare war on Japan. He still seemed to believe that a long war was to be expected out of which Russia might get some advantage if she delayed her intervention until the right moment. Yet such a belief would hardly seem to have been possible if he had received the reports that should have reached him. One wonders what had happened to all the information so secretly collected and so deviously passed on by Fuchs and the American atom spy, Greenglass. And what, one asks oneself, happens to all the other information transmitted by intelligence services in the one war that never stops? Can it be possible that, like more legitimate enterprises, spying suffers from clogged in-trays?

The hurdy-gurdy of Washington conversation had its hypnotic appeal. But I was glad all the same that when the *Observer* approached me I had suggested a rather unusual deal: they should pay me a lump sum down and instead of being a staff man I would regard myself as free to move about as I wished, although keeping a base in Washington. I have never believed that one can understand a country and the reactions of its people by reporting only what goes on in the capital and this is even less true of the United States than of other countries. We went on a sort of safari across the States hunting public opinion and the weather in the streets. I talked to Governors and politicians and newspapermen, and Jess, who had a grant from Great Ormond Street Children's Hospital, visited hospitals and universities and talked to doctors and research workers. In the evenings we pooled the day's experiences or went to parties where we met each other's friends, each of us finding an extension of our knowledge in the happy good fortune of the other's professional activities. We were driven high into the Rockies from Denver by the *Rocky Mountain News* and were glad we had first seen the great mountains from below as mountains should be seen. Then we flew over them to San Francisco, to which Jess gave her heart as I had done.

We went to Berkeley and while I discussed economics and political science Jess, whose capacity for friendship has always much enriched our lives, made the warmest of relationships which have grown and deepened over the years with Jean Macfarlane, Edith Katten and others engaged in a longitudinal social and psychological study which she found fascinating—as I did, too, when I learned about it.

When we got back to Washington Betty and John came to stay with us for the summer vacation and we hired a car and drove down to South Carolina. It was the first time any of us had seen cotton growing and made Jess and me think of our old acquaintance the boll-weevil. It was also the first time we had seen racial discrimination at its most stark. It made us ashamed of being white.

With Betty and John we went, also, to Williamsburg and in the evening to a huge pageant of the War of Independence in an open-air theatre. It ended with the English flag being torn down and trampled on, whereupon every man woman and child in the huge audience very properly rose to their feet and cheered—all but we four who felt that, far away from home, we must remain English patriots, even if we were torn limb from limb for it. However, no one minded and when the audience sat down again one of our neighbours said, 'You English, uh?' and offered us each a hot dog.

When we had seen Betty and John off to England again Jess and I went to Canada, about whose rapidly developing economy I had promised to write for the *Observer*. We went by train to Montreal where we were welcomed by the stationmaster in a tall hat and felt unexpected lumps come into our throats when we saw a Union Jack flying and heard 'God Save the King' being played at a theatre. When I had finished talking with businessmen and bankers in Montreal and Toronto and Ministers and Civil Servants in Ottawa we took train to Winnipeg and Edmonton across the vast sweep of the prairielands, and then north through the Rockies to Prince Rupert and by ship to Vancouver where Jack and Jeannie Wilkinson, whom we had scarcely seen since Middleton days, were waiting by the dockside to meet us.

Later we went to Chicago and to Bloomington to stay with Adlai Stevenson, who had been elected Governor of Illinois on a vote which had linked many progressive Republicans with his Democratic supporters.

I was delighted to see Adlai Stevenson again. He was one of the truly civilized people I knew—too civilized, I rather thought for the rough and tumble of politics and I wondered how he was enjoying the hard chores of Governorship. He had a mind which always saw both sides to any question—more if they were to be found. This made conversation with him stimulating and delightful but above all reasonable. He won Jess's affection because when she told him about the hospitals and other institutions she had been visiting in Chicago he was horrified and said: 'But they've only taken you to the best ones. That's quite wrong. You must see some of the really bad ones, too. I'll arrange it.'

Despite Adlai's charm and courtesy and that special lambent quality which made conversation with him so engaging, something uncomfortably tense became manifest in the atmosphere as we talked over dinner. When we arrived his wife had sent a message that she had a headache. But she came down to dinner and it soon became plain, despite the flickering brilliance of her conversation as we talked of art and literature and mutual friends, that we were participants in some sort of a domestic crisis. She made a particular point of asking us about people we all knew in London and of remarking with an edged glance at her husband, 'Their marriage is breaking up, you know. One can always tell.' She was just recovering, it turned out, from an attack of mumps which had caused some political concern because just before it she had been to a party of Democratic State Senators and had given one of the leading ones a hospitable kiss, with the result that it was feared he would get mumps too. 'If only I'd known,' she said regretfully, 'I would have kissed them all.' She then turned to me and said, 'Are politicians as dreadful in England as they are here? And their wives? But, of course, they all love dear Adlai.'

Throughout all this Adlai remained as courteous and civilized as he always was. Nor was the whole meal as bad as this. There were times during it when some idea or comment caught her fancy when his wife would change to a mood of pleased excitement that was extraordinarily attractive and gay, so that one found oneself thinking what a delightful person she must be when she was happy, and hoping—unavailingly as it turned out—that her present mood was merely a carry-over from the mumps or whatever it was.

After dinner a group of the Governor's friends who had been active in his election came in. Mrs Stevenson curled up in a corner of a settee from which she fired bursts of lightly flickering malice as the rest of us fell to talking about the political situation in America and Britain. Presently she retired to bed, expressing regret for the recurrence of her headache to Jess and me, but saying nothing to the others. She did not come down in the morning when we left.

After she had gone the tension relaxed and we began to talk

about a particular problem that was facing the Governor—a question of whether it would be morally right for him to do a deal with some elements in the State Senate linked, as he suspected to the crime syndicate in order to get through constitutional reforms which seemed to him vital to efficient government. The debate went on a long while. It was clear as Stevenson examined first one side of the dilemma and then the other that we were all participating in a genuine crisis of conscience which Stevenson, despite all the sympathy surrounding him, could only decide alone. Finally after the talk had been going on several hours and Jess and I were both beginning to feel more than a little sleepy he turned to me and said, 'What do you think Attlee would do in a case like this, Francis?' Before I realized how rude I must sound, I found myself saying, 'I'm not sure what he would do but I'm pretty sure he would have decided it quite a while back and said, "Well, ladies and gentlemen, thank you all very much for giving me your opinions. And now let us talk of something else."' Adlai responded with an amused shrug of the shoulders. 'I know,' he said, 'I do go on, don't I? I wish I had the capacity for deciding and to hell with it. But there are so many sides to see.'

I came to admire Stevenson enormously. In much that he did and said he seemed to me to add a new and loftier dimension to the political dialogue and to bring fresh grace and lucidity to its language. Like a great many English people I was very sad when he failed in his Presidential challenge, even although he pulled more votes than any Democratic candidate had since Roosevelt in 1936. Yet I cannot help but think that if he had got to the White House he would sometimes have found the heat of the kitchen intolerable. He lacked Truman's cheerful capacity to roll up his sleeves and get on with it whatever the temperature, or Eisenhower's ability to stay in the front parlour. But, of course, one cannot be sure. The office shapes the man. And there was wonderful metal there for tempering.

The last time I saw Adlai, although he was as stimulating and civilized as ever, he seemed rather sad and diminished. I had flown to New York at the invitation of Robert M. Hutchins to speak at the tenth anniversary symposium of The Fund for the Republic which was being held in a shiny new hotel on Sixth Avenue, of which someone aptly remarked that the only thing wrong with it was that it was a long way from the beach. Stevenson was a brilliant participant and I remember he concluded his own lecture with a quotation from Plutarch particularly dear to him. 'Only those persons who live in obedience to reason are worthy to be accounted free. Only they live as they will who have learned what they ought to will.'

He was then U.N. Representative of the Kennedy Administration, a job that did not stretch his powers and had on one or two occasions confronted him with the sort of moral dilemma he struggled so hard to resolve according to his own conscience. The night I arrived we met at a dinner given by the British Consul-General. Adlai Stevenson had asked, I found out later, that he should be seated next to me and we talked to each other engrossed through a very long dinner, discourteously ignoring our other partners most of the time. By the time the dinner ended I was beginning to feel conscious of the five hours' difference between London and New York but Stevenson insisted that I should go on with him to what turned out to be a party of some of his rich friends. Parties, I gathered, were coming to be more and more a part of the staple diet of his existence.

He was planning to come to London and when the symposium ended we arranged that he should lunch with me at the House of Lords as soon as he arrived. But when he came I was ill and we had to cancel our meeting. Later when I had recovered I had a note from him telling me when he expected to be in London again and hoping we could meet. I had news of his arrival but before we could arrange anything he collapsed and died walking from the American Embassy in Grosvenor Square. For me, as for many others, something of civilized virtue in the world died with him.

CHAPTER 15

Governor of the B.B.C.

David Astor asked me to stay on in Washington but much as we liked America we had no wish to live there on a semi-permanent basis and nor, we knew, would Betty and John. Betty was at Cambridge where she was finding Girton, which no doubt seemed fine and adult to young ladies from Roedean or Cheltenham Ladies College, somewhat stuffy after St Christopher. John was in his last year at school before he also went to Cambridge to St John's College. And there was Jess's work at Great Ormond Street Children's Hospital to think about.

Also we wanted to see my father and mother. Although now well again they had been seriously ill while we were away. They had both had an attack of food poisoning and had only just managed to call the doctor before collapsing. He sent for an ambulance and they were carried out on stretchers. My father was in a coma and my mother seemed to be in one too. But as they prepared to lift her stretcher into the ambulance, she suddenly opened her eyes and asked them what they were doing.

'You've been very ill and we're taking you both into hospital,' said the doctor soothingly. 'It will be easier to give you proper treatment there. Just relax and try not to worry.'

'Don't be silly,' said my mother, putting her feet on the ground. 'Who do you think will look after things if I'm not here?' and insisted on being helped back into the house. 'And Eddie would have something to say to you, too, if he was well enough,' she said. 'How can I help you if you won't do what I say?' asked the doctor, 'But I always do what you tell me,' said my mother opening wide her eyes. 'When it's sensible.'

It was the fall of the year and although we liked the country best and were trying to get a licence to build a house on a hillside in Abinger, London was lovely to look at and much pleasanter than most capital cities to live in. It seemed like a quiet village after New York. I settled down to work on a book and engaged myself to write a weekly column on current affairs for the *News Chronicle*, a newspaper soon to be killed for which I had great affection. Robin Cruickshank, its editor, was one of the most engaging and intelligent men to set foot in a newspaper office and was full of odd pieces of information about Victorian London and twentieth-century New York. The Cruickshanks came to dinner with us in Gordon Square to celebrate my writing for him and to meet some friends of ours from Princeton, and Jess produced what Robin justly described as a 'memorable' chicken pie.

Shortly afterwards I had a call from Herbert Morrison. There had been several cables while I was in Washington asking me to let my name go forward for a forthcoming by-election and I had refused and I was afraid that it might be Herbert Morrison, the party manager, rather than Herbert Morrison, Lord President of the Council, who wanted to see me. However, I was wrong. The purpose of the invitation was much more pleasant than I had anticipated. It was to ask me to serve as a Governor of the B.B.C.

I had already had a longish experience of the B.B.C. as a broadcaster. When I began in the early 1930s Sir John Reith was still Director-General and one embarked on a broadcast with awe and a sense of apostolic compulsion. The first time I broadcast—I was Financial Editor of the *Daily Herald* at the time and it was on some economic subject—I was met at Reception by a charming lady who clearly embodied in her svelte and courteous person the highest ideals of broadcasting. She conveyed me on tiptoe to a small studio and pointing to the microphone on the table at which I was to sit said in a reverential tone—but whether to encourage or subdue me I was not sure—'That is the microphone into which the Prince of Wales spoke.'

Since then I had broadcast on many occasions and on almost

all B.B.C. services and experienced to the full the subtle gradations of programme status conveyed by the kind of refreshments one was offered. There was coffee and an egg and cress sandwich on the overseas services, a drink from a locked cocktail cabinet, for the key of which the producer had to sign, on the European service, a couple of drinks in the Duty Room after a current affairs broadcast on the Home Service, an elaborate buffet supper after the 10 o'clock news, smoked salmon sandwiches and gin and tonic on the Third Programme and pleasant dinner parties at 'Any Questions'. To the last one was allowed to invite a guest, for whom, however, one had to pay—a matter discreetly arranged by a secretary when no one else was looking.

It was all very cosy. One met the same people and discussed very much the same subjects from month to month. It was like being a member of a repertory company.

Most of the producers were Oxford or Cambridge arts graduates. David Owen, co-administrator of the U.N. Development Programme, used to tell of how when he applied for a job with the B.B.C. as a young man and confessed that he had been to neither Oxford nor Cambridge but to Leeds an uncomfortable silence fell on the interview board. It was as though the Athenaeum had found itself considering an application for membership by a shopkeeper. Many of these producers were women: pleasant, earnest ladies who worried a good deal about many things but not much about listening figures. Those were thought to be rather vulgar.

However, things were changing. Television was on its way. It had had to be abandoned during the war but was now back on the air. I had appeared on television for the first time just before going to America, in a programme with Alan Bullock about a book I'd written on politics. We broadcast from a large gloomy studio at Alexandra Palace and there was still a fine amateur glow about things. Looking for a lavatory I found myself in a bathroom where there was an old man with a drooping moustache lying on his back in a bathtub of water who turned out to be a sea lion waiting for a nature programme. Everyone behaved as if they were pioneers staking out new frontiers and talked constantly about the fun they'd had in the old pre-war days—like the television interview with Jim

Mollison the flyer who came on from a party and swayed in front of the cameras with a smile on his face saying nothing so that the interviewer had to put the questions and then answer himself until the very end when Mollison, fixing him with a beady but wavering eye, gave voice and said, reasonably enough: 'What's the use of asking me all these bloody silly questions if you know the answers anyway? Let's all have another drink.'

On my programme with Alan Bullock the lights were terribly hot in the studio and the yellow make-up they had plastered on us soon began to run, but it was all very jolly and at the end the producer, who was Mrs Grace Wyndham-Goldie, later a very *grande dame* of television indeed, was presented with a bouquet by the grateful B.B.C. This shows how long ago and far away it was.

I looked forward, therefore, to being one of the Governors of the B.B.C., who were at that time a small body of seven who met once a fortnight. Three of them were old friends or acquaintances of mine: The Chairman, Lord Simon of Wythenshawe, the Vice-Chairman, Marshal of the Royal Air Force Lord Tedder, and Barbara Wootton, whom I had known for many years.

The Director-General was Sir William Haley, later Editor of *The Times*, whom I had known as Editor of the *Manchester Evening News* and as a Director of Reuters during the war. Lord Reith later told me that he considered Haley the only man of stature to be Director-General of the B.B.C. since himself. There was a brief period when it seemed just possible that he would include Sir Hugh Greene in his list too. But what with satire, permissiveness and one thing and another Sir Hugh was cast out, leaving Haley to his lonely eminence, below but in hailing distance of Reith himself.

Certainly Haley did a good deal for the B.B.C., especially in defence of its independence against erosion by Government influence. But whether all that he did for it was what the B.B.C. most needed at that exact time is another question. An extraordinarily shy man, of strong principles and unbending intellect, he found it difficult to display warmth towards those of his staff with whom he was not in direct contact and was known among them as the man with two glass eyes. Those who knew him better, however, sometimes found him one of the kindest as well as one of the most intelligent of men.

The day my appointment as a Governor was announced I received a formal but pressing invitation to lunch with him. We lunched simply but rather grandly in a private dining-room at the B.B.C. and he confided in me that his first act on hearing that I was to join the Board had been to send for all the books I had written and read them through from cover to cover—an exercise well within his competence, as I was later to discover, since he was one of the most rapid and voracious of readers. I was much complimented by this, although I could not help feeling that it might have been more tactful to pretend that he had read them before. I asked him whether he had enjoyed them, but received the strong impression that this was quite beside the point. Enjoyment had nothing to do with it. 'I thought I'd better get to know you,' he said.

Haley's idea of the responsibilities of the B.B.C. was very like Reith's. So was his view of the role of the Governors. When pressed he would observe that the Board of Governors was 'a reserve of wisdom'—a reserve, as Barbara Wootton once remarked, most useful when not drawn on, like the gold reserve of the Bank of England. Under his direction Governors were treated like constitutional monarchs. They were accorded great deference but not allowed any power. He did not take kindly to independent thinking among them, considering that their wisdom should be reserved to confirming his own.

Nor, I think, did he enjoy independent thinking among his staff. He thought their job was to preserve the Ark of the Covenant. When, after much irritating prodding by the conscientious Simon, several senior officers of the B.B.C. were dispatched on missions to the United States to see whether there was anything the B.B.C. could learn from American radio and television, they reported almost to a man that there was nothing. This view was confirmed by Haley himself after a hurried visit. 'I fear,' commented Simon sadly, 'that complacency is a real danger to the B.B.C.'

Haley wished to improve the taste of the masses and make people more serious-minded. He explained to me with some passion that his ambition, which he seemed to think readily achievable, was to lead listeners from the Light Programme to the Home and from the Home to the Third until eventually both Home and Light should wither away leaving the Third over all. For these reasons he regarded television with a suspicious eye. He did not like what was happening to it in America and wished to contain it by putting gentlemanly, scholarly men in charge. Perhaps because he had never been to a university himself he had an exaggerated respect for university men, if they came from one of the older universities and, oddly for a newspaperman, seemed to like to think of the B.B.C.'s affairs as being conducted by members of a senior commonroom.

These attitudes came to a head over the appointment of a Director of Television. The appointment was a reluctant admission that perhaps the new medium, although basically inferior to radio, which was the B.B.C.'s real business and more suited to raising the taste of the people, ought to be allowed a seat at the same table as sound radio which had three Directors, one for Talks and News, one for general Home Broadcasting and one for Overseas Broadcasting. Previously television had merely had a Controller—a lower rank in the hierarchy. The Controller, and as it seemed to many the natural Director, was Norman Collins, a man of much drive, energy and ambition, who had been a journalist and publisher and was a popular novelist. He was, however, suspected by Haley of being a little short in that unquestioning devotion to the higher purposes of the B.B.C. thought necessary in its chief officers and to have heretical ideas about making television popular. Haley was, therefore, determined to appoint to the new Directorship not Collins but George Barnes. Barnes had been Head of the Third Programme and was a much more senior-commonroom type than Collins, although not without his own politely concealed ambitions: when the B.B.C. later failed to yield him its richest prize, the Director-Generalship, he left to become Principal of Keele University.

Barnes was a man of courtesy and culture. There were few people it was pleasanter to spend an evening with. But he had no experience of television and to promote him over the head of Norman Collins, who had built the television service to the level at which it then stood, seemed to me both unfair and to be asking for trouble. However, by the time I attended my first Board meeting the decision had already been taken. The

Director-General had proffered his advice and the Board had loyally endorsed it. Norman Collins thereupon resigned and insisted on saying publicly that he disagreed with the B.B.C.'s television policy—a course which, Haley smugly told the Governors, confirmed his judgement that such a man had not the qualities required of a Director. Like the officers of a good regiment, members of the higher staffs of the B.B.C. were expected to salute the colours, bite on the bullet, back up the colonel, and keep quiet.

This particular episode had far-reaching consequences. Thwarted in his very proper B.B.C. ambitions Collins turned his mind to commercial television, becoming its most able and energetic exponent and doing perhaps more than any man to bring its campaign to early success, thus presenting the B.B.C with exactly the challenge that Haley most feared and detested.

I would not say that in my own—relatively brief—period as a Governor of the B.B.C. the Governors exercised no influence at all. But it was small and mainly retrospective. We were rarely, if ever, told what was to be done, only what had been done, and devoted ourselves to discussion of past programmes and policies laid before us by the various Directors behind the formidable shield of the Director-General. I can think of no major issue and only of one or two minor ones in which the Board did other than give its blessing to what the Director-General had already decided: indeed, in one absurdly minor matter which I happened to raise at the suggestion of Wilson Harris, then Editor of the *Spectator*, which was why the B.B.C. should insist on referring to the head of the German State as Mr Adenauer instead of Dr Adenauer as everyone else, including himself, did, it took, I think, three meetings to get the Director-General to reverse, not his opinion, that remained adamant, but his ruling.

This dictatorship of the B.B.C.'s affairs, great and small, by the Director-General worried the Chairman, Lord Simon, a good deal. He was a conscientious and simple-minded man—simple, I mean, in the sense that he lacked much of either guile or subtlety—and the fact that he had agreed to accept the part-time appointment of Chairman and, as required by its Charter, make the B.B.C. his 'main interest' nagged at him. The Director-

General, not the Chairman, whose name, indeed, most of them scarcely knew, was regarded by the staff as their master and it was the Director-General, not the Chairman, who was accepted by outside opinion, including that of politicians, as the presiding genius and voice of the Corporation whenever its activities roused either praise or criticism. Simon could find no parallel to this situation in any world he knew, whether that of industry where he was Chairman of a great family engineering concern, in politics where the Minister, not the Permanent Secretary, was the policy-maker, in the nationalized industries where the Chairman was the man at the top or in local government to which he had devoted himself with much success in Manchester, where officials were officials and policy came from the Council and the Committee Chairman.

Reith, although he stood no nonsense from the Chairman and regarded it as a law of nature that he himself was in every sense the B.B.C., had, nevertheless, paid his Chairmen the courtesy of inviting them to attend the meetings of the official Board of Management which had the executive running of the B.B.C. in its hands. Haley saw no reason even for this concession. Throughout his period of office Simon struggled in vain to get acceptance of the notion that the Chairman of the B.B.C. should be allowed to get his hand on any of the B.B.C.'s levers of power.

This conflict over the relative position of Chairman and Director-General continued after Simon—or would have done so but for the fact that until Lord Hill no Chairman even tried to fight. There would have been a chance to do so when the Governors—from whose company I had by then departed—chose Sir Ian Jacob, Director of the B.B.C.'s Overseas Services, rather than Barnes as Haley's successor. Jacob is a nice man, efficient in an undisturbing way and one of those soldiers you can never imagine firing a shot in anger. He had been Assistant Military Secretary of the Cabinet during the war and by temperament and training had a staff officer's attitudes. If there had been a strong positive Chairman a secondary role would have come naturally to him. But Sir Winston Churchill, who was by then again Prime Minister, chose instead to appoint as successor to Simon not, as many, including himself, had hoped and expected, the Vice-Chairman, Lord Tedder, who was used to command, but Sir Alexander Cadogan, the former Permanent Under-Secretary of State for Foreign Affairs, of whom I have already spoken. Cadogan was an intelligent and charming man, but an adviser by profession. He left things to Jacob. In due course Cadogan was succeeded by another Civil Servant, Lord Normanbrook, and Jacob by a stronger and more creative Director-General, Hugh Greene. Greene assumed first place as of right and Normanbrook did not challenge him. Not until Mr Wilson shocked the B.B.C. by sending them Lord Hill did the balance between Director-General and Chairman come under pressure.

Since Greene's dislodgement and the appointment of a sound administrative man as his successor the issue has become open again, but with a much more subtle operator in the Chairman's office than poor dear Simon of Wythenshawe. Despite the noise one now hears of men whistling to keep their courage up when one visits Broadcasting House or Television Centre all the odds are that for the first time in B.B.C. history it will this time be the Chairman who comes out on top.

I enjoyed being a B.B.C. Governor but despite its stately and enervating charm I was glad when my period of office—rather shorter than most because of a new Charter—came to an end and delighted to find when I parachuted back to earth that my services as a broadcaster were still in demand. This proved to be particularly the case in television.

The modern world has created few occupations odder than that of being a television personality. Marghanita Laski, I remember, opted out of it in the full flood of success as a popular panel member because she said it interfered too much with her private life, causing her to be constantly recognized and accosted by strangers. Few have her resolution. For most the easy appeal of television proves irresistible. Some it kills as it did poor Gilbert Harding, who found it necessary during the time I knew him to turn more and more to whisky to stave off the sense of being committed to something essentially phoney that was eroding his personality. Some it corrupts in both manners and personality. Some, like Richard Dimbleby, it enhances, so that they become larger than they formerly were. Yet even with those performers whose public personality television expands it diminishes the private one. Even with Dimbleby it became more and more difficult as time passed to find within the public personality the private person one used to know.

Fortunately I was never more than a part-time T.V. personality. I will not claim to have escaped all damage. It is not easy to be even a part-time professional pundit without some loss of sensitivity. To become a popular pipe-smoking image on a television screen has its character corruption even if one tries to keep to serious television. When Gilbert Harding died and it was found difficult to find anyone to replace him with the right blend of omnipotent grumpiness masking the promise of a kind heart underneath I was asked if I would take his place on 'What's My Line?' I answered with a clear conscience that this was not my line at all and for the same reason I kept clear of quiz programmes. All the same when a *Sunday Times* television critic referred sharply to the habits of television interviewers 'led by that redoubtable jack-in-the-box, Francis Williams' and commented, 'These household gods are all the same. They put their victims on trial for treason even when all that is at stake is the butter content of ice-cream,' I had to admit to myself that there was a good deal to say for the American observation: 'All cameras corrupt. Television cameras corrupt utterly.'

My most regular appearances were as a kind of playing captain of 'Press Conference', a somewhat less formalized version of the American 'Meet The Press'. Each week some prominent public figure, sometimes a politician, sometimes a dramatist, or artist, or author, sometimes a scientist, or educationist, or businessman, would be invited to be cross-examined by a group of three or four newspapermen and women, among whom I was the only constant element, the others being picked according to the nature of the examinee.

The programme had a large viewing audience and had the effect of making me known to many millions or people in almost every town and village in the country. But how much of what was actually said and discussed on these programmes got through I found it hard to decide. Most of the people who spoke to me, as a great many did wherever I went, clearly switched on much more in the hope of a clash or a quarrel than anything else. They saw it as a pleasurable form of jousting, but not, I think, as much more. Why, indeed, should they? We provided entertainment and gave viewers a superficial chance to judge all sorts of people. But I doubt if the sum total of public knowledge was much increased by our efforts and I sometimes think we may have done more harm than good by helping to foster the public myth, which has now reached a level where it may soon make both Britain and America virtually ungovernable, that there are, or ought to be, instant answers to all questions and that everything is, or ought to be, capable of simple explanation.

There were a few splendid moments like the one when A. P. Herbert—that dear delightful man—expressed his opinion of a Government Bill by putting a match to it and the fireman on duty in the studio rushed up with a bucket of water and was only just prevented from throwing it over him. There was also an evening long remembered when the Aga Khan talked about the most beautiful women he had known and tipped the messengers and liftmen a five-pound-note apiece as he made his princely way from the studio to his Rolls-Royce.

And there was a wonderful evening when Randolph Churchill, his eyes bulging, lost his temper and shouted in reply to a question of mine, 'Are you suggesting that I'm nothing but a miserable hack like that fellow—' (giving the name of a well-known employee of Beaverbrook newspapers)—'who'd change his opinions overnight if you offered to double his pay?' Not unnaturally this outburst was followed by a solicitor's letter with a threat of a libel suit by the unjustly attacked journalist. To this Randolph replied in terms which ran, as I remember: 'I have received your pompous letter. I frankly admit that I was wrong in saying that your client would change his opinions overnight for an offer to double his salary and I apologize. I am credibly informed by those who know him better than I do that he would do it for half the money.' This reply delighted Randolph but did not help to settle the affair and finally Randolph, who although partial to fighting libel suits liked to have some chance of winning them, decided that it might be useful to have a talk with Lord Beaverbrook. He made his way to Arlington House. Here, according to the report he gave me, for he loved to retell his own jokes, he was received by Nockels, Lord Beaverbrook's famous butler. 'The Lord,' said Nockels employing the phrase by which he always distinguished his master, 'is in St James's Park.' 'Ah,' said Randolph, giving birth to a *mot* subsequently much repeated in a slightly smudged form, 'walking on the lake, I presume.'

However, he eventually tracked Beaverbrook to dry land and Beaverbrook undertook to intervene with his employee who, although he had every reason for an action, agreed to drop it.

'Press Conference' had something of a reputation for stringent questioning. Kurt Hahn, the founder of Gordonstoun, told me that when he agreed to take part in it he was in such a state of nerves on his way to the studio that when he got out of the car at Lime Grove the B.B.C. driver patted him on the shoulder and said, 'There, there, sir. They're not as bad as all that.' In fact, however, the programme was usually concerned much more with extracting information than with dissecting reputations. The world had not reached the stage where television was thought to have a mandate to act as a public prosecutor.

Nor did politicians yet feel that their positions depended on doing whatever television asked of them. It would have been inconceivable for either Churchill or Attlee to have agreed to subject themselves to the sort of television inquisition to which Prime Ministers now avidly submit. When they sought to defend themselves they did it in the House of Commons. Macmillan did once take part in a 'Press Conference'. But it was a formal affair with the scope of questioning agreed beforehand. Nor, I think, in those innocent days did those of us who put the questions on 'Press Conference' have any very inflated view of our own importance. There was a view fairly commonly expressed at that time that those who appeared regularly on television might come to possess a dangerous influence over the popular mind. I found little evidence of this. Viewers were then too sensible, and probably still are, to take talking heads too seriously. At the best they seemed to regard us less as fountains of wisdom than as neighbours who had dropped in for a chat, at worst as household pets whose mannerisms were more important than their opinions.

I never found it possible to regard television either as a serious art or even, so far as I was concerned, as important a means of communication as written journalism. But I enjoyed the people I met and the places I went to for 'Panorama' and 'Gallery' and other documentary programmes on which I appeared in addition to 'Press Conference'. And I was interested to find that some of the programmes that appealed least to thrusting young producers like Michael Peacock, who thought that television should challenge and assert, lasted longest in the public memory just because they did not try to state absolutes. However, one must not, I suppose, discount the symbolic importance of the television set. In Kirkenes on the edge of the Arctic Circle I was taken by local communists to see a television set presented to them by their Russian comrades. There were no programmes it could receive. But it was treated as an object of veneration.

CHAPTER 16

A Firm Hand at the Top

The Labour Government was running out of steam. After the 1950 election it began to run out of manpower too. Most of its principal members had been in office steadily for nearly ten years with only a break of a few weeks between the end of the wartime coalition and the start of the Attlee administration. Its two strongest members, Bevin and Cripps, were seriously ill. Even Attlee himself, normally as tough as a piece of wire, was starting to show the strain. He began to suffer with ulcers and eczema. There were bitter quarrels among some of the younger members.

I went to see Cripps at the Treasury in 1951. I was shocked by his appearance. His skin was tightly stretched on the bones of his face and seemed almost transparent. He was very thin and obviously weary. As we talked he said, as if he had been thinking about it a long time, 'I think it's time I went, Francis.' He passed a hand over the Treasury papers in front of him. 'They put up such superb reports,' he said, 'you have to read them two or three times to find the snags. And now I'm so weary I just want to accept what they say. When that happens it's time to go.'

It seemed to me a sentiment of universal application. However, I tried to persuade him that he would be all right after a holiday. But he shook his head. 'I'm so tired,' he said. He smiled bleakly. 'You know,' he said, 'I often think modern governments need two teams of Ministers, one to take over when the first lot wear out.'

That was my last talk with him. He went to the Burcher-Benner Clinic in Zurich for examination and sent his resignation to Attlee. And there after a lingering illness he died. He urged Attlee to appoint as his successor Hugh Gaitskell, who had been his second-in-command at the Treasury—thereby ensuring, although he was, perhaps, too weary to realize it, that Aneurin Bevan, who had for long been his dearest disciple, should feel himself and his ideas snubbed and be driven into mischief.

Although Cripps had seemed to me when I first knew him a man whose common sense never matched his intellect, I had come in latter years to have both admiration and affection for him. He was a good deal more human than he let himself be thought. To Attlee and the Labour Government his loss at that time was most grievous.

Yet not so grievous as that of Ernest Bevin. Even before the 1950 election it was clear to everyone but Bevin himself that he could not long stay on as Foreign Secretary. But he would not believe it. He had it fixed in his mind that soon there would come a softening of Soviet suspicion of the West. He wanted to be there to make sure that it was recognized when it came and to persuade the Americans to soften in their turn. He would not accept the possibility that he might have to resign. From the Colombo Conference he wrote to Attlee, 'This morning I am much better, it is not the swan-song yet. Colombo will not be very strenuous and a steady journey home will help.' But the handwriting was woefully shaky. Three months later he was in Manor House Hospital, writing; 'Both doctors say I am nearly out of the wood so far as the angina pectoris is concerned and the treatment I have followed has been effective. I have some other trouble with the heart, fibrillations, or something of that kind, the cause of which I do not understand but which seems to take the breath out of me every now and again. However, the rest here is helping that and I am taking special treatment for it. Then I have got the swelling of the legs but they have something now which will take the place of the injections and so far the results have been satisfactory. The operation itself was a nasty one, but the pain has died down. . . . I am giving close attention to the Atlantic Pact and all the other papers for the Acheson visit. I want to turn that into a success if I can. . . .'

He ended, 'I believe I am going to make a good recovery.'

His illness had by now become the subject of constant debate in the newspapers, many of which were calling for his resignation. This made Attlee very bitter. Recalling it, he said to me, 'They are more generous in such matters in America. When Dulles was ill they cracked him up and urged he should stay on. But as soon as Ernie was ill people started howling for his blood.'

Bevin recovered enough to fight the 1950 election and to carry on for a time with what had become his driving ambition —the search for a crack in the cold war. But by 1951 it was clear that he could go on no longer and, hating what he had to do, Attlee, who normally moved Ministers without any show of emotion, had to tell him so. I went to see him two days after he had left the Foreign Office.

I had been asked by one of the Sunday papers to write a piece about his early days and was proud to do so. But he did not like it—or at least his wife did not. He asked me to go and see him at his Foreign Office flat in Carlton House Terrace from which he had not yet moved. When I got there he said, 'You shouldn't have written that, Francis.' 'What shouldn't I have written?' I asked. 'All that about when I was a boy. And stealing as a nipper in Bristol to keep alive.' 'Why not?' I asked. 'It's true. You told me yourself. I wanted to show them just how great a man you are.' 'I know,' he said and then with a self-conscious wave of the hand towards the next room he said, 'but it's not the sort of thing women like being reminded of. It upset her.' 'I'm sorry,' I said and he gave a half-embarrassed smile and said, 'I don't mind but I promised her I'd give you a ticking off. Now let's forget it. Have a drink. I can't, but you can.'

He looked ill but not as ill as I had feared. He was still brooding about the Foreign Office. 'I could have managed,' he said. 'No need for Clem to turn me into an elder statesman.' He had been succeeded by Herbert Morrison. This rankled, for his feud with Morrison was as lively as ever. The papers were carrying stories about lights burning in the Foreign Office until well after midnight as Morrison grappled with telegrams and brought himself up to date on international problems. Bevin waved contemptuously through the window across St James's

Park in the general direction of the Foreign Office. 'He's enjoying himself now,' he said. 'But let him wait a month or two. It'll be different then.' I asked him if not Morrison who? 'I'd have rather it had been Jim,' he said, meaning Jim Griffiths who was Secretary of State for the Colonies. I raised an eyebrow for although I was very fond of Griffiths and thought him one of the most truly single-minded and warm-hearted socialists in the Government I could not see him holding his own at the international negotiating table. Bevin chuckled when he saw my expression. 'He's tougher than you think,' he said. 'Well Nye, then. I'd sooner have had Nye than 'erbert. He might have turned out quite good.'

I tried to get him to talk about what he thought his own biggest achievements as Foreign Secretary had been but he would not. 'Tell them to wait twenty years,' he said. He was beginning to get tired and I left. He shook hands formally as he often did. 'Remember,' he said reverting to the beginning of our talk, 'Don't you go upsetting her again. You know what women are.' He went back to his chair and as I let myself out of the room I could see him sitting chewing a non-existent something as he often did and glowering through the window at the interloper, Morrison, across the park.

I saw him again about four weeks later on Wednesday 11 April in his room at the House of Commons. I had taken a small group to see him about some matter which fell within the province of his new office as Lord Privy Seal, so far as it had any province. I could see a great change in him even in those few weeks. He seemed shrunken in size. I kept the discussion short but when the others rose to go he beckoned to me to stay behind. He seemed to want to chat, as we often had in the past, about his old trade-union days. He began to talk about a pensions scheme he had got for workers in the milling industry many years before. 'It made all the difference in the world to them,' he said. 'I didn't think the bosses would agree. But they did. It was a nice day. I think they must have wanted to get away to the races.'

He swung back to the present. 'I'd have liked to stay until there was a chance of agreement with the Russians,' he said. 'Bringing them and the Americans nearer. I'd set my heart on it.'

His private secretary brought in some tea and as we drank

he said, 'I'm going to get away to the sun. I'll be all right if I get to the sun.' And then turning back to his trade-union days again he said, 'You remember, Francis. It's no use to start talking unless you've made up your mind what you'll do if the other fellow says no.'

On Saturday, three days later, he died. He had arranged to go to a football international between England and Scotland at Wembley but when the time came he did not feel up to it. He insisted on his wife going with Hector McNeil, the Secretary of State for Scotland, who had called for them. Shortly after they had left he had a heart attack. He died before a doctor could reach him.

He was, I think, one of the greatest men I have known—perhaps the greatest I have known intimately—for although I knew Churchill I never knew him so well as I did Bevin. They resembled each other in many ways—the aristocrat and the illegitimate son of a farm labourer and a village midwife—and especially so in the richness and strangeness of their characters. Above all they both possessed that quality which Goethe once thought to be especially English: 'The courage they have to be that which nature made them.'

After Bevin's death I was asked by the *Spectator* to write about him. I did so in words which for me still stand: 'As a man he was often ruthless, sometimes brutal, frequently childishly egotistical, at times needlessly vindictive. But he had a greatness of spirit, a fundamental magnanimity, that transcended all these defects and made them in the final count unimportant. ... On those who knew him the impact of his personality was so strong that it is hardly possible to believe he is no longer there to exercise his unfailing power over the imagination and the mind, to quarrel with and to love.'

The death of Bevin, the illness of Cripps, these alone would have been sufficient to disturb the balance that had so long kept the Government steady, especially as Attlee himself was ill; he was, in fact, in hospital undergoing treatment for a duodenal ulcer when Bevin died. But within a week of Bevin's death Aneurin Bevan, along with Harold Wilson and John Freeman, had resigned, all three of them as a protest against Hugh Gaitskell's first Budget and the policy regarding armament expenditure it reflected.

284

It was the beginning of the long internecine war between Bevanites and Gaitskellites which was to divide the Labour Party into warring factions for so long and help to keep it out of office for a decade and a half.

It is surprising in view of these losses by death and resignation and the evidence they provided of the irreconcilable nature of some of the disputes within the party that Labour did as well as it did when Attlee went to the country, especially since Herbert Morrison, who had wanted so much to be Foreign Secretary and insisted so stubbornly on his right to it when Bevin went, had made a worse showing at the Foreign Office than even Bevin at his most vindictive could have expected. Yet despite all this and the shortages and austerities imposed by the Korean War, Attlee had bigger meetings when he toured the country than he had ever had, amounting in some cases to 30,000 or more, and Labour increased its popular vote to 13,950,000, more than had ever been received by any political party in British history. It was about a quarter of a million more than the total received by the Conservatives and their allies and should have been enough to send Attlee back for a third time. Perhaps it would have been but for a redistribution of electoral boundaries to meet the effects of wartime changes in population distribution which he had initiated and which even in the 1950 election had resulted in doing away with a number of Labour constituencies in the East End of London, including Attlee's own Limehouse seat. In this election it had the result of substituting a Labour majority in the Commons of ten by a Conservative majority of sixteen, despite the greater number of votes cast for Labour.

'Some people thought we'd been too moral about redistribution,' Attlee said to me afterwards, 'but you had to take into account what bombing and wartime population movements had done and that was how it worked out. It would have been wrong to hold it up.'

As far as I was concerned the end of the Labour Government meant, I anticipated more freedom from politics. Ever since life in Bootle had turned me into a socialist political events had continued to creep up on me. Political activity had seemed a duty. But although I could not deny that I had often got much pleasure from it and hoped I had helped to do some good, I was glad to be more on the periphery of things. I was still, of course, a socialist and deeply committed to what seemed to me the moral principles it spoke for. Personal relations were what to me gave life its richness and quality and I could never tire of the pleasure of getting to know men and women in all their infinite strangeness and diversity. But I could not understand those who found it possible to disassociate themselves from social responsibility and live lives wholly centred on their own and their family's affairs. Such a person seemed to me to be a kind of monster.

Even after I had left Downing Street I had kept in touch with Attlee and many of his Ministers and had always felt that I must hold myself available if it should be felt that there was some particular contribution I could make. Now that they were out of things for the time being I felt more free of political commitment than for a long time.

Now, I thought, I can really retire into my own chosen activities—always supposing I can make a living by them. I was now a member of the management committee of the Society of Authors—that admirable body whose intelligent staff, led by the knowledgeable and delightful Elizabeth Barber, have done so much for the profession of authorship—so that I knew a good deal about the uncertainties of the author's life as well as its splendours and miseries. For such a life one needs strong nerves and a sympathetic bank manager. I thought I had the first and knew from long experience with the Westminster Bank that I had the second. Lord Thomson of Fleet once told me that in his experience the first essential of success was to have a bank manager who knew what you were about and was prepared to trust you. Lord Thomson has made a lot more money than I have. But I have found his advice re bankers as sound for authors as for businessmen.

After a good deal of trouble we had now managed to get a house built in Abinger and were back in the countryside we greatly loved and in which our children had been brought up. It had taken us a long time to get a licence to build which was then necessary because of the post-war shortage of building materials. Such were political feelings at that time that several Conservatives on the Rural District Council were by no means inclined, if they could help it, to give a building licence to someone thought to be so closely associated with what a subsequent Conservative Prime Minister with a wider grasp of affairs than they had, Mr Macmillan, was to call 'one of the most able Governments of modern times'. They would have liked to blackball me for being a friend of Attlee. In Britain it is only when a man is safely retired from politics that it becomes permissible to recognize his qualities. So strong, indeed, was the antagonism to Attlee and as a consequence to me in the darker reaches of the local Conservative Party that one councillor went so far as to say publicly that he saw no reason why Francis Williams should be allowed back into Surrey.

Fortunately this expression of prejudice deeply enraged my solicitor, Mr W. L. Pengelly, a man with an infinite capacity for making legal affairs exciting who is now a Master in Chancery and who had been, when I first met him, Tom Darlow's lawyer—a rich experience in itself. Pengelly, to whom I was devoted, was himself an active Conservative prominent in his local Conservative Party. He considered the attitude of some of these Dorking Conservatives an insult to Conservatism and determined to put it down.

Gordon Square, where we then lived, was in the Borough of St Pancras. There was very little private building in St Pancras which in consequence had at times a superfluity of private licences. Pengelly therefore approached Conservative friends of his on the St Pancras Council, where they had recently won a majority, and pointed out that by giving me a licence which could then be transferred to Dorking they could make the living accommodation I occupied in St Pancras available for people on their housing list. They agreed and since even the most prejudiced of the Dorking councillors could not quite bring themselves publicly to refuse a transfer from another Conservative Council, we were finally enabled to build our house on the piece of woodland we had bought some years before.

Abinger had altered little since we first knew it. There were still craftsmen like Mr Sherlock of Peaslake and his son, Denis, to turn to when you needed any building to be done, always providing you were prepared to wait for quality. As for the timber to be cleared, Mr Arrow, who always wore a bowler hat and talked to trees as if they were members of the family, was still there to deal with this.

Transactions with Mr Arrow took on the quality of a treasure hunt in reverse. The trees cut and the timber disposed of one would receive a summons to his cottage for a final accounting. There, three tins would be put on the table in front of him by his wife. From the first he would take a large wad of pound notes and count them out slowly, one by one, on to a pile in front of you. 'That,' he would say with much satisfaction, 'is what we got for the timber we sold.' He would give you a moment or two to stroke it and would then proceed to the next stage. 'But there's the cost of the haulage,' he would say and one by one he would take notes away from the pile and put them in the second tin. Even at the end of this a sizeable pile would still remain at which one looked hopefully. 'And then,' he would say, 'there's the cost of the felling,' and one by one what was left of the pile would go into the third tin. Not, if one was lucky, quite all. One or even two would remain. One would put them in one's pocket and, business over, Mr Arrow would beckon to his wife to put the kettle on and offer you a cup of tea.

Mr Arrow is now dead and his sons have taken over the business. He used to fuss a good deal about them when he was alive and would come and measure the 'thresholds' of the trees they cut and talk about young fellows being in a hurry, they being then in their forties and fifties. They have more modern accountancy methods, but I sometimes miss the old ways.

Howard Lobb, who had been Chairman of the Architectural Council of the Festival of Britain, was our architect and the result was both pleasant to look at and pleasing to live in. Because there are charcoal ovens in the woods from the old days when Abinger Hammer was a centre of the iron industry I wanted to call the house Ovens, but Jess thought it might put ideas into hungry visitors' heads, so we called it Griffins after my grandmother's farm in Shropshire. My brother-in-law, Phillip, later found a magnificent stone griffin on the gatepost of a Queen Anne house that was being demolished and had it sent to us. It now stands in a general attitude of watchfulness by our front door. The garden has become almost a bird sanctuary and was much approved of by Julian Huxley when he came to lunch. Over the hedge in the field of our neighbours, the Parkers, there are horses and a donkey, and in the wood there are deer which insist on eating our roses, although mothballs hung on a string deter them a little, and foxes and badgers and squirrels.

Also grandchildren. When John married he and Jean, his wife, much to our delight built a house at the top of the wood, with sweeping views across Holmbury Hill and Hurtwood Forest. They have four children, Mark and Adam and Cait and Huw, and one must expect at any time to hear a rushing noise and have them break out from the woods into the garden with many shrieks, especially when Betty and George, her husband, who live in Kew are staying with us with their two children, Nicholas and Sally. Six grandchildren fill quite a lot of wood and even more garden.

We also, for a time had two cats: a black cat called Sambo, which might, I suppose, be frowned upon as a name in these colour-status conscious days, but which was bestowed with deep affection and respect when he was a little black kitten, and his half-sister—a tortoiseshell called Susie.

Susie was beautiful and indolent and liked to lie in the sun and be given cream and receive the respect due to her looks, but Sambo would come for long walks with us and when I had been away he would hear my car long before anyone else and be sitting on the gatepost waiting to greet me. He would go off through the woods by himself for far distances but always returned if I called 'Samboooy'—a call based on P. G. Wodehouse's Pighooy—although sometimes it would be half an hour or more before he could traverse the journey back. He had the most beautiful golden eyes and when I was writing he would sometimes sit on my desk and look at me with an encouraging and loving look. When I stopped and lifted my head from the paper he would hold a long conversation with me, saying many things that only my dullness prevented me from understanding. He hated us to go away and when we came back he would punish me by ignoring me. But Jess, whom he adored and whom he seemed to think was in control of such matters, he would tantalize by leaping from behind chairs to catch her foot between his paws and bite her ankle. If we were packing to go away he would wait until he thought we were not looking and then jump into one of the cases and burrow his way under the clothes in the hope of remaining undiscovered and being taken with us. When Betty got married he was the very last person to see her off to the church and waited by the gate to be the first to welcome her back—very conscious, I always thought, of his role as a purveyor of good luck!

For many years he was a deeply loved part of our lives and Susie, too, in her lazy, lovely way and when they fell ill and had to be taken away Jess and I could not easily comfort each other. When people say to us, 'But why don't you get another cat if you're so fond of them?' we can only look at them in amazement as if when a dear friend died someone had said brightly, 'There are lots of people walking about why not make friends with one of them?'

In those days there was a steam train in the morning and one back in the evening between Gomshall Station and London Bridge along a line that ambled its peaceful private way between the chalk hills of the North Downs and there were also excellent fast trains between Dorking and London Bridge until time and Dr Beeching got to work, so that living at Griffins was quite handy for Jess when she joined the staff of Guy's Hospital. It was also convenient for the B.B.C. television studios at Lime Grove to which I could motor in the evening in forty minutes or so.

Here in Griffins, I thought, I could with a few excursions into television from time to time sit and write, soothed and inspired by the view across the valley and the infinite gradations of green and, for the time being, at any rate, put public affairs behind me. But, of course, it did not work out quite like that.

I had not long withdrawn myself from public preoccupations when there came a rather secretive, finger-on-lips approach from the Foreign Office asking whether I would be willing to visit Iraq at the invitation of the Iraqi Government, disguised, although that is altogether too cloak-and-daggerish a description, as a British Council lecturer, and advise on what was the best way to tell the Iraqi public what was being done with the money that came from oil royalties so that students would stop smashing the windows of the Ministry of Development. It seemed that it might be an interesting thing to do and so leaving snow and slush behind me in London I flew into the heat of Baghdad, slightly incommoded by the insistence of a large persistent man at London Airport that I was Randolph

Churchill. Randolph was, as has already been made clear, by way of being a friend of mine. I even forgave him when he developed a habit of ringing me in the middle of the night to listen to some article he had just finished writing. 'You weren't asleep,' he would say. 'Of course I was,' I would snap. 'Never mind,' he would reply happily, 'you're awake now.' I did not, however, think I looked or behaved like him and I began to fear that I was to be involved in some obscure, possibly sinister, Middle-Eastern conspiracy of identity. However, when I arrived in Baghdad I was glad to find that it was me they were expecting.

I suppose there are few cities more disconcerting to the romantic than modern Baghdad with its ugly concrete buildings and filthy streets. However, there are beautiful Turkish houses along the river and in one of these I stayed with the head of the British Council who, like most British Council officials I have met, was intelligent, cultured and worldly. I gave a rather grand lecture to which all the members of the Iraqi Government came and having thus established my identity went north to Mosul and Kirkuk and the borders of Kurdistan and then south to Basra. I saw a great deal of the country and was entertained by local sheiks to immensely long, highly-spiced meals so that I spent most of my time in anguished search for bicarbonate of soda, of which our efficient Consul at Kirkuk, I was glad to find when I arrived there, had a large supply.

In the shadow of great hydro-electric works in the north the thin sandy soil was being turned over by wooden ploughs drawn by oxen, and flying low across the desert from the oil fields at Kirkuk one saw the black tents of Bedouins to whom the oil fields were still centuries away. Baghdad itself was noisy and smelly and full of an appalling poverty which seemed to have no relationship whatever to the lives of those of the rich to whose parties I was invited. I drank innumerable cups of sweet black coffee followed by green tea in Government departments where nothing ever seemed to happen and met newspaper Editors who, like those of eighteenth-century London, lived dangerous and precarious lives on tiny circulations, subsisting on bribery while they could and reviving their journals under new names when they were suppressed, which was often.

I found it hard to think why I had been invited or what it

was supposed I could do with so small a knowledge of a country whose social fissures ran so deep and whose problems were endemic to the state of its society. Nevertheless, it did seem that a substantial portion of the royalties received from oil were being spent on sensible capital projects which could prove of long-term value and equally plain that a large proportion of the population of Baghdad and perhaps of the whole country, including most of the students and intellectuals, were convinced that most of this money was going into the pockets of Ministers and Court hangers-on, including particularly the ex-Regent and his circle. It was also plain enough that there was a good deal of anti-British feeling about and a seething and understandable discontent with what were felt to be the remnants of British suzerainty, although among the more educated the British Council with its library was excluded from this feeling.

That there was corruption was certain. Also a degree of nepotism in the staffing of Government departments which was shocking to a twentieth-century Westerner, but which, I reminded myself, would have appeared perfectly normal to an Englishman of a century or so previously, and which was accepted by most Iraqis as not only a natural but indeed an obligatory expression of family loyalty. It seemed to me that any report I made after a few weeks of travelling up and down the country could not help but be hopelessly superficial.

However, I did the best I could with suggestions for improved information services, with films and photographs and broadcasts in the cities and travelling vans to the villages which would record complaints and return with the recorded voices of Ministers and officials replying directly to the questioners by name.

This done I was taken to the palace for an audience with the young King Feisal II, who had been educated at Harrow. He was a well-mannered young man and clearly anxious to behave in all matters as an Harrovian should. He listened intently to all I had to say and asked intelligent questions. He was obviously desperately eager to do good to his people and to move his country into the modern world and yet, it seemed to me, was so lacking in the kind of toughness and subtlety that was necessary that I could not help but despair for him.

At the end of a long talk he asked me if I would be willing to discuss all these matters with Nuri as-Said who, although not then the Prime Minister, was the one man whose support it was necessary to have. I said I would be delighted to do so. I was, indeed, much excited by the prospect since in my youth my imagination, like that of many others, had been much affected by Lawrence of Arabia and I knew that Nuri as-Said had marched and fought with him.

I saw the young King once again at a picnic of sorts to celebrate a hunt of desert foxes by army officers which ended with a swim on horseback across a river to a terraced café where a magnificent buffet awaited. I was shocked to see how ostentatiously the young army officers kept apart from the King at this affair. One could smell hostility and conspiracy in the air. The King's isolation was so painful that ignoring all protocol I went to him and engaged him in conversation. To judge by the looks thrown by the army officers in the direction of the King and the Englishman this was probably not a very sensible thing to do.

I told the Ambassador that the King would like me to talk to Nuri Said and a rather ostentatiously innocuous dinner party was arranged at the end of which Nuri and I were left alone. I thought him an impressive but cold character, capable, perhaps, of almost any heroism or cruelty, but subtle in intrigue and adroit and ruthless in the usages of power and I guessed that the King was right in naming him as the one man who had to be placated in any reforms that were suggested. I also judged, quite wrongly as it turned out, that if the King could depend on him, he would be all right. Nuri Said listened politely to my repeated affirmations of the importance of devising means to tell the people what their Government was doing, how money was being spent, and what would be the effect on their lives. He remained impassive throughout and at the end nodded his head sharply. 'To tell the people,' he said. 'No doubt that is good. But most of all it is important to make them understand that there is a strong hand at the top.' And he brought his hand sharply down on the arm of the sofa on which we sat. I said nothing and he rose to his feet and bowed and we moved away to join the rest of the party.

I could not but think that if it was left to Nuri Said not much of what I proposed would come to pass. However, I thought that perhaps he knew what he was doing, and even that 'the Fox', as many people called him, would know how to contain the plottings and antagonisms which seemed so clearly to be alive in the army.

In this I was wrong. In the end it was the army, not Nuri, that won the day. Perhaps the strong hand at the top had not been strong enough. Or perhaps if Nuri Said had been more ready to take account of the people, or even of my recommendations for keeping them informed, the mob that chased him through the streets and tore him to bits and that killed the young King in his palace would have been more ready to be patient. But I do not have much conviction that this is so.

This adventure in advising external governments did not fill me with much confidence in my ability in that direction and I was somewhat dubious when I was approached some years later to do so again—this time by the Government of Mauritius in the Indian Ocean, the idyllic island of *Paul et Virginie*, once known as the Ile de France.

I was in Guy's Hospital recovering from an illness when the Commissioner for Mauritius, the very charming Dr Teelock, called to see me. He brought with him a large bunch of flowers and a letter from James Griffiths, the former Secretary of State for the Colonies, urging me to give a favourable ear to what he had to say. Dr Teelock had an invitation from the Mauritian Prime Minister, Sir Seeswoosagur Ramgoolam, known to all Mauritians and to his friends everywhere as Dr Ram. Dr Ram, it transpired, and I was much improved in health by the compliment, was a long-time admirer of my writings and a great believer in my judgement. He wanted to know if I would be willing to advise his Government on a number of matters which seemed likely to arise as they moved from colonial status to independence the following year and if Jess and I would visit Mauritius for this purpose. In particular he sought advice on what could best be done in the way of information and other services to help bind more closely together as Mauritians one of the most complex mixtures of races anywhere in the world: Hindus, Moslems, Creoles, Chinese, plus French sugar planters and some English, with a jumble of languages so diverse that each evening Mauritius radio had to transmit bulletins in thirteen languages and sub-languages.

'But as you will see,' I said to Dr Teelock, 'I am ill in hospital. You must let me find someone else.'

'But no,' said Dr Teelock, 'Dr Ram wants only you. We will wait until you are out of hospital and then the Mauritian sun and air will make you truly well. Besides the Prime Minister is a doctor also. He will keep you fit.'

And so it was arranged. Jess and I flew to one of the loveliest and most agreeable islands in the world inhabited by a hospitable and charming people who made every day we spent there an event. Pope-Hennessy, that most wayward and engaging of colonial servants in a service much given in its hey-day to the cultivation of eccentricity, was once Governor of Mauritius. He fell head over heels in love with it and fought Whitehall ferociously in its interests. I do not blame him. It is one of the most lovable of islands. Dr Ram, moreover, is surely one of the most remarkable of Prime Ministers. He still keeps the front room in his house for old patients to call and see him if they want his help before he goes off to govern his country at Parliament House among the palm trees of Port Louis. In his sitting-room there is a complete collection of T. S. Eliot's first editions, most of them signed, along with a good many of E. M. Forster's, and Virginia Woolf's—relics of the days when he was a medical student at University College, London and spent his money on poetry instead of lunch.

Ernest Bevin once remarked to me that the trouble about British colonialism was not exploitation but neglect. One did not have to be in Mauritius long to discover that despite the charm of its people, the dazzling silver of its beaches, the theatrical backdrop of its miniature mountains, the beauty and variety in little space, and the miles of sugar plantations on the central plateau, one of the heritages it would carry with it into independence was a shocking burden of poverty. Nor could the efforts made by Dr Ram and his government, helped by the Governor, Sir John Rennie, do much at this time to reduce it. It belonged to history: a built-in consequence of colonial dependence on a one-crop economy and a Catholic Creole population impervious to arguments about birth control. The disparities of wealth and poverty were appalling. Such disparities are not, of course, rare in former Colonies of the great European powers. One may find much the same thing in a great deal of Asia and in North Africa; indeed when a little later Jess and I went to Tunis—this time with Jess playing the lead and me as an attendant traveller as she helped to train students for an American-sponsored research into nutrition among young babies—we found conditions very similar to those in Mauritius, along, too, with some of the charm. But the fact that such conditions exist elsewhere do not make them any easier for those who suffer them and Jess would often return heartbroken from her visits to hospitals and schools in Mauritius and I much frustrated from my talks with Ministers and Civil Servants.

The high colonial society of the rich French planters was urbane, charming, cultured and formidably embedded in the eighteenth century.

'Things really are becoming terrible,' said our hostess at one dinner party. 'Do you know it will soon be impossible to get a chef. We shall have to put up with women cooks.' On the sugar estates many of the Creoles in their single-room shacks were still living in conditions not much better than when our hostess's ancestors had imported theirs from Madagascar and Africa. But the reforms proposed by Dr Ram were bitterly attacked by many of the planters and their friends.

Mauritius with its social cleavages: the French sugar planters with their town houses and their villas on the coast and their house-servants; the Hindu and Moslem middle classes in their neat new suburban houses, the Chinese traders chock-a-block in the narrow streets of Port Louis, the sugar workers crammed together in the villages: often seemed to us to contain within its area of 38 miles long by 29 miles broad and its three-quarters of a million population a microcosm of all the social and racial problems of the world, but tempered by sun and natural beauty and free of the special problems of urban industrialization. At Le Reduit, built with elegance for the occupation of the French Governors of the island before the British captured it in the Napoleonic wars, where we stayed with the Rennies, one was conscious of a colonial order on its death-bed. It was dying with ceremony, dedicated to the last to the best British principles of order, justice and paternalism; a little cold, a little remote, not easily given to love and warmth, somewhat surprised still that a people with the advantages of British rule should actually want to be done with it, anxious in the kindest way about how the children would manage if left to themselves, but honest, efficient and fair-minded. The Rennies themselves could not have been nicer and more charming: one could not help but feel anxious, as they were themselves, about how they would manage in an uninterested world when the Colonial Service which they had served so devotedly no longer had a place for them. It is not a happy thing to be part of a machine that is running down.

We had parties at Parliament House, parties at Dr Ram's, parties at the houses of sugar planters, parties with Hindu friends where the ladies of the family danced for us with a grave and dedicated beauty and were themselves as beautiful as the dances they performed, but of a greater gaiety. There was a vast dinner party in our honour at Le Reduit where when the ladies had withdrawn the Governor observed—for eighteenth-century grace and twentieth-century plumbing do not always co-habit—that perhaps we would care for a stroll in the garden, gentlemen, and we went through the long french windows across the lawns each to find a bush suitable to his needs.

But also in addition to the parties we did much work and in the end I drew up a report and presented it to the Prime Minister and Cabinet. They did not, as Nuri Said had done, talk about a strong hand at the top but instead about the need to bring all the classes and races of Mauritius into a genuine democracy to whom independence, if it were chosen at the following General Election, would be more than a symbol.

There were riots before independence and the visit of Princess Alexandra to represent the Queen at the independence ceremony was cancelled. I began to fear that for me to give advice to a government was to lay the hand of death upon it. But, in fact, the riots were not initially due to internal Mauritian conflicts but to the fact that even coral islands in the Indian Ocean cannot escape the back-wash of world events. In the odd way such things happen, the Mauritian riots had their roots in the closing of the Suez Canal. This brought many more ships to Port Louis to refuel and with them came the gangs formerly operating in drugs and prostitution in Suez. One of them, a Moslem gang based on Istanbul, found local partners among unemployed co-religionists in Port Louis and set to work to beat up its rivals, and Mauritius, little used to the world's violence, lost its chance of a royal fiesta on independence day.

However, the riots are over, some of my recommendations are gradually being put into operation, and Dr Ram, with Eliot by his bedside when he cannot sleep, is the democratically elected head of an independent state. I sometimes encourage myself with the hope that in one small island at least I may yet be found to have done something to help good government.

CHAPTER 17

Those Who Run Newspapers

It was a column on newspapers in the *New Statesman* that brought me into active contact again with my old friend and enemy Lord Beaverbrook. I called it 'Fleet Street' and when I started it I expected it to run for no more than a few months. It ran for fourteen years and Lord Beaverbrook became one of its most avid readers, fluctuating between a strong distaste for what I had to say and a flattering appreciation of it.

When I criticized the *Daily Express* dark comments would appear referring to my fatal—if, as it seemed, somewhat delayed —effect on all those newspapers and institutions for which I had worked. Sometimes there would be remarks on the 'Socialist' who had 'helped to break' the General Strike. This was a reference to the occasion recounted earlier, when Tom Darlow and I had rounded up a newsprint lorry. It caused me to warn young journalists never to help a newspaper baron even if they thought they were only helping a horse. On the other hand when I found cause to praise the *Daily Express*, quotations from what I had said would appear in black type on its front page or in italics above its leader column, or there would be flattering references to me in the 'Londoner's Diary' of the *Evening Standard*. One was followed, I remember, by a letter which said: 'The attached note from the *Evening Standard* Diary of last Tuesday was prepared by me: Don't bother to answer,' and was signed, 'Sincerely Beaverbrook.'

Our long ambivalent relationship finally moved into sunny waters when he wrote to me towards the end of his life thanking me for an article in which I had attempted to assess as honestly as I could his total impact, good and bad, on the British press. In terms astonishingly warm in view of much that had passed between us, and surprising, also, having regard to his general touchiness to any sort of criticism, he described what I had had to say as 'generous and perceptive' and went on: 'It combines criticism, acute analysis and kindly feeling. The final effect was, I think, favourable—and I think you meant it to be so. Need I say that I am glad to have the appraisal and the approval of one of the sternest critics in the trade to which we both belong.'

I could not but be moved by this letter. All the same I remained glad that as a young man I had had the good sense with Jess's support to break free of him and reject his invitations to return.

There was a magical quality about him that captivated and enthralled. But it was a dangerous magic. He was not a Celt although there may well have been some Celtic blood in his Scottish ancestry, but his magic was akin, I thought, to that which J. M. Keynes discerned in Lloyd George and wrote of in his *Essays in Biography*: 'How can I convey to the reader who does not know him any just impression of this extraordinary figure of our time, this siren, this goat-faced bard, this half human visitor to our age from the hag-ridden magic and enchanted woods of Celtic antiquity. One catches in his company that flavour of final purposelessness, inner irresponsibility, existence outside or away from our Saxon good or evil, mixed with cunning, remorselessness, love of power, that lend fascination, enthralment and terror to the fair-seeming magicians of North European folklore.'

Cunning, remorselessness, love of power, all these along with, as in Lloyd George's case, many more endearing qualities, were to be found in Beaverbrook, combined with a capricious contempt for any convenience or interest other than his own which is often seen in the very rich.

All these qualities were shown in the treatment accorded to Arthur Christiansen, Editor of the *Daily Express* for nearly a quarter of a century, when Beaverbrook decided to have done with him. Unwittingly I had a part in this affair because of a book I wrote on the press called *Dangerous Estate*.

Christiansen and I had been young reporters together on

Merseyside and had later seen a fair amount of each other when we both joined the *Sunday Express*. We got married around the same time and entertained each other to dinner and talked a good deal about Fleet Street. Later we went our separate ways and except on professional occasions had not seen much of each other since. We were old friends but not close ones and, if anything, rather disapproved of each other. I was, therefore, surprised to have a telephone call from Christiansen not long after *Dangerous Estate* was published asking if he could see me at once. He sounded very emotional. I knew he had been ill and had been away from the *Daily Express* and there were rumours that he was no longer to be its Editor. But he was so close to Beaverbrook and had served him so well that I assumed that if he did not go back to his Editor's seat it would be because he was moving to some even grander place in the Beaverbrook empire.

We met at the Reform Club where I had invited him to lunch. Almost as soon as we sat down he told me emotionally that he was leaving Beaverbrook. 'But what for?' I asked. 'He doesn't want me any more,' he said and I thought he was going to break down in the dining-room of the Reform. After lunch we found a quiet corner in the smoke-room and, frequently having to stop to control himself, he told me his story. 'It's partly your fault,' he said, summoning up a smile. 'So you ought to know. You and your blasted book.'

This is his version of what happened. If true, and I had no reason to doubt it, it throws a singular light on Beaverbrook's jealousy, even of those who worked for him.

Christiansen was staying with Beaverbrook in the Bahamas recuperating after an illness. He was making excellent progress and between him and Beaverbrook everything was going well: never had The Lord smiled so benignly on his servant. Then one day two copies of my book, *Dangerous Estate*, arrived by mail from the *Express*: one for Beaverbrook, one for Christiansen. They had dinner together and then retired to bed early, each taking his book with him. Christiansen read it with much pleasure, especially the chapter dealing with the rise of the *Daily Express*.

In this I said: 'Beaverbrook is the true creator of the *Express*. His personality is the one constant power that shapes its doings wherever he may be in the world.' But I went on to say that although the policy was Beaverbrook's, for Christiansen neither had nor wished to have political views of his own, the skill which made the *Express* such compulsive reading was Christiansen's. In close on twenty-four years as Editor he had, I said, stamped his personality on the paper, 'only a shade less indelibly than Beaverbrook himself'. I went on to devote some three pages to Christiansen's impact on modern journalism as one of the greatest newspaper technicians of all time and said that the answer to the question of why the *Express* had won for itself so large a part of the new reading public since the end of the war could be discovered in the daily bulletins issued by Christiansen to his staff: 'In these bulletins is to be found the philosophy of the *Express*.'

This appears to have been too much for Beaverbrook. He was not prepared to share the credit with anyone. When Christiansen came down to breakfast the next morning Beaverbrook was absent. He was handed a letter. It began: 'Dear Mr Christiansen,' a sure sign of Beaverbrook's displeasure, and said that as he was now recovered it would be best for him to return to London without delay. Christiansen tried to see Beaverbrook to say goodbye but was told that he was not available and left without meeting him. Even when Beaverbrook returned from the Bahamas Christiansen found it impossible to get to see him or even to speak to him on the telephone although formerly he had always been put through immediately. Although a remarkable popular newspaper editor in terms of new and sparkling techniques of presentation Chris was basically a simple and uncomplicated character. He had served Beaverbrook for nearly a quarter of a century, taken his opinions from him and given him his absolute loyalty. He was devastated by the breach between them and could not understand why it had happened. He longed for a restoration of the old relationship. Finally he received a formal message that Lord Beaverbrook had decided he was not well enough to edit the *Daily Express*, but was offering him another job—on the *Evening Standard*. It turned out to be an almost derisory post for a man of Christiansen's eminence, in charge of the syndication of *Evening Standard* features. 'I took it,' said Christiansen, 'because I hoped that if I hung on long enough the old man would forgive me for whatever it was I had done and things would be the same again. I couldn't believe everything could have ended between us.'

After a time, however, he could bear it no longer and wrote to Beaverbrook saying that he did not feel that he could go on as things were and perhaps it would be best if he faced a complete break and resigned. He then left the office and went to his house in Essex, Little Holland Hall. Late that night a messenger arrived by motor bicycle with a letter from Beaverbrook. It said, 'You must not feel like that, Chris. Come and see me tomorrow.' Full of hope and eager for a reconciliation Christiansen went next day to Beaverbrook's flat in Arlington House. The two of them had an emotional meeting. 'We both cried,' said Chris. He told Beaverbrook that he owed everything to him and Beaverbrook told him that he had always thought of him as a son. But the offer of a return to the *Express* editorship, or at any rate of something in keeping with his talent and experience, for which Christiansen had hoped did not come. Instead, after more talk about their long time together Beaverbrook said, 'I'm sorry it's come to this, Chris, but it can't be helped.' And taking him by the arm led him to the lift. He opened the lift gate and Christiansen got in. Beaverbrook closed the gate and pressed the button and as the lift began to descend he leaned forward and said, 'Well, goodbye, Chris. Sorry to see you going down.'

At the end of this story Christiansen was again near breakdown. I found it hard to believe that even Beaverbrook could behave in this way but Christiansen repeated again, 'Goodbye, Chris. Sorry to see you going down.' And then he said, 'And the worst of it is I can't get the old bastard out of my system. I know I'll never be able to work for anyone else.'

He asked me if I thought there was any chance of him getting into television and I said I would try to help and suggested we might have an interview about the press on a television 'Press Conference' for a start. He was delighted with this and I later arranged it, but it was not very successful because what came over most was how much he had come to be possessed by Beaverbrook over the years and how devastated he was by the separation.

Before this it was arranged that he should be the subject of a 'This Is Your Life' programme with Eamonn Andrews in which I would take part. A great many people who had known him and worked with him were assembled but the one man who would have made the programme for him, Beaverbrook,

refused to have anything to do with it. All through the programme I could see Christiansen waiting for the moment when
Beaverbrook would walk on the stage, or if he was not prepared
to do that then say a few recorded words on a television film as
had often been done on these programmes. But there was no word
from him, and the party that followed was shadowed by his
absence.

Later Beaverbrook did so far relent as to give a farewell dinner
for Christiansen at the Dorchester after the financial arrangements for his 'resignation' had been completed and the break
accepted as final. Even this small gesture filled Christiansen with
happiness. I was one of the guests and Beaverbrook greeted me
with what I could not help but regard, in view of everything, as
remarkable good-will. Afterwards Christiansen said to me,
'He's still fond of you. If you tried you could be one of his
white-headed boys again. Why don't you?' It seemed a surprising thing to come from Christiansen in the circumstances
and I could only reply, 'But I don't want to.' Christiansen,
however, had lived too long in his shadow ever to get the 'old
bastard' out of his system and could not understand me.

I suppose in fact none of us who had worked with him could
ever get him completely out of our systems. The magic persisted even when it seemed an evil magic. Possibly it was only
those like Christiansen who gave themselves wholly to it who
failed to survive. Beaverbrook's relations with Michael Foot,
who became for a time Editor of the *Evening Standard*, were,
for instance, very different. Michael remained always his own
man, compromising not one inch of his own individuality, and
had Beaverbrook's affectionate respect as a result. Beaverbrook's relationship was very different, too, with John Gordon,
Editor of the *Sunday Express*. Gordon invested his savings
wisely, some of them in Beaverbrook Newspapers, and won
Beaverbrook's respect both as a journalist and a man of
property. But those who allowed themselves to be swamped by
the magic, as Christiansen did, were wholly lost.

If it is true that there is nothing so strange as people, Beaverbrook was one of the strangest of them all. Despite everything
I could never bring myself to hate him, although, as in the
episode with Christiansen, there was a good deal to hate. I
often felt it must be some oddness in myself that made me

continue to feel affection for him. Yet I do not think anyone who was there will ever be able to forget the eighty-fifth birthday party given for him by Roy Thomson a few days before he died. He had been unable to move except in a wheelchair for many weeks. But he insisted on walking firmly and erect on the arm of his son Max between the crowded tables and the applauding guests to his seat at the top table. None of us, I think, will ever forget the final words of his speech. The speech would have been magnificent in content and delivery from any man. It was especially so because so characteristic of the man we had known in the full pride of his power. He ended: 'Now it is time for me to become an apprentice again. I have not settled in which direction. But somewhere, some time soon.' For such a departure it was possible to forgive much.

Beaverbrook was the last of the newspaper tycoons. There was no one else like him on either side of the Atlantic in his own day. Cecil Harmsworth King had leanings that way. But he made the mistake of not owning the newspapers he controlled. To be a tycoon you must own both your newspapers and your staff. In some ways King's relationship with Hugh Cudlipp on the *Daily Mirror* seemed for many years rather like Beaverbrook's with Christiansen on the *Daily Express*. King was the man with the last word and for that matter the first as well, Cudlipp the man with the editorial flair and expertise to translate the King ideas into dazzling journalistic techniques. But you have only to try to contemplate the possibility—at which the mind boggles—of Christiansen supplanting Beaverbrook, as Cudlipp eventually supplanted King, to see the difference between the two men.

King, like Beaverbrook, was one of the most avid readers of my column and a frequent correspondent. Cudlipp once described him as 'A shy man who has never achieved any successful relationship with the human race as a whole'. I never found this when we lunched together, as at one time we did fairly frequently. What I did find was that conversation with him was inclined to be a one-way street. He loved listening to ideas—so long as they were his own.

He had a great need to justify himself. He sometimes modestly claimed that the real key to his character was his discovery that it was possible to get more done if you allowed others to take the credit but he did not let much pass him by.

He seemed to me a lost man. Immensely egotistical, enormously able, but affectionless at the centre, his arrogance was a suit of chain armour to protect his brittle ego. One could not, at least I could not, help being fond of him. Somewhere inside, struggling to get out, there was, one felt, a man of acute sensitivity and delicate imagination.

King did not think much of Roy Thomson. He would often remark to me that he was an uneducated ignoramus who knew about nothing but money. But I find Thomson more mysterious than King. It may be that the mystery is of my own imagining and that there is really nothing to understand. I find it disconcerting however that he made no impression on me the first time I met him years ago when he was still, in Beaverbrook's phrase, 'A little guy with a lot of little newspapers'. Tycoonery on his scale ought to show even when it is only at the cocoon stage.

I have seen a good deal of him one way and another since he arrived in this country fifteen years ago but I still find it hard to judge what there is inside him. You might almost say he was an unpretentious man with a good deal to be unpretentious about. He likes money, of course. But not as Beaverbrook did because you can use it to buy almost anything, including men and women and power, but simply, so far as one can judge, for the satisfaction he gets in making it and the fact that having it enables him to make a lot more. I once asked him his recipe for making money. 'You've got to think about it all the time,' he said. 'Not just intermittently, but always.' 'I'll have to do without it,' I said. 'It's too boring.'

I asked him on another occasion why he wanted to make more money when he already had so much. 'Look,' he said, 'when you write a book I guess you're pleased if a critic you think well of says it's good. Balance sheets are my critics. When they tell me I've turned a loss into a profit, I know I'm good.' He also told me on another occasion when I was trying to persuade him that it was too early to go home to bed after a boring public dinner party that there wasn't anything he liked better than going to bed with a balance sheet—his own or another's. He turned down my offer of a lift in a taxi. 'We can take a bus,' he said. 'I don't like wasting money. Even yours.'

I thought at first that this was merely part of an act. But

although he now spends more freely and has a Rolls-Royce to take him places I think it was part of the real man. Money to him is a commodity you deal in. He has almost none of the vices of the very wealthy although only an innocent would miss the ruthlessness beneath the joviality. He sometimes seems driven by an unrelenting itch to buy, a greedy acquisitiveness almost without discrimination. Yet he clearly has an enormous talent for business and almost without meaning to has greatly affected the pattern of British quality journalism for the better, establishing for it a framework of commercial profitability in which editorial independence can function with remarkably little interference from him. Time, of course, has mellowed him. He is a nicer man than when I first knew him. Nicer, but not basically more interesting to be with—except as a phenomenon you find it hard to understand and keep thinking you will find the key to if only you try hard enough, but never do.

I wish I had been able to borrow his genius for making papers pay when I was persuaded to edit *Forward*.

Attlee had wanted to retire from the leadership of the Labour Party for some time. He had stayed on for a reason that many people, and especially Herbert Morrison, refused to accept: he felt an obligation to give Morrison a chance at the Leadership. In 1951, when it would have been reasonable enough for Attlee to retire, Morrison's reputation was in the doldrums. His showing as Foreign Secretary had shadowed all his hopes of the Leadership. Even without it he would, in fact, probably not have had much chance. He had continued to think of himself as Attlee's natural successor but as early as 1949 Arthur Moyle, a shrewd judge in such matters, reported to Attlee that it had now become extremely unlikely that the Parliamentary Party would ever turn to Morrison again. However, Morrison had so long thought of himself as the man robbed of the Leadership by a fluke that Attlee felt it only right to leave time for his reputation to recover. In the event, when Attlee did finally go in 1955 Morrison suffered humiliating defeat and Hugh Gaitskell, his junior by eighteen years, became Leader instead.

He could have been influential as an elder statesman but his political judgement, so sharp in other things, was off beam when it came to himself. Right up to the last he expected to win. When he failed he was convinced he was the victim of a conspiracy with which everyone associated with Attlee had been involved. He cut me dead when I met him in the street. Later when we were both members of the House of Lords we became friends again. But always with reservations. His resentment never died. He and Attlee had the same birthday, 3 January, but although Attlee was always punctilious about sending a birthday card to Morrison, Morrison never sent him one after 1955.

What mattered more than the feuds of the past, however, were those of the present. With Gaitskell's victory the great Bevanite battle for control of the constituency parties and of the annual party conference began.

Bevan's phrases could sometimes hit like lightning. But they could also sometimes be woefully superficial. He called Gaitskell 'a desiccated calculating machine' which was about as big a misjudgement as anyone could make of a man, most of whose political weaknesses came from too much emotionalism. But, as a weapon, the phrase served. It helped to deepen the bitterness.

In these struggles I was a Gaitskell man. I believed his conception of the modern Labour Party as a radical, reforming party freed of dogmas was right. I knew very well the extent to which it had been forced in the past to fight a class war in the interests of the most depressed classes in the nation. But I thought it was time to leave class to the Conservatives.

Some years before I had been invited by *Fortune* to write an article on 'The Moral Case For Socialism' (subsequently reprinted by Professor Ebenstein of Princeton in his book *Modern Political Thought*). I had begun by saying that I knew no better definition of this moral case than the opening of the second paragraph of the American Declaration of Independence and was a socialist because I believed that only within a socialist society could these rights be assured for everyone. That was the way I still felt and that was the way I believed Gaitskell wished to lead the Labour Party.

Feeling thus I could scarcely refuse when he asked me to help him.

I did not regard him as an exciting political leader. And although the ability to excite and amuse is often derided it is one of the most precious of all political qualities. But I knew him to be an honest and intelligent one. Some of the antennae that catch the swirl and movement of ideas and transmit them into vivid action were in his case missing. He had a head for politics rather than an instinct for them. And although he usually got there in the end he was sometimes a little late in arriving.

Although these were drawbacks in a leader, there was, however, much to set on the other side. He combined idealism with intellectual conviction and had great courage. He could understand the material problems of the age without losing touch with its moral imperatives. He had a genuine nobility of character.

A small group among those closest to him—and he was, perhaps, too prone to cultivate intimate groups—was ready, he told me, to put up the money to finance a weekly paper to put the case for the Gaitskell changes to the constituency parties which were at this time being saturated with the Bevanite point of view. They proposed to buy the Scottish socialist weekly, *Forward*—known to all Scots as *The Forward*—and bring it to London and turn it into a national weekly. Would I edit it? I tried to argue myself out of the proposition but in the end I said yes. Feeling as I did, it was hard not to.

Alan Sainsbury, Chairman of Sainsburys, Henry Walston, who owned estates in Cambridgeshire and the West Indies, Charles Forte, who owned the Café Royal and a chain of restaurants, put up some money and John Diamond, later Chief Secretary to the Treasury, was Chairman and Financial Director. Alfred Robens was adviser and circulation promoter. The regular editorial staff consisted of George Thomson, later Secretary of State for the Commonwealth, who had been Editor of the old *Forward* and brought great balance and integrity as well as much humanity and good humour to its doings; John Harris, a young man of energy and charm who later became Gaitskell's press officer and close intimate and is now a Special Assistant to the Chancellor of the Exchequer; Douglas Jay, subsequently President of the Board of Trade, who had been my successor as Financial Editor of the *Herald*; Alma Birk, now Baroness Birk, who wrote a dashing column called 'Here's Alma'; Roy Roebuck, now an M.P. but then a make-up sub-editor on the *Daily Mirror* in Manchester, in which city *Forward* was printed by the Co-op Press; and George Wright, Barbara

Wootton's husband who had been a taxi-driver in his youth and wrote us a Cockney column full of warm beer and arguments in public bars called the 'Adventures of Henry Dubb'.

We also had a secretary called Judith who is one of the kindest, most warm-hearted girls I know. Unfortunately, however, she could not always manage to find things. Articles waiting to be typed would get mysteriously mislaid, notes would be lost for days and would sometimes turn up in the oddest places like under the bed in Judith's flat where she would eventually triumphantly find them. This and the fact that searches for what had mysteriously gone would sometimes make her late in the morning worried George Thomson, an orderly man, and infuriated John Harris. But I thought it added a pleasant fantasy to life. I took the view that if one article, for which the printers were waiting, could not be found the odds were that another about which we had forgotten would turn up, thus giving the contents of the paper a pleasant unexpectedness.

Judith, who had a sweet character, worked long hours for very little pay, for we could not afford to pay anyone much. Sometimes she would feel, and I could not blame her, that some of the sympathy for the poor in distant countries which came so readily to the pens of *Forward* writers ought to be diverted in her direction and as I read through the typescript of an article on, say, Uganda, I would come across the plaintive words, 'But who cares for poor Judith, who can't even afford to get her hair done?' When I would point out to Judith that she really must not insert remarks like this in the articles she typed and say, 'Why, if I'd been rushed and hadn't noticed it, it might actually have got into the paper,' she would reply, 'And a jolly good thing, too. Then you'd all have felt ashamed.'

With this glittering crew list we ought to have sailed into sunny and prosperous seas. Instead we quickly found ourselves becalmed. We had insufficient money to spend on promotion and distribution and could get very little advertising. We might have managed if we could have been content to grow slowly. But if we were to have any early effect on the course of the civil war waging in the constituency Labour parties, we had to establish ourselves quickly and get newsstand sales if we could.

Nature had designed Jack Diamond, our finance controller, to be an excellent First Secretary to the Treasury. What we needed was a tycoon. Alf Robens was the nearest to that we had and if we had had the nerve to do some of the things he wanted we might have gone further—or bust sooner. But he got little support and in the end he grew discouraged and went off to run the National Coal Board instead!

There are those, including himself, who think that if Robens had not abandoned politics to demonstrate remarkable commercial ability for running a great nationalized industry and become a peer he would have succeeded to the Leadership of the Labour Party when Gaitskell died and would have become Prime Minister instead of Harold Wilson. I doubt this. His political career had already been overcast, like Herbert Morrison's, by foreign affairs. Gaitskell had made him shadow Foreign Secretary and he was not a success. 'Here comes Fleet Street's favourite flop,' he said to me as he came into *Forward*'s office after one disastrous debate. I tried to cheer him up by saying that one bad speech never killed any politician and told him how Attlee, walking from the Commons after a debate on one occasion, had said to me, 'I made a mess of that, Francis.' Nevertheless, he had reached the dangerous point in a politician's career when even his enemies were beginning to feel sorry for him. I doubt if he could have recovered. What he had was great energy and warmth and a rather slap-dash approach to affairs which made him very attractive but not, I think, a serious contender for the highest political office. Since then he has become less slap-dash but also, perhaps, less attractive.

Wilson himself was one of our most reliable contributors. I could always depend on his word. Wilson's cleverness and self-confidence tends, I think, to deceive people. He is given more credit for his ability as a political tactician than he deserves, for he is not a terribly good one, but less perhaps than his due as a man of principle. He was the only one of those resigning from the Attlee administration in 1951 to risk serious personal damage. Aneurin Bevan had so large a majority behind him in Ebbw Vale that his seat and his career was safe whatever happened. John Freeman had grown tired of the parliamentary life and wanted to turn to journalism on the *New Statesman*. But Harold Wilson, to whom politics meant everything, had only a tiny majority in his constituency and risked sacrificing his whole political career for what seemed to him, rightly or wrongly, a matter of principle.

I admired him for this but, although on the Christian name terms customary in Labour circles, he and I had never been particularly close and I would not have been surprised if he had found some reason to refuse when I asked him to write for *Forward*. However, he agreed and thereafter did so fairly regularly. So did George Brown, whose company I enjoyed more, but who was often maddening as a contributor. He would agree with great enthusiasm to write articles which never turned up. If Wilson agreed his article would always arrive in time and be exactly what was wanted. Moreover, I found that he would often turn down much better offers in order to keep his promise to me. It would sometimes happen that other Editors would get the same idea for an article by him as I had and he would refuse offers of fifty or a hundred guineas from Sunday newspapers because he felt committed to *Forward*.

This was in pleasant contrast to several of the prominent pro-Gaitskell intellectuals in the party who when approached would explain in a superior fashion that they would have liked to write an article for *Forward* but were unfortunately busy on a piece for *Encounter*. Among the intellectuals, I could depend only on Douglas Jay. He came into the office two or three times a week and in addition to writing many serious articles for us developed a highly agreeable talent for corrosive political gossip.

Most of the leaders of the big trade unions were friendly. But not Frank Cousins, who had just become General Secretary of the Transport and General Workers Union. Cousins was determined to be different from Ernest Bevin and Arthur Deakin, his massive predecessors. He had even gone to the trouble of moving out of the office they had both used in order to demonstrate that a new régime had begun.

When *Forward* was first launched it was thought to be a good idea to have a private dinner party for some of the leading trade unionists to discuss it. Charles Forte, who was more Alf Robens's friend than Gaitskell's but anxious to help, arranged it at the Café Royal. Cousins came but shattered what had been intended as a friendly get-together by announcing harshly, that he had no intention of helping *Forward* if it meant helping Gaitskell.

It often seemed to me at this time that the political feuds I had lived with in the thirties had been no more than friendly family squabbles compared with those that now existed. There was a personal bitterness in the air that had scarcely been known then and that far exceeded anything even between Bevin and Morrison. It was also very plain that the balance of forces on which Attlee had been able to rely had gone for ever.

Through all this Gaitskell, although often badly hurt, comported himself with dignity and common sense. In the end he came to terms with Bevan who proved more ready to accept the nature of political action than his disciples. It is hard to say whether the truce between them would have lasted. But it might. Bevan was a bigger man than most of his followers and a more practical politician. Politics, he had said, was about power and he came to appreciate, as some of his disciples never did, or could, that power requires some compromises and that neither strong governments nor strong oppositions are possible without it.

There was, however, much hard battering before this comparative calm—transient and vulnerable as calm in the Labour Party always is—was reached and the weather proved too harsh for *Forward*. In the end George Thomson and I sailed it into harbour and merged it with the monthly *Socialist Commentary* before we climbed from the bridge. As a last office George arranged for its files to be kept in a safe place for future political historians of those acrimonious days. I hope they will find some of its records useful.

CHAPTER 18

Interlude in America

We flew by the polar route and came down at Reykjavik to refuel. In the darkness the frozen earth was like black ice and the wind burned our ears as we walked to the airport lounge. But the airport lounge itself was like airport lounges all across the world. It had the same drinks and the same custom-free shop and the same people buying last-minute presents, although here you could buy sheepskins as well as the usual kind of mementoes and some of the passengers did. Much later we came in low over the neon-lit desert of Los Angeles and went through customs before flying on to San Francisco.

This was the trip on which we first learned to love America. Not just to find it interesting and stimulating as on other trips but to love it with all the occasional mixture of hate and despair and excitement and disillusion and longing and warm companionship and sense of total commitment that goes with love. Mostly it was six months in Berkeley that made us feel like this, but not Berkeley alone because we travelled around a good deal as well, south to Santa Barbara and north to Oregon and east to Chicago and to Boston and Philadelphia, where we stayed with Margaret Parton, and to Washington and New York. Everywhere we went we found ourselves on this occasion in love with America and subject to that swirl of emotions I mentioned.

In a book I later wrote called *The American Invasion* I listed in a nostalgic sort of way some of the things that America meant to me:

... a summer evening in Carmel, long talks in white-frame houses in Georgetown, Washington, the cold fierce grandeur of the Sierra Nevadas and the black fangs of granite through the snow-covered hills, little tucked-away bars in New York, a saloon in Virginia City, hot, hot days in Charleston, South Carolina, cold, clear ones in Denver, Colorado, fireflies dancing over the trees in a garden in Philadelphia, the silver lances of the moon striking down to the dark heart of Yosemite, the click of dice and the clatter of fruit machines at two o'clock in the morning in Harrah's at Lake Tahoe, breakfast on the quayside at Sausaleto and fishing boats at anchor at Glouces-ter, Mass., a drive up the switch-back hills of San Francisco in a Thunderbird and along the lake shore at Chicago, a house in Berkeley with the quilted carpet of lights below and talk beside a fig tree in the garden of another, a picnic by the lake at Madison, Wisconsin, another on Mount Baker, the long high whistle of a train across the prairie and the stillness of a summer afternoon in a garden on the hills above Palo Alto, rain in Portland, Oregon and a barbecue in Orinda, the blue haze on the mountains of Virginia, a restaurant in Occidental and the sun slanting across the Pacific at Big Sur . . .

Most, although not all of these memories go back to that spring and summer in Berkeley and the journeys we made and the friends we found during it.

Unlike my immediate predecessor in the attractive office of Regents' Professor, C. P. Snow—a natural professorial figure if there ever was one, heavy with the weight of revealed opinion and the certainty of worth—I lacked donnish instincts and had never expected to find myself a professor of any sort, even the most transient. I had been much startled, therefore, when approached by the American Embassy in London and asked whether, if the University of California, Berkeley, invited me to spend a semester there as Regents' Professor, I would be in-terested. However, when I protested that I was not an academic, it was made plain to me that Regents' Professors were not hard-working professors of the ordinary sort, but campus birds of paradise expected only to amuse, entertain and stimulate. It was hoped I would give one open lecture on some subject of public importance, have a seminar with a small group of graduates, and for the rest be available to be entertained by members of the faculty and to sit around and, as they nicely said, exchange minds with whoever wanted to while, of course, taking time off to travel about when I felt like it. It seemed a highly civilized assignment.

It was arranged that we should rent the house of one of the many Nobel prize-winners at Berkeley who was going to Europe with his family and we left the slush of an English January for a Californian spring with limes and lemons growing in our own garden when we felt like a whisky sour.

Although it is only eight years ago it is hard to recapture the Berkeley or even the America of that time. Riots had not yet become a campus way of life. Most of the students were polite. They even seemed interested in what one said. Kennedy was at the White House and even Republicans were saying: well yes, maybe it had been time for a change. Newspapermen, scarred by many a tough engagement trying to find out what Eisenhower meant—'If you just listen and let your mind go blank like it was music or something,' one said to me, 'you sometimes think you know what he means. But if you ask to look at a transcript, you're done for'—were talking ecstatically about the Kennedy style, and the word charisma was beginning to creep into the language. Clark Kerr was still President of Cal and was making a good deal of sense, or so it seemed, with his talk of the multi-university, and John W. Gardener, whom Jess and I had met in New York, was explaining to everyone's satisfaction how it was possible to be equal and excellent too.

Vietnam was still merely a small country in South-East Asia where the United States had sent a handful of American advisers to help the goodies against the baddies and no one doubted either American morality or American power. McCarthy was dead and McCarthyism with him. He had given the tree one hell of a shake but it had survived and was growing taller and the young were up there among the branches reaching for the stars. Bliss was it in that dawn to be alive, and to be with the young was very heaven.

As one walked about the Berkeley campus the young were everywhere. Most of the young men had books under one arm and a girl on the other and very often a baby in a pram, and Margaret Mead, who came to lecture, warned them against the

American sickness of getting married and tied down too young. 'Do you want us to marry *old* men?' asked a sweet young thing in the audience tragically. 'Yes,' said Dr Mead, 'old men of twenty-two or maybe twenty-three.'

The Bay of Pigs came as a shock to all this. Momentarily it shattered the image of Kennedy, the young hero. But it was only momentary. One could blame the C.I.A. and when he saw what they had gotten him into Kennedy pulled out quickly. It was only a passing slip and when I was asked to address a vast open-air meeting of the students about its effects on world opinion I was able to conclude a difficult assignment—in which I was much helped by frankly confessing that the English and French had got into an even bigger mess over Suez—by proclaiming in all sincerity and to thunderous applause that America would serve mankind best by remembering not only her present strength but her revolutionary past. Even the junior Chamber of Commerce asked me a couple of days later for a talk on the same theme.

It really did seem at this time that this vast and powerful country with which it was so easy to fall in love had found her way ahead, and, linking material prosperity with idealism, would save the world by her example. I daresay she still may. But it was to get to look a lot less likely over the next few years than it did in that wonderful spring.

I was attached to the Journalism Department at Berkeley but with a foot also in the political sciences and I could not have been better cared for and cosseted. Charles Hulton, who had been at the Office of War Information during the war, was Chairman of the Department and he and his wife, Bobby, who had survived being a Daughter of the American Revolution with a light heart and a bubbling wit, lived near us and would constantly drop in with suggestions for wonderful things to do. Then there were Bob and Emily Desmond, who had come to see us in Abinger before we left so that they were almost old friends and rapidly became better ones, and Alan Temko who with his family added a touch of cheerful madness to life while he discoursed learnedly on urban planning, and Phil Griffen and his wife, old Californians who introduced us to the then still undeveloped, still traffic-free silences and magnificent coastline of Northern California. One is always lucky to find congenial colleagues in a strange environment; it is a bonus not to be expected or easily assessed when you find friends who become closer than those you have known at home.

Nor was this the half of our good fortune, for Jess was immediately welcomed, with arms wide open, to the Institute of Human Development which she had visited when last we were in Berkeley. Jean MacFarlane and Edith Katten now became among her dearest friends—and mine too—together with a whole galaxy of others whom we came to know through the Institute, like Wanda Bronson and her husband, Gordon, who was at Mills College, and Catherine Landreth and Mary Cover Jones and Marjorie Honzik and the Livsons and Nancy Bayley with whom Jess worked on her baby tests. And to make things even better there was Rosamund Gardner, who had been a student of Jess's and was as English as Joyce Grenfell, and was trying to make up her mind whether to settle permanently in Berkeley or not. One way and another Berkeley soon became a place of special meaning to us.

This was even more the case when we struck up a close friendship with Alexander Meiklejohn, on any rating one of America's greatest liberal philosophers and teachers, and his wife, Helen, whose iconoclastic wit, uttered in a gravelly and sinister whisper because of an operation on her throat, exactly complemented his serene good temper.

I would put Alec Meiklejohn alongside Leonard Woolf as one of the two most civilized men I have met. He had a similar belief in reason as the best lubricant of human relations but was less pessimistic about man's readiness to accept it than Woolf. His testimony before the Sub-Committee on Constitutional Rights of the Senate Committee on Judiciary, in which he argued that no abridgement of freedom of speech on any grounds whatever was permissible under the First Amendment, still seems to me one of the great classic statements of the case for freedom of ideas.

When we got to know him he was already nearing his eighties but was still as open and lively in mind as he can ever have been. What shone out from him above everything else was the quality of goodness. This combined with his intellectual integrity and his readiness to put all questions to the most rigorous tests of free discussion made him a most impressive person to be with. His influence on the American young was still profound. One had only to mention his name at a student meeting for it to bring cheers. By now, I suppose, it has become less so, for otherwise I do not see how the current fashion of unreason among the young would have got so far as it has, although I think Alec Meiklejohn would still have tried to be on their side.

His daughter, Ann Stout, was on the staff of the Institute of Human Development and was married to a remarkable longshoreman, a member of Harry Bridges's West Coast Longshoreman's Union, who had chosen this way of life because it gave him a larger degree of independence than he could hope for in most other occupations. Bridges at this time was engaged in a rather remarkable transaction, the sale of the Union's rule book to the port employers for a substantial sum. The basis of the deal was that if the employers wanted to do away with the union restrictions and speed up handling in the docks that was all right with Bridges but they must be prepared to pay the union in dollars—a great many dollars—for its investment in working conditions in the hard days.

Stout was opposing him. He thought Bridges was trading principle for profit and was, anyway, altogether too dictatorial in his handling of things. He took me to a meeting of the San Francisco Local which was to vote on the matter. As I went in Bridges recognized me. We had met during the U.N. Conference and he knew me as a one-time Editor of the *Daily Herald*. He hauled me on to the platform to sit beside him. 'That man,' said Bridges when Stout went to the rostrum to speak, 'is a damn nuisance. He's the Michael Foot of the Longshoreman's Union.' Stout's speech brought a lot of applause. But it was Bridges who got the votes.

Across the Bay from Berkeley, San Francisco was as golden as ever, although less accessible, it seemed to us, than it used to be, at any rate to those untrained in free-ways and clover leafs. The first evening we ventured across the Bay Bridge in the Oldsmobile we had taken over with the house we got in the wrong stream of traffic. Down below we could see San Francisco. But how to reach it? To do so seemed far beyond our competence and we began to think we would hit Seattle before we could find a way off. However, in the end we managed to get down and drove around a bit and found Union Square and parking our car took a cab to the Mark Hopkins Hotel. I wanted Jess to see the Mark Hopkins because this was where I had been when the war against Hitler ended and she was in London and I thought it would be a good place to eat and restore our nerves. We ordered dinner and I told the wine waiter it was a celebration and I wanted a bottle of Californian wine to go with it but I did not know Californian wines and would he pick one for me. He said, 'Certainly, sir,' and went away and then he came back carrying a bottle very proudly in front of him. 'You'll like this, sir,' he said, 'it's homogenized.' No wine waiter had ever said this to me before and I thought it ought to tell me something about the American character, or maybe the Californian character, or maybe simply about the character of the Californian wine trade. But I could not think what.

We had a lot of friends in San Francisco as well as Berkeley, mainly television people or journalists, or people who went to the Hungry I. or the Press Club where I spoke and was given a model of a black cat. One of these friends was Walker, who had been City Editor of the *Examiner* in 1945 and had got the United Fruit Company to send round a roomful of bananas for me to take back to my children. He was dying of cancer, although we did not know it, and had put off an operation so that he could take us around. And there was Bill Hall of the *Sunday Examiner*, who asked me to write a column for him while I was there and who had a Thunderbird. I asked him when he had a chance to drive it as fast as it would go and he said, 'Always in my dreams.'

Because this was Berkeley and San Francisco, we spent a good deal of time just talking. And the odd thing is that although we talked a lot and worried a good deal about the future almost none of the things we talked about were the things that in the end actually happened.

What particularly worried many of our friends on the Berkeley campus was that they thought the young were getting too orthodox. It seemed to them that what most of them wanted from life were jobs as junior executives in big corporations or as wives of junior executives. The fire, they thought, had gone out of the belly of American youth.

There were a few protesters. There was a student protest
against the House Un-American Activities Committee which
was at that time perambulating around the country and had
stopped off for hearings in San Francisco. And there was some
excitement when a student group in Berkeley invited a young
man who was awaiting committal to prison on a contempt charge
to come and speak to them. President Clark Kerr defended the
right of the students to do this. It was, he said, the business of a
university 'to make students safe for ideas, not ideas safe for
students'. It seemed a good but innocuous remark suitable for a
Y.M.C.A. prizegiving. But it made several State Congressmen
denounce Clark Kerr as a communist and many of his friends
began to get worried that he was storing up trouble for himself
in the future. This seemed to us absurd. But in the end it
turned out he was.

Many of the young seemed armoured against thought by the
clichés of authority. To open a discussion with many of them
was as unrewarding as to debate with a young Russian communist. One stubbed one's toes on minds closed to everything
except the winning of a three-car home. It was impossible to
foresee—or at least we did not foresee it—that very soon their
successors would be hippies and drop-outs and that conformity
would become a dirty word. I find myself wondering what clues
we overlooked. Was the rejection there already, even while we
worried about the too great acceptance? Did the war in Vietnam
create it or release it, acting, as Lenin saw the First World War
doing, as a great all-powerful *régisseur*, a mighty accelerator of
events not only in Berkeley but almost all across the world?

It is amazing to think how different were the questions we
asked each other then from those that are asked now, a mere
nine years later: how unrelated to the current mood of the
Berkeley campus and other university campuses across America
and the world is what then most concerned us. It may be that
we were too much beguiled by friendship and pleasant conversation to see what was going on under our noses. But it does
not seem to me that the mood of protest that has since become a
way of life existed in any significant measure then. It was,
indeed, as I have said, its absence that perturbed us. We had no
suspicion of the nature of the genie in the bottle.

Nor do I even remember us discussing problems of racial

discrimination except as something that existed in the Southern States, but not to any real extent outside them. If such discrimination was still to be found here and there in California or in the Mid-West or in the East it was taken for granted that it would disperse under the pure idealism of liberal ideas. We had been shocked when we lived in Washington that there was no theatre except in the summer because black and white could not sit together. But that had passed. The Theatre Guild had won. The races could now sit side by side to watch plays in the Nation's capital even in winter. Progress was on the march. Some of our friends, it is true were a little sheepish about the lack of any sizeable number of black students in the Berkeley campus. But this was to be explained, we were assured, not by any discrimination on the part of the university itself but by the failure of more than a small handful to come up to the necessary academic standard—although why this should be so no one seemed anxious to say.

What happened in the South and the attitude of the South were horrible and did not bear thinking about. But the Southern States still seemed a long way from California and even the South would have to give way in the end to the feelings of the rest of America. And we—Jess and I—would nod sympathetically and accept modestly our friends' congratulations on how fortunate we were because the tolerant and civilized British did not—eight years ago—have any racial hatreds, or at any rate none that showed.

In Chicago you felt racial antagonism in the air as you never did in the Bay Area. People we knew there complained about the arrogance of the blacks. They would tell you how the young bucks swaggered along the sidewalks and how those driving around in beaten-up automobiles would gun their engines when they were waiting at lights and a white girl passed to smear her nylons with smoke from the exhaust. But even in Chicago the people we met were sure things were getting better. It was all a matter of time—peaceful time.

Black Power had not yet been born. Or if it had we had not heard about it. The idea that there would come a day when a sizeable number of black people would spit in the face of white America and say they wanted no part of the values of American civilization would have seemed as absurd to most of our friends as the idea that a sizeable number of the young would do the same.

Looking back I find it astonishing how innocent we all were. We had wonderful talks about almost everything except, as it turned out, what was brewing underneath. I do not even remember the generation gap being mentioned. Perhaps no one had yet invented it. Nor—but this may have been out of deference to the well-known modesty of the English, for London had not begun to swing—did we discuss sex much so far as I can remember. We were worried about the hydrogen bomb, and about whether there would ever be any way of achieving peaceful co-existence with the Russians, and about the need to keep a close watch on the John Birch society, and about the quality of education and whether universities were getting dangerously swollen in size, and the poor level of television entertainment and the perils of a consumer society and the deterioration of public taste. But of most of the things that have been making the headlines over the last four or five years we had no premonition at all. I find this rather odd. As a newspaperman it fills me with shame and as a professor, even of an exotic, temporary sort, it shakes my confidence in the view from the faculty club.

We returned to America six years later. To another professorship—this time as Kemper Knapp Professor at Madison, Wisconsin. Then the things of which there had seemed so little reason to talk when we were at Berkeley were the only things there were to talk about. Especially, of course, Vietnam. And after Vietnam, Black Power, and after Black Power, student power or perhaps the other way round, depending on who you were talking to. And the generation gap. And, of course, the credibility gap.

When we were in Madison we flew to Berkeley for a visit. Charles Hulton had invited me to give the annual university journalism lecture. But he died of a heart attack a few weeks before we arrived and Bobby Hulton, whom we had loved so dearly, had died earlier and so had Phil Griffin, so that it was a sad coming back, although the Desmonds met us at the airport as kind and welcoming as ever and it was good to see them. We stayed with Edith Katten and that made up for much. Edith had been seriously ill and had had a major operation. She could not at this time move from the house, although she is able to do so again now, and much of the time she was in great pain. But she had such courage as gives dignity to the human condition and in the mornings we breakfasted together in our dressing-gowns and talked of innumerable things, and in the evenings when we came back from our various enterprises we sat under the fig tree in her garden and drank strong gin and tonic and told her of our doings, and her wit and pleasure brought a revived edge to life.

When I went to the university campus now it was not the distant view of a Nobel prize-winner that was pointed out to me, but the scenes of student battles. Clark Kerr, whom we had learned both to like and admire during our previous visit, had gone from the President's office. Governor Reagan had made it untenable by him. And although some of the worst of the student battles, with National Guards in the streets and a helicopter spraying tear gas over the campus, were still to come, Berkeley had the air of a battlefield stilled by an armistice everyone knew to be temporary. When we went to parties, for in Berkeley it is always necessary to go to parties, most of those we met were angry, some of them neurotically so. One smelt frustration everywhere as the disillusion and anger swirled from one group to another and we were glad to get back to Edith's intelligent concern.

There was a march in the streets on the Saturday after we arrived and Edith asked a group of people in to meet us—twenty or more, I suppose. Each one of them as they came in said, 'Have you heard about our demonstration?' Then they told us about it and what they had done and what they had said so that by the time the party ended we had been told all about this demonstration twenty times or more and asked as frequently whether we thought such things were any use or was there no longer anything intelligent people could do to influence the course of things.

I have been mixed up, one way or another, in public affairs most of my life. But I have never known anything—not the unemployment and depression of the thirties, nor the Civil War in Spain, nor Munich—that had so disintegrating an effect on a nation as Vietnam. Perhaps only on the intellectuals of a nation. But I do not think so, for it seemed far wider than this. It was as though America, this country we had grown to love so much, was suffering from a death of the will and in this death of the will not only this war, that could neither be won nor lost, but the rebellion of youth and the terrible clash of race had temporarily robbed the American people of the ability to think or act or do anything except let the waters of frustration sweep over their heads.

We flew from San Francisco to Los Angeles to stay briefly with a friend before returning to Madison. The scene and the company changed. The mood and the conversation did not—except that here one flash of macabre humour broke the frozen surface of the American dialogue, caught as it seemed for ever in the same dark pool. Our hostess had been to Watts to help clear up after the racial riots. Some of the Negroes she reported were trying to raise money to start an African restaurant in a gutted warehouse and when she asked them what its speciality would be—every restaurant must have a speciality she said—they said, 'Missionaries, of course.'

We had thought when we accepted the invitation to go to Madison, Wisconsin, that it would help to fill in our knowledge of the U.S.A. We had lived in the East and on the West Coast and had visited the South, but we did not, except for brief trips to Chicago, know the Middle-West at all—and the Mid-West, we thought, would show us the grass roots of American life. Moreover, we knew of Wisconsin as a fine progressive university, one of the shapers of the New Deal and one of the bulwarks of academic freedom when the Junior Senator of that State was rampaging around trying to trap the whole nation in a net of suspicion and fear.

We had visited Madison briefly on an earlier visit to the States and had picnicked on the shores of Lake Mendota with the Ragsdales who are, perhaps, the most dedicated picnickers in two hemispheres. Rags, whom I had first known as a newspaperman in London, was on the staff of the Journalism School. Also we had met Harold Nelson, who had just become Director of the School, and his wife, Ann, in London and enjoyed their company and their pleasure in the London scene.

But although we made good friends in Madison, among them Scott Cutlip, one of the best academic authorities in the States on the fascinating subject of public relations, and his wife, Erna, who carries an ever-bubbling fountain of human kindness about with her wherever she goes, and Martin and Dorothy Loeb, who sustained us constantly with conversation and hospitality, and many others, Madison never jelled for us as Berkeley had.

Perhaps it was the wrong moment in history. Or perhaps just the wrong time of year. When we flew into Chicago on our way there frozen snow was piled along the streets and my cousin, Molly, and her husband Walter, who met us and to whom we turned again and again during our visit whenever we were in any difficulty, told us that for several days they had been afraid they might not be able to get to us because the airport had been completely cut off. In Madison itself the streets were frozen and whenever we went out the wind blew across the lakes as though from Siberia. The weather scarcely let up all the time we were there, except towards the very end, and we both acquired a strong admiration for the pioneers who had settled this country and made it a great agricultural state, but without any desire to emulate them.

Here, too, although less neurotically than in Berkeley, one was conscious of the deep scar on the American conscience, the painful trauma of Vietnam and the credibility gap between government and people as Johnson's Presidency wound towards its disillusioned end. I was amazed when I returned to London to find how many of the same stories that were being whispered about Johnson were being told against Harold Wilson. It was as though some disease of politics was manifesting right across the world and the human imagination was incapable of doing anything but react with a similar outbreak of intellectual boils.

Many of the students of Wisconsin seemed to have lost direction in a peculiarly unhappy way. They had not, at this time, turned, except spasmodically, to the violence that was sweeping Berkeley, although that was soon to come to Madison too. But they seemed frustrated and disassociated, as if the university was both too big and, for many of them, too meaningless to give any centre to their lives. They could find no answer to their questions about the purpose of life, or even the promise that somewhere, sometime, such an answer might be found to exist. When a meeting was arranged to give representatives of disaffected students a chance to put their grievances before faculty members what was most sad about it was the inarticulateness of the students, the sense one got of something lost and hopeless yet somehow incapable of being put into words.

I must not give too sombre a picture of our stay in Madison. We had some fine days and made some good friends and as a sort of spin-off from my activities as a speaker I picked up one of the compliments I most treasure. I was speaking to a group of editors and publishers at a weekend conference and, as is often my habit, I was denouncing the failure of much of the press to live up to its possibilities. Jess was in the body of the audience. She was sitting behind two newspaper publishers who became increasingly angry as I proceeded. Finally after much muttering they fell into an indignant silence broken as I reached my peroration by one saying to the other, 'I'm damned if I accept a word he says, but you've got to admit it, the guy's got grammar.' I have often thought it would be a fine thing to put on one's tombstone, 'The guy had grammar.'

There was, of course, from time to time a good deal to enjoy. I remember a dinner at the Milwaukee Press Club, where they invited me to sign a shingle to be hung next to that of a much earlier visitor, Clement Attlee, and a trip with the Cutlips to the wonderful Circus World Museum at Baraboo run by Mr Fox, a man completely happy because he has escaped out of an office to live a dream and is doing what he most wants to do in the world—and how many of us can say that? And we went with the Nelsons to Minneapolis to speak at a centenary celebration for the *Minneapolis Tribune* and drove for miles beside the Mississippi. It was not at its widest but it gave me a sharper sense than ever before of how it must have been for Huckleberry Finn going down river on the raft.

The *Tribune* had fixed a dinner at the Minneapolis Club that evening as a preparation for the speeches and discussion next day. Because the Minneapolis Club is the Minneapolis Club it was to be a men-only affair and Jess and Ann Nelson had arranged to go out by themselves. But when we got to the hotel there was a message asking if they would come to the dinner after all. It turned out that the Managing Editor of the *Washington Post*, who was to have been one of the speakers, could not make it and Mrs Frances Graham, the *Post*'s pub-lisher, had decided to come instead and the *Tribune* could not just turn her out on her own for the evening, so there had to be some women guests after all, although only Mrs Graham and Ann and Jess. When we arrived at the Minneapolis Club a doorman was looking out for us. He ushered Bud Nelson and me through the main entrance but Jess and Ann were taken round the back and through the kitchens and up in a service lift so that the club should not be seen to be contaminated by them. It made me feel that my own club in London, the Reform, which would only allow you to invite women to dinner on Friday and Saturday, and then stowed you away at one end of the dining-room carefully segregated from honest members not subject to feminine influence, was wildly progressive and had not, after all, come to a dead stop at the second Reform Bill as I had sometimes thought.

The lakes had opened before we left Madison and we heard the wild geese flying over, and the green and rolling countryside was pleasant to see. But we came back sad from America and could only hope, not for its own sake only but for that of all of us, that some day soon it would find its sense of direction again.

CHAPTER 19

To Be a Lord

To want to be a lord had always seemed to me the silliest of ambitions. I had been amazed when I found Harold Nicolson anxious for someone to make him one. It seemed an odd wish for an intelligent man and I could only put it down to that streak of snobbery that had always been a blemish in his character, although in a curious way an endearing one since it was so obvious that one did not even have to pretend that it was not there.

I had defended Attlee against the scorn of Michael Foot when he became an Earl after giving up active politics. But I had been more than a little surprised myself. However, Attlee after all was a parliamentary man and I could understand that he might still want a platform without seeming to be getting in the way of his successor in the Commons. Also Earldoms for ex-Prime Ministers were a matter of tradition and Attlee had always been strong on tradition. But when, shortly after we came back from Berkeley the first time, Gaitskell asked me if I would let him put my name forward to Macmillan for a Life Peerage I looked at him as if he had gone mad and said no.

'I thought you'd say that,' said Gaitskell. 'You're an old-fashioned ILP'er at heart. But do please think it over. I'm not offering it as an honour but as an invitation to do something politically useful without being too involved. And after all, it's only for life!'

Life Peers at that time were still comparatively new and few: the first had been created only some three years before. I could see they might be regarded as somewhat less obnoxious to equalitarians than hereditary ones. Indeed, my friend Barbara Wootton, who had always been very strong for equality, had been one of the first of them. But that was different again because in her case what added zest to the whole thing was that she was being asked to be one of the first women to sit in the House of Lords in its nine hundred years or so of history and that was not something that any one so ardent for sex equality as she was could be expected lightly to let pass.

But no special circumstance existed for me. If I had wanted to be a politician I would have stood for the Commons years ago. I saw no good reason for keeping the House of Lords in existence and no merit in reforming its composition to make it more acceptable to public opinion. In brief, I thought that so far as I was concerned a title would be a social encumbrance and a political nuisance and I felt annoyed at Hugh Gaitskell for suggesting it.

But Gaitskell refused to drop the idea. His argument was that so long as the House of Lords existed—and if it was reformed it might, in the British way, go on existing for a long time and even be useful, for there was much merit in a second chamber—then it was necessary to make it work and important to have among its members some Labour people who were well known apart from politics and would be listened to on general issues. 'I'm not asking you to become a full-time politician,' he said. 'And I don't expect you always to support the party line. I know you're your own man and I know you'll go on being. But we need more Socialists there and I'd very much like you to be one of them.' And then he grinned and said, 'And I thought it might interest you to be the first Press Lord who didn't own a newspaper.'

I think it must have been this that clinched it. He went on arguing for a while longer but I think it was this that did it. In the end I promised to talk it over with Jess and let him know.

When I told Jess she said, 'You really do get us into some awful jams. Do we have to?' In the end we decided that perhaps we did. I daresay we were both flattered by Gaitskell's arguments and I thought to myself that being a member of the House of Lords would be in a way an extension of journalism.

It would give me a platform. Some of the pleasures of politics without the pains.

So in 1962 I became a Life Peer along with one or two other people I knew: Oliver Franks who had been Ambassador in Washington when I was there, Alan Sainsbury, Tom Williamson who was one of the trade-union leaders I liked best and Elaine Burton—there were eight in the list altogether.

I wished my mother were still alive. I thought she was probably the one member of the family who would have enjoyed the whole thing unreservedly. She was always the one for new things and for making a splash. Also I don't suppose she would have had much truck with a new idea like a life peerage. She would have taken it for granted that if you were a lord you were one of the old kind which meant, according to her reading of life, a stake in the country and no one so rude as to ask you to pay your debts. But she was dead and so was my father who would have thought the whole thing rather a joke.

Garter King of Arms seemed to be cherishing some of my mother's ideas when I went to see him: at least so far as a stake in the country was concerned. He opened by saying he hoped I would choose a territorial title. I said no, I was not a territorial baron and what I really wanted was my own name. After some head-shaking and much consideration of precedents, of whom the main one I could suggest was Lloyd George—and he, it turned out, although born George and christened David Lloyd had been baptised at a camp fire revivalist meeting at the age of five as David Lloyd-George which made it easier to accept that name as a title when the time came—Garter agreed that I could be Francis Williams since Francis was not only my Christian name but my mother's family name too. This gave my mother a role in the affair after all. I was pleased about this and I thought she would have been. But there would, said Garter, have to be a hyphen. Without a hyphen, he observed sombrely, I might find myself being taken for the younger son of a Marquess. Even with it I could not entirely escape the risk when announced at receptions. For, as he said, although a hyphen could be printed it could not be pronounced. However, I said rather arrogantly, that I was satisfied that whenever and wherever I was announced I would never be mistaken for anyone but myself and we parted amiably. Indeed, at the end Garter, whose office had perhaps tended in my mind to disguise the fact that he was a most intelligent and agreeable person, warmed my heart by telling me how much he enjoyed my writings in the *New Statesman*.

As dressed in scarlet and ermine with two friends, Lord Shackleton and Lord Taylor, to support me and the Gentleman Usher of the Black Rod, the Earl Marshal, the Lord Great Chamberlain and Garter King of Arms to guide my way, I was introduced to the House of Lords and bowed three times to the Lord Chancellor, I could not help feeling that I had reached a watershed in my life and put some of my youth behind me. It had been on the whole an amusing journey so far. But the train had pulled in at a station I had had no intention of going to and I could not think why I had got out. I was in a somewhat thoughtful and elderly mood therefore when I walked from the Prince's Chamber to the library a day or two after my introduction and felt a martial clap on my shoulder. It was Field-Marshal Montgomery. 'Nice to see you again, my boy,' he said, cheering me up no end by the assumption of my continuing youthfulness, and then in a voice that went echoing through the corridors of their Lordships' House, he said, 'You'll like it here. All decent chaps here.'

So indeed they have proved to be, although some of them are sometimes in my view decent chaps with indecent opinions. I have come to have a considerable respect for the House of Lords, and much regret that a fit of petulance on Harold Wilson's part, when the Conservative Peers temporarily held up an order imposing Rhodesian sanctions, played into the hands of the extreme right and the extreme left and destroyed the best chance for years of carrying through changes in the constitution and powers of the Lords which would have begun to make it a genuinely viable and effective second chamber.

As now constituted the House of Lords is in an impossible position as an effective legislative body. The dead weight of Conservative hereditary peers gives any Conservative opposition a built-in majority, but one which cannot be evoked without constitutional crisis. It is not, however, the hereditary peers who now stand in the way of reform but the old musket men like Michael Foot and Enoch Powell linked on this matter in a blimpish alliance of opposites in the Commons. With exemplary fortitude and a huge majority the hereditary peers approved proposals which would have ended for ever the hereditary principle as a legislative instrument and destroyed their political lives. But for Mr Wilson's flash of temper and Mr Heath's eagerness to find in it an excuse for not tangling with his right wing the House of Lords would by now have been a workable second chamber.

Even unreformed the Lords is often a useful revising chamber for repairing slap-dash work in the Commons. At the hack rate of $4\frac{1}{2}$ guineas' subsistence a day (recently raised to £6 10s) it sometimes brings to bear on legislative affairs a concentration of expert opinion not easily matched elsewhere.

Apart from this the Lords puts on each week, usually on Wednesdays, debates on general issues which, perhaps because there is by long convention no vote, manage at times to bring together in a civilized and literate fashion—forbearing for honour's sake according to the usage of the House since 13 June 1626 all 'personal, sharp and taxing speeches'—independent and authoritative views of a kind rarely given much time or space in the Commons.

It is argued by some, including some members of the House of Lords itself, that this is no more than kids' stuff; talking for talking's sake, appropriate to a university debating society but not a proper occupation for adults. I do not share this view. I do not think everything in life needs to have an immediate purpose or that talking for talking's sake is more to be despised than loving for loving's sake or, for that matter, doing anything for the pleasure of doing it well. The practice of civilized debate has, I cannot help but think, a political and social value of its own, if only to show that it is possible even when people feel strongly. Moreover, to argue that it is not worth saying anything unless there is a possibility of immediate result—as in a vote— seems to me to misunderstand the use of language and the way in which ideas permeate a society.

I do not want to put the claims too high. The House of Lords has many lapses into ennui. It is frequently boring, sometimes silly, often sententious. The habit of putting one's name down for a debate in advance and being given a batting order some- times means that speeches prepared ahead have little relevance to what has just been said. The most frequent opening sentence in many Lords' debates is: 'I have listened with great interest to what the Noble Lord has had to say, but I do not intend to follow him.' Some of the cut and sparkle of genuine debate is often lost. But it is difficult to sit through a Wednesday debate without learning something new or catching an idea worth turning over in one's mind. Although such debates commonly get small coverage in the daily newspapers they may reach through *Hansard* some of those who help to direct action and may help to make their contribution to the pool of ideas by which we live. And on some great moral and social issues the House of Lords has given genuine leadership to the country.

One way and another it will be seen that despite my original feelings I have by now fallen a victim to the Lords' seductive charm. Only in comparatively small doses. If I went more often I might like it less. On the other hand I might like it more. Some do. But I think if I were there all the time the feeling of taking part in an elaborate charade would be too much for me so long as the Lords remains unreformed. It is very proper that the Commons should have all the power, the Lords most of the pomp. But to someone who does not go much for pomp it can become a little boring. Yet in an increasingly professional world it is nice to have a few amateur institutions around and the House of Lords remains magnificently amateur.

I could not have afforded to be a full-time peer even if I had wanted to be and scarcely had I agreed to become one—indeed the public announcement had not yet been made—than I found myself involved in other matters which although they did not, as I had at first hoped, bring me much profit added for a time to the incidental fascinations of life.

This was a television enterprise of a co-operative sort with Malcolm Muggeridge, Robert Kee, Ludovic Kennedy, James Mossman and a young producer from B.B.C. 'Panorama', Jeremy Murray-Brown, with whom we had all worked at one time or another. We called it Television Reporters International, T.R.I., and our idea was to break free of the administrators and make the sort of television programmes we wanted to. I can see now that although we were professionals in programme-making we were as innocent about the facts of life in the entertainment world as others strayed into it from programme-making have proved to be since. We believed that all that mattered was quality and that if we made films of quality it would be easy to sell them. Also, I suppose, we were all a bit vain about our reputations and felt that any television service in its senses —but we did not realize how many were not—would be glad to get hold of what we made.

We sat for a long time through many late nights before we decided to form our company. During our talks Malcolm Muggeridge would frequently remark that he hated television and that as intelligent, literate men we must surely all do likewise. 'The important thing is to hate the tele,' he would say.

Many might think he has adopted a curious way of showing this. But I think that maybe what he said was true and that he really does hate it because it and malice are the only vices he has found it impossible to give up on that compulsive journey to Christian asceticism which now commands his life and which he talks about so much.

The rest of us took a less extreme view. We thought much of the creative urge in television, especially in public affairs television which was our main interest, was running down and that if one was to do anything worth while it was necessary to break away from the big machines. None of us had much capital. But Robert Kee knew Michael Astor and he invited him to a meeting at Jim Mossman's house and Michael Astor was very keen and anxious to join us and put up some money. Moreover, he had several friends who he felt sure would like to do the same. We formed a company in which the investors of talent had half the share capital and the investors of money the other half. The most active of the investors of money were Michael Astor, Colin Tennant and Miki Sekers and I do not think we could have had a nicer group of financial backers. By the end we were scarcely on speaking terms with any of them.

I became very fond of Michael Astor and pitied him for having all that Astor money around his neck. I have known several Astors of both the British and American branches of the family but I have known only one able to break free of the money and make himself a person in his own right: David Astor, the Editor of the *Observer*. Michael tried but he never quite succeeded. I would not go so far as Hemingway in hating the rich, although there is a good deal, I think, in that sad ending to *A Moveable Feast*: 'Then you have the rich and nothing is ever as it was again.' But it is very difficult for those who are not rich and who think that there are a lot more interesting things to be than rich to get on well with them for long. I do not mean the rich like Miki Sekers. He had made his own money and is a great designer and creative artist too— although even on him some of the richness has rubbed off. I mean those who have been born to it, whether they live by dealing in it and adding to it like Colin Tennant or going along with it like Michael Astor.

If Michael Astor had not had all that money, I think he might have made a good writer. His *Tribal Feelings* was a good book which never got the attention it deserved. Even there the Astors stood in his way. It came out just when the newspapers were plastered with stories of Cliveden as the place where Profumo met Christine Keeler in the bathing-pool and people were thinking of Astors in quite a different connotation from literary style.

Michael Astor did not only invest money in T.R.I. I think he also invested a lot of his anxiety to show that he was more than just someone who had inherited money, and I was sorry for his sake it did not come off. If you overlooked the blank areas all the rich have, he was a sensitive man and did his best to pick his way among the temperaments. It was not easy. Our board meetings were gatherings of prima donnas. It was rarely possible to get through them without a great swopping of insults. These did not go deep between the investors of talent. We might fall out but we accepted each other as fellow professionals: animals of the same kind. Not so with those on the other side of the table. However much we tried to avoid it there was almost always a gap in understanding between us and them.

What really hit us was, however, something we had been too naïve to anticipate. This was the opposition in the B.B.C. and in all but one of the commercial companies. We were all individually well known as television commentators and 'personalities'. Our services were in much demand. But as an independent group we were quite a different matter. We had to be frozen out. We had expected to be able to sell T.R.I. productions to both the B.B.C. and the independent television companies, sometimes one, sometimes the other. And we thought we would have a good chance of some overseas sales to American networks and to television services in Europe, Canada, Australia and the newly developing countries, most of which we reckoned were starved of good material.

At first the B.B.C., in the person of Kenneth Adam, Director of Television, was sympathetic. I rang him and then we called on him and told him our plans. He thought the B.B.C. would be very interested in taking some of our programmes. But he was going abroad and he arranged that we should next meet Stuart Hood, Controller of Television Programmes, to discuss plans. Stuart Hood was sympathetic to the idea, too. But it soon became plain that the young lions just below him, notably Donald Baverstock, were not.

Hood is a remarkable man and his wartime autobiography, *Pebbles from Inside my Skull*, is a fine and sensitive and remarkable book. But he was not cut out for administration and has now escaped from it. It runs contrary to his real nature, which is that of an artist. As Controller of Television he was, as Kenneth Adam was later to observe, 'inscrutable in many ways, a solitary, not a committee man, an isolationist, not a collabora-tionist'. Forceful and even excessively abrupt on some occasions he was on others, 'absent-mindedly indifferent to what was going on around him'. Also, although we did not know it, he was already in process of deciding to leave a job he did not like. When he found that Baverstock, who was in charge of B.B.C. I, regarded the suggestion that the B.B.C. should buy current affairs documentaries from outside as an insult, even though they were made by people he knew and with most of whom he had worked at one time and another, Hood withdrew into inscrutability. The meeting at which Baverstock defended his interests with hostile vigour ended in vague platitudes of good-will in which, to his credit, Baverstock did not pretend to join.

Malcolm Muggeridge had done programmes for Granada Television and knew its chief, Sidney Bernstein, well. Bernstein, he thought, might be interested. But Bernstein was not. Bern-stein, as he was to show in emphatic manner, wanted nothing to do with independence either.

In fact there was, it turned out, only one man interested in a venture of our kind and that the man most people would have thought most unlikely, Lew Grade (now very deservedly Sir Lew) of A.T.V. Lew Grade looks like a caricature of any

337

high-brow's idea of a movie tycoon. He acts a good deal like one, too. He is the only man, other than Winston Churchill, who has made a long cigar into an extension of his personality. Unlike Churchill, he hands his cigars out to everyone he meets. This is a habit I find endearing as a cigar smoker who has not attained the income bracket to support cigars of the length and quality of Lew's.

I once asked his wife, Kathleen, how long he had been smoking these cigars. It all began, she said, when he was an agent and not yet doing all that well. An old music-hall comedian they knew who was down on his luck called round to their flat. He had a box of these big cigars with him and he asked her to buy them. So she did, just to help him along, although Lew didn't smoke and she didn't know what to do with them. When Lew came home she told him he'd better take the cigars to his office and put them on his desk to impress people. He said well, they'd certainly smarten up the furniture and after he'd taken them she forgot all about them until one evening he came home and started bouncing about the place like a ball that had just scored the winning goal in a cup final. 'I pulled off a big deal with Val Parnell this afternoon,' he told her and she asked him how. And he said, 'Well, I was sitting there thinking how big he was and why would he be interested in any of my artistes and then I saw this box of cigars and I opened it and stuck one in my mouth and lit it just to give me something to do. And then I got through to Parnell and you know I always called him Mr Parnell, but with that cigar in my mouth I found myself just naturally saying, 'Hi, Val' and then I started selling like I've never sold before and you know what, he was really avid to sign.' 'And that,' said Lew's wife, 'is how Lew started with his cigars.' I thought it a fine story, creditable to all concerned, and since hearing it I have smoked Lew's cigars with even more pleasure than before.

When it was clear that we were getting nowhere with either the B.B.C. or Bernstein we talked to Hugh Cudlipp, who was on the A.T.V. board for the *Mirror* group, and he said, 'Come and see Lew'—so we did. Lew handed cigars all round and began to talk. He did not listen, or only by mischance very occasionally, and we found we weren't selling T.R.I. to him, he was selling it to us. In the end he negotiated a deal with himself on our behalf for £110,000 and we took one of his cigars back to frame it but somehow never got around to it.

I can never hope to do business with a man I liked better than Lew Grade. His taste in television is of a sort to cause dedicated members of the B.B.C. to wake up sweating in the night; I don't much like it myself either. To him television is entirely a branch of show biz and show biz is giving people what they want and then putting it on to film so you can sell to America. But he has the immense virtue of never pretending to be what he is not. He has no truck with hypocrisy. He stays true to his own personality which is pretty much the same, I should guess, as when he was born Winogradsky in the East End of London and started getting into show business the hard way with his brothers, Leslie and Bernard. He is not easily prejudiced or intimidated. When someone complained that there was a man on A.T.V. who had been a communist, Lew replied, 'He's a communist. I'm a Jew. And we're both in television. So what?'

His standards are commercial and he puts no gloss on them. But it is not just making money that makes Lew run. It is making entertainment. And above all selling it. To be in his office when he is on the line to New York or Los Angeles with a series to sell is to have the high privilege of watching a great artist at work. Every part of him is engaged: voice, face, hands, feet, every inch of his body. He generates salesmanship like an elemental force. Randolph Churchill used to ask whether someone you mentioned was the sort of fellow you'd go tiger shooting with. I would go on a tiger hunt with Lew any day of the week in the certain knowledge that it would not be necessary to shoot. He would have that tiger booked up for a personal appearance before it had time to lick its lips.

I suppose we made a mistake in signing an exclusive one year's contract for T.R.I. productions with A.T.V. It put us out of the open market. But then we were out of it anyway, since no one would buy from us. We still had foreign rights and in fact we did good business abroad. Our films were shown in Germany, France, Italy, Scandinavia, Australia and a great many other places to considerable acclaim. Not, however, in the United States. The American networks would not touch us.

When I was in New York on a lecture engagement I saw

James Haggerty, whom I'd known as Eisenhower's press secretary. He was Vice-President of the American Broadcasting Corporation, in charge of all its current affairs activities. At first he was interested. But finally he reported that good as the films I had shown him were his Board felt that the American public would not accept an international background report that was not in an American accent. They did not want to hear about the world from anyone who was not an American. I said we aimed in the end to make T.R.I. truly international by bringing in television men from America and Europe to join us and we could speed this up if A.B.C. was really interested. But he said that even so there would be considerable difficulty in using anything regularly in the news documentary line that the company did not itself control. The other American networks were chillier still. N.E.T., on the other hand, was enthusiastic and several of our films were shown on educational television to considerable public acclaim. But not, of course, for much money.

All this was disappointing, especially when we got 'rave notices' for several of our documentaries in *Variety*. But the response of the British television companies hit us even harder. Here the amazing situation developed that A.T.V. was informed at the T.V. network committee that no T.R.I. programme would be accepted by the other companies for networking. The motto was: no independents need apply. Lew Grade and Norman Collins fought hard to get this ban lifted and I raised the freezing of independent producers by big companies in a debate on television in the Lords, after duly declaring my interest. In the end Associated Rediffusion relented slightly and so did A.B.C. which had been the most sympathetic from the start. Granada never did.

The result of this was that T.R.I. found itself denied a national audience and Lew Grade found himself with a very bad bargain indeed. He had made his contract with us on the assumption that he would network our programmes in the usual way. The price had been fixed on this assumption. We were well-known. The pilot films we had made were of high quality. Robert Heller, A.T.V.'s Head of Factual Programming, was happy about our plans and was in regular consultation on subjects. But the refusal of the other companies to accept independently-made current affairs programmes made it inevitable that A.T.V. should lose heavily on every T.R.I. film it put on. Without networking it could not expect to get the advertising revenue it needed for prime time.

No doubt in making his original deal Lew had been attracted by all those well-known names in one group. He was buying names the public knew to make the sorts of films the public service element in his I.T.V. contract required of him. He was backing talent and new ideas. But when his package-deal turned sour on him he made no complaint. He not only kept his bargain to the letter but helped and encouraged us in every way, as did also Bob Heller, who had had great experience in television and radio in America before coming to this country and whom I found invariably stimulating. A.T.V. continued to give us peak showing-times and all the publicity it could mobilize. No one could have guessed from the co-operation we got that it was losing money on every film of ours it put on.

The refusal to network plus the cold-shouldering by the B.B.C. effectively destroyed T.R.I.'s chances of survival. Apart from America, which was not allowed to see them on any of the commercial channels, our films proved even more acceptable abroad than we had hoped. But without either a domestic or American market they could not earn sufficient to make the company viable—and with the best will in the world we could not expect A.T.V. to go on supporting us at a loss once our original contract ended. So T.R.I., which we had conceived with a good deal of hope and excitement, died.

As soon as this venture in co-operative independence was over none of us met with any further difficulty in getting on the screen. Malcolm Muggeridge went to the B.B.C. to bare his soul to vast public acclaim in a seemingly endless series of television instalments all drippingly sincere, and Mossman and Kennedy were welcomed back to Auntie with similar if less emotive enthusiasm. Robert Kee went to 'This Week', the best of the independent news documentary programmes and I was asked by Lew Grade and Bob Heller to continue making documentaries for them. I thus had the interesting experience of seeing several films I had originally planned for T.R.I. produced as A.T.V. productions and given the full network coverage that would have been denied them if they had had a T.R.I. credit line.

Perhaps if we had been better diplomats—or more united

among ourselves—we might have fared better. But I am not sure how. Unfortunately the person nominated as our chief diplomat, because supposedly the most experienced in negotiation in public affairs, proved useless during the most critical phase of the affair. This was me. I was lying flat on my back in bed.

It had been a cold day and a rushed one. Robert Kee and I had spent much of it with Norman Collins trying to think up ways of out-flanking the networking ban announced by Granada and Associated Rediffusion without doing anything that might erode T.R.I.'s independence. After this we had met our financial directors and fallen as we nearly always did into acrimonious dispute with them for reasons mostly foolish or obscure and rising mainly from temperamental differences. After that I had discussed with Malcolm Muggeridge and Ludovic Kennedy a film the three of us were to make on 'What's Happened to the English'. I had arranged to start filming some of my first sequences two days later in Nottingham, where I was to go from Oxford where I was speaking in a Union debate. Tony Essex (later famous for his Great War film series) had just joined us from the B.B.C. as a producer and was already in Nottingham surveying the field. He rang up to report that he had found a wonderful gang of ton-up boys. It was latish when I got home and I felt tired and cold as I got out of the car but otherwise all right.

'Dinner is just ready,' Jess said. 'Shall we have a drink first?' I said 'Yes' and poured a couple of sherries, and Jess and I had just sat down to drink them and tell each other about our day's adventures as we always did when a bomb exploded in my chest. I clutched the chair to keep myself steady until the pain, which was so acute as to be almost unbearable, passed. Neither of us realized what it was, only that I was very ill and had better get to bed. We thought it might be bronchitis. When I was strong enough to move Jess helped me upstairs and I said, 'I'm so sorry about your nice dinner, darling. I'll be all right tomorrow.' But when tomorrow came we learned from the consultant who had been called in that I had had a coronary and would have to stay flat on my back in bed for six weeks.

The first two weeks were the critical ones. It was during them that there was most danger of a second attack and if there

should be one, it might be fatal. If I got through without another attack I would probably be all right but I would have to
be away from my office for at least three months. Jess told the
consultant, who was from Guy's and who was wonderful to us
then and later, that she would try to nurse me at home: 'He
would hate it in hospital,' she said. 'I was wondering about that,'
the consultant said. 'It would be safer not to move him if we
don't have to, but it is bound to be an immense strain on you.'

I was not allowed to move in the slightest way. Everything
had to be done for me. I do not know how Jess managed. But
John and Jean were not far away and friends helped where they
could, especially Sylvia Sprigge. And Betty, who was not yet
married but was in process of getting engaged, although we did
not know it until I was well again and she brought George to see
us, came with unfailing loyalty every weekend and whenever
else she could get away from her newspaper which was very
generous about giving her time off.

It is a curious experience in the middle of an active life to
find oneself lying in bed waiting to see whether one is going to
live. I cannot remember being in any way worried about dying.
I thought it quite possible I would die but the expectation of
death did not disturb me, except for leaving Jess and worrying
how she would manage after we had been together so long and
had been so close and done so many things together. I had no
belief in immortality or a personal God. I had been a humanist
all my thinking life and I saw no reason to change now.

Nor had I any wish to. It had been a cold winter and I
remembered how one morning I had found a tiny blue-tit
frozen in the snow. I took it in my hand and tried to revive it
and then I found an old piece of woollen rag in the garage and
made a nest to warm it. It lifted its head momentarily and then
without further commotion lay back on the rough wool and was
still. Lying in bed I thought that to die with the dignity and lack
of fuss of that small bird ought not to be beyond one.

The idea of being frightened because one's own personality
was coming to an end seemed to me mean and small-minded. I
thought the least one owed to oneself and those closest to you
was to face the ending of oneself stoically. I was friends with
many sincere Christians, among them Frank Pakenham (Lord
Longford), whom I regard as one of the most truly good men I

have known, and Clifford Chapman, the former Rector of Abinger, who was now Canon of Guildford Cathedral, of whom I was deeply fond and whose intelligence I much respected. I did not share their views. Nor did they expect me to. Lying in bed I found myself remembering pleasantly a small dining and discussion group that Julian Huxley and I had organized to see if it were possible to arrive at any reasonably succinct humanist alternative to the idealogical slogans that divided the world, particularly those of Christianity and Communism. These, it seemed to us, often deadened thought and replaced it by a dangerous confrontation of irreconcilables like that in which Foster Dulles gloried when he said to me at an international conference that he knew himself to be fighting 'absolute evil'.

Those who came fairly regularly to these dinner discussions in a small unostentatious restaurant included in addition to Julian Huxley and myself A. J. Ayer, Barbara Wootton, Jacob Bronowski and Max Nicholson, Director-General of the Nature Conservancy, and more irregular visitors included Denis Brogan and Stephen Spender. We ate some modestly pleasant meals, drank some modest but agreeable wine and talked a good deal, and in the end we came to the conclusion that if Humanism ever had to be sloganized the best one could hope for was to say it stood for 'Limited Certainty'. This did not seem to any of us likely to offer a great rallying cry and we did not see ourselves marching to Trafalgar Square with it emblazoned on our banners. But it expressed reasonably satisfactorily, we thought, and in limited space what we all believed, which was that it was important to appreciate that the alternative to absolutist religions or doctrines was not anarchy, as their adherents sometimes argued. On the contrary one should recognize that at any moment in time there were 'certainties' that derived from existing human knowledge and experience and which it was sensible to accept as guides. But it was equally necessary to recognize that these 'certainties' were relative and limited. They might have to be modified at any time in the light of new knowledge. The real sin against humanity was to seek to establish absolutes for all time and to close one's mind to change.

I could not pretend to myself as I lay in bed that this slogan

344

was of any particular value to me in my present condition. But I thought that so far as any slogan could it expressed a basic and important truth and I found a good deal of pleasure in recalling the Humanist discussions that had led up to it. I saw no reason to reject this Humanism because my own life might be coming to an end and, indeed, could not have rejected it without intellectual dishonesty. I had enjoyed my life and hoped it would go on longer. I had learned from my mother to greet life with romantic expectancy and from my father to look at it with a cool, sceptical but friendly regard, and both attitudes had served me well. But I thought that one should not be excessively concerned about dying. I preferred the Shakespearean spirit and said to myself with a small, ironic Humanist smile, 'A man can die but once; we owe God a death.'

However, I did not have a second attack. I survived the critical two weeks and at the end of another four was allowed downstairs again. I was warned that since one of the muscles of my heart had gone I must not indulge in violent exercise and should avoid extremes of heat and cold and not get into situations over which I had no control. Otherwise there seemed no reason why I should not continue to do much as I had been doing before, although at a more deliberate pace and with some bouts of ill health to put up with.

This has proved to be so. I have been to America, Mauritius, Canada, Czechoslovakia, Tunis and several other places since that sudden shock of pain on that cold February evening, have written and published three books, made several television films and sat on more committees, delivered more speeches, and written more newspaper columns than I can count. It is a nuisance finding illness like 'flu magnified by heart weakness, but one has to learn to bear with such things. I am not allowed to run after a bus. But I bear this deprivation with patience for I gave up the habit many years ago in favour of hailing a taxi.

I am a good deal better off than was my friend Douglas Ritchie, Director of Publicity for the B.B.C., who was 'Colonel Britain' of the wartime broadcasts to Occupied France. He had had a stroke that paralysed his right side eight years before my coronary and I doubt whether I could have brought to such a condition the courage and cheerfulness that he did and that is recorded with such modesty in his remarkable book, *Stroke*. We first knew Douglas and his wife, Ev, in New York when he was on loan from the B.B.C. to the British Information Services. He won Jess's heart by his quick understanding and sensitivity at a crowded party into which she was shuttle-cocked knowing no one. I count him one of the most remarkable men I have known, as well as one of the most delightful and engaging of friends. He and Ev Ritchie between them succeeded in turning a grievous blow at the height of his powers and ambitions into a crucible of the human spirit from which they emerged larger and more serene in personality than before—and more delightful and engaging to be with. I was called on to make no such effort. Like a car missing on one cylinder I could no longer accelerate as I used to do. But otherwise I was not greatly impaired: no longer a racing model but fairly feasible for ordinary transport.

In a curious way the biggest diminution I have felt is in my phantasy life. I can no longer, as I sometimes used to do, imagine myself climbing mountains or tall trees, or winning hard-fought tennis matches or scattering toughs who have attacked an old lady. I am no longer a knight errant and have had to trim my romanticism, for in all my imaginings I am now constrained by the awkward awareness that any sudden eruption of energy would leave me lying on the ground fighting for breath. I feel this a good deal. But I cannot pretend that my ordinary life is badly diminished by it.

When I was well enough and had been downstairs for several weeks Jess and I went abroad to recuperate. We went to a small inn by the sea near Jerez and sat in the sun and ate Mediterranean prawns and visited sherry bodegas. There is a habit at some such bodegas of asking guests to sign their names on a barrel. When I signed mine I found that it was next to that of Sir Alexander Fleming, the discoverer of penicillin. He had written alongside his name, 'Penicillin heals the sick but sherry brings the dead to life.' So Jess and I bought another bottle of sherry, cold and dry, and sat in the sun under a tree and drank to each other and thought how lucky we were.

Index

Abdication, the, 140–2
Abinger, 127, 129, 214, 286–90
Acland, Sir Richard, 159
Adam, Kenneth, 337
Adams, Mary, 161
Aga Khan, 277
Agate, James, 60
Alanbrook, Field-Marshal Lord, 233
Alexander, Field-Marshal (later Lord Alexander of Tunis), 234
Alexander, A. V., 227, 257
Alexandra, Queen, 17
America, legendary family fortune in, 8–9, 21
American Invasion, The (Williams), 314–15
Andrews, Bert, 259
Andrews, Eamonn, 303
Appeasement, 118, 145. *See also* Hitler; Munich; National Socialism
Astor, David, 184, 267, 335
Astor, Michael, 335–6
Astor, Nancy, 155, 160
Atom bomb, atomic energy, 230–2, 237–8, 241–2, 261
Attlee, Clement Richard (later Lord Attlee), 4, 106, 119, 135, 141, 144, 233–4, 258, 278, 280, 282, 285, 286, 307, 308, 329; elected Prime Minister (1945), 210–14; asks Francis Williams to become his P.R. Adviser, 215–16; his association with Williams, 217–27; his friendship with Bevin, 217, 222–3; his relationship and work with Truman, 230–2, 235–8, 241–50; and India, 251–3; and celebration of Burmese Independence, 254; his retirement from leadership, 307
Attlee, Janet, 226

Attlee, Violet (later Lady Attlee), 216
Austin, A. B., 188
Austin, S. A. V., 60–6
Ayer, A. J. (later Sir Alfred), 344

Bacup, 19, 27, 28, 31
Baghdad, 291
Baldwin, Stanley, 96, 118–19, 144, 198
Bank of England, 90, 95–101, 112
Barber, Elizabeth, 286
Barnes, George, 272
Barnes-Brand, Amy, 126
Barnstaple, 26
Barrie, J. M., 57, 71
Bartlett, Vernon, 62
Battle of Britain, 162
Batty Farm, 31–2
Baverstock, Donald, 337
Bay of Pigs, 317
Bayley, Nancy, 318
Beaverbrook, Lord, 69, 91–2, 101–2, 116–17, 132, 169, 183, 277–8, 299–300; Francis Williams's first introduction to, 84–5; sends Williams to the City, 86–7; offers Williams a regular column, 92–4; sacks Arthur Christiansen, 300–5; his 85th birthday party, 305
Bell, Clive, 122
Beresford, Admiral Lord Charles, 4
Beresford, Dr, 4
Berkeley (California), 262, 314–22, 323–4
Bermondsey Book, the, 72
Bermondsey Bookshop, the, 71–2
Bernstein, Sidney, 337
Berry, H. V. (later Sir Vaughan), 111–12, 113